The Customer is the Planet: A handbook for sustainable business is a powerful blueprint that redefines business success by putting the planet first. The book explores urgent issues such as climate change, pollution, water resources, and biodiversity, and offers sharp insights and actionable strategies for businesses to embed sustainability at every level. With a strong focus on emerging regulatory frameworks and reporting obligations, the book is an essential resource for forward-thinking leaders committed to long-term, planet-friendly growth. A must-read for anyone serious about integrating sustainability into their business model.

ROBERTA BOSCOLO, Climate & Energy Leader, World Meteorological Organization

What an incredible book! It's easy to read and clearly explains what's at stake for companies in terms of sustainability, offering valuable insights on how to embark on this journey. Highly inspiring for ESG practitioners, it's a must-read for decision-makers and employees aiming to position their company in a rapidly changing world where sustainability is crucial.

SEBASTIAN JURAS, Sustainability & Transformation Director, Alcatel-Lucent Enterprise

A brilliant dissection of what we are getting so very wrong in today's society and economy and how we can put it right. It brings structure and clarity to the complex amalgam of science, policy, reporting and standards that so often acts as an impediment to action. And, crucially, it puts people at the heart of the problem and the solution.

MIKE BARRY, Strategic Advisor on Sustainable Business and former Director of Sustainable Business, Marks & Spencer

A 'how to' handbook that is a great read for any sustainability and circular economy professional – for beginners and experts alike. It's great to see various practices, topics and new trends that we have to manage in a business on a daily basis come together in one piece. It's an easy and practical read – and sharpens the vision: why we are all doing this. A 'purpose book' that hopefully many get to read!

HARALD TEPPER, Global Lead – Circular Economy, EcoDesign & ESG Transformation, Royal Philips

The Customer is the Planet is a must-read for any business leader serious about sustainability. It's not just a guide – it's a call to action that challenges us to rethink our impact and make meaningful changes that benefit both people and the planet.

GEOFF HUCKER, CEO & Founder, Work for Impact

If you're looking to get serious about sustainability in your business, *The Customer is the Planet* is the guide you need. It's packed with practical tips and real talk on how to put the planet at the heart of what you do. Honestly, it's a must-read if you care about making a difference while staying successful.

DAN SHERRARD-SMITH, Founder & CEO, MotherTree

The authors skilfully guide readers through the history of climate change, offering a clear explanation of its key drivers while sharing their insightful vision for the future. *The Customer is the Planet* provides crucial illumination for businesses navigating the increasing tide of regulations and shifting public sentiment. As a company committed to decarbonising cement, reducing the environmental footprint of steel manufacturing and aggregates processing, and conserving vital natural resources, this book has been instrumental in refining our strategic approach to an ever-evolving business landscape. *The Customer is the Planet* outlines a comprehensive roadmap of forthcoming laws, regulations, expectations, and enforcement, empowering business leaders to prepare effectively for the challenges ahead.

REUBEN MAXBAUER, Director, Edw. C. Levy Co.

A compelling and thorough guide to transforming every aspect of our businesses to truly reach sustainability. *The Customer is the Planet* also provides motivation, a moral case for change and a hopeful image of the future world we could leave our descendants. Great work.

MARK SCHRUPP, Executive Director, Detroit/Wayne County Port Authority

The Customer is the Planet is a transformative guide that flips the script on traditional business thinking, making it clear that the planet isn't just a stakeholder – it's the ultimate customer. The book masterfully illustrates how aligning with natural systems isn't just ethical; it's a strategic necessity for businesses to thrive in a world where sustainability drives success. It's a wake-up call for companies to rethink their impact and see environmental stewardship as the core of their business model. This book aligns perfectly with our ethos at Oxygen Conservation, where we believe that businesses can – and must – be a force for good. By integrating environmental considerations into every decision, companies can unlock new opportunities and contribute to a regenerative economy. *The Customer is the Planet* is essential reading for anyone serious about leading their business into a sustainable future.

RICH STOCKDALE, Ph.D., Founder & CEO, Oxygen Conservation

The Customer is the Planet will help you navigate a path from why, to what if, to how might we? The book gives you space to really think about what's possible and the confidence that together we can shape a much better world where everyone and everything thrives.

DONNA OKELL, CEO, UK for Good

The Customer is the Planet is not just a book; it is a manifesto calling on us to act with urgency and hope for our environment. As a repository of insightful contributions from leading sustainability thought-leaders, this book stands as a beacon of inspiration. It underscores that the journey towards sustainability isn't just about individual action but about global collaboration. At illuminem.com, we resonate deeply with this message, seeing it reflected in the dedication of our global community who look up to these thought-leaders for guidance and example. This extraordinary book serves not only as a message of hope but as a profound symbol of collaborative potential across countries and topics, united in a singular mission for our planet.

ANDREA GORI, Founder & CEO, Illuminem

An innovative sustainability book structured around the European Sustainability Reporting Standards (ESRS) framework. Renowned interdisciplinary experts connect together their pieces of knowledge and experience, offering us an enlightened vision of the sustainability challenges and ways to act. An inspiration for anyone leading or supporting businesses through their sustainable transition.

SABRINA DEDEURWAERDER, ESG Consultant, SuReal

I read the book with a very open mind. Daily, I am developing biobased construction-materials, and there is no doubt that we have to shift from the oil-based to a bio-based economy. This book is a fantastic guide to help businesses transition and find a balance between a healthy planet and a future for us and our next generations.

FREDERIK VERSTRAETE, CEO, C-biotech

At long last, a book has emerged that captures the essence of a truly Earth-centric perspective: **The Customer is the Planet** *is a guerilla guide for world changers, impact entrepreneurs, and passionate activists. Collaboratively penned by 17 visionary thought-leaders, it generously delves into every crucial sustainability concept, illuminating them with clear examples. Now every adventurer eager to shape a sustainable future has a navigation map.*

STEFAAN VANDIST, author & keynote speaker; Senior Storytelling Coach, We Are Impact Collective

The Customer Is the Planet *is a book that truly understands the challenges faced by sustainability leaders today, offering a timely shift in focus from carbon to ecosystems, nature, and biodiversity. The authors provide practical strategies to help business leaders consider their reliance on the more-than-human world, and how to reconcile this crucial relationship.*

LARA BIRKES, former Chief Sustainability Officer, Hewlett Packard Enterprise; Sonder Inc., Director of Strategic Partnerships & Initiatives, Virgin Unite, Biomimicry enthusiast, ESG advisor, board member, and wildlife advocate

At a perplexing and worrying time, we at last get a single powerful book that brings together everything that a genuinely sustainable business should think about and act on. It's all here: personal insights, deep expertise, clear explanations and, above all, the reassuring sense that sympathetic hands are guiding and nudging us towards a safer pathway.

DAVID SHUKMAN, Science Editor, BBC News, turned independent consultant, speaker and moderator

Now more than ever, sustainability is becoming a moral imperative. I am honoured to provide a testimonial for this book. Referencing the European Sustainability Reporting Standards (ESRS) as guiding principles, **The Customer is the Planet** *takes us on a journey through key sustainability topics to a key message: the planet is our first and ultimate customer and stakeholder. Through thought-provoking questions and frameworks, the authors use storytelling to inspire us to live a truly sustainable life with our planet. Whether you are a seasoned sustainability professional or a newcomer, there is something you can learn from this book. The collective effort of* **The Customer is the Planet** *is a stark reminder of what we need now the most: a collective effort to curb carbon emissions, reverse climate change and set ourselves on a path of true sustainability.*

GIULIA MARZETTI, former European Commission Policy Officer and TEDx Speaker

THE CUSTOMER IS THE PLANET

A handbook for sustainable business

DONAL DALY
INGRID DE DONCKER
DAVID CARLIN
CARLOS TEROL
HARALD FRIEDL
ELENA DOMS
Dr WILLIAM BEER
TARA GARRATY
OLIVER DAUERT
MARIJE DE ROOS
ELIN BERGMAN
ANNA TRIPONEL
MINOU SCHILLINGS
JOY NJERI
KOWAWA KAPUKAJA APURINÃ
TIAGO PAES VILAS BOAS
ORLA CAROLAN

·OAK·TREE·PRESS·

Published by Oak Tree Press, Cork T12 XY2N, Ireland.
www.oaktreepress.com / www.SuccessStore.com

© 2024 Donal Daly, Ingrid De Doncker, David Carlin, Carlos Terol, Harald Friedl, Elena Doms, Dr William Beer, T.A.O. Garraty, Oliver Dauert, Marije De Roos, Elin Bergman, Anna Triponel, Minou Schillings, Joy Njeri, Kowawa Kapukaja Apurinã, Tiago Paes Vilas Boas, Orla Carolan

Cover design & images: Sophie Morris.

A catalogue record for this book is available from the British Library.

ISBN 978-1-78119-636-6 Paperback
ISBN 978-1-78119-637-0 PDF
ISBN 978-1-78119-638-0 ePub
ISBN 978-1-78119-639-7 Kindle

DISCLAIMER

It's important that you read this page ...

The information and advice provided in this book is based on the personal experiences and knowledge of the authors and is intended for general educational purposes only. It is not a substitute for professional legal, accounting, financial, sustainability, general management, or other advice. Since every company and situation is unique, the reader is solely responsible for evaluating the applicability of any information or advice to their own specific circumstances and should seek the advice of qualified professionals before taking any action related to the topics covered in this book. The authors, editor and publisher disclaim all liability in connection with the use of this book.

*If you do not agree, please stop reading **now**.*

CONTENTS

Contents

THE AUTHORS

DONAL DALY

INGRID DE
DONCKER

DAVID CARLIN

CARLOS TEROL

HARALD FRIEDL

ELENA DOMS

Dr WILLIAM BEER

TARA GARRATY

OLIVER DAUERT

MARIJE DE ROOS

ELIN BERGMAN

ANNA TRIPONEL

MINOU SCHILLINGS

JOY NJERI

KOWAWA KAPUKAJA
APURINÃ

TIAGO PAES VILAS
BOAS

ORLA CAROLAN

For more information on each author and their expertise, see **About the Authors** at the end of the book.

PREFACE

In an era of mounting global challenges, sustainable change will only happen, if we all decide to make it happen. That fact is often forgotten.

One key ingredient that not many want to talk about is that this necessitates all of us to dare to look beyond our own interests: to create real spaces for collaboration, where sustainable change can emerge.

This book exemplifies such a new approach; written by building on the collective wisdom of LinkedIn's top sustainability thought-leaders and content-creators who represent the voices of 100.000s of followers.

Our diverse voices, often unheard in mainstream discourse, offer a fresh perspective on building trust and driving positive change. By bridging divides and fostering collaboration, we aim to accelerate progress towards a sustainable future.

This book embodies the power of community and knowledge-sharing, challenging readers to look beyond self-interest and embrace the collaborative spirit needed for transformative action.

Donal Daly, Ingrid De Doncker, David Carlin, Carlos Terol, Harald Friedl, Elena Doms, Dr William Beer, T.A.O. Garraty, Oliver Dauert, Marije De Roos, Elin Bergman, Anna Triponel, Minou Schillings, Joy Njeri, Kowawa Kapukaja Apurinã, Tiago Paes Vilas Boas, Orla Carolan

INTRODUCTION

Donal Daly

D ad", my son said, "should I be worried?"

"Why would you be worried?", I responded.

In my mind I was wondering what might be causing concern. Christian was 15, and while I recognise that for teenagers these days there are many more distractions, pressures and expectations than there were when I was his age, I had no indication that there might be something up. He wasn't struggling in school, he seemed to have a healthy social life and he was doing pretty well in sports. What could be on his mind?

We were just finished dinner, so I looked at him, my head cocked, as if to say, "Well, go on."

He looked at me and then posed "The Question".

"Will the planet still be OK when I am your age?"

I was floored. Not because he asked The Question – he was intellectually curious and I enjoyed our frequent discussions about an eclectic range of topics – but because I did not have an honest answer that I wanted to give to a 15-year old boy.

The age gap between us is 44 years. This was 2018. *Will* the planet still be in a good shape in 2062? Well, not at the current course and speed. Not unless we act. So my question to myself was, "What could I do about it?" I certainly couldn't sit by and do nothing.

The New York satirist Fran Lebowitz said:

Think before you speak. Read before you think.
This will give you something to think about that you didn't
make up yourself.

So, I got to reading, and thinking, and listening, and now I am ready to speak.

I feel terribly privileged to have been able to pull together the outstanding list of creators and collaborators who you see here as co-authors of this book. The knowledge, experience and generosity they bring to this project is extraordinary.

I have been actively engaged in human rights for a few decades and have a reasonably well-developed sense of social and environmental justice. But, until the moment of The Question, I did nothing to address the systemic environmental, social and governance changes that I now know have long been necessary. How we use the limited resources of the planet, the inequity of resource distribution, the consequences on the Global South of the over-consumption by the Global North, the perilous state of our air, water and food infrastructures were not actively on my daily To Do list. That is not an excuse, just a statement of fact.

By contrast, most of the collaborators in this book have made the mission of saving the planet for future generations their life's work. The work of these climate pioneers – they are not just climate activists pursuing a once-off single topic, but career-long climate pioneers forging a path forward for the benefit of humankind – is a privilege to witness.

These collaborators, who are working for your future, could have been the "crazy ones, the misfits, the rebels, the troublemakers, the round pegs in the square holes ... the ones who see things differently ... the ones who are crazy enough to think that they can change the world" referenced in the iconic Apple ad from Steve Jobs in 1997. They, and their kin, will change the world. These are my "crazy ones".

But changing the world isn't easy. It was in fact Steve Jobs who proclaimed:

> You can't connect the dots looking forward, you can
> only connect them looking backwards. So you have to trust
> that the dots will somehow connect in your future.

To trust that connection, you must understand the forces at play. First, you must consider and understand the dots, before you can connect them. This is part of the challenge of transforming a business for sustainable performance. If you do the work, expand your knowledge, learn from others, collaborate and co-create, deliberate on the details, then you can trust your informed instinct to connect the dots. This book can be the link to make your connections.

Albert Einstein defined insanity as doing the same thing over and over again and expecting different results. If I extrapolate Einstein's point, patterns that repeat can matter and inform but only when they point to informed causations, and not spurious correlations. Anthropogenic activities – human behaviour – have been a causative contributor to climate change for over a century.[1] If we are to believe Einstein, it follows that, by doing more of the same activity, we will likely get more of the same outcome. Bearing in mind that the global population has doubled in the last 50 years – from 4 billion on April 1974 to 8.1 billion in April 2024 – we don't really want twice the number of people doing the same things over and over again. That would not be good. In fact, based on the increasing pace of climate change, that would be a disaster.

Imagine that you are in a room just big enough, with just enough food, and just enough oxygen, to comfortably accommodate four people who are moderately active and consuming responsibly. Now imagine four more people entered the room, and everyone's activity level is increasing, and the consumption – of food, oxygen, or both – is out of control. The room quickly runs out of food and oxygen, and it becomes uncomfortably warm. That's what is happening on our planet.

There are a lot more of us, and we are all busier and consuming more than our ancestors.[2] Unless you subscribe to population control, our only option is to reduce our consumption and activity levels. In our homes, our workplaces and our nations, we need to stop doing the same things over and over again – consuming more than we need, burning vast quantities of fossil fuels, eating an increasingly meat-based diet. We can choose to do different and better things.

To opt for a better way means first we need to have a vision for the future and then we must acquire the knowledge that shows us how to get there: how to live, work and play differently. That's what this book is about.

Pierre-Simon Laplace, a 19th century French mathematician, theorised that, given perfect knowledge, we could make perfect predictions. Wouldn't that be wonderful, being omniscient, having all the answers? We know, however, that the pursuit of perfect knowledge is an endless and thankless task, but the pursuit of domain-specific knowledge in the area of sustainability can be less of a Sisyphean task than it may first appear.

While 'sustainability' is wide and deep – it is after all a planet-sized problem – there are structures, frameworks and experts to help you lead your organisation through your sustainability / environmental, social and governance (ESG) strategy, execution, reporting, measurement and compliance. Our hope is that much of that fount of knowledge is found here and in the related resources. Our wish for this book is that it will be a fellow-traveller and support for your endeavour, and your compass on your sustainability journey to build a vision for the future and a transition plan to get there.

Perhaps somewhere in the mélange of the perspectives of these three geniuses – Jobs, Einstein and Laplace – lies the truth. As we trend towards imperfect knowledge, but the best knowledge available, albeit in the limited domain of sustainability for business, we increase our ability to shape our future behaviour, and our actual future, through intelligently derived and more informed insights and strategies.

This time, this time today, right now, is a time to stop and think, to consider the dots, and to evaluate the patterns. It is time to value and respect the need for knowledge and critical assessment, and then do something about it. Reacting to time pressures, the need for immediate corporate results and personal gratification, rewarding ourselves or being rewarded by others, getting the job done and moving on – we don't always take the time to deliberate. In corporate-land, sometimes we juggle the fridge-magnet vocabulary of business-speak without critical assessment, consume bumper sticker pronouncements in the time it takes us to swipe to the next screen, often without taking the time to digest or reflect or consider the fact that, while we each have individual, family, corporate, or national pursuits, we are all part of the same planet, looking to solve the same problem for the same future.

Together, through this book and other related resources, we are seeking to collaborate with businesses to make it easier to respond to the challenges of the climate crisis, the attendant social upheaval, and the corporate challenges – strategy, execution and compliance – that accompany the greatest business transformation challenge of our generation. This book is intended to equip changemakers in business with the knowledge to make better choices for their business, for people and for the planet, and to ease their journey. This book is intended to chart the path, educate the changemakers and collaborators, and to entice others to make this the new normal.

Paraphrasing and combining Francois Guizot and Noam Chomsky:[3]

The future belongs to the optimists. Unless you believe that the future can be better, you are unlikely to step up and take responsibility for making it so.

Delivering a sustainable future for today's generation and future generations is within our grasp. We need to face forward, shoulders back, our faces to the wind, and the goodwill of future generations at our backs.

Whoever our customers are, whatever markets we serve, whether we are consumer or manufacturer, legislator or regulator, environmentalist or activist, politician or voter, parent or child, we know that we only have one planet.

This planet is our only source of resource, and its resources are finite. In business, and in everything we do, to serve current and future generations, we must acknowledge that the customer is the planet and the planet is our customer – a customer that we must unswervingly serve and support.

We need to be optimistic, to believe in the possibility of a better future for people and planet.

Can you do this?

This book aims to show you how.

Donal Daly
Cork, August 2024

---

[1] National Oceanic & Atmospheric Administration. ESRL Global Monitoring Division – *Global Greenhouse Gas Reference Network* (2005). Available at: http://www.esrl.noaa.gov/gmd/ccgg/trends/history.html.

[2] Over the last 50 years, there has been a significant global increase in consumption *per capita*. The availability of food, measured in average caloric supply, has consistently increased globally since 1961, notably in Asia and Africa (https://ourworldindata.org/food-supply). Water withdrawal and freshwater use has grown over the last 50 years (https://www.worldometers.info/water). There has been an increase in *per capita* energy consumption, as the world transitioned from coal to oil and then to natural gas https://transportgeography.org/contents/chapter4/transportation-and-energy/world-energy-consumption/.

[3] Francois Guizot said, "The future belongs to the optimists. Pessimists are only spectators". Noam Chomsky said, "Optimism is strategy for making a better future. Unless you believe that the future can be better, you are unlikely to step up and take responsibility for making it so".

1

THE CUSTOMER IS THE PLANET

Donal Daly

THE HISTORY & FUTURE OF SUSTAINABILITY

Climate change isn't a distant storm on the horizon; it's a relentless force reshaping our world. The unapologetic rise in temperatures, erratic weather patterns, and the increasing frequency of extreme events are the alarm bells Nature rings in our ears. We know that we need to do something. We know that a sustainability mindset is no longer an option; it's a survival strategy.

The good news is that we can stand on the shoulder of giants to lift us up, those sustainability evangelists who have come up with ways to mitigate the harm that we are doing and evolve a process of adjustment to the increasing climate effects. Their history begins hundreds of years ago and takes a long path to bring us the structured sustainability frameworks we have today, like the European Sustainability Reporting Standards (ESRS) in Europe and International Sustainability Standards Board (ISSB) in the US. Let's go through that journey now, but first let's agree on what sustainability means.

Although there are many definitions of sustainability, my favourite comes from the Brundtland Commission[1]:

Sustainable development is development that meets the needs of the present without compromising the ability of future generations to meet their own needs

The commission – a sub-organisation of the United Nations (UN), founded by Javier Pérez de Cuéllar, the then UN Secretary-General, who appointed Gro Harlem Brundtland, former Prime Minister of Norway, as chairperson – is best known for its report *Our Common Future*,[2] also known as the *Brundtland Report*. Released in 1987, this report was one of the most significant events in the history of sustainability, as it was influential in popularising the concept of sustainable development. The Brundtland definition emphasises the need to balance economic growth, environmental protection, and social equity.

Brundtland argued that:

... the "environment" is where we live; and the "development", what we all do in attempting to improve our lot within that abode, are inseparable."

We try to encapsulate that philosophy in the title of this book, *The Customer is the Planet*, which we sometimes reverse as "The Planet is the Customer." In either case, we know the two are interlinked and inseparable.

The Brundtland Commission's mandate was to:

- Re-examine the critical issues of environment and development and to formulate innovative, concrete, and realistic action proposals to deal with them;

- Strengthen international cooperation on environment and development and assess and propose new forms of cooperation that can break out of existing patterns and influence policies and events in the direction of needed change; and to

- Raise the level of understanding and commitment to action on the part of individuals, voluntary organisations, businesses, institutes, and governments.

Sitting here in 2024, 37 years later, after a year of record temperatures, extreme weather and many climate-related deaths, it is clear that we still have a long way to go to integrate this thinking into how we act, and how we reimagine the systems and behaviours that underpin our future.

But Brundtland wasn't the beginning of sustainability thinking. If we consider that sustainability has three core principles – economic, environmental, and social – and that the equal consideration of, and a balance of impacts between, all three principles create the holistic sustainable development concept that Brundtland espoused, then we need to go way further back.

The origins of socially responsible or ethical investing (SRI) may date back to the Religious Society of Friends (Quakers).[3] In 1758, the Quaker Philadelphia Yearly Meeting prohibited members from participating in the slave trade: buying or selling humans.

John Wesley (1703-1791), one of the founders of Methodism, outlined his basic tenets of social investing: not to harm your neighbour through your business practices and to avoid industries like tanning and chemical production, which can harm the health of workers.

In modern times, in the 1960s, economic development projects started or managed by Dr Martin Luther King, like the Montgomery Bus Boycott and the Operation Breadbasket Project in Chicago, established the model for future socially responsible investing.

Since Brundtland, sustainable business models, regulatory frameworks and social contract models have progressed in multiple dimensions and in most jurisdictions in the world, though the progress has been marred by social and environmental conflicts that continue to remind us why changes are necessary. Developments includes:

- **1988:** The Intergovernmental Panel on Climate Change (IPCC) was established by the United Nations Environment Programme (UNEP) and the World Meteorological Organization (WMO), charged with advancing scientific knowledge about climate change caused by human activities;

- **1989:** The grounding of the *Exxon Valdez* oil tanker was a major environmental disaster, spilling 11 million gallons of oil and damaging 2,100 km of coastline in Alaska's Prince William Sound on 24 March, 1989. The human and natural losses were immense;

- **1992:** The Earth Summit was a UN conference held in Rio de Janeiro in June. With 30,000 attendees, it was the largest environmentally focussed event in history. A key achievement was the establishment of the *United Nations Framework Convention on Climate Change* (UNFCCC) to combat dangerous human interference with the climate system and to stabilise greenhouse gas (GHG) concentrations;

- **1996:** Nike got caught up in a child labour scandal when *Life* magazine[4] published an article featuring a photo of a young boy named Tariq from Pakistan, who was reportedly sewing Nike footballs for 60 cents a day. Nike subsequently cleaned up its act;

- **1997:** Adopted at the third Conference of the Parties (COP 3) in Kyoto, Japan, on 11 December 1997, the *Kyoto Protocol* extended the 1992 UNFCCC. Although the *Protocol* shares the objective and institutions of the *Convention*, the major distinction between the two is that while the *Convention* encouraged countries to stabilise GHG emissions, the Protocol commits them to do so.

From the turn of the century, momentum really started building, weaving sustainability into the tapestry of government, business and consumer lives: regulation by regulation, standard by standard, directive by directive. The givers and takers gave and took, but the sustainability frameworks marched inexorably on, seeking to chart a path to a planet that would work for all:

- **2000:** The Carbon Disclosure Project (CDP) was created, the Global Reporting Initiative (GRI) started, and the Millennium Development Goals (MDGs), a precursor to the 2015 Sustainable Development Goals (SDGs), were established to improve the lives of the world's poorest people.

   In July, the *United Nations Global Compact* established a non-binding pact to get businesses and firms worldwide to adopt sustainable and socially responsible policies;

- **2002:** The World Summit on Sustainable Development in Johannesburg established the critical principle that sustainable development is a bridge concept, connecting economics, ecology and ethics, and pointing out that, to get real action, the ownership of the concept of sustainable development must extend to all sectoral agencies and – most importantly – to private-sector stake holders;

- **2006:** Echoing the activities of the Quakers and John Wesley in the 1700s, the *UN Principles for Responsible Investment*[5] launched with the aim of making financial investment more sustainable, its signatories agreeing to work to implement its six aspirational principles;

- **2011:** The Sustainability Accounting Standards Board (SASB) was founded. Its mission is to establish industry-specific disclosure standards across ESG topics that facilitate communication between companies and investors about financially material, decision-useful information. In 2022, all SASB standards were transitioned to the ISSB;

- **2014:** The *Non-Financial Reporting Directive* (NFRD) was adopted by the European Union (EU), requiring certain companies to provide non-financial disclosure documents along with their annual reports. This was the pre-cursor to the 2024 implementation of the *Corporate Sustainability Reporting Directive* (CSRD) – the gold standard for sustainability reporting;

- **2015:** The UN SDGs – 17 interlinked goals – were developed as a shared blueprint for peace and prosperity for people and the planet, now and into the future. In the *Paris Agreement*, governments pledged to meet new goals by 2030 – the target being to restrict the global temperature increase relative to pre-industrial times to 1.5°C, a level deemed critical by many of the world's climate scientists.

  The Task Force on Climate-related Financial Disclosures (TCFD) was created to provide information to investors about what companies are doing to mitigate the risks of climate change, as well as be transparent about the way in which they are governed.

But all the while, as **Figure 1.1** shows, the imprint of climate change was becoming more evident. The mercury rose, seas roiled, and floods, storms, and droughts devastated communities in the most vulnerable parts of the world. By 2015, we had already seen our first days above the 1.5°C average temperature change over pre-industrial times.

Figure 1.1: The Impact of Climate Change

Global daily average temperature anomalies relative to a preindustrial baseline, C

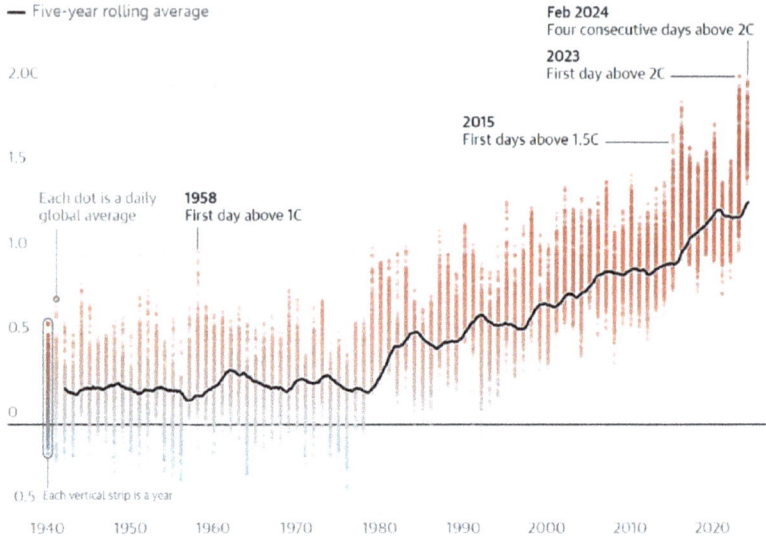

Guardian graphic. Source: Copernicus C3S/ECMWF ERA5. Note: Preindustrial baseline = 1850-1900

Clearly more had to be done – and it was:

- **2020:** The *European Green Deal* was approved: a set of policy initiatives by the European Commission that aims (a) to make the EU climate neutral by 2050 and (b) to achieve a 55% reduction in the EU's emissions by 2030 when compared with 1990. The *Green Deal* also supports the transformation of the EU into a fair and prosperous society with a modern and competitive economy;

- **2021:** The *Sustainable Finance Disclosure Regulation* (SFDR) is a EU regulation that aims to integrate sustainability considerations into the financial sector, to foster investment in projects and companies that contribute positively to ESG factors, enhance transparency, mitigate greenwashing and encourage accountability.

  The US Securities & Exchange Commission (SEC) issued a proposed disclosure rule for public companies. That rule has been through the wars with multiple objections, reviews and redrafts, and now in mid-2024 it is once again the victim of legal challenges.

Those of you who are familiar with the ESRS might have spotted in the *Contents* page of this book that, once we get past this introductory chapter, the following chapters follow the ESRS structure. There are five Environmental chapters, followed by three Social chapters (**Chapter 7** combines ESRS 1 and ESRS 2), and then one Governance chapter. This is not an accident.

ESRS is based largely on a blend that has evolved from the GRI and the TCFD. Moreover, as there is increased interoperability between ISSB – the natural descendant of SASB – and CSRD, the reporting directive based on ESRS, the overarching super-standard is really ESRS. There is very little in any of the other standards around the world that is not generally covered by ESRS. It is logical therefore, and we hope more helpful as a reference guide, that the table of contents mirrors ESRS.

So, to the final phase of our journey through sustainability time:

- **2021:** In the US, the International Financial Reporting Standards (IFRS), which is responsible for developing global accounting standards, created a new sustainability standard-setting board, the ISSB. A number of the US standards came together under the International Integrated Reporting Council (IIRC), which later joined forces with SASB as the Value Reporting Framework (VRF). ISSB subsequently brought VRF into the fold.

- **2022:** On 3 May, the ESRS was released in draft form for public comment by the European Financial Reporting Advisory Group (EFRAG). One of my colleagues was an advisor to EFRAG, so I have reports at first-hand of how the ESRS was debated, massaged and negotiated to be an appropriate standard for all companies and a powerful framework for change. ESRS came into force on 5 January, 2024, and all EU member states were required to transpose it into law by 6 July, 2024;

  The ESRS is part of the CSRD and applies to a broad set of large companies, including listed SMEs, within the EU. Companies subject to the CSRD will have to report according to ESRS for the first time in the 2024 financial year, with reports published in 2025. The ESRS aim to enhance transparency and provide investors and other stakeholders with the necessary information to assess the sustainability performance of companies. CSRD updates and replaces NFRD and has been in practical effect throughout the EU since 1 January, 2024. The roll-out follows a practical timeline, running to 2029.

We are generally taught that there is an arc of history: an inevitable path of progress that leads to modern society. The arc that we are currently travelling is certainly not a rainbow. Our projected destination is not a pot of gold.

Figure 1.2: The CSRD Roll-out Schedule

2025 Based on FY2024 data	2026 Based on FY2025 data	2027 Based on FY2026 data	2028 Based on FY2027 data
Entities already subject to the **NFRD**, which includes entities with listed securities on an EU-regulated market and more than 500 employees. WE ARE HERE	Other **large** undertaking. Large means ... if two of these criteria are met: • Total assets > €25m • Revenues > €50m • Employees > 250.	**Small and medium** sized undertakings listed on an EU exchange; small and non-complex credit institutions; and captive insurance undertakings.	**Non-EU companies** with EU revenues > €150m, and either: • EU subsidiary meets 'large' criteria • EU branch with revenue > €40m.

In fact, we know that, if we don't change, if the 8.1 billion of us on the planet today – or at least those of us who are consuming way beyond our fair share – don't do a better job of looking after our resources, we will cross more of the planetary boundaries that are neither negotiable nor retrievable. Let's talk about that.

IT'S NOT JUST CARBON!

First proposed by the Stockholm Resilience Centre in 2009, the Planetary Boundaries concept presents a set of nine planetary boundaries within which humanity can safely operate to avoid destabilising the Earth system – in other words, there are global environmental limits which, if crossed, could lead to abrupt, and potentially irreversible, environmental changes.

As of the latest official update, in September 2023, six out of the nine planetary boundaries have been crossed:

• Climate Change;

• Biosphere Integrity;

• Land-System Change;

- Biogeochemical Flows;
- Freshwater Use,; and
- Novel Entities.

Figure 1.3: The Nine Planetary Boundaries (updated 2023) – 1

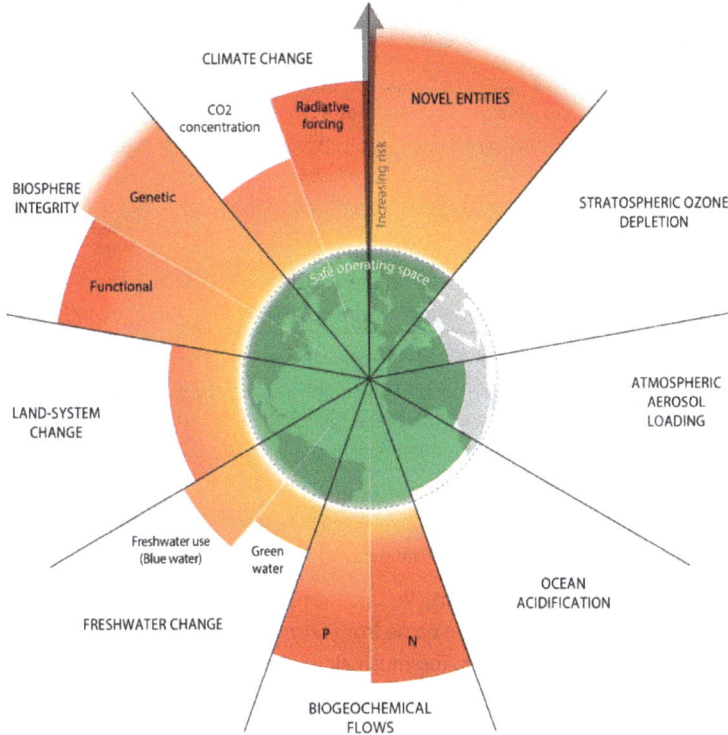

Credit: Azote for Stockholm Resilience Centre, based on analysis in Richardson *et al.* (2023).[6]

The boundary for Ocean Acidification is very close to being breached, indicating a significant change in the chemistry of the ocean, which can have widespread impacts on marine life. Also, the Atmospheric Aerosol Loading measure is being breached in certain regions.

It is important to note that these boundaries are interconnected, and crossing one can influence others, leading to a domino effect that can impact the entire Earth system. Nations, businesses and individuals alike have a role to play in understanding and addressing these challenges to ensure the planet remains safe and stable for all.

Figure 1.4: The Nine Planetary Boundaries – 2

Boundary	Explanation	Status
Climate Change	The amount of greenhouse gases like CO2 in the atmosphere. Too much traps heat, causing global warming and disrupting weather patterns.	☹
Biosphere Integrity	The rate at which species are disappearing. Losing too many species disrupts ecosystems and threatens food security.	☹
Land-System Change	Conversion of natural land (forests, grasslands) to human uses like agriculture and cities. Excessive conversion disrupts ecosystems and reduces the planet's ability to absorb CO2.	☹
Freshwater Use	The amount of freshwater humans withdraw from rivers, lakes, and aquifers. Using freshwater faster than it can be replenished can lead to water scarcity.	☹
Biogeo-chemical Flows	Natural cycles of nitrogen and phosphorus, important nutrients for plants. Adding too much fertilizer disrupts these cycles, leading to water pollution and algal blooms.	☹
Ocean Acidification	Acidity of the oceans caused by absorbing CO2 from the atmosphere. More acidic oceans harm marine life, especially shellfish.	😐
Atmospheric Aerosol Pollution	Those tiny particles and droplets suspended in the air, which can come from burning fossil fuels and dust storms. Too much air pollution affects human health, reduces crop yields, and disrupts weather patterns.	☺
Stratospheric Ozone Depletion	The thinning of the ozone layer in the upper atmosphere, which protects us from harmful ultraviolet radiation. Ozone depletion is mainly caused by chemicals used in refrigerants and aerosols.	☺
Release of Novel Entities	This refers to introducing new human-made chemicals and materials into the environment, such as plastics and pesticides. These can have unforeseen negative consequences for ecosystems and human health.	☹

As a Business Leader, Why Should I Care about Planetary Boundaries?

Crossing boundaries increases the risk of generating large-scale abrupt or irreversible changes. An unstable system always brings risk. Apart from the humanitarian catastrophes that will inevitably accompany the breaching of planetary boundaries, the very fact that the risk exists, means that all leaders of any collective – globe, continent, nation, institution or company – need to be aware of the holistic nature of the changes that are emerging. Drastic changes will not necessarily happen overnight, but together the boundaries mark a critical threshold for increasing risks to people and the ecosystems of which we are part. Just as businesses must manage financial or operational risks, planetary boundaries represent environmental risks that, if crossed, could lead to systemic failures with severe consequences for economies and societies.

This is a shift from 'business as usual' to 'business as unusual'.

Leaders who innovate, who consider new products, services, or processes, or indeed design whole new business models, will thrive. Those forward-looking leaders are already anticipating regulations that will inevitably arrive to respond to existing planetary boundary breaches, or that might arrive in the face of new or more extreme breaches, and they are creating solutions.

This 'business as unusual' brings with it a responsibility to operate within these boundaries. It recalls the Brundtland definition of sustainability referenced earlier in this chapter:

> *Sustainable development is development that meets the needs of the present without compromising the ability of future generations to meet their own needs.*

From a business, or a global economy perspective, which needs to consider all of the globe – the Global South as well as the Global North – for it to be sustainable, the future is about integrating sustainability into your core strategy within Earth's limits, the planetary boundaries – remembering that the boundaries are interrelated. It is not just about climate.

Carbon Tunnel Vision

In November 2021, Dr Jan Konietzko posted on LinkedIn a graphic (**Figure 1.5**) that highlighted a concern that still is valid today. Companies, and sustainability practitioners and consultants, are overly and narrowly focused on carbon emissions. Carbon Tunnel

Vision, the term describing this predisposition, was coined by Dr Konietzko at that time.

Companies that suffer from Carbon Tunnel Vision ignore the connections between the environmental impacts evident from the planetary boundaries but, equally and possibly more importantly, do not truly consider the social impacts, the people, the affected communities, the consumers and end-users, the 'you and me', our family and friends.

Figure 1.5: Carbon Tunnel Vision

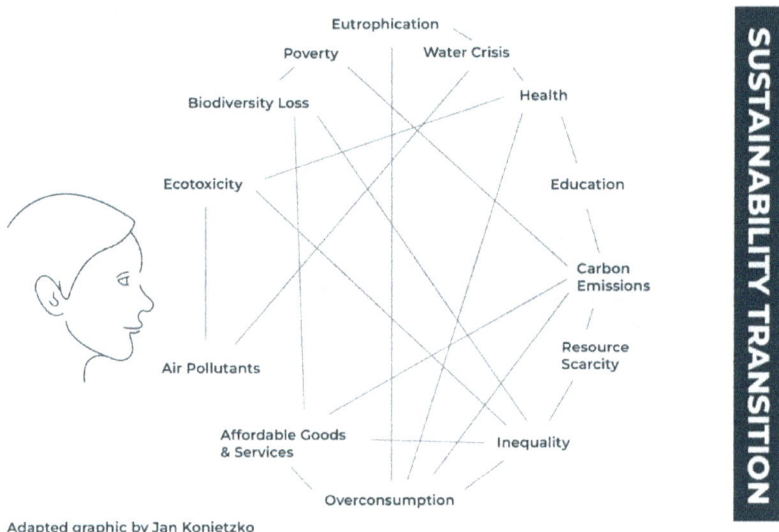

Adapted graphic by Jan Konietzko

Konietzko's graphic highlights how a 'tunnel vision' focus on carbon emissions misses out on the breadth of sustainability. The reality is that emissions are, in many cases, the consequence of what you do in the other areas. When you create waste, you generate emissions. When employees commute to work, or take business trips, they generate emissions. The design of your products, the degree to which they are designed with circularity in mind, greatly influences the impact those products have on people and the planet. From the components and labour used to make the products, to the distribution systems used to get the products into the hands of the customers, to the resources used when the product is being used, all are contributing factors to the impact on people and planet. These impacts may be measured in emissions of carbon, or methane, or other GHG. And that is before we consider the land used, the forests displaced, the oceans polluted or the imbalance in food and resource distribution that has its own embodied social cost.

Our task, as we move forward through the book, is to widen the aperture for you, to let more light in, and to help you to reflect on the breadth of the sustainability landscape. That way, you will see the path forward more clearly, visualise the opportunities as well as understand the obligations, and inspire and motivate others to travel this new and textured journey with you.

The best way to begin a journey is to have a map. For that, we will use the ESRS and its related reporting regulation, the CSRD.

THE CORPORATE SUSTAINABILITY REPORTING DIRECTIVE & THE EUROPEAN SUSTAINABILITY REPORTING STANDARDS

Ingrid De Doncker

The CSRD and the ESRS were the last two stops on our tour of sustainability history earlier in the chapter. They are two sides of the same coin in the EU's push for greater transparency and standardised sustainability reporting. CSRD is the 'what' and ESRS is the 'how'.

More specifically, CSRD is the overarching *legislation*. It mandates that certain companies in the EU must report on their sustainability performance. It is the law that requires companies to disclose sustainability information. The ESRS is the *framework*, outlining what information and metrics companies need to report on and how they should be presented to comply with the CSRD. The goal of the ESRS is to create a more sustainable economy by making companies accountable for their environmental and social practices.

The ESRS Framework

The ESRS framework allows a consistent approach to be used by all companies. This book follows that structure closely. **Chapters 2** to **10**, map directly to the ESRS topical standards, of which there are five Environmental, four Social, and one Governance.[7] The intention is that each topic is dealt with in enough detail for you to understand *what* it is, *why* it might be important, and *how* you might engage with it. At the end of each chapter, you will also find high-level reporting guidelines for that topic.

Figure 1.6: The Structure of the European Sustainability Reporting Standards

EUROPEAN SUSTAINABILITY REPORTING STANDARDS

ESRS 1: General Requirements

How ESRS operates; Double materiality, due diligence, value chain, time, preparation and structure, links with other reporting, transition provisions

ESRS 2: General Disclosures

Basis for preparation · Governance · Strategy · IRO Management · Metrics & Targets

E

ESRS E1 Climate Change
· Climate change adaptation
· GHG emissions (mitigation)
· Energy

ESRS E2 Pollution
· Pollution of air
· Pollution of water
· Pollution of soil
· Pollution of living organisms
· Substances of concern
· Substances of very high concern
· Micro-plastics

ESRS E3 Water + Marine resources
· Water consumption
· Marine resources

ESRS E4 Biodiversity + Ecosystems
· Direct impact drivers of biodiversity loss
· Impact on the state of species
· Impact on extent and condition of ecosystems
· Impacts and dependencies on ecosystem services

ESRS E Resources + Circular economy
· Resources inflows, resource use
· Resource outflows of products and services
· Waste

S

ESRS S1: Own Workforce
· Working conditions
· Equal treatment and opportunities for all
· Other work-related rights

ESRS S2: Value chain workers
· Working conditions
· Equal treatment and opportunities for all
· Other work-related rights

ESRS S3: Affected communities
· Civil and political rights
· Economic, social and cultural rights
· Rights of indigenous communities

ESRS S4: Consumers, end users
· Information-related impacts
· Personal safety
· Social inclusion

G

ESRS G1: Business Conduct

Corporate culture · Supplier relationship management, incl payment terms · Animal welfare
Protection of whistle-blowers · Political engagement, lobbying · Corruption and bribery

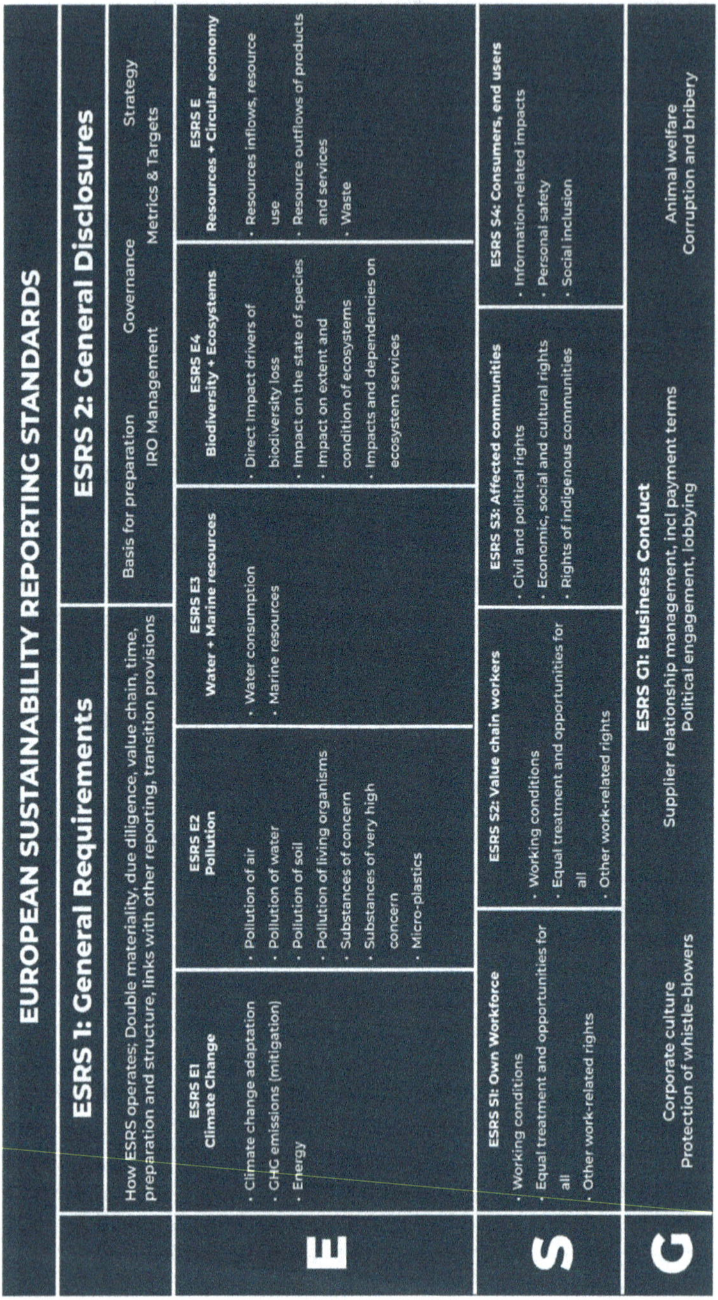

In the ESRS, each of the 10 topical standards reflect the three dimensions of sustainable development: Environmental (E), Social (S) and Governance (G), indicated by a letter and a number. For instance, ESRS-E4 deals with *Biodiversity & Ecosystems*, whereas ESRS-S2 covers *Value Chain Workers*. Each topical standard is itself structured into sustainability topics, sub-topics and sub-sub-topics, collectively called 'sustainability matters'.

In addition to the 10 topical standards (which only apply when the topic is material to the company or its stakeholders), there are two general cross-cutting standards, that always apply to all companies: ESRS 1 and ESRS 2.

As of 2024, all standards are common across industries, and are referred to as sector-agnostic. Sector-specific standards and requirements will follow in the coming years.

ESRS 1 – General Requirements

ESRS 1 is the first part of the reporting standards that make up the *European Sustainability Reporting Standards* (ESRS) for companies to comply with the CSRD. Its primary purpose is to establish the general principles and requirements for sustainability reporting, ensuring that companies disclose comprehensive and relevant sustainability information. This standard does not contain specific disclosure requirements but provides the overarching guidelines and concepts that underpin the entire ESRS framework.

Let's deep dive in to the 10 sections of this general requirements standard:

- **Categories of ESRS standards, reporting areas and drafting conventions:** The ESRS are categorised into three main types:
  - o Cross-cutting standards;
  - o Topical standards (covering Environmental, Social, and Governance issues); and
  - o Sector-specific standards, with the first two being applicable across all sectors.

  Cross-cutting standards, such as ESRS 1 and ESRS 2, set general requirements and disclosures that apply to all sustainability matters, while topical and sector-specific standards provide more detailed guidance tailored to specific sustainability topics and sectors. The drafting conventions emphasise clarity and consistency in reporting, ensuring that sustainability information is presented in a structured manner that enhances understanding and comparability;

- **Qualitative characteristics of information:** The qualitative characteristics of information outlined in the ESRS highlight the need for sustainability disclosures to be relevant and faithfully represented, ensuring that they can influence user decisions under a double materiality approach. Key characteristics include **relevance**, which ensures that information can impact decision-making; **faithful representation**, requiring that information is complete, neutral, and accurate; and **enhancing characteristics** such as comparability, verifiability, and understandability. These characteristics collectively aim to provide users with reliable, coherent, and meaningful sustainability information that supports informed decision-making;

- **Double materiality as the basis for sustainability disclosures:** Double materiality serves as the foundational principle for sustainability disclosures, encompassing two dimensions:
  o Impact materiality;
  o Financial materiality.

  Impact materiality assesses the impact of an organisation's activities on the environment and society, while financial materiality evaluates how sustainability issues can affect the organisation's financial performance and position. The regulation mandates that organisations consider both dimensions in their reporting, ensuring a comprehensive understanding of sustainability impacts and risks, which ultimately informs stakeholders and supports better decision-making;

- **Due diligence:** The due diligence process outlined in the ESRS involves a systematic approach for organisations to identify, prevent, mitigate, and account for actual and potential negative impacts on the environment and people associated with their operations and value chain. It emphasises the importance of engaging with affected stakeholders and assessing negative impacts to inform the organisation's materiality assessment and sustainability reporting. The process is ongoing and may lead to changes in the organisation's strategy, business model, and operations, ensuring that sustainability considerations are integrated into decision-making and governance frameworks;

- **Value chain:** The value chain section of the ESRS highlights the importance of reporting on material impacts, risks, and opportunities associated with both upstream and downstream business relationships. It requires organisations to extend their sustainability disclosures to include relevant information about their value chain, following a double materiality approach that considers both the organisation's impacts on sustainability and the sustainability impacts on the organisation. Additionally, it acknowledges the challenges in obtaining value chain information, particularly from SMEs, and allows for the use of estimates and sector averages when direct data collection is not feasible, ensuring that material sustainability matters are adequately reported;

- **Time horizons:** The time horizon section of the ESRS defines specific intervals for short-term, medium-term, and long-term reporting periods, with short-term aligning with the organisation's financial reporting period, medium-term extending up to five years, and long-term exceeding five years. It outlines the need for organisations to provide additional breakdowns for long-term impacts or actions when relevant, ensuring that users receive pertinent information for sustainability assessments. It allows for flexibility in defining these time horizons based on industry-specific characteristics and the organisation's unique processes, ensuring that the information remains relevant and useful for stakeholders;

- **Preparation and presentation of sustainability information:** The preparation and presentation of sustainability information requires organisations to disclose comparative information for quantitative metrics and monetary amounts from previous periods, ensuring clarity and consistency in reporting. It calls out the importance of coherence, clarity, and comparability in sustainability disclosures, encouraging a structured approach that connects sustainability-related impacts, risks, and opportunities to financial statements. The section outlines the need for concise, material disclosures that avoid unnecessary duplication and use clear language, enhancing the overall understanding of sustainability information for users;

- **Structure of sustainability statement:** The structure of the sustainability statement mandates that it be presented in a dedicated section of the management report, clearly distinguishing between ESRS-required disclosures and other information. To facilitate easy access and understanding, it should be organised into four main parts:
  - General information;
  - Environmental information;
  - Social information;
  - Governance information.

The statement must also ensure that disclosures related to environmental objectives are clearly identifiable and may incorporate information by reference, provided it maintains readability and cohesiveness;

- **Linkages with other parts of corporate reporting and connected information:** The section on linkages with other parts of corporate reporting outlines the need for organisations to provide clear connections between sustainability statements and other corporate disclosures, enhancing the coherence of information presented. It requires that sustainability-related impacts, risks, and opportunities be linked to financial statements, allowing users to understand the implications of sustainability on financial performance. This section highlights the importance of incorporating information by reference, ensuring that all relevant disclosures are accessible and aligned with the overall corporate reporting framework;

- **Transitional provisions:** The transitional provisions section eases the implementation of sustainability reporting requirements, allowing for phased-in disclosure obligations over the initial years. It permits organisations to omit certain disclosure requirements or adapt their reporting based on prior disclosures, particularly in the first three annual sustainability statements, to facilitate a smoother transition. It acknowledges the challenges in gathering comprehensive data, especially for SMEs, and encourages explanations of efforts made to obtain necessary information regarding the value chain during the initial reporting period.

Overall, ESRS 1 is crucial for ensuring that companies within the scope of the CSRD provide transparent, accurate, and comprehensive sustainability reports, aligning with the EU's broader goals of enhancing corporate accountability and promoting sustainable business practices.

ESRS 2 – General Disclosures

ESRS 2 is the mandatory standard designed to standardise sustainability reporting across all sectors. Developed by EFRAG and enforced by the CSRD, ESRS 2 mandates that all companies, regardless of their industry, disclose specific sustainability information. This standard is sector-agnostic and cross-cutting, meaning it applies universally across various sustainability topics, ensuring a consistent and comprehensive approach to sustainability reporting.

ESRS 2 is designed to ensure that sustainability reporting is comprehensive, consistent, and comparable across different organisations, thereby enhancing transparency and accountability in corporate sustainability practices. The key objectives of ESRS 2 are:

- **Standardisation of reporting**: ESRS 2 sets out the disclosure requirements that apply universally to all undertakings, ensuring that sustainability information is reported in a standardised manner. This includes general characteristics of the company, an overview of its business operations, and specific disclosures on compliance matters;

- **Comprehensive coverage**: The standard covers various aspects of sustainability reporting, including governance, strategy, impact, risk and opportunity management, and metrics and targets. This comprehensive approach ensures that all relevant areas of sustainability are addressed, providing a holistic view of a company's sustainability performance;

- **Alignment with other standards**: ESRS 2 aligns with frameworks such as the TCFD and the ISSB, fostering consistency and comparability across different reporting standards. This alignment helps companies streamline their reporting processes and meet multiple regulatory requirements simultaneously;

- **Double materiality**: ESRS 2 incorporates the concept of double materiality, which requires companies to report not only on how sustainability issues impact their financial performance (financial materiality) but also on how their operations affect the environment and society (impact materiality). This dual focus ensures a comprehensive view of a company's sustainability impacts and responsibilities;

- **Enhanced transparency and accountability**: By mandating detailed disclosures on governance structures, strategies, materiality assessments, and performance indicators, ESRS 2 aims to enhance the transparency and accountability of corporate sustainability reporting. This helps stakeholders, including investors, regulators, and the public, to better understand and evaluate a company's sustainability performance;

- **Facilitation of compliance**: ESRS 2 provides clear guidelines and minimum disclosure requirements, making it easier for companies to comply with the CSRD. This includes specific instructions on how to prepare and present sustainability statements, ensuring that companies can meet their reporting obligations effectively and efficiently.

ESRS 2 is structured into five key reporting sections, each addressing different aspects of sustainability reporting:

- **The BP section** includes two key disclosure requirements:
  - BP-1, which mandates the general basis for the preparation of sustainability statements;
  - BP-2, which addresses disclosures related to specific circumstances;

  BP-1 requires entities to disclose whether their sustainability statements are prepared on a consolidated or individual basis, the scope of consolidation, and any exemptions used, such as those related to intellectual property or sensitive information. BP-2 focuses on providing context for specific circumstances that affect the preparation of the sustainability statement, such as deviations from standard time horizons or the use of value chain estimations;

- **The Governance section (GOV)** focuses on the roles, responsibilities, and expertise of the administrative, management, and supervisory bodies in relation to sustainability matters. It includes disclosures on the composition and diversity of these bodies, their oversight of sustainability processes, and the integration of sustainability-related performance in incentive schemes. This section aims to provide transparency on how governance structures support sustainability initiatives within the organisation;

- **The Strategy & Business Model section (SBM)** requires companies to disclose how their strategy and business model interact with and impact sustainability matters. This includes information on the company's market position, key elements of its strategy, and how it addresses material impacts, risks, and opportunities. The section also covers how stakeholder interests and views are integrated into the company's strategy and business model, ensuring that the company's approach to sustainability is aligned with broader societal and environmental goals;

- **The Impact, Risk & Opportunity Management section (IRO)** outlines the processes by which companies identify, assess, and manage sustainability-related impacts, risks, and opportunities. This includes a detailed description of the methodologies and assumptions used in these processes, as well as how these processes are integrated into the company's overall risk management framework. The section also requires companies to disclose the outcomes of their materiality assessments, providing a clear understanding of the most significant sustainability issues they face. Under the IRO section, you will find detailed disclosure datapoints in relation to policies (MDR-P), and also actions and allocated resources (MDR-A) when an organisation has policies and action plans in place and for when they don't;

- **The Metrics & Targets section (MT)** focuses on the specific metrics and targets that companies use to track their sustainability performance. This includes both standardised metrics defined in the ESRS, and entity-specific metrics developed by the company. Companies must disclose the methodologies and assumptions behind these metrics, as well as their progress towards achieving their sustainability targets. This section ensures that companies are held accountable for their sustainability commitments and provides stakeholders with clear, comparable data on sustainability performance. The MDR data points under this section relate to the metrics, and targets for material sustainability matters. These requirements ensure that companies provide a clear, transparent, and accountable report on their sustainability practices and performance.

This structure ensures that all relevant areas of sustainability are covered comprehensively.

This Standard should be read in conjunction with ESRS 1 *General Requirements*. ESRS 2 outlines clearly, in five *Disclosure Requirements* (DRs), the narrative and numeric data points (DPs) an organisation should comply with. There are 127 *Shall* DPs, irrespective of materiality. Of these, 24 are numeric, 89 narrative and 14 semi-narrative. There are 12 additional *May* DPs.

Figure 1.7 shows the structure of the ESRS 2 DRs and DPs that must be reported, irrespective of materiality.

Even though ESRS is predominantly a European standard, the requirements of other standards are closely aligned. Already, at time of writing, there are significant interoperability activities between the ESRS and the standards from the main US-based standards body, the ISSB. Between ESRS and ISSB, most other major economies outside of the EU and the US are covered by some variation of one of the two.

EFRAG is the advisory body charged with the definition of the ESRS. It provides extensive guidance material to aid implementation of ESRS, and by extension CSRD. Also, as the standards evolve, and new requirements emerge – for example, sector-specific standards – EFRAG's website (efrag.org) is a tremendously valuable resource.

Figure 1.7: ESRS 2 – Mandatory Disclosure Requirements

ESRS 2	General disclosures
	BASIS FOR PREPARATION
ESRS2-BP-1	General basis for preparation of sustainability statements.
ESRS2-BP-2	Disclosures in relation to specific circumstances.
	GOVERNANCE
ESRS2-GOV-1	The role of the administrative, management and supervisory bodies.
ESRS2-GOV-2	Information provided to and sustainability matters addressed by the organisation's administrative, management and supervisory bodies.
ESRS2-GOV-3	Integration of sustainability-related performance in incentive schemes.
ESRS2-GOV-4	Statement on due diligence.
ESRS2-GOV-5	Risk management and internal controls over sustainability reporting.
	STRATEGY
ESRS2-SBM-1	Strategy, business model and value chain.
ESRS2-SBM-2	Interests and views of stakeholders.
ESRS2-SBM-3	Material impacts, risks and opportunities and their interaction with strategy and business model.
	IMPACT, RISK & OPPORTUNITY MANAGEMENT
	4.1 Disclosure on the materiality assessment process
ESRS2-IRO-1	Description of the processes to identify and assess material climate-related impacts, risks and opportunities.
ESRS2-IRO-2	Disclosure requirements in ESRS covered by the undertaking's sustainability statement.
	4.2 Minimum Disclosure requirement on policies and actions
ESRS2-IRO-MDR-P	Policies adopted to manage material sustainability matters.
ESRS2-IRO-MDR-A	Actions and resources in relation to material sustainability matters.

	METRICS & TARGETS
ESRS2-IRO-MDR-M	Metrics in relation to material sustainability matters.
ESRS2-IRO-MDR-T	Tracking effectiveness of policies and actions through targets.

LOOKING BACK FROM 2062

Big Yellow Taxi was written, composed, and recorded by Canadian singer-songwriter Joni Mitchell in 1970, after she noticed a huge parking lot that tarnished the natural beauty of the islands in the middle of the northern Pacific Ocean.

> *They paved paradise and put up a parking lot*
> *With a pink hotel, a boutique, and a swinging hot spot.*

> *Don't it always seem to go*
> *That you don't know what you got 'til it's gone?*
> *They paved paradise and put up a parking lot.*

The song bemoans environmental destruction and excessive urban development. It goes on to caution about the destruction of trees and exhorts farmers to "put away your DDT", one of the most infamous insecticides linked to a range of diseases.[8]

In the same year, Neil Young, coincidentally another Canadian, released *After the Goldrush*, with the simple line:

> *Look at Mother Nature on the run, in the nineteen-seventies.*

I expect that some of the readers may be too young, like my son – he of The Question – to remember these songs, or even know who Joni Mitchell is. But I expect everyone will understand the message. We understood in the 1970s that we were causing irreparable harm to the planet. Maybe we did not know at that point that it was irreparable, but we knew we were causing harm.

In 1970, the global population was 3.7 billion and the intensity of carbon in the atmosphere was about 325 ppm.

The increase in atmospheric concentrations of carbon dioxide (CO_2) and other long-lived GHG, such as methane, increase the absorption and emission of infrared radiation by the atmosphere, so the world gets hotter.

In 2024, the global population is 8.1 billion and the CO_2 ppm number is gone up to 425ppm.

Figure 1.7: The Keeling Curve

Monthly mean CO_2 concentration

Mauna Loa 1958-2023

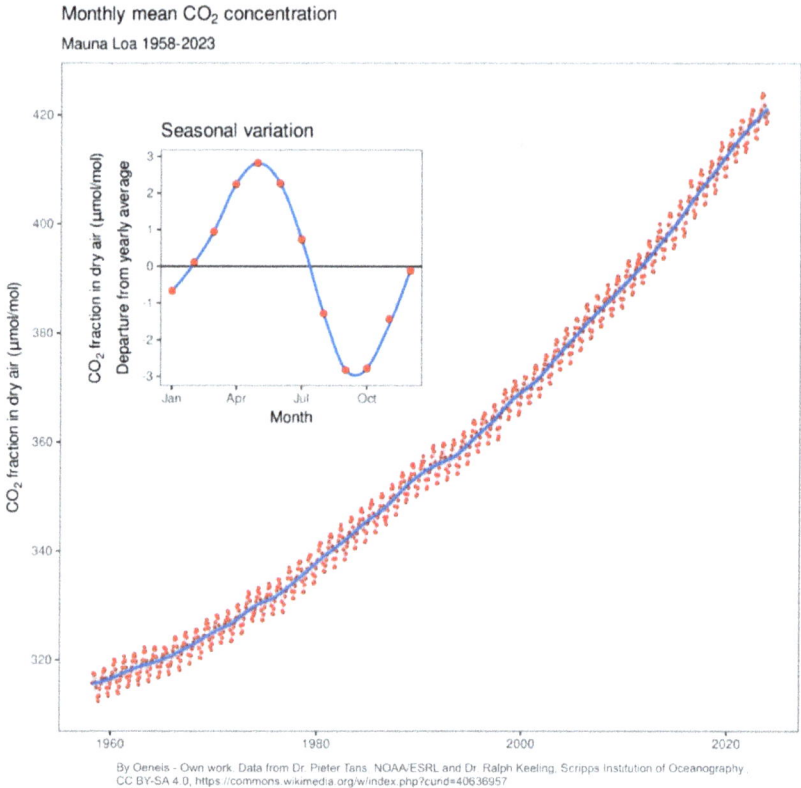

By Oeneis - Own work. Data from Dr. Pieter Tans, NOAA/ESRL and Dr. Ralph Keeling, Scripps Institution of Oceanography. CC BY-SA 4.0, https://commons.wikimedia.org/w/index.php?cund=40636957

In 1953, Dave Keeling started sampling the atmosphere near Monterey in California. He began to take air samples throughout the day and night and soon detected an intriguing diurnal pattern. The air contained more CO_2 at night than during the day and, after correcting for the effects of water vapour, had about the same amount of CO_2 every afternoon, 310 ppm. He repeated these measurements in the rain forests of the Olympic peninsula and in the high mountain forests in Arizona. Everywhere, the data were the same, so he began a daily routine, and start to draw the now famous Keeling curve, shown in **Figure 1.7**.

By the early 1970s, the curve was getting serious attention and played a key role in launching a research programme into the effect of rising CO_2 on climate. Since then, the rise has been relentless and shows a remarkably constant relationship with fossil-fuel burning that can be accounted for based on the simple premise that 57% of fossil-fuel emissions remain airborne.[9]

Keeling's research was funded in part by the fossil fuel industry. So, as early as 1954, the fossil fuel industry was aware of its contribution to increased concentration of CO_2 in the atmosphere.

Whether the fossil fuel industry, or the rest of us, knew back then, or in the intervening decades, that we were causing irreparable harm to the planet is a matter of conjecture. Some would argue that Carl Sagan's 1985 speech to the US Congress, where he advised on the dangers of the burning of fossil fuels intensifying what was then called the 'greenhouse effect', should have set off alarm bells. In any case, what we know for sure is that we cannot continue along the same path. We now need to look into the future, let's say 2062, and look back from there to design today's path forward.

Learning from the Iroquois & the Japanese

Long before Dave Keeling, Carl Sagan, and even the industrial age, were the Iroquois. Established in the earlier part of the last millennium, the Iroquois were a confederacy of multiple Indian tribes in Ontario and upstate New York. Their strategising was governed by what has become known as the Seventh Generation Principle of the *Great Law of the Iroquois*:

> *In every deliberation, we must consider the impact on the seventh generation.*

That's really not much different from Brundtland's definition of sustainability. It just provides a little bit more structure to our thinking. If you considered how the actions in your business today would impact the world seven generations hence, how would that change what you do? Even if we reduced the timeframe to seven decades, the minimum likely lifespan of today's children, can we look that far ahead?

Tatsuyoshi Saijo, a Japanese economist, inspired by the Iroquois' Seventh Generation Principle, is at the forefront of the 'Future Design' movement. He is designing methods to have the voice of decision-makers from the future – who, by definition, would care more about future generations – in today's boardrooms and strategy sessions. The lives of future generations will be directly affected by the decisions we make today, yet they don't have a voice in politics or business today – so how can we make sure their needs are considered? Saijo's principles are simple and elegant, and best explained by an example.

In 2015, at a town hall of 20 residents in the small community of Yahaba, in north-eastern Japan, the community wanted to design policies to shape the future of Yahaba. Would it be better to invest in infrastructure or childcare? Should they promote renewable energy or industrial farming?

Half the citizens were invited to be themselves, and the other half were asked to put on special ceremonial robes and play the part of people from 2060, meaning they'd be representing the interests of a future generation during group deliberations.

What unfolded was striking. The citizens who were just being themselves advocated for policies that would boost their lifestyle in the short-term. But the people in robes advocated for much more radical policies – from massive healthcare investments to climate change action – that would be better for the town in the long-term. They managed to convince their fellow citizens that taking that approach would benefit their grandkids. In the end, the entire group reached a consensus that they should, in some ways, act against their own immediate self-interest in order to help the future.

Looking Forward

Can we replicate Saijo's decision-making process in our homes, offices, businesses or countries? In some ways, it is not too big a leap. Instead of building a three-, five- or 10-year plan, what if we looked out 30 years, and let the magic of imagination, spirit and generosity put ourselves in that frame of mind, and look back at the plans and strategies being made today, and then we can be the voice of 2062 in the room.

We hope you use this book as your occasional companion to deal with today, tomorrow and the future. Each chapter, from **Chapter 2: Climate Change** to **Chapter 10: Business Conduct** maps to the ESRS and the expertise from my co-authors here is extreme. It really is the best of the best, and given with a willing heart to help you on your sustainability journey.

In **Chapter 11: What If...?**, you are invited to consider scenarios that you may not have imagined before, ideas that may help you envision a more sustainable future, and that may help you answer the question my son Christian asked me: "Will the planet still be OK when I am your age?"

The online resources available at the accompanying website (**www.thecustomeristheplanet.com**) will be updated and augmented as long as people still need them. Please drop in there and let us know what you think and how your journey is going.

See you in 2062.

1   *This Norwegian's past may connect with your future*
    https://web.archive.org/web/20100623004236/;
    http://oregonfuture.oregonstate.edu/part1/pf1_03.html.

2   World Commission on Environment & Development (1987). *Our Common*
    Future.

3   *The history of socially responsible and ethical investment* http://www.the-
    ethical-partnership.co.uk/HistoryofEthicalInvestment.htm.

4   *Nike child labour scandal* https://www.studysmarter.co.uk/explanations/
    business-studies/business-case-studies/nike-sweatshop-scandal/.

5   *Principle of Responsible Investment* https://www.unpri.org/about-us/what-
    are-the-principles-for-responsible-investment.

6   Richardson et al. (2023). Earth beyond six of nine planetary boundaries,
    ScienceAdvances, 9(37). Doi 10.1126/sciadv.adh2458.

7   There are different sets of ESRS to be used by different companies in the
    CSRD's scope: the full ESRS as shown here – to be used by listed and large
    companies; a standard for listed SMEs; and a standard for third-country
    companies. A guide is available from the GRI at globalreporting.org that
    explains CSRD in detail and how it is applied to entities of different sizes.

8   In 1972, EPA issued a cancellation order for DDT based on its adverse
    environmental effects, such as those to wildlife, as well as its potential human
    health risks.

9   *The history of the Keeling Curve* https://keelingcurve.ucsd.edu/2013/04/03/the-
    history-of-the-keeling-curve/.

2

CLIMATE CHANGE

David Carlin

I sometimes joke that climate is the perfect field for a generalist to pretend to be a specialist. When people ask "What do you work on?", they aren't expecting an answer like "Well, finance, policy, environment, economics, psychology, and science". However, if you insert 'climate' before each of those words, an understanding seems to grow in their eyes: "Oh, you're a climate person." How ridiculous is the idea of a 'climate person' – aren't all of us on this planet 'climate people'? Climate change and other sustainability challenges demand interdisciplinary and systemic solutions. Those interconnections suit me well, as someone whose academic work has been in behavioural science, whose passions lie in history and natural sciences, whose work experiences have been in finance, and whose earliest parental lessons were in social action.

My career began in the field of quantitative risk at a bank, as I contemplated an academic career. From there, I moved into management consulting, but found an outlet for my pent-up social activism by founding a non-profit. My combination of professional and personal experiences led me to overseeing a programme in Geneva with the United Nations Environment Programme (UNEP) and financial institutions on climate-related financial risks. There, I found that climate brought together my various passions, interests, and experiences across finance, psychology, science, political economy, and policy. From my work at UNEP, I began to believe in something I call 'ecosystems theory'. Whether in a rainforest or within the field of climate action, we cannot evaluate the effects of a single action or actor without considering the system as a whole. Balancing this systemic view is an appreciation that individuals have far greater impacts than they often realise. A small number of vocal climate advocates can drive a policy shift and a committed executive can drive climate strategy forward at their firm. My greatest desire is to take these lessons about systems and individuals to help empower organisations and individuals to create positive change.

David Carlin

THE CLIMATE CHALLENGE FOR BUSINESS

How Has Our Climate Changed?

Climate change refers to long-term alterations in the average weather patterns that have come to define Earth's local, regional, and global climates. These alterations have a broad range of observed effects that are synonymous with the term.

Global warming is the long-term heating of Earth's surface observed since the pre-industrial period (between 1850 and 1900) due to human activities, primarily fossil-fuel burning, that increase levels of heat-trapping greenhouse gases (GHGs) in Earth's atmosphere.[1]

Increase in global temperatures and record CO_2 levels

Since the pre-industrial period, human activities are estimated to have increased Earth's global average temperature. We know that, in 2024, this increase will likely exceed 1.5°C – the watershed number that the scientists have been using as a guiding threshold, and which is currently increasing by more than 0.2°C (0.36°F) per decade. The overwhelming scientific consensus is that the current warming trend is unequivocally caused by human activity since the 1950s. Furthermore, scientists concur that current warming is proceeding at a rate unseen for millennia.

The extra heat is driving regional and seasonal temperature extremes. Among other effects, this reduces snow cover and sea ice, intensifies heavy rainfall, and changes habitat ranges for plants and animals – with some expanding and others shrinking. As the map in **Figure 2.1** shows, most land areas have warmed faster than most ocean areas, and the Arctic is warming faster than most other regions. Alarmingly, it is also clear that the rate of warming over the past few decades is much faster than the average rate since the start of the 20th century.[2]

The main driver of climate change is the 'greenhouse effect', which is what causes global warming.[3] Some gases in the Earth's atmosphere absorb and radiate heat, acting like the glass in a greenhouse (hence the name), trapping the sun's heat and stopping it from leaking back into space. Many of these GHGs occur naturally, but human activities are increasing the concentrations of some. Of particular concern are carbon dioxide (CO_2), methane (CH_4), nitrous oxide (N_2O), hydrofluorocarbons (HFCs), perfluorocarbons (PFCs), and sulphur hexafluoride (SF_6). Importantly, CO_2 comprises Earth's most important GHG. Unlike oxygen or nitrogen (which make up most of our atmosphere), GHGs absorb heat radiating from the Earth's surface and re-release it in all directions – including back toward Earth's surface.

Figure 2.1: Global Warming, 1994 - 2023[4]

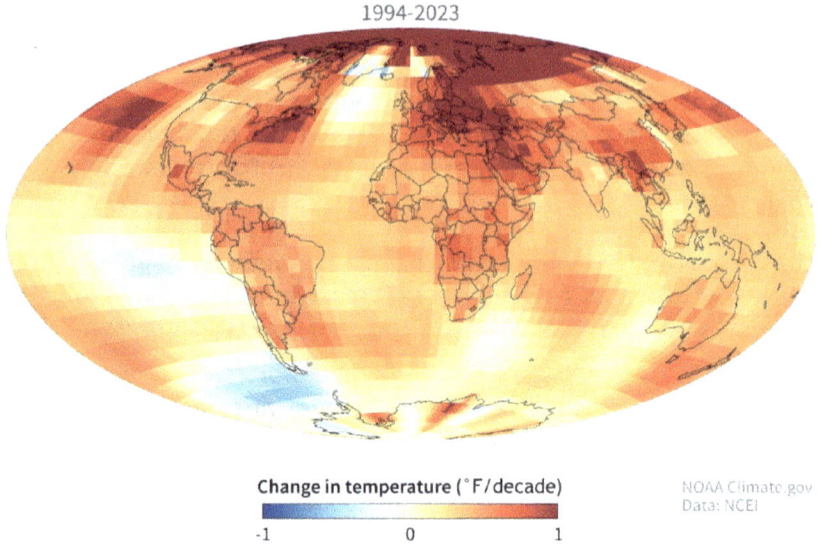

1994-2023

Change in temperature (°F/decade)

-1   0   1

NOAA Climate.gov
Data: NCEI

Figure 2.2: The Keeling Curve Overlaid with Temperature Change[5]

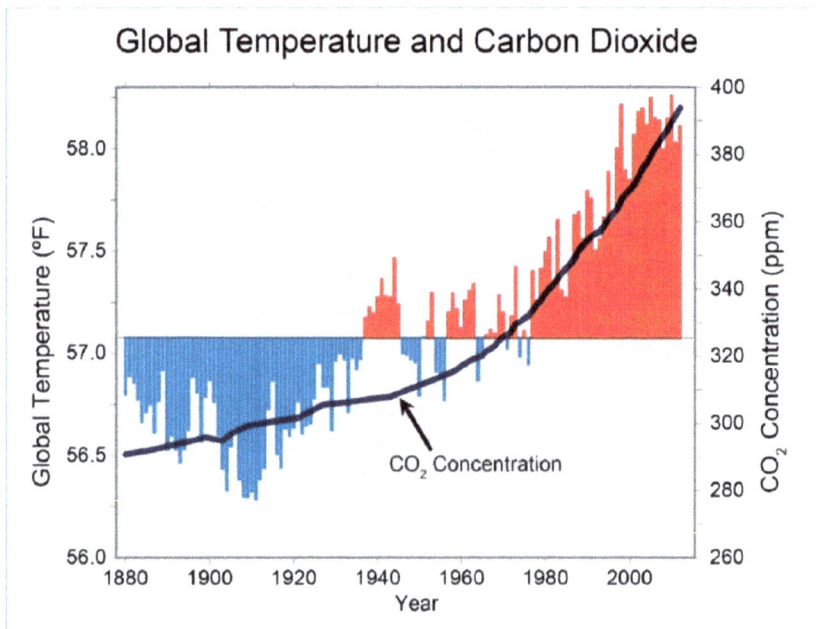

Global Temperature and Carbon Dioxide

CO$_2$ Concentration

But by adding more CO_2 to the atmosphere, people are supercharging the natural greenhouse effect, causing global temperature to rise. According to observations by the US National Oceanic & Atmospheric Administration's (NOAA) Global Monitoring Lab, CO_2 alone accounted for about two-thirds of the total heating influence of all human-produced GHGs in 2021.[6] This is also illustrated by **Figure 2.2**, which shows the correlation of CO_2 concentration and global temperature since 1880.

The effects of climate change
According to the UN,[7] climate change leads to changing weather patterns and disruptions in the usual balance of nature. These effects pose many risks to human beings, as well as all other forms of life on Earth. Some of these impacts include:

- **Hotter temperatures:** As GHG concentrations rise, so does the global surface temperature. Among other effects, higher temperatures increase heat-related illnesses and make working outdoors more difficult. Wildfires are another worrying result of hotter temperatures;

- **More severe storms:** As temperatures rise, moisture evaporates, exacerbating extreme rainfall and flooding, leading to more frequent and more severe destructive storms, which can cause deaths and leave individuals, businesses, and governments facing huge economic losses;

- **Increased drought:** Global warming exacerbates water shortages in already water-stressed regions, bringing an increased risk of agricultural droughts, which can cause harvests to fail and lead to food insecurity, and ecological droughts, which increase the vulnerability of a wide range of ecosystems. This process of desertification in turn reduces the amount of land available for growing food;

- **A warming, rising ocean:** The ocean soaks up most of the heat from global warming. As oceans warm, their volume increases since water expands as it gets warmer, and so we are seeing the level of the world's oceans and seas rise. This is exacerbated by the melting of the ice sheets in Earth's polar regions. Higher sea levels are a concern for coastal and island communities, with life in some areas becoming untenable. In addition, as CO_2 in the oceans builds up towards its capacity point, the acidity of seawater increases, putting the world's marine life and coral reefs at risk. Most concerning is the fact that we rely on oceans to absorb CO_2 from the atmosphere but, as oceans warm, their absorption capacity reduces, resulting in higher concentrations of atmospheric CO_2;

- **Loss of species:** Exacerbated by climate change, the world is losing species at a greater rate than at any other time in recorded human history;

- **Food shortages**: Changes in the climate and increases in extreme weather events are among the reasons behind a global rise in hunger and poor nutrition. A warmer world will see fisheries, crops, and livestock becoming less productive – and potentially being destroyed completely. With the ocean becoming more acidic, marine resources that feed billions of people are also at risk;

- **Growing public health challenges**: Climate impacts are already harming health in many ways: greater air pollution, disease, extreme weather events, forced displacement, and pressures on mental health. There is also an increase in hunger and poor nutrition in places where people are struggling to grow or find sufficient food;

- **Poverty and displacement**: Climate change increases the factors that force people into poverty and cements the factors that keep them there. Floods may sweep away urban slums, for example, destroying homes and livelihoods. Equally, heat can make it difficult to work in outdoor jobs, while water scarcity reduces income from farming. Between 2010 and 2019, weather-related events are estimated to have annually displaced 23.1 million people.[8] Most refugees come from countries that are most vulnerable and least ready to adapt to the impacts of climate change.

How Do We Know Human Activities Are Driving Climate Change?

Evidence of the role of fossil-fuel combustion

In the Industrial Revolution, people started engaging in many activities that use fossil fuels. Using fossil fuels takes carbon out of the ground and burning it puts CO_2 into the atmosphere. When levels of CO_2 in the atmosphere increase, heat becomes trapped – thereby pushing up the temperature. As a direct cause of humans adding more CO_2 to the atmosphere, temperatures around the world are increasing. Since the middle of the 20th century, annual emissions from burning fossil fuels have increased every decade, from close to 11 billion tons of CO_2 per year in the 1960s to an estimated 36.6 billion tons in 2022.[9]

The more we overshoot the level of atmospheric CO_2 that natural processes can remove, the faster the concentration of that CO_2 rises. The annual rate of increase in atmospheric CO_2 over the past 60 years is about 100 times faster than previous natural increases, such as those at the end of the last Ice Age 11,000 to 17,000 years ago.[10]

Figure 2.3: Global Atmospheric Carbon Dioxide Compared to Annual Emissions, 1751 - 2022[11]

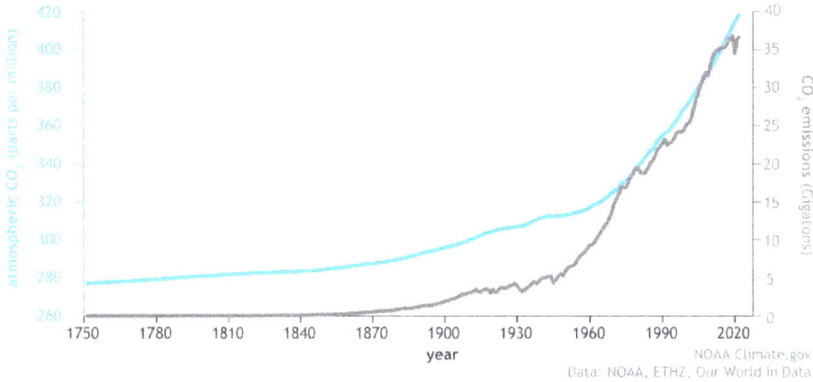

NOAA Climate.gov
Data: NOAA, ETHZ, Our World in Data

The role of deforestation

Land use change, principally deforestation, contributes between 12% and 20% of global GHG emissions. When deforestation – the purposeful clearing or thinning of trees and forests – occurs, much of the carbon stored by trees is released back into the atmosphere as CO_2, which contributes to climate change. In the last decade, most deforestation occurred across the humid tropics, in Africa and South America. Its key driver is the global demand for agricultural commodities: agribusinesses clear huge tracts of forest and use the land for the cultivation of high-value cash crops (such as palm oil and soya) and for cattle ranching.[12]

Note that, according to the Center for Global Development, avoiding deforestation Is better for the climate than reforestation.[13]

Climate change's impact on our planet is undeniable, with clear scientific evidence highlighting the role of human activities in driving this change. The overwhelming conclusion of peer-reviewed research is that phenomena such as the increasing temperature, retreating ice, and rising sea levels stem directly from human-produced GHGs.

What Are the Financial Risks of Climate Change?

For companies of all kinds and sizes, climate-related disasters can no longer be considered isolated or random events: they are a symptom of our global ecological emergency and a threat to people, the planet, and businesses. Companies that want to stay in business need to prioritise efforts to assess and address their short- and long-term climate risks.[14]

The Task Force on Climate-related Financial Disclosures (TCFD) was created in 2015 by the Basel-based Financial Stability Board (FSB), whose role has been to promote international financial stability since its creation in 2009 following the global financial crisis. The FSB seeks to make firms' climate-related disclosures more consistent and therefore more comparable.[15] By following the TCFD framework, companies can better understand, manage and disclose their exposure to climate-related financial risks. According to the TCFD, there are two categories of climate risks:

- **Physical risks** are driven by the rising temperature level and describe material risks that result from climate change, including potential damage to facilities and infrastructure, negative impacts on operations, reduced availability of water and raw material, and disruptions to business supply chains;
  - o Acute physical risks are event-driven, including a rise in the severity and frequency of extreme weather events – heatwaves, hurricanes, fires, floods, etc – that are increasingly resulting from climate change.
  - o Chronic physical risks (or 'incremental' climate impact) are the knock-on effects of longer-term shifts in climate patterns, such as a rise in sea levels, chronic heatwaves, and changes in seasons (shorter winters and longer summers) with accompanying changes in annual average precipitation;[16]
- **Transition risks** arise from the changes needed to transition to a low-carbon economy. Depending on the nature, speed, and focus of these changes, they may pose varying levels of risk to organisations. Alternatively, if an organisation is a low-carbon emitter and in the renewable energy or climate transition market, it could find opportunities in transition.

Transition risks are influenced by the speed and scale of emissions reductions, while physical risks are directly linked to temperature changes. The magnitude and severity of both physical and transition risks vary depending on the chosen path towards net zero that countries and companies take, making it crucial to understand the trade-offs between the various options for climate action. Here are some examples of how businesses in certain sectors might be exposed:[17]

- **Energy:** With the push for greener energy sources – and energy security – governments are increasingly shifting to a reliance on renewable energy sources and demanding net zero carbon emissions from energy producers. Companies in this industry must also navigate the potential for stranded assets, where fossil fuel-based energy investments may lose value or turn into liabilities due to regulatory changes and the evolving energy market dynamics;

- **Mining:** Precious metal mining could be at financial risk from policies that introduce carbon pricing. The negative effects of mining on the climate and the environment are a reputational issue for mining companies, making investors nervous;

- **Agriculture:** Vulnerable to risks from regulatory changes aimed at reducing emissions and sustainable farm practices which may lead to increased costs;

- **Real estate:** An increasing need for energy-efficient buildings and infrastructures can bring extra costs and devalue existing properties;

- **Consumer goods:** Changing consumer behaviour and demand for sustainable products bring risks in this sector.

The TCFD categorises transition risks into four major types: policy and legal, technology, markets, and reputational risks.[18]

Policy and legal risks are a significant component of climate-related transition risks. Policy risks arise from the possibility that changes in policies, regulations, and laws will affect the operations, financial performance, or market positions of businesses. For example, a new carbon tax could increase operational costs for companies reliant on fossil fuels. Legal risks encompass the threat of legal action related to climate change. This can include litigation for failing to mitigate risks associated with climate change, for inadequate disclosure of climate-related financial risks, or for causing environmental damage.

Technological risks under climate-related transition refer to the challenges and uncertainties businesses face as they adapt to new technologies required for the transition to a low-carbon economy. These risks can emerge from various factors, including the pace of technological change, the adoption and scalability of new technologies, and potential dependencies on unproven or costly innovations.

Figure 2.4: Climate-Related Risks, Opportunities & Financial Impact[19]

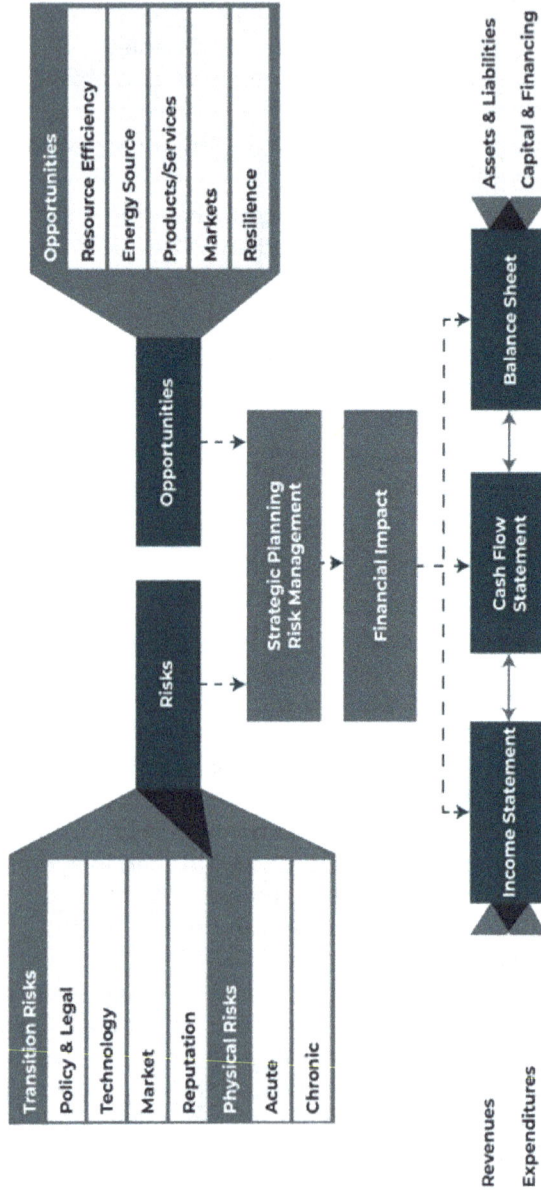

For example, a utility company transitioning to renewable energy, such as wind and solar, faces potential problems due to the unpredictable nature of these energy sources or due to the challenges of integrating them into the existing grid. Retrofitting old infrastructure to accommodate new, fluctuating energy sources requires significant investment and strategic planning. As technology rapidly evolves, current investments risk becoming obsolete, requiring a delicate balancing act between advancing towards sustainability and maintaining operational efficiency and cost-effectiveness.

As public awareness of climate change increases, consumer preferences are shifting towards more sustainable products and services. Corporations that are slow to adapt to these changing preferences face a market risk of becoming less attractive to consumers, leading to decreased sales and reduced market share.

On the other hand, financial institutions are intensifying their scrutiny of environmental risks when evaluating investment, lending and insurance decisions. Corporations that fail to demonstrate a commitment to sustainable operations or to mitigate climate change risks may find it increasingly difficult to secure financing and may see impacts on their valuation.[20]

Why Net Zero?

Net zero means cutting GHG emissions to as close to zero as possible, with any remaining emissions re-absorbed from the atmosphere. The commonly-used analogy of a bathtub may help to explain the emissions challenge. The water in the bathtub represents emissions already in the atmosphere and the water from the tap represents new emissions. The drain represents natural carbon sinks like forests and human activities like carbon capture, all of which remove emissions from the atmosphere. The drain can be increasingly clogged by cutting down forests and overburdening the oceans with CO_2. If the tap runs faster than the tub drains, the water level rises. In this analogy, when the water reaches the top of the tub, temperature rise will likely exceed 1.5°C. In the meantime, the quantity of water that can come out of the tap (the new anthropogenic emissions) before the tub overflows represents the remaining carbon budget.

However, if the rate of the tap and the rate of the drain are balanced, the water level will no longer rise. This steady state is called net zero[21] or carbon neutrality.[22] According to the Intergovernmental Panel on Climate Change (IPCC), net zero CO_2 emissions are achieved when anthropogenic CO_2 emissions are balanced globally by anthropogenic CO_2 removals over a specified period.

Figure 2.5: Projected Impacts of Climate Change on GDP *per capita*[23]

| | Temperature rise scenario, by mid century | | | |
| | Well-below 2°C increase | 2°C increase | 2.6°C increase | 3.2°C increase |
	Paris target	The likely range of global temperature gains		Severe case
Simulating for economic loss impacts from rising temperatures in % GDP, relative to a world without climate change (0°C)				
World	-4.2%	-11.0%	-13.9%	-18.1%
OECD	-3.1%	-7.6%	-8.1%	-10.6%
North America	-3.1%	-6.9%	-7.4%	-9.5%
South America	-4.1%	-10.8%	-13.0%	-17.0%
Europe	-2.8%	-7.7%	-8.0%	-10.5%
Middle East & Africa	-4.7%	-14.0%	-21.5%	-27.6%
Asia	-5.5%	-14.9%	-20.4%	-26.5%
Advanced Asia	-3.3%	-9.5%	-11.7%	-15.4%
ASEAN	-4.2%	-17.0%	-29.0%	-37.4%
Oceania	-4.3%	-11.2%	-12.3%	-16.3%

What the science says

Climate science is clear that the extent of global warming is proportional to the total amount of CO_2 added to the atmosphere by human activities. It is also clear that to avert the worst impacts of climate change and preserve a liveable planet, global temperature increase needs to be limited to 1.5°C above pre-industrial levels.

The World Meteorological Organization (WMO) confirmed that 2023 was the hottest year on record (with the average global temperature reaching 1.45°C higher than it was in the late 1800s) and that emissions are continuing to rise.[24] To stabilise climate change, net CO_2 emissions need to fall close to zero. The longer it takes to achieve this, the more the climate will change. In addition, emissions of other GHGs (such as methane, for instance) also need to be constrained.[25]

As part of the *Paris Agreement*, governments agreed to keep global warming "well below" 2°C, and to "make efforts" to keep it to 1.5°C. The IPCC, in a report in October 2018 on the 1.5°C target, concluded that global emissions need to reach net zero around mid-century to give a reasonable chance of limiting warming to 1.5°C.[26] Parties signed up to the Pact recognise that:

> *... limiting global warming to 1.5°C requires rapid, deep and sustained reductions in global greenhouse gas emissions, including reducing global carbon dioxide emissions ... to net zero around mid-century.*

The distinction might sound minor but the difference in consequences between 2°C and 1.5°C is vast. Holding warming to 1.5°C could mean 11 million fewer people exposed to extreme heat, 61 million fewer to drought, and 10 million fewer to the impacts of sea level rise. In addition to these human benefits, it could also halve the number of vertebrate and plant species facing severe range loss by the end of the century. With studies showing that the value of services provided by a functioning biosphere averages approximately US$125 trillion a year, it is clear that restricting warming to 1.5°C could also shield us from severe global economic losses.[27]

Achieving net zero

Achieving net zero will require a two-part approach. First and foremost, human-caused emissions (such as those from fossil-fuelled vehicles and factories) should be reduced to as close to zero as possible. Any remaining emissions should then be balanced with an equivalent amount of carbon removal, through natural approaches, such as restoring forests or peatlands, or through technologies, such as direct air capture and storage (DACS), which scrubs carbon directly from the atmosphere.[28]

Decarbonisation is essential in the global drive towards net zero. Some sectors will be able to decarbonise more easily than others. However, with the necessary support for environmental sustainability, green investments, and climate innovation, it is possible for all key sectors in the economy to make positive strides towards a net-zero future.

Figure 2.6: 10 Key Solutions Needed to Mitigate Climate Change[29]

1. **RETIRE** coal plants

2. **INVEST** in clean energy & efficiency

3. **RETROFIT** and **DECARBONIZE** buildings

4. **DECARBONIZE** cement, steel & plastics

5. **SHIFT** to electric vehicles

6. **INCREASE** public transport, biking and walking

7. **DECARBONIZE** aviation and shipping

8. **HALT** deforestation & **RESTORE** degraded lands

9. **REDUCE** food loss and waste and **IMPROVE** agricultural practices

10. **EAT** more plants & less meat

Source: IPCC AR6.　　　　　WORLD RESOURCES INSTITUTE

For companies, the transition to net zero brings challenges and opportunities. Companies are increasingly seeing the commercial value of large-scale climate action, which has been described as the century's "biggest financial and business opportunity".[30] While the risks posed to companies by even half a degree of global warming would be monumental, bold climate action could also yield material economic gains. And many millions of new jobs will likely be created. Though the challenge may seem daunting, the solution requires humanity to do what it does best: innovate.

From renewable energy to electric vehicles, companies are pioneering ingenious new solutions to the climate crisis that are becoming increasingly available in the market. Decisive business leadership and investment in climate solutions must also be supported by ambitious government policies.

TAKING ACTION ON CLIMATE CHANGE

As we address the pressing challenges of climate change, it is evident that our current system lacks the robustness needed to fulfil the objectives of equity, well-being, and ecosystem health as set out in the *Paris Agreement* and the United Nations' Sustainable Development Goals (SDGs). There is an urgent need to shift towards a more resilient state. Systemic change is required to realign our economic structures and policies to support these goals.

Figure 2.7: Systemic Change Required to Build Resilience[31]

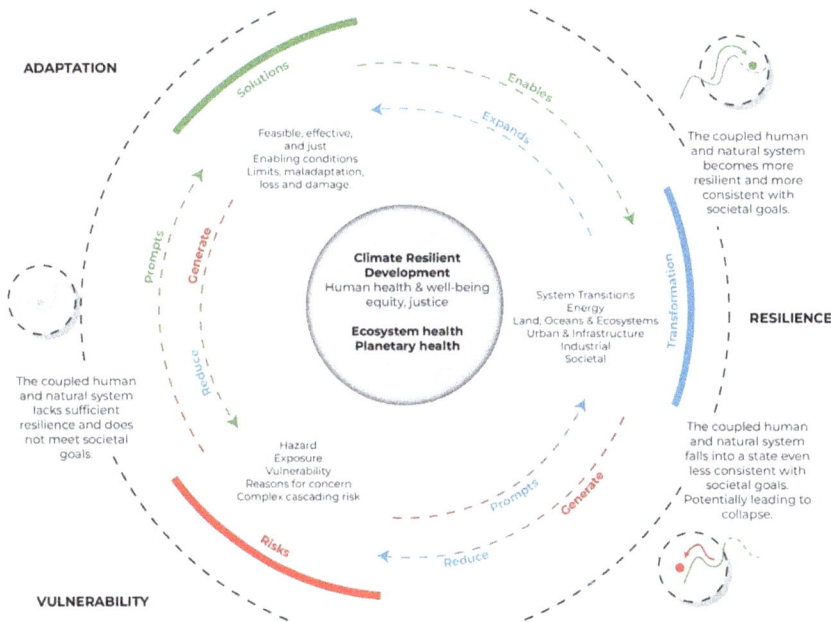

What does Resiliency Mean?

In the context of climate change, resiliency involves the ability of systems, communities, and economies to anticipate, withstand, and adaptively respond to environmental stresses and changes. Resiliency is crucial for sustaining development and mitigating global vulnerability to the unpredictability of natural disasters and extreme weather events.

We need to consider five types of resilience:

- **Ecological:** The ability of ecosystems to resist, absorb, and recover from climate change, while maintaining their essential functions and structures;
- **Economic:** The capacity of economies to withstand, adapt to, and recover from environmental shocks;
- **Social:** The ability of communities to manage and recover from the impacts of climate change;
- **Infrastructural:** Building and adapting physical structures that can withstand extreme weather events and other climate-related risks;
- **Institutional:** Policies and regulations that governments implement to mitigate climate risks and manage disaster responses effectively.

Where Is Adaptation Needed Most?

Fragile elements of the global economy

The economic losses from climate-related extreme events have reached over $1.5 trillion, according to a report released in April 2024 by the Organisation for Economic Co-operation & Development (OECD) (**Figure 2.8**).

Sectors within the global economy that could be particularly vulnerable to the impacts of climate change include:

- **Agriculture:** Heavily dependent on climate conditions, such as rainfall patterns, temperature, and extreme weather events;
- **Coastal tourism:** An economic pillar for many island and coastal nations, but increasingly at risk due to rising sea levels and deteriorating marine ecosystems;
- **Energy production:** Water availability affects hydropower generation, while cooling processes in thermal plants are susceptible to variations in water temperature and availability;
- **Insurance:** Crucial in managing risk, but vulnerable as the frequency and severity of climate-related disasters increase. Investments and underwriting are both exposed to climate risks;
- **Telecommunications:** Vulnerable to climate change, as disruptions caused by extreme weather can severely impact infrastructure, including data centres and wireless networks;
- **Water resources:** Changes in precipitation patterns and the frequency of extreme weather events can lead to water scarcity

or flooding, impacting not only drinking water supply but also agriculture and hydropower.

Figure 2.8: Economic Losses from Climate-related Extreme Events[32]

Billion USD, 2021 base year

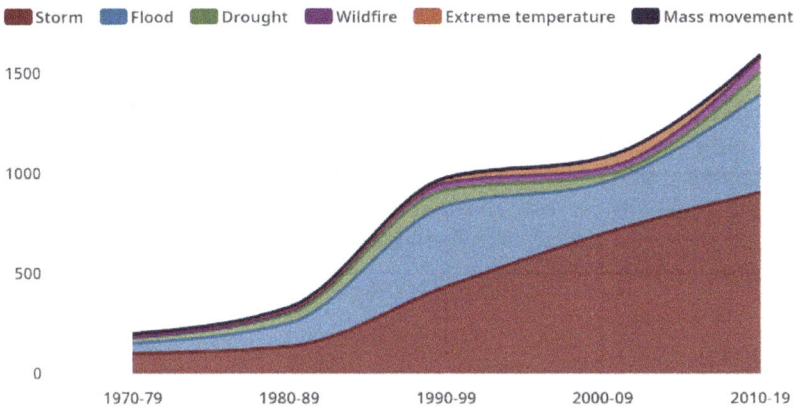

| Storm | Flood | Drought | Wildfire | Extreme temperature | Mass movement |

Note: Mass movement: Hydrology-related events include avalanches, landslides, mudslides, rockfalls and sudden subsidence.

Climate-ready infrastructure
Infrastructure systems form the backbone of modern economies, but they are also highly dependent on stable climatic conditions. As climate change intensifies, traditional infrastructure systems face increasing risks from extreme weather events, sea level rise, and other climate-related challenges. Climate-ready infrastructure is designed to withstand these challenges, ensuring resilience and continuity in service delivery and includes:

- **Durability and flexibility:** Infrastructure must not only be strong but also flexible enough to adapt to changing conditions without significant degradation;
- **Energy efficiency and sustainability:** Integrating energy efficiency reduces the carbon footprint and operational costs of infrastructure, contributing to overall sustainability;
- **Disaster resilience:** Infrastructure must be equipped to handle natural disasters.

Vulnerable communities and the climate finance shortfall
Vulnerable communities, often located in geographically and economically disadvantaged areas, could face disproportionate risks

from climate change. While they are especially susceptible to extreme weather events, rising sea levels, and other climate impacts, these communities also often lack the means to adapt sufficiently to changing environmental conditions. They often suffer from poor housing, limited access to services, and lack economic diversification, which exacerbates their vulnerability to climate change. Governments and international organisations need to prioritise these areas in their adaptation strategies.

Although the need for climate adaptation is increasingly recognised, a significant shortfall remains in the funding required to protect the world's most vulnerable communities. The United Nations (UN) estimates that the cost of adapting to climate change could range from $140 billion to $300 billion per year by 2030; current investments are far below these levels. This funding gap poses a serious threat to the ability of vulnerable communities to withstand climate impacts.[33]

Who Needs to Be Involved in Supporting Adaptation to Climate Change?

Public and private finance and projects
Adapting to climate change requires substantial financial investments and collaborative projects, involving both public and private sectors. Recognising the complementary roles of public and private entities in financing and implementing these strategies is crucial for a comprehensive approach to climate resilience.

An example of how this can be implemented is through public-private partnerships (PPPs). In the first half of 2023, investments totalling $36.4 billion were committed through PPPs, with a significant focus on energy and transport sectors.

To address the growing impacts of climate change on infrastructure, governments around the world can implement a series of strategic actions to enhance resilience and sustainability. The OECD recommends the following for governments' consideration:[34]

- **Integrate climate risks into infrastructure planning:** Governments should incorporate climate risk assessments into the planning and development of infrastructure projects;

- **Mainstream climate resilience into financing and investments:** Governments can incentivise investment in climate-resilient infrastructure projects and implement policies that require consideration of climate resilience in public and private investments;

- **Unlock the potential of nature-based solutions:** Governments should integrate nature-based solutions into their policy, regulatory, and financial frameworks that guide infrastructure development to mitigate climate impacts through natural processes;
- **Address challenges and opportunities in developing countries:** Governments in developed countries can facilitate knowledge sharing, provide technical assistance, and promote research and development to support developing nations in building climate resilience;
- **Integrate climate resilience approaches across all levels of government:** Governments should harness multi-level governance to ensure that actions are coordinated across different levels of government.

The role of communities

Communities, especially those in vulnerable regions, play a critical role in local efforts to adapt to climate change. Communities possess unique insights into local environmental conditions and historical climate patterns; leveraging this knowledge can lead to more effective and sustainable adaptation strategies. They are often the first to respond to climate impacts and can initiate grassroots adaptation projects, like early warning systems or ecosystem restoration projects, and can advocate for their needs and perspectives in broader climate adaptation planning. Community education also can play a key role; increasing awareness and knowledge about climate change within communities empowers individuals to make informed decisions and take proactive measures.

The role of the private sector

Businesses have a crucial role in addressing climate change through adaptation strategies that not only protect their own operations and supply chains but also contribute to broader societal and systemic climate resilience. Engaging the private sector in climate change adaptation can drive innovation, enhance competitiveness, and ensure sustainable business practices.

It is critical that businesses conduct comprehensive risk assessments to understand potential impacts from climate change, identify vulnerabilities, like more frequent extreme weather events, and implement appropriate risk management strategies. Additionally, they should invest in resilient infrastructure, leverage innovation to develop new solutions that facilitate climate adaptation and engage in partnerships across all stakeholders – public bodies, private enterprise and communities – to optimise outcomes.

The financial sector plays a key role in climate change adaptation and mitigation by mobilising resources, innovating financial products, and integrating climate risks into investment decisions. Given their role as the gatekeepers of capital flow, financial institutions are well-positioned to influence global efforts towards a sustainable future. The development of innovative financial products such as sustainability-linked loans, green bonds, social bonds and loans is also crucial to support climate adaptation and mitigation efforts.

What Can Companies Do to Improve Resiliency?

The World Business Council for Sustainable Development (WBCSD) recommends three practical steps for businesses to achieve business climate resilience:[35]

- **Step 1:** Develop ambitious mitigative efforts;
- **Step 2:** Adapt to ensure business continuity;
- **Step 3:** Assess dependencies and value to society.

To implement these three steps, companies could consider:

- **Business resiliency planning:** Business resiliency planning is crucial for mitigating climate change risks and capitalising on opportunities. Key elements include risk identification and assessment (for example, ISO 31000: 2018 guidelines), business continuity strategies (for example, backup systems and alternate supply chains, supported by the Business Continuity Institute), and employee training and engagement;
- **Scenario analysis:** Scenario analysis helps businesses prepare for potential futures by understanding impacts, informing decisions, and enhancing adaptive capacity. By simulating different climate scenarios, companies can use climate data and trend projections to identify risks and opportunities that may arise and model future scenarios.

Cemex's climate resilience strategy evaluation through scenario analysis

Cemex is a global building materials company exposed to a variety of climate transition and physical risks, given complex supply chain considerations. It actively assesses the resilience of its climate strategy against a variety of climate-related scenarios, aligning with both medium and long-term climate goals.

Cemex leverages multiple scenarios to test the robustness of its strategies, including:

- **Historical scenarios:** Until 2020, Cemex used the RCP 6.0 and RCP 4.5 from the IPCC, and the 2DS and B2DS from the International Energy Agency's (IEA) Energy Technology Perspectives;

- **Updated scenarios (2021):** As the IEA updated its set of climate scenarios with the publication of the *World Energy Outlook* in 2020 and 2021, Cemex used these updated scenarios to identify the risks and opportunities of its resilience strategies:

  o *Stated Policies Scenario (STEPS):* Assesses impacts based on current and developing policies without assuming complete goal achievement;

  o *Sustainable Development Scenario (SDS):* Considers more stringent climate actions aligned with sustainable development;

  o *Net Zero Emissions by 2050 Scenario (NZE):* Evaluates the feasibility of achieving net zero emissions by 2050 under the most restrictive conditions.

Under each of the updated scenarios, Cemex identified potential risks and opportunities that were crucial for building resilience. The company assessed the likelihood and potential impact of these risks, categorising them with a rating system of 'low', 'medium', and 'high'.

The analysis confirmed that Cemex's strategy is generally robust across various temperature projections and policy landscapes, particularly highlighting the resilience in the more stringent SDS and NZE scenarios. This has supported Cemex's pursuit of the following resilience-building activities:

- **Future in Action programme:** A commitment to net zero CO_2 emissions by 2050, promoting sustainable and circular economy practices;

- **2030 CO_2 reduction goal:** A target to reduce net-specific CO_2 emissions by 47% from the 1990 baseline, validated under the Science-Based Targets Initiative's (SBTi) 1.5°C scenario;

- **Innovation funding and R&D investments:** Continued focus on developing sustainable building materials and solutions for climate-smart construction and resilient infrastructures, including leveraging Cemex's CX Ventures and Urbanization Solutions to foster strategic partnerships and technology advancements.

Cemex's approach in aligning its climate resilience strategy with dynamic and rigorous scenario analyses ensures that the company is prepared to meet future climate challenges and is positioned to adapt to varying future climates and regulatory environments. Doing so will help it secure its operational continuity, while also contributing to global climate goals.

Integration of climate risks into strategy and operations

Integrating climate risks into business strategy and operations is essential for companies aiming to enhance their resilience and sustainability. This integration helps businesses not only to mitigate risks but also to capitalise on opportunities arising from the shift towards a low-carbon economy.

The following key steps can be considered when businesses integrate climate risks into their strategies and operations:

- **Risk identification and prioritisation:** Useful resources businesses can consider using include the Sustainability Accounting Standards Board's (SASB) materiality maps,[36] which form part of the IFRS Foundation's industry-based guidance for International Financial Reporting Standards (IFRS) S1 and S2,[37] among the most influential international voluntary disclosure standards for sustainability-related reporting;

- **Strategic planning and adaptation:** Once risks are identified and prioritised, developing strategies to adapt to these risks is essential. For instance, when managing supply chain risks, companies might conduct detailed supplier risk assessments to pinpoint potential weak links and to strategise accordingly. A useful resource is the Climate Adaptation Knowledge Exchange;[38]

- **Monitoring and reporting**: Effective monitoring and reporting ensure that companies can respond dynamically to both evolving risks and regulations, as well as communicating their progress and challenges in managing climate impacts.

A range of adaptation options

Adaptation to climate change involves a spectrum of strategies that companies can deploy to not only cope with current impacts but also prepare for future conditions. Exploring a range of adaptation options allows businesses to tailor their approaches based on specific vulnerabilities and opportunities:

- **Technological innovations:** Investing in new technologies, such as water recycling systems or heat-resistant materials, that reduce vulnerability to climate impacts.;

- **Operational adjustments:** Modifying operational practices for better alignment with sustainability practices and hence lower operational risks;

- **Ecosystem-based approaches:** Using natural systems to mitigate the impacts of climate change, enhancing both ecological and business resilience – for example, implementing green roofs, restoring wetlands, and maintaining buffer zones along waterways can reduce flood risk and enhance biodiversity.

CLIMATE MITIGATION: REDUCING EMISSIONS & GETTING TO NET ZERO

What Does Decarbonisation Mean for Different Sectors?

Energy

Decarbonisation of the energy sector is crucial for global efforts to combat climate change. This involves transitioning from fossil fuel-based energy production to renewable and less carbon-intensive energy sources.

The IEA has developed a set of scenarios that indicate the potential conditions that need to be met to realise net zero by 2050. These conditions include measures that should be taken for energy production and consumption, through policy-making, adjustments in industrial processes, changes in transportation means, and the undertaking of retrofits. Meeting these conditions could involve transitioning to renewable energy, enhancing energy efficiency, and/or carbon capture and storage.

Transportation

The transportation sector is a significant contributor to global carbon emissions, primarily due to its heavy reliance on fossil fuels. Decarbonisation in this sector involves transitioning to more sustainable modes of transport and fuels – for example:

- **Electrification of vehicles:** EVs offer an effective alternative to traditional fossil fuel-powered vehicles, significantly reducing emissions;

Figure 2.9: Key Milestones in the Pathway to Net Zero[39]

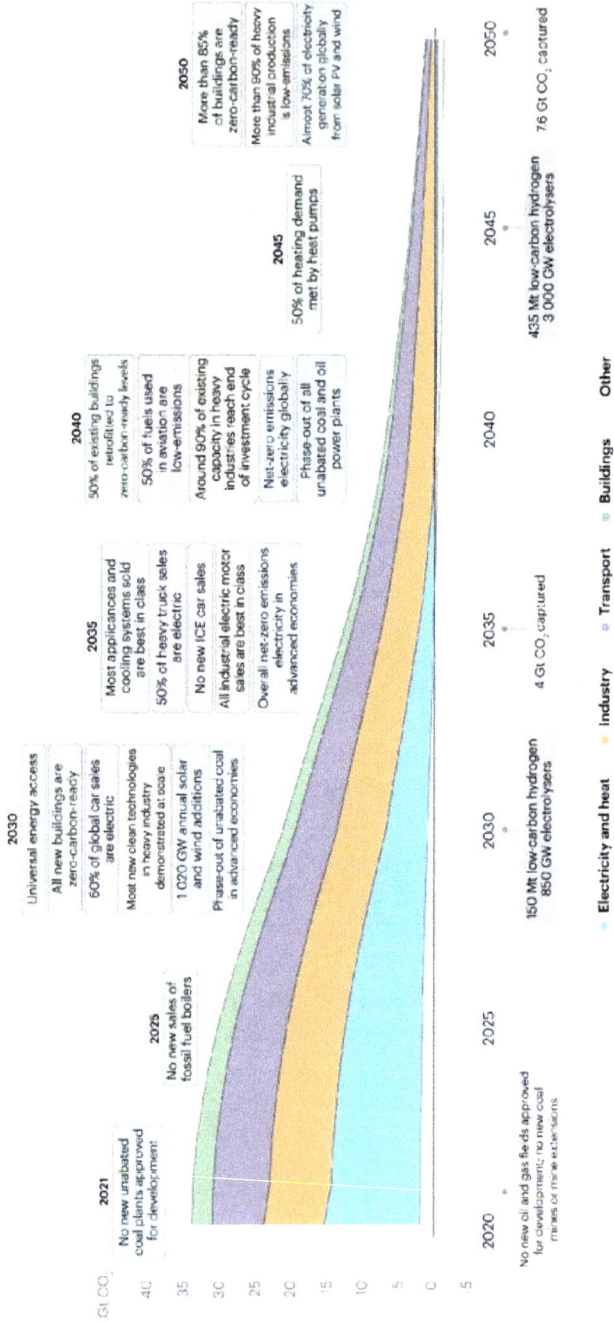

2021
No new unabated coal plants approved for development

2025
No new sales of fossil fuel boilers

2030
Universal energy access
All new buildings are zero-carbon-ready
60% of global car sales are electric
Most new clean technologies in heavy industry demonstrated at scale
1 020 GW annual solar and wind additions
Phase-out of unabated coal in advanced economies

2035
Most appliances and cooling systems sold are best in class
50% of heavy truck sales are electric
No new ICE car sales
All industrial electric motor sales are best in class
Overall net-zero emissions electricity in advanced economies

2040
50% of existing buildings retrofitted to zero-carbon-ready levels
50% of fuels used in aviation are low-emissions
Around 90% of existing capacity in heavy industries reach end of investment cycle
Net-zero emissions electricity globally
Phase-out of all unabated coal and oil power plants

2045
50% of heating demand met by heat pumps

2050
More than 85% of buildings are zero-carbon-ready
More than 90% of heavy industrial production is low-emissions
Almost 70% of electricity generation globally from solar PV and wind

No new oil and gas fields approved for development; no new coal mines or mine extensions

$Gt\ CO_2$

150 Mt low-carbon hydrogen
850 GW electrolysers

4 Gt CO_2 captured

435 Mt low-carbon hydrogen
3 000 GW electrolysers

7.6 Gt CO_2 captured

Electricity and heat   Industry   Transport   Buildings   Other

- **Public transport and infrastructure:** Enhancing and expanding public transport systems can reduce reliance on private vehicles. Additionally, investing in cycling and walking infrastructure encourages more sustainable urban mobility;
- **Alternative fuels:** Biofuels and hydrogen are emerging as viable alternatives to diesel and petrol in vehicles.

Industry

The industrial sector, which encompasses manufacturing, construction, and heavy industry, is a significant source of global GHG emissions. Decarbonising this sector involves adopting cleaner production methods, energy efficiency enhancements, and technological innovations, including deploying carbon capture, use, and storage (CCUS) technologies.

Agriculture

Agriculture contributes significantly to global emissions through livestock, fertiliser use, and land management practices. Potential ways for the sector to decarbonise include:

- **Improved land management:** Adopting sustainable land management practices such as no-till farming, cover cropping, and agroforestry;
- **Livestock emissions reduction:** Improving feed efficiency, breeding practices, and manure management; methane digesters can be used to capture and convert livestock methane emissions into renewable energy;
- **Energy use in agriculture:** Transitioning to renewable energy sources for agricultural operations, including solar and wind power.

Rockwell Automation's Decarbonisation Strategy through Technology & Automation[40]

In 2019, the world generated approximately 53.6 million tonnes of electronic waste (e-waste), with over 80% of it discarded, traded, or recycled in environmentally harmful ways. As a leader in industrial automation and digital transformation, Rockwell Automation (RA) found itself well-positioned to influence sustainable practices within the industry by promoting the circular economy through its technologies. RA adopted a dual strategy to tackle this challenge:

- **Sustainability calculator:** An analytical dashboard that quantifies the waste and carbon emissions reduced by repairing automation assets instead of replacing them. It provides customers with valuable insights that can help optimise their maintenance, repair, and operation costs;

- **Repair and remanufacturing services:** RA operates 14 repair centres and eight exchange hubs globally, where it remanufactures products to like-new or better condition. The remanufacturing process involves thorough inspection, revisions, upgrades, and functional load testing to ensure operability and quality. These services support a 'fix-it-first' approach, encouraging customers to reuse existing resources rather than purchasing new ones.

RA partnered with a global consumer packaged goods (CPG) company to implement these solutions in one of the CPG company's UK plants, significantly reducing the plant's environmental impact. The outcomes included:

- A reduction in the CPG company's carbon footprint and e-waste;
- Contributions to the circular economy by repairing and reusing assets rather than acquiring new ones;
- An estimated 91% reduction in avoided CO_2 equivalent Scope 3 emissions (compared to purchasing new equipment);
- An 8% reduction in hazardous waste sent to landfill, as calculated by RA's sustainability calculator for repairs.

Moreover, the remanufacturing process preserved 85% of the energy that would have been expended in producing new equipment and used 90% fewer raw materials compared to original manufacturing processes, substantially extending equipment life.

RA's initiative demonstrates how technological innovation and sustainable business models can effectively contribute to environmental conservation and the circular economy, setting a benchmark in the industrial sector for reducing carbon emissions and managing e-waste.

More generally, firms are stepping up their commitments to decarbonise through:

- **Understanding science-based targets (SBTs):** Companies are increasingly setting emission reduction targets based on the latest climate science, conducting comprehensive emissions inventories, setting reduction targets, and periodically reviewing progress. The SBTi provides step-by-step and sector-specific guidance to help companies set these targets;
- **Industry alliances for decarbonisation:** Industry alliances are crucial for scaling decarbonisation efforts across sectors. These

alliances enable companies to pool resources, share best practices, and drive innovation in reducing carbon emissions. By collaborating, companies can influence policy decisions and market trends, leading to broader changes in industry standards and practices. Examples include Tech Zero for the tech sector, Pledge to Net Zero for the environmental sector, and Healthcare Without Harm for the healthcare sector, among others. These alliances help companies commit to ambitious emissions reductions and foster collective progress towards sustainability goals;

- **Conducting emissions audits:** By identifying all emission sources, collecting accurate data, calculating total CO_2 equivalent emissions, analysing and reporting findings, and benchmarking against industry standards to set realistic reduction targets, companies establish a baseline for tracking progress over time;

- **Developing clear action plans and timelines:** To transition to lower carbon operations, firms set specific emission reduction targets influenced by policies and standards, create detailed roadmaps with timelines, invest in technology and process improvements, and regularly monitor and report emissions to track progress and ensure accountability.

Schneider Electric's Journey Towards a Net Zero Supply Chain with the Zero Carbon Project[41]

Schneider Electric (SE) is committed to reducing its absolute GHG emissions by 25% by 2030 from a 2021 baseline, with an ultimate goal of achieving net zero CO_2 emissions across its entire value chain by 2050. Despite reducing its Scope 1 and Scope 2 emissions by 67% since 2017, SE recognised that achieving this ambitious target would be unattainable without the collaboration of its suppliers, who contribute 70% of its upstream carbon emissions. Thus, in 2021, SE initiated the Zero Carbon Project, specifically to help its top suppliers reduce their operational emissions (Scope 1 and 2) by 50% by 2025. The project offered capacity building, thought leadership, resources, digital tools, and direct assistance and guidance, as well as the exchange of best practices through:

- **Regular interactive sessions:** Live engagements and training sessions, with resources made available on the Schneider Supplier Portal;

- **Core principles of the project:** Widely-disseminated markers to help inform decision-making and consistency:

- o *Analytics:* Assisting suppliers in quantifying their GHG emissions, establishing baselines, and identifying major emission sources;
- o *Ambition:* Motivating suppliers to set robust emissions reduction targets;
- o *Action:* Supporting suppliers in implementing action plans to meet these targets.

The project was launched globally *via* a live webcast featuring top executives from SE and its leading suppliers, who communicated the vision and expectations for the initiative, underscoring SE's significant experience in rapid CO_2 reduction and the adaptable nature of the programme to fit various supplier contexts.

SE's Zero Carbon Project has seen remarkable engagement, with over 1,000 companies joining and 1,300 supplier participants trained. By the end of the third quarter of 2023, these efforts had resulted in a 24% reduction in emissions. Notably, 70% of the suppliers had not previously assessed their carbon footprints. SE continues to support these companies, helping them at different stages of their decarbonisation journeys and steering them towards the 50% reduction target by 2025.

WHAT OPPORTUNITIES DOES TRANSITION PRESENT?

New Business Models & Markets

Climate transition is catalysing a broad spectrum of opportunities across multiple sectors, from renewable energy to sustainable agriculture. These sectors are pivotal in driving innovation, sustainability, and economic growth, thus contributing significantly to a climate-resilient future. Embracing these opportunities can mitigate climate risks and foster a transition towards a more sustainable and environmentally friendly global economy.

Real Estate

Environmental, Social, and Governance (ESG) integration is vital within the real estate sector. As governments intensify their focus on decarbonisation objectives, heightened standards (particularly regarding energy efficiency in building construction) are likely to raise operational costs for real estate companies. Nonetheless, the rationale for incorporating ESG factors into corporate strategies and risk management within this sector is compelling, with numerous professionals in the industry recognising that ESG initiatives are unlocking new business prospects.[42]

Research supports the positive influence of ESG factors on real estate investment outcomes. A meta-analysis conducted in 2015 found that, while 57% of equity-related studies observed a positive impact from ESG integration, this rate was slightly higher at 64% for investments and bonds.[43] In real estate, the positive effects were even more significant, with 71% of studies noting a beneficial impact. Additionally, a 2014 study revealed a 2.8% difference in return spread between the highest-rated properties in the Global Real Estate Sustainability Benchmark (GRESB) and the lowest-rated properties.[44] Additionally, regulatory changes are prompting increased attention and engagement with ESG considerations in the real estate sector.

The sector could leverage climate-related opportunities by considering:

- **Local energy production and storage**: Real estate companies can use their properties to produce and store energy. For instance, developers have started equipping buildings with batteries as well as solar panels, which contributes to grid stability and reduces clean energy costs;

- **Green buildings**: Developers and property managers can invest in constructing green buildings or retrofitting older structures to align with the growing demand for sustainable workspaces and residences;

- **Green building materials**: Players in the industry can investigate eco-friendly materials like green steel, tall timber, modular construction, and emerging technologies to achieve faster and more cost-effective construction;

- **Additional on-site services**: Firms can introduce new income streams by offering services such as EV charging, eco-friendly facility management, and other sustainable amenities that cater to occupants' preferences;

- **Emission reduction and monitoring services**: Real estate companies can support occupants by monitoring emissions and providing solutions to reduce their carbon footprints. This may involve using smart sensors to track energy consumption related to heating, cooling, lighting, and space management.

Technology

In the technological sector, there are significant climate-related opportunities projected to spur substantial investments, which are expected to reach $56 trillion by 2050, according to a Goldman Sachs report.[45] A study by the EU[46] provides several key considerations for investors looking to capitalise on these opportunities.

One major area is the development of 'green cloud' and 'green data centres'. Digital technologies continue to consume a significant portion of global electricity; this is likely to increase with further digitisation and new technologies. In light of these trends, there is a strong push towards making IT infrastructures more sustainable. According to the European Commission,[47] improving cooling and data transmission technologies has proven to substantially reduce energy waste and emissions.[48] The European Commission is also promoting the establishment of energy-efficient cloud computing and data centres as part of its climate strategy. Such initiatives are linked to a variety of funding programmes, including Horizon Europe, Connecting Europe Facility 2, Digital Europe programme, InvestEU, and the Recovery & Resilience Facility (which was set up to support the deployment of an innovative, green, and secure cloud).

Another key strategy is enhancing the efficiency of cloud computing technologies. Cloud computing, which is noted for its scalability and automated resource management, also can be optimised to save energy. This is particularly true when using pay-per-use strategies that allow for more precise usage aligned with demand, thereby reducing unnecessary energy consumption.[49] Moreover, adopting cloud-native development practices, along with strict scaling rules and orchestration tools, can further minimise energy use.

Improving software efficiency marks another critical approach. The EU points out that the design of application programme codes can lead to high energy consumption, as applications with similar functions can vary significantly in their IT resource demands, such as CPU load, RAM, and network use. To address this, it suggests pursuing energy-efficient programming practices,[50] which could include adopting 'green' coding languages known for better energy efficiency[51] and implementing code refactoring techniques.[52]

Competitive Advantages to Sustainability Leaders

One of the major challenges companies currently face is maintaining their operational capacity and economic viability amid shifting conditions. This requires a significant level of resilience, largely derived from a company's capacity for adaptation and change. Companies that quickly adjust to evolving circumstances can access new markets, enhance their efficiency, and thereby increase their competitiveness. Companies that spearhead sustainability efforts gain significant competitive advantages in their business operations, across:

- Brand enhancement and customer loyalty;
- Operational cost efficiency;
- Expansion into new markets;
- Attractiveness to investors;
- Navigating regulatory landscapes.

CLIMATE COMMUNICATIONS & EDUCATION

Carlos Terol

I'm passionate about inspiring and empowering changemakers from all paths of life to make a positive impact. My tools of choice are climate communications and education.

I started my changemaker journey back in 2015 when a trip to Western Sahara opened my eyes to different realities and perspectives. As a civil engineer by background, I went on to found the Engineers Without Borders Reading Regional Network. I volunteered as a Team Leader in rural Nepal for three months, delivering water and sanitation projects, which led me to start my first company, a sustainable fashion brand.

Most recently, I founded Good Ripple, a platform with more than 3,000 changemakers from over 100 countries. I'm also a Climate Fresk facilitator, a role that I use to help educate more people about climate change and empower them to take action. And I share content on LinkedIn daily to try and inspire more changemakers like you.

Climate Communications & Education Matter

If the deep knowledge of climate change is like a library, then climate communications and education are the skilled librarians and storytellers who make that knowledge accessible and understandable to diverse audiences.

Climate communication focuses on disseminating information about climate change to different audiences, whilst climate education creates learning opportunities to enhance people's understanding of climate change, its causes, consequences, mitigation strategies and solutions. Climate communications and climate education play a critical role in activating people's agency, fostering behavioural change and driving collective action.

Think about it for a second: do you feel more compelled to take climate action after reading a technical, scientific paper full of acronyms, jargon and numbers, or when you hear an inspiring story of how someone has made a difference by taking action?

If you are like me (and like most people), you are probably more inspired by the story. Research by Stanford Professor Jennifer Aaker found that stories are remembered up to 22 times more than facts alone.[53] If we don't learn to communicate effectively and educate others in an inspiring and memorable way, we are going to have little impact. In order to create real change and impact in your organisation, you need to mobilise your colleagues, teams, departments, clients, suppliers and the rest of your stakeholders.

How to Start

These are eight top tips to get you started on your climate communications and education journey:

- **Know your audience:** *You cannot communicate the same way if you are talking to the Chief Sustainability Officer as when you are talking to a customer with little sustainability awareness. Do your homework to try and learn more about them beforehand, or ask them questions directly;*

- **Meet them where they are:** *Everyone is on a different stage on their own sustainability journey. You cannot tell a colleague who has never heard about net zero to stop flying or to go vegan. Similarly, you cannot tell the CEO of a climate company to just focus on recycling – they can do a lot more than that! Adapting your message is key;*

- **Talk like a human:** *Research by the Potential Energy Coalition found that the best way to get people on board with the climate crisis is to talk like a human, avoiding jargon, numbers or statistics.[54] Use storytelling;*

- **Keep it local:** *Emphasising the impacts on local communities, economies and ecosystems helps inspire more people. For the vast majority of people, knowing that polar bears don't have enough ice or that tropical islands are going underwater is not relatable and does not spark action;*

- ***Identify champions and empower them:*** *You cannot go alone in this race. And the sooner you get people on your side, the more you can influence how fast your organisation changes;*
- ***Don't talk doom and gloom:*** *Doom and gloom is proven to be ineffective when it comes to triggering action;*
- ***Make it fun:*** *Everyone enjoys a laugh. If you can communicate and educate about climate change in a fun and interactive way, you are more likely to get more support and people on board;*
- ***Be honest and transparent:*** *This should be an overarching theme in all communications and education.*

Examples & Stories

Here are some success stories of organisations that have used climate communications and education very effectively:

- ***Patagonia*** *leads the way in climate change and sustainability practices and communications. When it decided to put Earth as its only shareholder, Patagonia was all over the news and articles. It communicated the decision in a very simple way, understanding its audience and being very honest and transparent;*
- ***Climate Outreach*** *is one of the go-to organisations for climate communications and training. Its approach emphasises understanding people's values, beliefs, and cultural contexts to tailor messaging and foster constructive dialogue;*
- ***Climate Fresk*** *focuses on climate education, in a fun and interactive way. It has scaled from being a small team in France to having educated over 1.6 million people worldwide, with facilitators in 161 countries and over 75,000 volunteers.*

You now have the knowledge and tools to communicate and educate. Next, you need to take action. Share what you learned in this chapter (and the rest of the book) with colleagues and engage a group of like-minded colleagues in your organisation to make climate change part of the ongoing conversation in your company. Leverage all the resources mentioned throughout the book and in the accompanying website.

What if I told you that you can actually do something about the challenges we all face? Would you take action today? Our future is in your hands. Go build it.

ESRS-E1 – CLIMATE CHANGE REPORTING OBLIGATIONS

Ingrid De Doncker

ESRS-E1 is the standard for organisations to report on their climate-related matters. It aims to equip an organisation with the necessary disclosure requirements to enable users of sustainability statements to understand:

- How the organisation affects climate change, in terms of material positive and negative actual and potential impacts;
- Its past, current, and future mitigation efforts in line with the Paris Agreement and compatible with limiting global warming to 1.5°C;
- Its plans and capacity to adapt its strategy and business model, in line with the transition to a sustainable economy and to contribute to limiting global warming to 1.5°C;
- Any other actions taken, and the result of such actions to prevent, mitigate or remediate actual or potential negative impacts, and to address risks and opportunities;
- The nature, type and extent of the organisation's material risks and opportunities arising from its impacts and dependencies on climate change, and how it manages them; and
- The financial effects of risks and opportunities (arising from its own impacts and dependencies on climate change), on the organisation over the short-, medium- and long-term.

Climate Change Sub-topics

Per ESRS 1 Article 16, when considering E1 impacts, risks and opportunities, organisations should consider three sub-topics: climate adaptation, climate mitigation and energy. As words matters, let's understand what they refer to:

- **Climate mitigation:** This relates to the endeavours an organisation can undertake to limit the increase in the global average temperature to 1.5°C in line with the *Paris Agreement*. It includes disclosure requirements related, but not limited, to seven GHGs: carbon dioxide (CO_2), methane (CH_4), nitrous oxide (N_2O), hydrofluorocarbons (HFCs), perfluorocarbons (PFCs), sulphur hexafluoride (SF_6) and nitrogen trifluoride (NF_3). It also covers

Disclosure Requirements on how organisations can addresses GHG emissions as well as the associated transition risks;

- **Climate adaptation:** This relates to the process of adjusting to the actual or expected effects of climate change, such as rising sea levels, extreme weather events, and changing ecosystems. Organisations can implement strategies to reduce dependencies or vulnerabilities and build resilience to these impacts. This may involve taking proactive measures to cope with the consequences of climate change, including modifying infrastructure, ecosystems, and human systems;

- **Energy:** This subtopic covers energy-related matters, to the extent that they are relevant to climate change. It includes all types of energy production and consumption by an organisation, from sources such as fossil fuels, nuclear, and renewables. The reporting on energy use aims to provide more transparency and is intended to enable stakeholders to assess the undertaking's energy consumption or production patterns and its sustainability performance.

This Standard should be read in conjunction with ESRS 1 *General Requirements* and the requirements of this section should be read and applied in conjunction with the disclosures required by ESRS 2 on *Chapter 2: Governance*, *Chapter 3: Strategy* and *Chapter 4: Impact, Risk & Opportunity Management*. The resulting disclosures shall be presented in the sustainability statement alongside the disclosures required by ESRS 2, except for ESRS 2 SBM-3 Material impacts, risks and opportunities and their interaction with SBM, for which the organisation may, in accordance with ESRS 2, paragraph 46, present the disclosures alongside the other disclosures required in this topical standard.

It is important to further understand ESRS 2, Chapter 4.2, which outlines the *Minimum Disclosure Requirements* (MDRs). When an organisation identifies a sustainability matter as material, 34 MDR data points (DPs) for Policies, Actions, Targets, and Metrics (PAT-M) are applicable if the organisation discloses on policies, actions and targets. If it does not provide disclosure on policies, targets or actions, then it needs to disclose the reasons for not doing so, as per the corresponding 10 DPs of ESRS 2 MDR PAT, paragraphs 62 and 81.

ESRS-E1 outlines clearly, in nine *Disclosure Requirements* (DRs), the narrative and numeric DPs an organisation should comply with. There are 187 *Shall* DPs, of which 111 are numeric, 51 narrative and 25 semi-narrative, as well as 15 additional *May* DPs. The MDR PAT DPs are to be disclosed under E1-2; E1-3; E1-4 when the sustainability matters is material.

Figure 2.10 shows the structure of the ESRS-E1 DR and DP that must be reported, if deemed material by the double materiality assessment.

Figure 2.10: ESRS-E1 – Climate Change Disclosure Requirements

ESRS-E1	Climate Change		
	Climate mitigation	Climate Adaptation	Energy
	With the exception of DPs in IRO-1, none of these DPs are applicable if the topic is not material.		
	GOVERNANCE		
ESRS2-E1-GOV-3	Integration of sustainability- related performance in incentive schemes.		
	STRATEGY		
ESRS-E1-1	**Transition plan** for climate change mitigation.		
ESRS2-E1-SBM-3	Material impacts, risks and opportunities and their interaction with strategy and business model.		
	IMPACT, RISK & OPPORTUNITY MANAGEMENT		
ESRS2- E1-IRO-1	Description of the processes to identify and assess material climate-related impacts, risks and opportunities.		
	The DPs reported in ESRS E1 are subject to Materiality Assessment.		
ESRS-E1-2	**Policies** to manage IRO related to climate change mitigation and adaptation.		
ESRS-E1-3	**Actions** and resources in relation to climate change policies.		
	METRICS & TARGETS		
ESRS-E1-4	**Targets** related to climate change mitigation and adaptation.		
ESRS-E1-5	**Energy** consumption and mix.		
ESRS-E1-6	**Gross Scopes 1, 2, 3** and Total GHG emissions.		
ESRS-E1-7	**GHG removals** and GHG mitigation projects financed through carbon credits.		
ESRS-E1-8	Internal carbon pricing.		
ESRS-E1-9	**Anticipated financial effects** from material physical and transition risks and potential climate-related opportunities.		

1. https://science.nasa.gov/climate-change/what-is-climate-change/.
2. https://www.climate.gov/news-features/understanding-climate/climate-change-global-temperature.
3. https://climate.ec.europa.eu/climate-change/causes-climate-change_en.
4. https://www.climate.gov/news-features/understanding-climate/climate-change-global-temperature.
5. https://link.springer.com/chapter/10.1007/978-3-031-12354-2_2.
6. https://www.climate.gov/news-features/understanding-climate/climate-change-global-temperature.
7. https://www.un.org/en/climatechange/science/causes-effects-climate-change.
8. https://www.un.org/en/climatechange/science/causes-effects-climate-change#:~:text=Over%20the%20past%20decade%20(2010,the%20impacts%20of%20climate%20change.
9. https://www.globalcarbonproject.org/carbonbudget/22/files/GCP_CarbonBudget_2022.pdf.
10. https://www.climate.gov/news-features/understanding-climate/climate-change-atmospheric-carbon-dioxide.
11. https://www.climate.gov/news-features/understanding-climate/climate-change-atmospheric-carbon-dioxide.
12. https://www.fao.org/state-of-forests/en/.
13. https://www.cgdev.org/publication/ft/why-forests-why-now-preview-science-economics-politics-tropical-forests-climate-change.
14. https://quantis.com/news/bridging-the-gap-between-climate-risk-and-corporate-resilience/.
15. https://assets.bbhub.io/company/sites/60/2021/10/FINAL-2017-TCFD-Report.pdf.
16. https://assets.bbhub.io/company/sites/60/2021/10/FINAL-2017-TCFD-Report.pdf.
17. https://www.zurich.com/en/knowledge/topics/climate-change/how-climate-change-will-impact-business-everywhere.
18. https://www.tcfdhub.org/Downloads/pdfs/E06%20-%20Climate%20related%20risks%20and%20opportunities.pdf,
19. https://assets.bbhub.io/company/sites/60/2021/10/FINAL-2017-TCFD-Report.pdf.
20. https://www.tcfdhub.org/Downloads/pdfs/E06%20-%20Climate%20related%20risks%20and%20opportunities.pdf.
21. https://www.forbes.com/sites/davidcarlin/2022/04/18/how-net-zero-became-our-global-climate-goal/.
22. https://www.ipcc.ch/sr15/chapter/glossary/.
23. https://www.weforum.org/agenda/2021/06/impact-climate-change-global-gdp/#:~:text=URL%3A%20https%3A%2F%2Fwww.weforum.org%2Fagenda%2F2021%2F06%2Fimpact.
24. https://wmo.int/news/media-centre/climate-change-indicators-reached-record-levels-2023-wmo.
25. https://eciu.net/analysis/briefings/net-zero/net-zero-why.
26. https://www.ipcc.ch/sr15/.
27. https://wwf.panda.org/discover/our_focus/climate_and_energy_practice/ipcc152/.
28. https://www.wri.org/insights/direct-air-capture-resource-considerations-and-costs-carbon-removal.
29. https://www.wri.org/insights/net-zero-ghg-emissions-questions-answered.
30. https://www.thegef.org/news/how-low-carbon-economy-centurys-biggest-business-opportunity.
31. https://report.ipcc.ch/ar6/wg2/IPCC_AR6_WGII_FullReport.pdf.
32. https://www.oecd.org/en/publications/2024/04/infrastructure-for-a-climate-resilient-future_c6c0dc64.html.

33   https://www.unep.org/resources/adaptation-gap-report-2023.

34   https://www.oecd.org/en/publications/2024/04/infrastructure-for-a-climate-resilient-future_c6c0dc64.html.

35   https://docs.wbcsd.org/2019/09/WBCSD_Business-Climate-Resilience.pdf.

36   https://sasb.ifrs.org/standards/materiality-map/.

37   https://www.ifrs.org/issued-standards/ifrs-sustainability-standards-navigator/.

38   https://www.cakex.org.

39   https://iea.blob.core.windows.net/assets/deebef5d-0c34-4539-9d0c-10b13d84 0027/NetZeroby2050-ARoadmapfortheGlobalEnergySector_CORR.pdf.

40   This case study is based on publicly disclosed information from Rockwell Automation published in a report released by the UN Institute for Training & Research (UNITAR) (https://ewastemonitor.info/gem-2020/ – Forti V., Baldé C.P., Kuehr R., Bel G. *The Global E-waste Monitor 2020: Quantities, flows and the circular economy potential*. United Nations University/UNITAR – co-hosted SCYCLE Programme, International Telecommunication Union & International Solid Waste Association, Bonn/Geneva/Rotterdam).

41   This case study is prepared with reference to publicly disclosed information on Schneider Electric's Zero Carbon Project available on its official website (https://www.se.com/ww/en/about-us/sustainability/zero-carbon-project.jsp).

42   https://www.deloitte.com/ce/en/Industries/real-estate/perspectives/incorporating-esg-living-up-to-stakeholder-expectations-and-business-opportunities.html.

43   https://papers.ssrn.com/sol3/papers.cfm?abstract_id=2699610.

44   https://www.inrev.org/library/transparency-and-performance-european-non-listed-real-estate-fund-market.

45   https://www.goldmansachs.com/intelligence/pages/gs-research/carbonomics-security-of-supply-and-the-return-of-energy-capex/report.pdf.

46   https://digital-strategy.ec.europa.eu/en/library/energy-efficient-cloud-computing-technologies-and-policies-eco-friendly-cloud-market.

47   Montevecchi, F., Stickler, T., Hintemann, R. & Hinterholzer, S. (2020). *Energy-efficient Cloud Computing Technologies and Policies for an Eco-friendly Cloud Market.* Final Study Report. Vienna. doi:10.2759/3320.

48   https://joint-research-centre.ec.europa.eu/jrc-news-and-updates/eu-code-conduct-data-centres-towards-more-innovative-sustainable-and-secure-data-centre-facilities-2023-09-05_en.

49   https://nvlpubs.nist.gov/nistpubs/legacy/sp/nistspecialpublication800-145.pdf.

50   Montevecchi, F., Stickler, T., Hintemann, R. & Hinterholzer, S. (2020). *Energy-efficient Cloud Computing Technologies and Policies for an Eco-friendly Cloud Market.* Final Study Report. Vienna. doi:10.2759/3320.

51   https://www.washington.edu/news/2011/05/31/code-green-energy-efficient-programming-to-curb-computers-power-use/.

52   https://www.mdpi.com/2079-9292/11/3/442.

53   https://womensleadership.stanford.edu/node/796/harnessing-power-stories.

54   https://potentialenergycoalition.org/wp-content/uploads/2024/01/Talk-Like-a-Human.pdf.

3

POLLUTION

Harald Friedl & Elena Doms

Working in executive positions in government, business and civil society, I was frustrated how everything is run in silos. Learning about the circular economy 10 years ago enabled me to think and act in systems. A just economy that works for the people and the planet became the goal; and the flip-side of the circular economy is the global waste and pollution problem. I then began visiting landfills and dumpsites and treatment plants wherever I was working globally – from Asia to Africa to Europe. Pollution and waste are like the identity cards of our society. The amount of trash we produce in support of our ever-accelerating lifestyle has become a trap we have to escape. It has become the neglected mega-crisis of our times.

Harald Friedl

Fifteen years ago, I moved to Belgium. It seemed like a beautiful country, with wonderful traditions. Only a couple of years ago, I discovered how contaminated it is, especially with 'forever chemicals'. I started digging deeper and realised these chemicals spread throughout the whole world. And, honestly, after the tests from soils and water that I have seen, I don't know which food is safe for my kids anymore. Strawberries, beans, eggs, salads, meats, mussels... When I look at them, I see contamination statistics. And I wonder: "How did we get ourselves here? And how do we get ourselves out of this mess?" Because it's not OK. Our kids deserve better parents.

Elena Doms

POLLUTION & WASTE

Pollution is the introduction of harmful substances or contaminants into the environment, causing adverse effects on human health, ecosystems, and the overall quality of air, water, and soil. It is a pervasive and multifaceted crisis that has far-reaching consequences.

While waste and pollution are often used interchangeably, there is a crucial distinction between the two. Waste refers to discarded materials or substances that are no longer needed, while pollution is the result of harmful substances being released into the environment.

However, improper waste management and disposal can lead to pollution, highlighting the interconnectedness of these issues.

According to the World Bank, global waste generation is expected to increase by 70% by 2050, reaching 3.4 billion tons annually, while mismanaged waste is a significant contributor to pollution, with an estimated 8 million tons of plastic waste entering the oceans every year.[1]

Pollution is a cross-cutting crisis that aggregates the issues of inequality, climate and social degradation. Plastic pollution is a crisis that knows no borders. It's a challenge that impacts every corner of our globe, with no exception. We need to stand together to address this man-made pollution crisis.

Paula Francisco Coelho, Secretary of State of Climate Action & Sustainable Development, Republic of Angola

How Our Linear Economic System Fuels Pollution

Our current economic model is based on a linear 'take-make-waste' approach, which is a significant contributor to pollution. This model relies on the continuous extraction of finite resources, their transformation into products, and the eventual disposal of those products as waste. The relentless pursuit of economic growth and consumerism has led to unsustainable production and consumption patterns, generating vast amounts of waste and emissions that overwhelm the planet's capacity to absorb and process them. According to the United Nations Environment Programme (UNEP), the extraction and processing of natural resources account for more than 90% of global biodiversity loss and water stress, as well as approximately half of global greenhouse gas (GHG) emissions.[2]

How Our Fast Consumer Society & Behaviour Fuel Pollution

But it's not an anonymous 'model' that is causing global pollution. It's us. Our modern consumer society is characterised by a culture of disposability and overconsumption, fuelled by planned obsolescence, fast fashion, and a constant desire for the latest products and trends.

This throwaway mentality has led to a significant increase in waste generation, with the average American producing over 4.9 pounds of municipal solid waste per day.[3] Much of this waste ends up in landfills or the environment, contributing to pollution and environmental degradation.

Furthermore, our consumption habits extend beyond physical products. The digital age has brought about new forms of pollution, such as electronic waste (e-waste) and the carbon footprint associated with data centres and digital services, with only 17.4% being officially recycled.[4]

Why Should We Care Now?

Pollution is not just an environmental issue; it is a crisis that affects every aspect of our lives, from our health and well-being to our economic prosperity and social stability.

The impacts of pollution are far-reaching and severe:

- **Health consequences:** Water and soil pollution contribute to health issues, including respiratory diseases, cancer, and birth defects, while the estimated cost of the health damage caused by air pollution amounts to $8.1 trillion annually, equivalent to 6.1% of global GDP;[5]

- **Economic costs:** The economic costs of pollution are staggering. According to a study by the Lancet Commission on Pollution & Health, pollution-related diseases result in annual costs of $4.6 trillion, equivalent to 6.2% of global economic output;[6]

- **Environmental degradation:** Pollution is a leading cause of biodiversity loss, ecosystem destruction, and climate change. The effects of pollution on the environment threaten our food and water security, as well as the overall stability of our planet's life-support systems;

- **Social inequalities:** The burden of pollution disproportionately affects marginalised communities and developing nations, exacerbating existing social and economic inequalities.

The time to act is now. Ignoring the pollution crisis will only lead to further environmental degradation, economic losses, and human suffering. By addressing pollution, we can create a more sustainable, equitable, and prosperous future for all.

HOW POLLUTED IS THE PLANET?

Overview: 10 Most Important Facts & Figures

The scale of pollution afflicting the planet is staggering, with far-reaching consequences for human health, ecosystems, and the global economy. Here are 10 sobering facts that underscore the gravity of the situation:

- Air pollution is responsible for an estimated 7 million premature deaths annually, according to the World Health Organization (WHO).[7] This accounts for nearly one in nine deaths globally, making air pollution the single greatest environmental health risk;

- While plastic pollution is already at epidemic proportions, it is projected to triple by 2040 if no action is taken;[8]

- Water pollution affects more than 40% of the global population, with over 80% of wastewater being discharged untreated into the environment, according to the UN;[9]

- Soil pollution poses a significant threat to global food security, with an estimated 52% of soils worldwide already degraded;[10]

- The global cost of fossil fuel air pollution is estimated at $8 billion per day, or 3.3% of global GDP;[11]

- Microplastics have been found in the air, water, and food supply, with a recent study by the University of Newcastle, Australia, detecting microplastics in human blood for the first time;[12]

- The Great Pacific Garbage Patch, a vast accumulation of plastic debris in the Pacific Ocean, is estimated to cover an area twice the size of Texas, according to a study by The Ocean Cleanup;[13]

- The Arctic region is experiencing rapid warming due to climate change and pollution, with temperatures rising at nearly four times the global average rate;[14]

- E-waste is one of the fastest-growing waste streams globally, with an estimated 53.6 million metric tons generated in 2019, according to *Global E-waste Monitor 2020*;[15]

- The cost of addressing the global plastic crisis is estimated at $100 billion per year, according to UNEP.[16] And the cost of addressing 'forever chemical' pollution at current production rates would likely exceed global GDP.[17]

The Different Types of Pollution

Pollution manifests in various forms, each with its unique sources, impacts, and challenges. Understanding the different types of pollution is crucial for developing targeted solutions and mitigation strategies:

- **Air:** Air pollution refers to the presence of harmful substances in the atmosphere, such as particulate matter, nitrogen oxides, sulphur dioxide, and ground-level ozone. The primary sources of air pollution include transportation, industrial activities, power generation, and agricultural practices. Air pollution has been linked to respiratory diseases, cardiovascular problems, and increased mortality rates;

- **Water:** Water pollution occurs when harmful substances, such as chemicals, nutrients, pathogens, and plastics contaminate water bodies, including rivers, lakes, and oceans. Major sources of water pollution include industrial effluents, agricultural runoff, sewage discharge, and oil spills. Water pollution poses significant risks to aquatic ecosystems, human health, and water security;

- **Food:** Food pollution refers to the contamination of food sources by harmful substances, such as pesticides, heavy metals, and microplastics. The primary sources of food pollution include agricultural practices, industrial activities, and improper waste management. Food pollution can lead to health issues, including cancer, reproductive problems, and developmental disorders;

- **Soil:** Soil pollution occurs when harmful substances, such as heavy metals, pesticides, and industrial waste, contaminate the soil. The primary sources of soil pollution include industrial activities, improper waste disposal, and agricultural practices. Soil pollution can have severe impacts on food production, ecosystem health, and human well-being;

- **Noise:** Noise pollution refers to excessive or unwanted sound that can have detrimental effects on human health and the environment. The primary sources of noise pollution include transportation, industrial activities, and construction. Noise pollution has been linked to health issues, including hearing loss, stress, and sleep disturbances.

The Main Pollution Creators

These are the top five biggest polluting industries, ranked by their GHG emissions:[18]

- **Energy (fossil fuels):** 37.5 billion tons of GHG emissions per year, including emissions from the burning of coal (14.98 billion tons), oil (11.84 billion tons), natural gas (7.92 billion tons), and flaring (416.53 million tons) for energy production;

- **Transport:** 7.29 billion tons; including emissions from road vehicles, aviation, shipping, etc., with road transport making up 74.5% of the sector's emissions;

- **Manufacturing and construction:** 6.22 billion tons, accounting for 50% of global natural resource extraction, 25% of wood harvesting, and 25% of total waste generation;

- **Agriculture:** 5.79 billion tons, caused by agricultural activities like livestock rearing and crop cultivation that lead to emissions of methane and nitrous oxide;

- **Food retail:** 3.1 billion tons, including emissions from food waste, plastic packaging, and transportation in supermarkets and restaurants.

Figure 3.1: The Worst Polluting Countries[19]

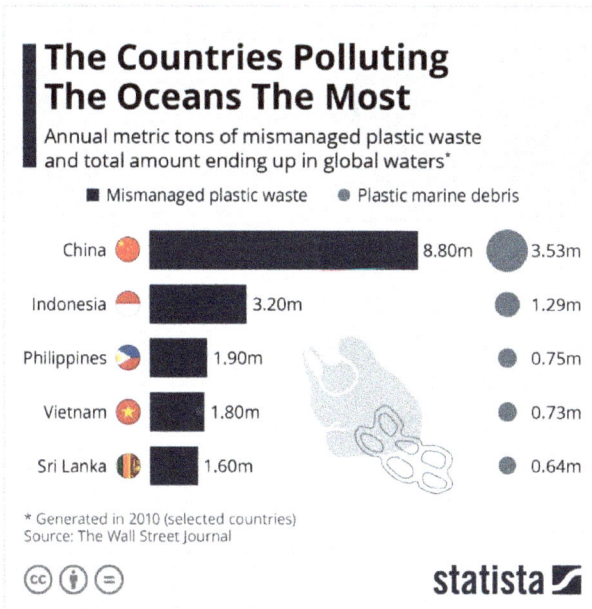

The Countries Polluting The Oceans The Most

Annual metric tons of mismanaged plastic waste and total amount ending up in global waters*

■ Mismanaged plastic waste   ● Plastic marine debris

Country	Mismanaged plastic waste	Plastic marine debris
China	8.80m	3.53m
Indonesia	3.20m	1.29m
Philippines	1.90m	0.75m
Vietnam	1.80m	0.73m
Sri Lanka	1.60m	0.64m

* Generated in 2010 (selected countries)
Source: The Wall Street Journal

statista

THE FACE OF GLOBAL WASTE: INFORMAL WASTE PICKERS

Photo: Harald Friedl.

Informal waste pickers, often overlooked and marginalised, play a vital role in the global waste management sector. These individuals, driven by economic necessity, collect, sort, and recycle valuable materials from the waste stream, contributing significantly to resource recovery and environmental sustainability.

The Global Issue
Informal waste picking is a widespread phenomenon, particularly in developing countries where formal waste management systems are inadequate or non-existent. Millions of people worldwide, including women, children, and

the elderly, rely on this informal sector for their livelihood. However, they often face numerous challenges, including hazardous working conditions, lack of recognition, and social stigma.

Relevance for Waste Management

Informal waste pickers are essential contributors to the circular economy and sustainable waste management practices. They divert a substantial volume of recyclable materials from landfills and incinerators, reducing the environmental impact of waste disposal. Their efforts also conserve natural resources and energy by feeding valuable materials back into the production cycle.

Economic & Social Implications

The informal waste picking sector represents a significant economic activity, generating income for millions of people who would otherwise have limited opportunities. However, these workers often operate in precarious conditions, lacking access to basic services, social protection, and fair wages. Addressing the challenges faced by informal waste pickers is crucial for promoting social inclusion, decent work, and sustainable livelihoods.

Five Key Facts

- *__Global workforce:__ It is estimated that around 15 million people worldwide are engaged in informal waste picking, with a significant concentration in developing countries;*

- *__Resource recovery:__ Informal waste pickers are responsible for recovering a substantial portion of recyclable materials, ranging from plastics and paper to metals and electronic waste, contributing to resource conservation and environmental protection;*

- *__Hazardous working conditions:__ Informal waste pickers often work in hazardous environments, exposed to toxic substances, sharp objects, and potential injuries, with limited access to protective equipment and healthcare;*

- *__Economic contribution:__ The informal waste picking sector generates billions of dollars in economic value annually, highlighting its significance as a source of income and employment for marginalised communities;*

- *__Organisational efforts:__ Waste pickers are increasingly organising themselves into cooperatives and associations, advocating for their rights, improving working conditions, and gaining recognition for their essential role in waste management.*

HOW POLLUTED ARE WE?

Pollution is not just an abstract concept; it is a tangible reality that permeates our daily lives, from the water we drink to the air we breathe. As consumers, we are directly exposed to the consequences of pollution, often without realising the extent of its impact on our health and well-being. We have literally polluted ourselves: a study published in May 2024 showed microplastics were found in the testicles of dogs and humans.[20]

How Polluted is our Drinking Water?

Access to clean and safe drinking water is a fundamental human right, yet millions of people worldwide are exposed to contaminated water sources. According to the WHO, unsafe drinking water is a leading cause of diarrheal diseases, which claim the lives of nearly 829,000 people annually.[21]

In the US, despite stringent regulations, water pollution remains a significant concern. The Environmental Working Group (EWG) found that more than 200 million Americans are exposed to drinking water containing potentially harmful levels of contaminants.[22]

Pollution in the Food We Eat

The food we consume is not immune to the impacts of pollution. From pesticide residues to heavy metal contamination, our diets are increasingly tainted by harmful substances that can have severe health consequences. In 2024, EWG determined that 75% of all conventional fresh produce sampled had residues of potentially harmful pesticides,[23] while globally maximum residue levels of pesticide found in food continues to be of concern, with some regions experiencing higher levels of exposure than others.[24]

Furthermore, the presence of microplastics in our food supply is a growing concern. In a 2022 study microplastic pollution has been detected in human blood for the first time, with scientists finding the tiny particles in almost 80% of the people tested.[25]

Pollution in Apartments & Houses

The very buildings we call home can harbour hidden sources of pollution. Construction materials, such as paints, insulation, and flooring, often contain harmful chemicals and substances that can contribute to indoor air pollution and potentially cause adverse health effects.

According to the US Environmental Protection Agency (EPA), indoor air pollution levels can be two to five times higher than outdoor levels, and in some cases, even higher.[26] Common indoor pollutants include volatile organic compounds (VOCs), formaldehyde, and particulate matter, which can exacerbate respiratory issues, allergies, and even increase the risk of certain cancers.

How Polluted Are Our Clothes & Cosmetics?

Even the products we use for personal care and adornment can be sources of pollution. Cosmetics and clothing often contain harmful chemicals and synthetic materials that can have detrimental effects on both human health and the environment.

The cosmetics industry has come under scrutiny for the use of potentially toxic ingredients, such as parabens, phthalates, and synthetic fragrances, which have been linked to health issues, including endocrine disruption and reproductive problems.

Similarly, the fashion industry's reliance on synthetic fibres, such as polyester and nylon, contributes to microplastic pollution. According to a study by the International Union for Conservation of Nature, an estimated 35% of primary microplastics released into the environment come from the laundering of synthetic textiles.[27]

BAD BOYS & GOOD SOLUTIONS

There is no throwing away on our planet. Every toxic non-degradable chemical, every piece of plastic, is still there. They spread throughout the environment, accumulating there and, increasingly as we're now finding, in our bodies. And it's not going to be a walk in the park to clean them and transition to better alternatives. But progress *is* being made. And in this part of the chapter, we'll explore how we could – and must – do better.

Let's look at two types of pollution: 'forever chemicals' and plastic.

'Forever chemicals'

Per- and polyfluoroalkyl substances (PFAS) are a group of over 10,000 synthetic chemicals that have been widely used in various industrial and consumer products due to their water- and grease-resistant properties. Often known as 'forever chemicals', we find them in our everyday items, like phones, frying pans, winter jackets, cosmetics, child car seats, fast food containers and even toilet paper.

However, because of their useful properties, they do not decompose in nature and create toxic pollution that spreads really far and which scientists fear will stay there for millennia. Forever chemicals have been found in the Arctic ice and in the blood of polar bears. It is estimated that 97% of us have forever chemicals in our blood too.[28] PFAS tend to accumulate in our bodies and can cause a variety of diseases. Studies have linked PFAS to cancers, reproductive and development disorders, liver diseases and other health issues.[29]

Figure 3.2: The Effects of PFAS on Human Health[30]

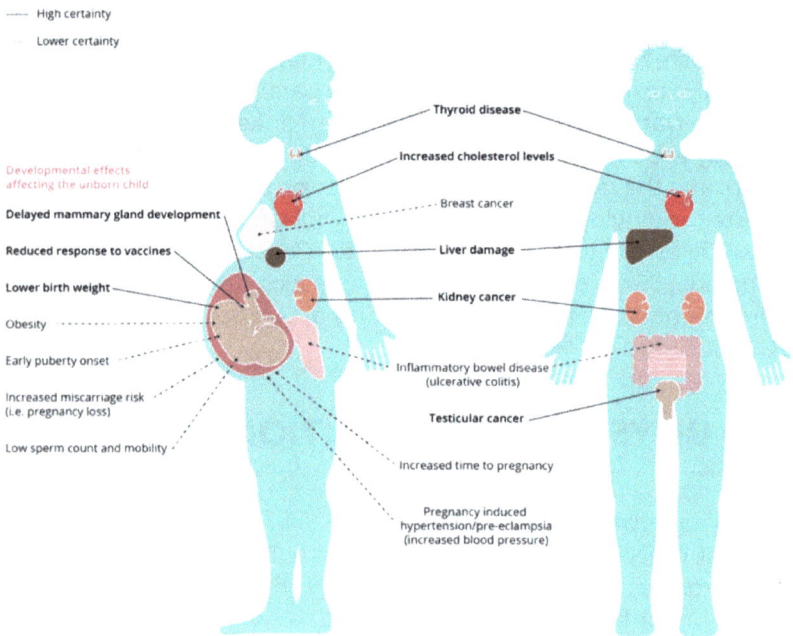

PFAS pollution is only starting to come to our attention through a couple of big scandals. One of them happened in Belgium in 2021. 3M is one of top PFAS producers in the world, along with Chemours, Honeywell, Daikin, Solvay, Merck, BASF, Arkema, Archroma, AGC and Dongue. 3M's Belgian plant is located in Zwijndrecht, close to Antwerp. The company has been releasing toxic wastewater into the nearby river for years. When the pollution hit the news, tests were carried out on soils around 3M's site – and because of high soil pollution, local residents were advised not to eat food from their gardens or eggs from their chickens. It didn't stop there: the blood of citizens living around the site were found to have concentrations of 10 to 100 times higher than the safe limit.[31]

In Belgium, 3M agreed to pay €500m. The company is also accelerating the closure of its production site. In the US, the settlement was higher: $12.5 billion.[32]

But even this money won't be enough to restore the damage. The Swedish NGO ChemSec calculated the global societal costs of PFAS at €16 trillion per year[33] – but that number only includes healthcare and remediation of soils and water, leaving out nature and property impacts. Another research study estimated that, at current emission rates, it would likely take more than global GDP to remove PFAS from the environment.[34]

Surprisingly, markets haven't caught on yet. PFAS cost about €19 per kg – yet it costs up to €60 million to destroy the same kilogram with existing technologies.[35] Hopefully, you can see how flawed this business model is.

Figure 3.3: A Map of PFAS Pollution in Europe[36]

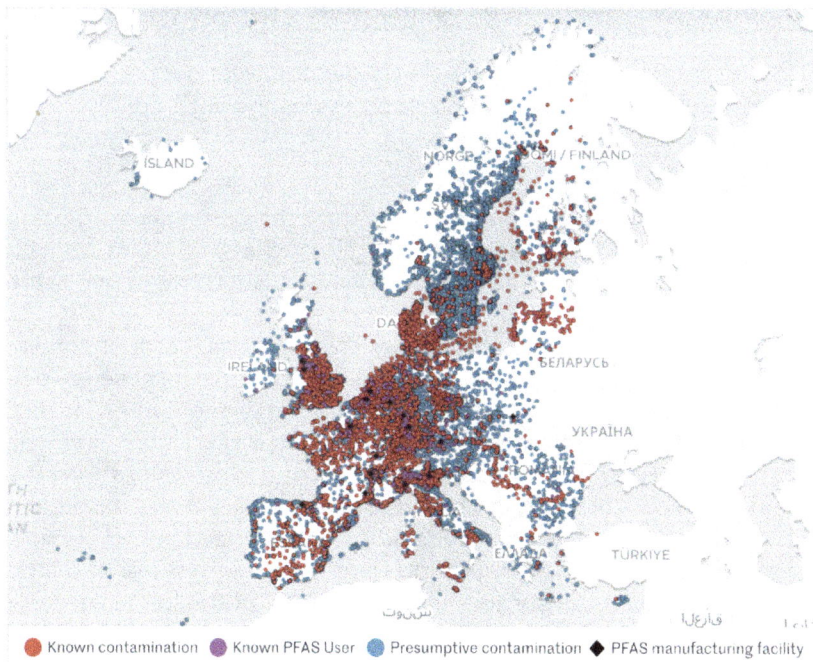

Known contamination   Known PFAS User   Presumptive contamination   ◆ PFAS manufacturing facility

We might think that PFAS scandals are unfortunate but far away. However, that's not the case. In 2023, the Forever Pollution Project and *Le Monde* published a map of contamination in Europe (**see Figure 3.3**), showing over 2,000 hotspots and over 40,000 known and presumed contaminated sites.[37] A PFAS pollution map of the US shows over 7,000 known contaminated sites,[38] while EWG has pinpointed wildlife exposure to PFAS, citing 600 species at risk.[39]

PFAS contamination leads to our potential exposure through water and food. The European Pesticide Network has been measuring PFAS in fruits and vegetables since 2011. Average fruit contamination in the EU jumped from 3.8% in 2011 to 14% in 2021. Strawberries were at an astonishing 37%. Vegetables did slightly better with 7.1% contamination overall; but chicory (*witloof*) ranked highest of all, at 42%.[40] The countries with the highest fruit and vegetable contamination within the EU are Belgium, The Netherlands and Austria, while the most polluted imported products come from Costa Rica, India and South Africa.

And worse, our fruits and vegetables aren't just contaminated because of environmental PFAS pollution; they are also contaminated because of residues of PFAS pesticides. That means we are literally spraying forever chemicals on our food. And then putting them in our bodies.

So what do we do now? How do we get ourselves out of this mess?

We suggest a three-step approach to dealing with pollution and creating a positive story of action.

Step 1: Close the tap

As long as we keep 'producing' pollution, things will keep getting worse. Imagine a water leak. We can get buckets, fill them up with water and carry them out as much as we want. But the leak won't stop until we close the tap.

That's why it's important to say "No". In the case of forever chemicals, only around 8% of use cases are essential.[41] Those include semiconductors, pharmaceuticals and renewable energy. For the rest, mostly, there are alternatives.

That means regulators need to step up and 'close the tap' on the remaining 92%. Certain types of forever chemicals already have been restricted globally through the *Stockholm Convention* and more new laws are starting to appear, limiting PFAS in drinking water and food in order to protect consumers, like in the EU and the US. France will prohibit PFAS in cosmetics, textiles and ski waxes from 2026, while New Zealand has banned PFAS in cosmetics with effect from 2027. The EU is considering a complete ban, which is being heavily opposed by the industry. But we need more. The tap is still running at full speed.

Organisations like ChemSec are actively working on education and lobbying for safer chemicals. It has done extensive research on PFAS societal costs, dug into the main shareholders behind top 12 producers and even organised PFAS blood testing of high-level European politicians together with the European Environmental Agency. Every test showed PFAS contamination, because no one is immune. And the message was clear: we need more action.

As a company you can actively support the PFAS ban too. A PFAS movement is gathering pace globally, with H&M, Intersport, Lyreco, Levi Strauss, Ralph Lauren and many other businesses on board. Make your voice heard too.[42]

Step 2: Find better alternatives
It's not enough to just close the tap. Let's face it, forever chemicals have been invented for a reason. We still need substances that protect us from the rain or help paper not stick together. But these substances can be better and safer for us and nature.

If your company currently uses forever chemicals (or any other harmful chemicals), you can check this SIN (Substitute It Now) list from ChemSec,[43] which is already being used by companies, investors and regulators around the globe. If you find a match, look into alternatives. ChemSec is there to help.

Not every toxic chemical has a safer alternative already. Or maybe it does, but the production scale is not there yet. Investment in, and adoption of, better alternatives is the most direct action you can take as a company to transition to safer practices.

Step 3: Clean up the pollution
Cleaning forever chemicals requires solutions for both water and soils.

Successful treatments are being implemented for waste water, drinking water and landfill leakage. They include electrochemical oxidation, activated carbon absorption, nanofiltration and others. Several start-ups are leading the way, including Allonia[44] and Aclarity.[45]

Soils are harder to clean. Traditionally, PFAS soil hotspots have been excavated and put somewhere else. But if you remember the maps of Europe or the US, you will see that we can't literally excavate so much land. Besides, what would it do except to create extra emissions as we send trucks from one place to another?

Organisations like +EARTH+[46] and C-biotech[47] in Belgium came up with an innovative approach, which proved successful on polluted sites close to 3M. They use plants like industrial hemp and willows to extract forever chemicals from soils and groundwater, in a process called phytoremediation. Plants pick up pollution from the soil and transfer it to their leaves. Leaves are then separated and treated at very high temperatures to get rid of the pollution. But the stems remain absolutely clean and can be used to make circular bio-based construction materials, removing carbon in the process. With more and more industrial and farming lands testing positively for PFAS across the globe, this approach could help bring restoration at scale.

Figure 3.4: An Example of Circular Bio-based Construction Materials

If your business has been involved in production or use of harmful substances like PFAS, look for and support clean-up solutions. Taking responsibility and a proactive approach will work better for your reputation than waiting for a potential court case.

Plastic pollution

Plastic pollution has been on our radar for a while now. Awareness is rising. You might have seen the pictures of the Great Pacific Garbage Patch, or a turtle stuck in plastic fishing nets, or flowing rivers full of plastic, or the belly of whale with almost 40 kg of plastic waste in it. You might have noticed the overwhelming amount of plastic in your home or office too. It comes with food, packaging, toys, clothes, electronics and just about anything we buy.

Almost all (99%) plastic is made from fossil fuels. Between 2000 and 2019, plastic production has doubled, and it is expected to quadruple by 2050. By now, all the plastic we've produced already outweighs the total weight of all the animals on Earth. Only about 9% of it has ever been recycled and 19% incinerated. The rest came back to our environment and is breaking down into microplastics and nanoplastics.[48]

Scientists are still researching what all of this means. But we already know that microplastics and nanoplastics release toxic chemicals and gather more toxins on their surface. They are then digested by plankton, which are at the start of our food chain.

So who are the bad boys of plastic pollution? Let's look at it on two levels (see **Figure 3.5**):

- The largest **plastic producers** in the world, that manufacture plastic from fossil fuels, include Exxon Mobil, Dow, BASF, Total and other fossil fuel and chemical companies;[49]

- The largest **plastic polluters** in the world, that widely use plastic in their products, are just 56 companies who together are responsible for more than 50% of branded plastic pollution. The top five are Coca-Cola, PepsiCo, Nestlé, Danone and Altria.[50]

Now if we apply the same system to solve the plastic pollution crisis as we did to forever chemicals, how do we get ourselves out of this mess?

Figure 3.5: The Worst Plastic Polluters, 2020[51]

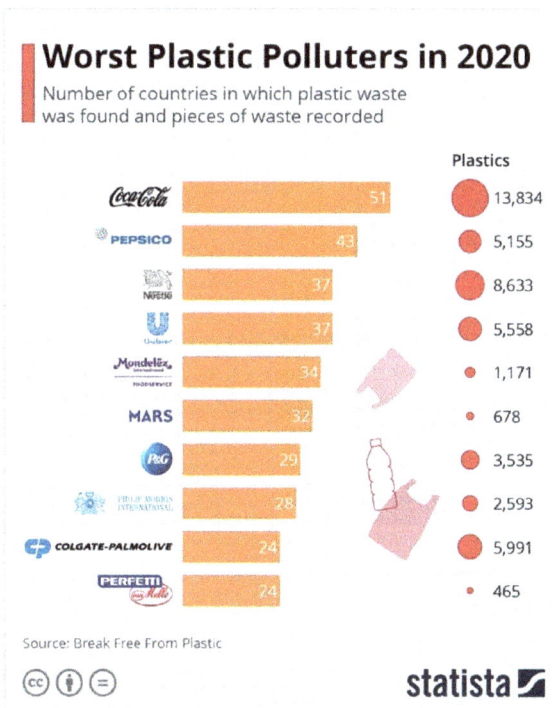

Worst Plastic Polluters in 2020

Number of countries in which plastic waste was found and pieces of waste recorded

	Number of countries	Plastics
Coca-Cola	51	13,834
PEPSICO	43	5,155
Nestlé	37	8,633
Unilever	37	5,558
Mondelēz International	34	1,171
MARS	32	678
P&G	29	3,535
Philip Morris International	28	2,593
COLGATE-PALMOLIVE	24	5,991
PERFETTI Van Melle	24	465

Source: Break Free From Plastic

statista

Step 1: Close the tap
Once again, we need to stop the outflow of plastics into our environment.

Single-use plastics are the easiest to start with. They comprise one-third of all the plastics produced and are only used for a few seconds before being discarded. Many countries have already banned certain types of single-use plastic: Kenya, India, China banned single-use plastic bags; the UK banned products with microbeads; the EU banned single-use straws, plates and cutlery. And the movement is growing further.

The *Global Plastics Treaty* is expected to be adopted in 2024. It will be legally binding and will focus on ending plastic pollution as a whole. That means cutting unnecessary polluting plastic products (including single-use plastic and plastic packaging) and setting specific requirements for plastic products aimed at reducing plastic consumption.[52]

As a business, don't wait for the *Global Plastics Treaty*. Analyse your supply chains and products and cut unnecessary plastic use now.

Step 2: Find better alternatives
Once unnecessary production is cut, we need different plastic systems. That means better materials, better collection and circular models. Some examples:

- Site Zero, the biggest plastic sorting plant in Sweden, has the capacity to sort the whole country's households plastic packaging waste, preparing it for proper recycling and saving plastic from incineration;[53]
- Rubbish Ideas helps companies track their materials journey, waste streams and recycling rates with material tracking software. The results are analysed to understand problems and identify lowest cost circular optimisations;[54]
- Sway decided to walk away from fossil fuel-based plastic altogether. The company develops bio-based compostable replacements from plastic out of seaweed. Instead of polluting the environment, its products contribute to biodiversity, ocean health and livelihoods;[55]
- BMW, Porsche and Harley-Davidson implement hemp biocomposite materials in cars and motorcycles. These natural composite materials help substitute fossil-fuel based plastic and cut carbon emissions.

What types of plastic are you using in your company? Can you find better alternatives and implement them already now?

Important notice: Please focus on cutting unnecessary plastic use first. Sometimes, we mean well, but fail to improve things. An example is drinking straws: plastic straws are being replaced by paper straws. But did you know that paper straws contain forever chemicals?[56] Not good news! Instead of switching to other single-use materials, eliminate them in the first place.

Step 3: Clean up the pollution
Even though we see a lot of plastic in our streets, rivers and oceans, most of it sinks to the bottom. That's why it's important to intercept it as quickly as possible.

The Ocean Cleanup[57] does large-scale plastic clean-up, catching plastic in rivers and oceans by building huge barriers and interceptors, then sending it for recycling with local partners. Every year, the technology gets more efficient. In April 2024, The Ocean Cleanup hit a new milestone by removing 10 million kg of plastic. And it hopes to be out of business eventually by having no plastics left to clean. Other organisations are joining plastic clean-up too. Among them are River Cleanup,[58] Plastic Odyssey[59] and lots of group and individual volunteer initiatives.

Once plastic is gone, magic starts happening. Previously heavily polluted Mumbai beach now sees vulnerable turtle species hatching for the first time in decades.[60]

Again, as an organisation, engage in supporting clean-up activities. Most of them are non-commercial and need your funding. After all, they are cleaning up someone else's trash and need all the help they can get.

Good Solutions Are Based on Systemic Approaches

To address the big challenges, we all must not only think – but also act – systemically.

Systemic government collaborations
Systems change is about problem-solving. Your initiative may change how the system functions, such as through policy change or resource allocation, but you should be clear that the changes are being made to solve specific problems, in order to achieve better outcomes for workers, businesses, and communities.

Here are some examples of successful government collaborations to address global pollution:

- The *Montreal Protocol on Substances that Deplete the Ozone Layer* (1987): A global agreement to phase out ozone-depleting substances like chlorofluorocarbons (CFCs), signed by 198 countries, and considered one of the most successful environmental treaties, helping to repair the ozone layer. Collaboration between governments, scientists and industry led to affordable alternatives;

- The *Minamata Convention on Mercury* (2013): A global treaty to protect human health and the environment from mercury pollution, ratified by 137 countries, that requires parties to phase out mercury mining, regulate emissions/releases, and promote mercury-free alternatives. It facilitated technology transfer and capacity building in developing nations;

- The *Paris Agreement on Climate Change* (2015): A landmark accord to limit global warming through emissions reductions, signed by 195 countries, that established common rules for transparency, reporting and review of national climate action plans and includes mechanisms for climate finance, technology transfer and capacity building.

Figure 3.6: Addressing Systems Change[61]

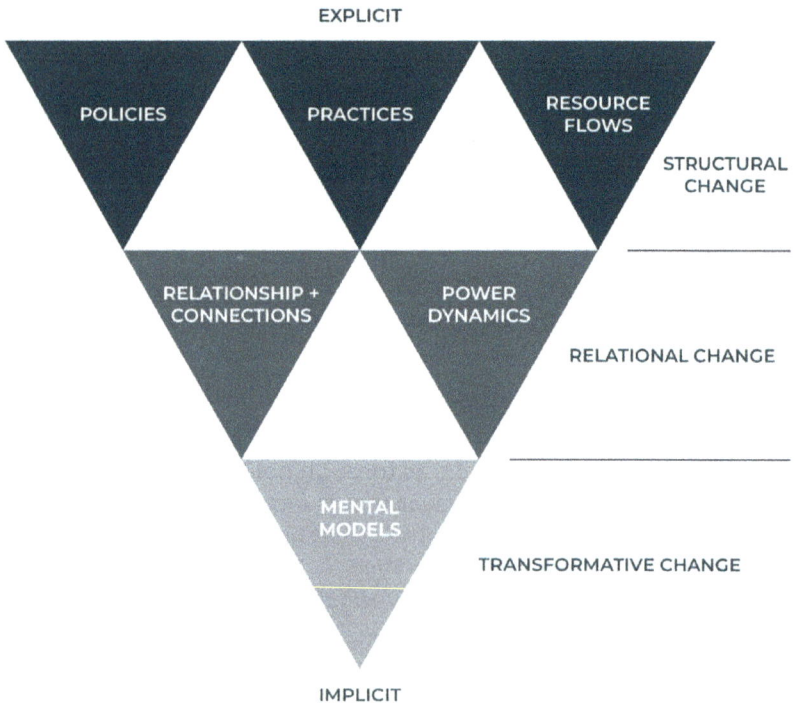

EXPLICIT

POLICIES

PRACTICES

RESOURCE FLOWS

STRUCTURAL CHANGE

RELATIONSHIP + CONNECTIONS

POWER DYNAMICS

RELATIONAL CHANGE

MENTAL MODELS

TRANSFORMATIVE CHANGE

IMPLICIT

These collaborations demonstrate how coordinated international efforts, underpinned by scientific evidence, can drive impactful solutions to address global pollution challenges through policy interventions, knowledge sharing and capacity building across borders.

The private sector as a driver of systemic change

The private sector can drive systemic solutions to address global pollution by:

- Implementing circular business models;
- Investing in new technologies, systems and materials;
- Collaborating, advocating for, and participating in eco-systems for systemic change.

Companies can transition from linear to circular business models that keep materials and products in use for as long as possible, eliminating waste and pollution at the source, through:

- **Product-as-a-Service:** Companies retain ownership of products and provide them through leasing or subscription models, incentivising durability, repair, and easy maintenance. For example, Philips' 'Light-as-a-Service' leases energy-efficient LED lights, keeping materials in a closed loop;
- **Product life extension:** Manufacturers facilitate repair, refurbishment, and remanufacturing to maximise product lifespans. Patagonia's 'Worn Wear' programme repairs and resells used clothing; it diverted 135 tons of apparel from landfills in 2022;
- **Investing in circular material flows:** For example, BMW is working on a 'Second First' approach to increase secondary materials in vehicles over time.

Companies can invest in advanced recycling technologies, material tracking systems, and renewable bio-based materials to keep materials cycling at their highest value through:

- **Better recycling technologies:** New approaches are transforming material waste back into high-quality feedstock. C-battery monitors every small battery cell of a few grams – and when it cannot be repaired, it is shredded and separated into components to go back to cell manufacturing. Mycocycle uses the power of fungi to transform construction waste into low-carbon materials for the built environment;
- **Material tracking:** Platforms like Atma.io connect physical products with digital IDs, helping to create transparency, tracking materials from source to consumer and enabling circularity;

- **Bio-based materials:** Renewable materials like seaweed (Sway), hemp composites (Harley-Davidson, Porsche), and mushroom construction materials and packaging can substitute for fossil-based plastics (C-biotech, Mykor).

Companies can collaborate across sectors, advocate for supportive policies, and participate in circular innovation ecosystems to drive systemic change through:

- **Extended producer responsibility (EPR):** Companies support policies that make manufacturers responsible for product end-of-life, incentivising circular design from the start. EPR policies are gaining momentum globally;
- *Global Plastics Treaty:* Businesses can advocate for an ambitious, legally binding treaty to reduce plastic pollution through product design requirements and waste management standards, expected in 2024;
- **Circular innovation ecosystems:** Public-private partnerships and industrial symbiosis create shared value from circular material flows and by-product exchanges. For example, Kalundborg Symbiosis in Denmark facilitates resource exchanges among companies, saving €635m in costs annually.

By redesigning business models, material flows, and enabling system conditions through collaboration, the private sector can drive the systemic changes needed to transition towards a circular, zero-pollution economy.

EMERGING GLOBAL HOPE

The international community is now rallying around several key frameworks aimed at mitigating pollution and promoting sustainable practices. Among these, the Global Framework on Chemicals, the Global Biodiversity Framework, and the *Global Plastics Treaty* stand out as beacons of hope. These initiatives represent comprehensive, multi-stakeholder approaches to addressing some of the most pressing environmental issues of our time.

Global Framework on Chemicals

The Global Framework on Chemicals is a pivotal initiative aimed at ensuring the sound management of chemicals throughout their life cycle. This framework is designed to prevent harm from chemicals and waste, promoting a safe, healthy, and sustainable future. It encompasses a broad range of activities, from the production and use of chemicals to their disposal and the management of chemical waste.

One of the key strengths of the Framework is its multi-stakeholder and multisectoral nature. It involves various sectors, including environment, health, agriculture, and labour, and engages stakeholders at local, national, regional, and global levels. This inclusive approach ensures that diverse perspectives and expertise are incorporated into the management strategies, enhancing their effectiveness and sustainability.

The Global Framework on Chemicals also emphasises the importance of integrating environmental and social considerations into chemical management practices. By doing so, it aims to protect not only the environment but also the health and well-being of communities worldwide. The *Bonn Declaration*, a key component of this framework, underscores the commitment to a planet free of harm from chemicals and waste, setting a clear vision for the future.

Global Biodiversity Framework

The Global Biodiversity Framework is another critical initiative that addresses the urgent need to protect and restore biodiversity. This framework was developed under the auspices of the *Convention on Biological Diversity* (CBD) and aims to halt and reverse biodiversity loss by 2030. It sets out ambitious targets for the conservation and sustainable use of biodiversity, recognising the intrinsic value of nature and its essential role in human well-being.

This Framework is structured around several key goals, including the protection of ecosystems, the sustainable management of natural resources, and the equitable sharing of benefits arising from the use of genetic resources. It also emphasises the need for transformative changes in how we interact with nature, calling for the integration of biodiversity considerations into all sectors of society.

One of the notable aspects of the Global Biodiversity Framework is its focus on implementation and accountability. It includes mechanisms for monitoring progress and ensuring that countries are held accountable for their commitments. This is crucial for translating the Framework's ambitious goals into tangible actions on the ground.

The *Global Plastics Treaty*

The *Global Plastics Treaty* represents a groundbreaking effort to tackle the pervasive issue of plastic pollution. This Treaty, currently under negotiation, aims to establish legally binding commitments to reduce plastic production, enhance waste management, and promote the circular economy. It seeks to address the entire life cycle of plastics, from production and consumption to disposal and recycling.

A key feature is its emphasis on international cooperation and coordination. Plastic pollution is a global problem that requires a unified response, and the Treaty aims to foster collaboration among countries, industries, and civil society. It highlights the importance of innovation and the development of sustainable alternatives to conventional plastics.

The *Global Plastics Treaty's* focus on the circular economy is particularly significant. By promoting the principles of reduce, reuse, and recycle, it aims to create a more sustainable and resilient system for managing plastic waste. This approach not only helps to reduce pollution but also conserves resources and supports economic development.

UPCOMING HOT TOPICS

Current hot topics shaping the discourse around environmental sustainability and influencing policy, business practices, and public awareness include pollution prevention, liability risks and circular models.

Pollution Prevention is Key

Pollution prevention is increasingly recognised as a fundamental strategy for reducing the emissions of pollutants and mitigating their impact on the environment and human health. Unlike traditional approaches that focus on managing pollution after it has been created, pollution prevention aims to eliminate or reduce the generation of pollutants at source, through:

- **Source reduction:** One of the primary methods of pollution prevention is source reduction, which involves modifying production processes, using less harmful substances, and improving efficiency. For example, industries can adopt cleaner technologies and practices that minimise waste and emissions, which not only reduces the environmental footprint but also often leads to cost savings and improved operational efficiency;

- **Regulatory frameworks:** Governments and international bodies are increasingly implementing regulatory frameworks that prioritise pollution prevention. Policies such as the EU's *Industrial Emissions Directive* and the US *Pollution Prevention Act* encourage industries to adopt preventive measures, promote sustainable practices and reduce the burden of pollution on ecosystems and communities;

- **Public awareness and education:** Raising public awareness about the importance of pollution prevention is crucial. Educational campaigns and initiatives can help individuals and businesses understand the benefits of reducing pollution at the source. By fostering a culture of sustainability, we can drive collective action towards a cleaner and healthier environment.

Liability Risks for Businesses: The Case of PFAS

PFAS are persistent in the environment and have been linked to adverse health effects, leading to growing concerns and regulatory scrutiny. Emerging liability risks include:

- **Legal and financial risks:** Businesses that manufacture, use, or dispose of PFAS are facing increasing liability risks. Legal actions and regulatory measures are being taken to hold companies accountable for PFAS contamination. For instance, several high-profile lawsuits have been filed against manufacturers for environmental damage and health impacts caused by PFAS. These legal challenges can result in significant financial liabilities, including fines, clean-up costs, and compensation for affected communities;

- **Regulatory developments:** Governments around the world are tightening regulations on PFAS. The EU has proposed a comprehensive ban on PFAS in firefighting foams, and the US EPA is developing stricter standards for PFAS in drinking water. These regulatory developments are likely to increase operational challenges and compliance costs for businesses;

- **Proactive measures:** To mitigate liability risks, businesses need to adopt proactive measures. This includes phasing out the use of PFAS, investing in research and development of safer alternatives, and implementing robust environmental management systems. By taking these steps, companies can reduce their exposure to legal and financial risks, while demonstrating their commitment to sustainability.

How Circular Business Models Help Reduce Pollution

Circular business models are gaining traction as a powerful approach to reducing pollution and promoting sustainability. Unlike the traditional linear economy, which follows a 'take-make-waste' pattern, the circular economy emphasises the continuous use of resources through recycling, reusing, and remanufacturing.

The benefits of circular business models include:

- **Waste reduction:** By designing products for durability, repairability, and recyclability, businesses can minimise the amount of waste generated. For example, companies in the electronics industry are developing modular products that can be easily upgraded or repaired, extending their lifespan and reducing e-waste;

- **Resource efficiency:** Circular business models promote resource efficiency by maximising the value extracted from materials and products, *via* practices such as closed-loop recycling, where materials are continuously cycled back into production processes. By reducing the need for virgin materials, businesses can lower their environmental impact and conserve natural resources;

- **Innovation and collaboration:** The transition to a circular economy requires innovation and collaboration across the value chain. Businesses, governments, and other stakeholders need to work together to develop new technologies, business models, and regulatory frameworks that support circular practices. For instance, the Ellen MacArthur Foundation's Circular Economy 100 programme brings together companies, policymakers, and academia to accelerate the adoption of circular economy principles;

- **Economic opportunities:** Embracing circular business models also can create economic opportunities. By tapping into new markets for recycled materials and sustainable products, businesses can drive growth and competitiveness. Additionally, circular practices can lead to cost savings through improved resource efficiency and waste reduction.

By prioritising pollution prevention, addressing liability risks, and embracing circular economy principles, we can make significant strides in the fight against global pollution and pave the way for a more sustainable future.

ESRS-E2 – POLLUTION REPORTING OBLIGATIONS

Ingrid De Doncker

The ESRS-E2 standard specifies the disclosure requirements in relation to pollution. It enables users of the sustainability statement to understand:

- How the organisation affects pollution of air, water and soil, in terms of material positive and negative actual or potential impacts;

- What actions are taken, and the result of such actions, to prevent or mitigate actual or potential negative impacts, and to address risks and opportunities;

- Its plans and capacity to adapt its strategy and business model in line with the transition to a sustainable economy and with the need to prevent, control and eliminate pollution. This is to create a toxic-free environment with zero pollution;

- The nature, type and extent of its material risks and opportunities related to the organisation's pollution-related impacts and dependencies, as well as the prevention, control, elimination or reduction of pollution, including where this results from the application of regulations, and how this is managed; and

- The financial effects on the organisation over the short-, medium- and long-term of material risks and opportunities arising from the organisation's pollution-related impacts and dependencies.

Pollution Sub-topics

Under ESRS 1 Article 16, there are seven sub-topics to consider. The wording is not always clear, so we have expanded the descriptions here for clarity:

- **Air pollution:** This refers to the contamination of the atmosphere by harmful substances or pollutants in the form of gases, liquids, or solid particles that are released into the air, often as a result of human activities such as industrial processes, transportation, and agricultural practices. We think here of particulate matter (PM), nitrogen oxides (NOx), sulphur oxides (SOx), carbon monoxide (CO) and volatile organic compounds (VOCs);

- **Water pollution:** This covers the contamination of water bodies, such as rivers, lakes, oceans, and groundwater, by harmful substances or pollutants, which can occur through industrial discharges, agricultural runoff, improper waste disposal, sewage discharge, etc;

- **Soil pollution:** The contamination of soil by harmful substances or pollutants, which can occur through industrial activities, agricultural practices, improper waste disposal, accidental spills, etc. Soil pollutants include heavy metals, pesticides and herbicides, petroleum products, industrial chemicals and solvents, and plastic waste;

- **Pollution of living organisms and food resources:** This relates to the contamination of the environment by substances that can accumulate in the bodies of living organisms, including plants and animals used for food production;

- **Substances of concern:** This refers to heavy metals, persistent organic pollutants (POPs), pesticides and herbicides, plastics and volatile organic compounds (VOCs) that have potential negative effects, because of their toxicity or harm to living organisms;

- **Substances of very high concern:** These materials are identified as particularly hazardous due to their properties or potential risks to human health and the environment. They are subject to stringent scrutiny because of their severe impact, due to their toxicity, persistence, bioaccumulation, and potential for long-term harm on people and planet;

- **Microplastics:** Microplastics are tiny plastic particles less than 5 millimetres in size that can be found in various environments, including water bodies, soil, and even the air. These particles can come from the breakdown of larger plastic items or be intentionally manufactured at a small scale. Microplastics pose environmental risks as they can be ingested by marine life, animals, and even humans, causing harm to ecosystems and health.

This Standard should be read in conjunction with ESRS 1 *General Requirements* and the requirements of this section should be read in conjunction with and reported alongside the disclosures required by ESRS 2, *Chapter 4: Impact, Risk & Opportunity Management*.

It is important to understand the *Minimum Disclosure Requirements* (MDRs) in ESRS 2, Chapter 4.2. When an organisation identifies a sustainability matter as material, 34 MDR datapoints (DPDs) for Policies, Actions, Targets, and Metrics (PAT-M) are applicable if the organisation discloses on policies, actions and targets. If it does not provide disclosure on policies, targets or actions, then it needs to disclose the reasons for not doling so, as per the corresponding 10 DPs of ESRS 2 MDR PAT, paragraphs 62 and 81.

The ESRS-E2 outlines clearly, in six *Disclosure Requirements* (DRs), the narrative and numeric DPs an organisation should comply with. There are 44 *Shall* DPs, of which 24 are numeric, 18 narrative and 2 semi-narrative, as well as 20 additional *May* DPs. The MDR PAT DPs are to be disclosed under E2-1, E2-2, E2-3 when the sustainability matters is material.

Figure 3.7 shows the structure of the ESRS-E2 DR and DP that must be reported, if deemed material by the double materiality assessment.

Figure 3.7: ESRS-E2 Reporting Requirements

ESRS-E2	Pollution
	Air, Water, Soil, Pollution of living organisms and food resources, Substances of Concern, Substances of Very High Concern, Microplastics
	With the exception of DPs in IRO-1, none of these DPs are applicable if the topic is not material.
	IMPACT, RISK & OPPORTUNITY MANAGEMENT
ESRS2-E2-IRO-1	Description of the processes to identify and assess material pollution-related impacts, risks and opportunities.
ESRS-E2-1	**Policies** related to pollution.
ESRS-E2-2	**Actions** and resources related to pollution.
	METRICS & TARGETS
ESRS-E2-3	**Targets** related to pollution.
ESRS-E2-4	**Pollution** of air, water and soil.
ESRS-E2-5	**Substances of concern** and substances of very high concern.
ESRS-E2-6	**Anticipated financial effects** from pollution related impacts, risks and opportunities.

1   https://sustainabledevelopment.un.org/content/documents/
    Ocean_Factsheet_Pollution.pdf.

2   https://www.unep.org/news-and-stories/press-release/un-calls-urgent-rethink-resource-use-skyrockets.
3   https://www.epa.gov/facts-and-figures-about-materials-waste-and-recycling/national-overview-facts-and-figures-materials.
4   V. Forti, C.P. Baldé, R. Kuehr, & G. Bel (2020). *The Global E-waste Monitor 2020: Quantities, Flows & the Circular Economy Potential*. https://ewastemonitor.info/wp-content/uploads/2020/11/GEM_2020_def_july1_low.pdf.
5   https://www.worldbank.org/en/news/feature/2022/09/01/what-you-need-to-know-about-climate-change-and-air-pollution.
6   https://www.ncbi.nlm.nih.gov/pmc/articles/PMC8294505/.
7   https://www.who.int/teams/environment-climate-change-and-health/air-quality-energy-and-health/health-impacts/exposure-air-pollution.
8   https://www.nationalgeographic.com/science/article/plastic-trash-in-seas-will-nearly-triple-by-2040-if-nothing-done.
9   UN *World Water Development Report 2022*.
10 https://www.eld-initiative.org/fileadmin/pdf/ELD-pm-report_08_web_72dpi.pdf.
11 https://energyandcleanair.org/wp/wp-content/uploads/2020/02/Cost-of-fossil-fuels-briefing.pdf.
12 https://www.sciencedirect.com/science/article/pii/S0160412022001258.
13 https://theoceancleanup.com/great-pacific-garbage-patch/.
14 https://www.nature.com/articles/s43247-022-00498-3.
15 V. Forti, C.P. Baldé, R. Kuehr, & G. Bel (2020). *The Global E-waste Monitor 2020: Quantities, Flows & the Circular Economy Potential*. https://ewastemonitor.info/wp-content/uploads/2020/11/GEM_2020_def_july1_low.pdf.
16 https://news.un.org/en/story/2021/10/1103692.
17 https://www.sciencedirect.com/science/article/abs/pii/S0048969724007861.
18 https://www.greenmatch.co.uk/blog/most-polluting-industries.
19 https://www.statista.com/chart/12211/the-countries-polluting-the-oceans-the-most/.
20 https://pubmed.ncbi.nlm.nih.gov/38745431/.
21 https://www.unicef.org/media/137206/file/triple-threat-wash-EN.pdf.
22 https://www.ewg.org/research/forever-chemicals-found-water-coast-coast-builds-case-strict-epa-limits.
23 https://www.ewg.org/foodnews/summary.php.
24 https://www.ncbi.nlm.nih.gov/pmc/articles/PMC10379487/.
25 https://www.sciencedirect.com/science/article/pii/S0160412022001258.
26 https://www.epa.gov/iaq-schools/why-indoor-air-quality-important-schools.
27 https://www.eea.europa.eu/publications/microplastics-from-textiles-towards.
28 https://chemsec.org/knowledge/all-you-need-to-know-about-pfas/.
29 https://www.researchgate.net/publication/345920639_Per-_and_Polyfluoroalkyl_Substance_Toxicity_and_Human_Health_Review_Current_State_of_Knowledge_and_Strategies_for_Informing_Future_Research.
30 Used with permission from the European Environment Agency (2019). Original sources for this figure: National Toxicology Program (2016), C8 Science Panel (2012), IARC Working Group on the Evaluation of Carcinogenic Risks to Humans (2017), Barry *et al.* (2013), Fenton *et al.* (2009) and White *et al.* (2011b).
31 https://meta.eeb.org/2021/09/23/surreally-serious-pfas-paralysis-follows-astonishing-scandal/.
32 https://www.wsj.com/business/3m-being-investigated-in-belgium-over-forever-chemicals-emissions-cd99b802.
33 https://chemsec.org/reports/the-top-12-pfas-producers-in-the-world-and-the-staggering-societal-costs-of-pfas-pollution/.

34   https://www.sciencedirect.com/science/article/abs/pii/S0048969724007861.

35   https://www.sciencedirect.com/science/article/abs/pii/
     S0048969724007861?dgcid=author.

36   *Source:* Forever Pollution Project and *Le Monde*.

37   https://www.lemonde.fr/en/les-decodeurs/article/2023/02/23/forever-pollution-
     explore-the-map-of-europe-s-pfas-contamination_6016905_8.html.

38   https://www.ewg.org/interactive-maps/pfas_contamination/.

39   https://www.ewg.org/interactive-maps/pfas_in_wildlife/map/.

40   https://www.pan-europe.info/sites/pan-europe.info/files/public/resources/
     reports/Report_Toxic%20Harvest%20The%20rise%20of%20forever%20PFAS%2
     0pesticides%20in%20fruit%20and%20vegetables%20in%20Europe%2027022
     024%20%281%29.pdf.

41   https://chemsec.org/reports/the-top-12-pfas-producers-in-the-world-and-the-
     staggering-societal-costs-of-pfas-pollution/.

42   https://chemsec.org/pfas/.

43   https://sinlist.chemsec.org/.

44   https://allonnia.com/.

45   https://www.aclaritywater.com/.

46   www.earthplus.eu.

47   https://www.c-biotech.eu.

48   https://www.technologyreview.com/2023/10/12/1081129/plastic-recycling-
     climate-change-microplastics/.

49   https://www.minderoo.org/plastic-waste-makers-index/.

50   https://www.science.org/doi/10.1126/sciadv.adj8275.

51   https://www.statista.com/chart/23720/worst-polluting-companies/.

52   https://www.worldwildlife.org/pages/global-plastics-treaty.

53   https://www.svenskplastatervinning.se/en/site-zero/.

54   https://rubbish-ideas.com/.

55   https://swaythefuture.com/.

56   https://pubmed.ncbi.nlm.nih.gov/33770693/.

57   https://theoceancleanup.com/.

58   https://www.river-cleanup.org/en.

59   https://plasticodyssey.org/en/.

60   https://www.theguardian.com/world/2018/mar/30/mumbai-beach-goes-from-
     dump-to-turtle-hatchery-in-two-years.

61   https://www.wfound.org/change/.

4

WATER & MARINE RESOURCES

Dr William Beer &
T.A.O. Garraty[1]

F ascinated by the ocean as a child, going on fishing and scuba diving trips from an early age and witnessing the reduction of fish stocks first-hand at the age of 15, I made the decision never to eat seafood again. Growing up in the UK, I never saw the direct impacts of climate change until my career led me to a Ph.D. on reducing the environmental impact of mining. The more I learnt, the more shocked I became. Learning the tools of the trade in managing large teams, I founded Tunley Engineering (now Tunley Environmental), a global team of sustainability scientists reducing the environmental impact of organisations and their products.

Dr William Beer

I have dedicated my career to understanding and mitigating the impacts of climate change on vital ecosystems. My research, particularly within the Peruvian Amazon, has given me profound insights into the intricate connections between biodiversity, hydrological patterns, and climate dynamics. I care deeply about water resources because they are the lifeblood of both terrestrial and aquatic ecosystems, supporting countless species and human communities. Driven by a passion for conservation, my work aims to promote sustainable practices that protect these essential resources.

T.A.O. Garraty

WHAT ARE WATER & MARINE RESOURCES?

Water resources encompass all the water present on Earth, whether in the form of liquid, solid (ice), or vapour. They are the lifeblood of our planet, essential for the sustenance of all living organisms and the functioning of ecosystems. From the vast expanses of oceans to the smallest creeks trickling through forests, water plays a crucial role in supporting life and biodiversity and in shaping ecosystems and landscapes. Broadly categorised into freshwater and marine resources, water reservoirs encompass a diverse array of habitats, each with its own unique characteristics and importance.

Figure 4.1: The Water Cycle

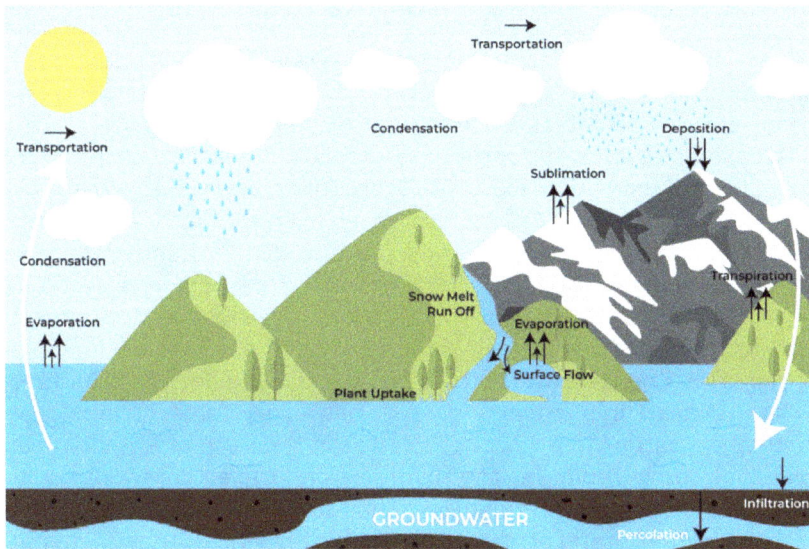

Freshwater resources, comprising lakes, rivers, streams, wetlands and groundwater, are vital for human survival and development. In particular, groundwater, stored beneath the Earth's surface in aquifers, serves as a vital source of drinking water for many communities, supports agricultural irrigation, and sustains ecosystems through baseflow to streams and wetlands. Additionally, freshwater resources provide irrigation for agriculture, energy generation through hydroelectric power, and habitat for diverse aquatic species – from fish to amphibians and insects, contributing to both ecological balance and human well-being.

Marine resources, covering more than 70% of the Earth's surface, are vast reservoirs of saltwater teeming with life. Oceans and seas regulate the planet's climate, absorb carbon dioxide (CO_2), and provide crucial ecosystem services such as nutrient cycling and oxygen production. These saline waters support diverse habitats, from deep-sea trenches to coral reefs, hosting a staggering array of species adapted to various ecological niches, from microscopic plankton to majestic whales. Marine ecosystems provide food, livelihoods, and recreational opportunities for millions of people worldwide, while also regulating the planet's climate and nutrient cycles.

Coastal zones, where land meets the sea, are among the most productive and biodiverse ecosystems on Earth. Mangroves, salt marshes, and estuaries provide critical habitats for marine and terrestrial species, serve as nurseries for fish and other aquatic organisms, and protect coastlines from erosion and storm surges. Moreover, oceans play a crucial role in global transportation, trade, and communication networks, serving as highways for shipping and laying submarine cables.

Coastal areas also support human communities through fisheries, tourism, and recreation. Exclusive Economic Zones (EEZs) – maritime areas extending up to 200 nautical miles from a country's coastline – are rich in resources such as fish, oil, gas, and minerals, and are subject to national jurisdiction for resource management and conservation.

Glacial and polar ice, stored in ice caps, glaciers, and ice sheets, constitute significant freshwater reserves, particularly in polar regions. Melting ice contributes to sea levels rising and alters regional water availability, impacting marine ecosystems and ocean circulation patterns. Atmospheric water, in the form of water vapour, plays a crucial role in the hydrological cycle, contributing to precipitation such as rain, snow, and hail. It cycles constantly between the atmosphere, land, and oceans. Human-made reservoirs, created for water storage, flood control, and hydropower generation, provide benefits like water supply and renewable energy but also can have significant ecological and social impacts, including habitat loss and displacement of communities.

WHAT ARE THE CHALLENGES?

Despite their immense importance, both freshwater and marine resources face an array of challenges that threaten their sustainability. Pollution from industrial runoff, agricultural pesticides, and plastic waste poses significant risks to water quality and marine life. Overfishing and destructive fishing practices deplete fish stocks and harm sensitive habitats such as coral reefs and seagrass meadows. Furthermore, the impacts of climate change, including rising temperatures, sea levels rising, and ocean acidification, exacerbate these threats, putting additional pressure on already stressed ecosystems. This all highlights the need for sustainable management practices to ensure their continued availability.

Water is a fundamental component in industrial processes, playing a pivotal role in a wide range of operations within sectors such as manufacturing, energy production, and mining. In manufacturing, water is essential for cooling equipment such as compressors, turbines, and reactors. It is also a vital part of cleaning and rinsing processes in industries like food and beverage, pharmaceuticals, and electronics. Additionally, water is a critical ingredient in chemical reactions and serves as a solvent for various raw materials and products. The energy sector heavily relies on water for the generation of electricity, as it is used in hydropower generation and for cooling in thermal power plants. Furthermore, mining operations require large volumes of water for processes such as mineral extraction, dust suppression, and transportation.

However, the extensive use of water in industrial processes raises concerns about its sustainable management, particularly in the context of global water scarcity and environmental impact. The extraction, treatment, and disposal of water involve energy consumption and can contribute to carbon emissions. Furthermore, the discharge of industrial wastewater can lead to pollution of water bodies, impacting aquatic ecosystems and human health. Additionally, the high demand for water in industrial activities can strain local water sources, leading to conflicts with other users such as communities. Embracing water-efficient practices and investing in innovative technologies are essential for mitigating the impact of water usage in industrial processes.

The oldest industrial use of water, agriculture, has been a cornerstone of human civilisation for millennia. Globally, agriculture is the largest consumer of water. In crop cultivation, water is essential for irrigation to support the growth of various plants, ensuring their hydration and promoting healthy yields. Additionally, livestock farming necessitates substantial water supplies for drinking and general husbandry, contributing to the overall water consumption in agriculture.

Water usage in agriculture can lead to pollution through surface runoff, particularly when excess water carrying agricultural chemicals, such as fertilisers and pesticides, flows over the land and into nearby water bodies. This runoff can introduce harmful substances into rivers, lakes, and streams, impacting aquatic ecosystems and water quality. The chemicals from agricultural activities can contribute to eutrophication, where an excess of nutrients leads to the overgrowth of algae and other aquatic plants, depleting oxygen levels and harming aquatic life. Additionally, sediment from eroded soils can be carried by the runoff, further degrading water quality.

The historical and ongoing significance of water in agriculture underscores its fundamental role in providing sustenance for human and animal populations and highlights the critical need for sustainable water management practices within this vital sector.

Water behaves as an enormous logistical system (the process is called 'advection'). To explain, ink is water with particles called pigment suspended in it; water provides the mechanism to transport the pigment to whatever the ink is used for (for example, this book). After transporting the pigment, the water changes state, evaporating and leaving the pigment (and a binder – for example, resin or glue) behind. This happens every day on a global scale but, instead of pigment, the suspended 'stuff' is plastic, microplastics, pollutants, toxins, effluent, etc. Thus our water systems are transporting human junk all over the world, and in many cases simply leaving it not just in the ocean but also in soil, where it ultimately can make its way into our food. Bioaccumulation is where food chains increasingly absorb higher and higher concentrations of 'stuff' – for example, the dangerous levels of some heavy metals in fish.

Algal bloom events occur when algae grows excessively in a body of water.[2] During these bloom events, algae can deplete the oxygen levels and produce harmful toxins, posing a risk to human and pet health, as well as leading to mass fish deaths, and posing a risk to other surrounding wildlife. Further, these organisms block sunlight to other plants, further limiting the capacity of the water body to recover oxygen levels. This eutrophication is driven by the availability of nutrients (primarily nitrogen and phosphorous compounds) and prolonged warm temperatures. Unsurprisingly, human activity is a major contributory factor, in both nutrient runoff and increasing temperatures driven by climate change.[3]

A large proportion of these nutrients arise from agricultural sources, including chemical fertilisers and manure, alongside sewage overflows and industrial pollution. Approximately 20% of nitrogen-based fertiliser is lost from surface runoff,[4] and intensification of animal livestock has led to increased manure application to food crops. Gardeners also can contribute unwittingly to nitrogen runoff, by the overuse of chemical fertilisers. In addition, several high-profile incidents have highlighted the use of combined sewage overflows, where raw sewage can be discharged into lakes and rivers when surface runoff would otherwise overwhelm current infrastructure.

The solutions require the use of best practices for fertiliser application, considering precipitation forecasts, regular soil testing and other measures, such as growing cover crops in winter. Of course, investment in sewage infrastructure to reduce the raw sewage contribution will reduce impact; however this is likely to need years of sustained investment. More ambitious projects include using floating solar panels to reduce water temperatures. Last, decarbonisation will limit further warming and mitigate the worst of impacts to come.

In the face of these challenges, concerted efforts are needed to conserve and manage water resources effectively, including implementing policies to reduce pollution, promote sustainable water use, and protect vulnerable habitats. International cooperation is also essential to address transboundary water issues and ensure equitable access to water resources for all communities. By adopting a holistic and inclusive approach to water management, we can safeguard these invaluable resources for future generations, while maintaining the health and integrity of our planet's ecosystems.

WHY DO WE CARE?

In the intricate web of life on Earth, water serves as the linchpin that sustains ecosystems, drives economies, and nurtures societies. From the deepest ocean trenches to the highest mountain peaks, water resources, both freshwater and marine, are the lifeblood of our planet. Understanding why we should care about these resources is not merely a matter of environmental concern; it is a fundamental imperative for the well-being of humanity and the health of the planet.

First, water is essential for human survival. Access to clean, safe drinking water is a basic human right, yet millions of people around the world still lack this fundamental necessity. Without adequate freshwater resources, communities face heightened risks of waterborne diseases, malnutrition, and poverty. Moreover, water scarcity and contamination exacerbate social inequalities, disproportionately affecting vulnerable populations such as women, children, and marginalised communities.

Beyond its direct impact on human health, water resources underpin global food security and agricultural productivity. Agriculture accounts for the largest share of freshwater withdrawals globally, with irrigation systems supporting crop cultivation on arable land. Whether it's rice paddies in Asia, maize fields in Africa, or vineyards in Europe, water is the lifeblood of agricultural production. Without sufficient water, crop yields dwindle, food prices soar, and livelihoods are threatened, leading to food insecurity and societal unrest.

Moreover, marine and freshwater resources play a crucial role in global food systems and economic development. Fish and seafood are essential sources of protein and nutrients for billions of people worldwide, particularly in coastal and freshwater adjacent communities, and developing countries. The fishing industry provides employment and income for millions of individuals, from small-scale artisanal fishers to industrial fleets.

The oceans and freshwater systems provides protein consumed by humans, further consolidating their vital importance for our survival. The global demand for protein from both ocean and freshwater systems has increased dramatically in recent years. This increase in demand, and the consequent reduction in fish stocks due to overfishing and anthropogenic impacts, represents significant risk. Additionally, aquatic ecosystems contribute to climate regulation, carbon sequestration, and shoreline protection, providing invaluable services for human well-being and environmental sustainability.

However anthropogenic pressures are causing climate change to become exacerbated to rates 1,000 times higher than natural climate change, which has a serious knock-on effect to our natural world, and more specifically natural resources such as water systems.

Climate Change & Marine Ecosystems

The current rise in sea surface temperatures and the looming threat of ocean acidification are urgent issues with profound implications for marine ecosystems, human livelihoods, global climate stability, and water resources. Since the onset of the Industrial Revolution, the ocean has absorbed nearly half of all anthropogenic CO_2 emissions. When atmospheric CO_2 dissolves into seawater, it forms carbonic acid, which lowers the pH of seawater, making it more acidic. This phenomenon, known as ocean acidification, has led to a 0.1 unit drop in seawater pH since pre-industrial times.

Ocean acidification significantly affects marine organisms that rely on calcium carbonate ($CaCO_3$) for their shells and skeletons, such as corals, molluscs, and calcifying plankton species. The increased acidity of seawater hampers the formation and maintenance of these skeletons, potentially leading to reduced growth rates and the dissolution of existing coral structures.

In addition to acidification, coral reefs have experienced significant declines in total coverage, with at least a 50% reduction since the first mass coral bleaching event in the early 1980s. The most recent mass bleaching event occurred in early 2024. These events are triggered by extreme heat waves resulting from rising sea surface temperatures, causing corals to expel the symbiotic algae that provide them with energy, leading to bleaching and often coral death. As ocean temperatures continue to rise, many marine species migrate towards cooler waters, disrupting local ecosystems and causing declines in species unable to adapt quickly enough.

The combined effects of ocean acidification and rising sea temperatures could lead to the extinction of coral reefs, resulting in the loss of critical marine habitats vital for the survival of many marine species. Coral reefs are biodiversity hotspots and serve as nursery grounds for a wide range of marine organisms.

Healthy coral reefs also act as natural barriers against storm surges and erosion, protecting coastal areas from the impacts of storms and rising sea levels. Their degradation leaves these areas more vulnerable. Furthermore, coral reefs are significant tourist attractions, generating substantial revenue for coastal economies.

The importance of coral reefs extends to their role in water resources. Coral reefs help maintain the quality of coastal waters by filtering pollutants and providing habitats for species that regulate water quality. The loss of coral reefs can lead to the deterioration of these water resources and have a knock-down impact on essential ecosystem services they provide thus impacting not only marine life but also the human populations that rely on clean water for drinking, agriculture, and industry.

Additionally, many human communities depend on seafood as a primary source of food and income. The decline of marine habitats and populations due to climate change threatens food security and economic stability, particularly in coastal regions reliant on fishing. As coral reefs represent key biodiversity hotspots, their decline would result in the loss of critical nursery grounds for many marine species, further exacerbating the impact on fisheries and water resources.

Therefore, mitigating ocean acidification and rising sea temperatures is crucial not only for environmental preservation but also for maintaining water resources, economic stability, and social well-being on a global scale. The preservation of coral reefs and the broader marine environment is essential to ensure the health and sustainability of our planet's water resources.

Climate Change & Freshwater

The ongoing effects of climate change also pose significant threats to freshwater ecosystems, with far-reaching implications for biodiversity, human livelihoods, and global water resources.

Freshwater ecosystems, including rivers, lakes, wetlands, and aquifers, are particularly vulnerable to changes in temperature and precipitation patterns caused by climate change.

Higher temperatures increase the rate of evaporation, reducing water levels in lakes and rivers and contributing to the desiccation of wetlands. This reduction in water availability can lead to more concentrated pollutants, adversely affecting water quality and the health of aquatic organisms.

Increased temperatures also influence the thermal stratification of lakes, leading to changes in oxygen distribution. Warmer surface waters can create a barrier that prevents the mixing of oxygen-rich surface water with deeper, cooler water layers. This stratification can result in hypoxic or anoxic conditions (low or no oxygen) in deeper waters, threatening fish and other aquatic life that depend on oxygenated water.

Changes in precipitation patterns, another consequence of climate change, can exacerbate these issues. More intense and frequent storms can lead to increased runoff, which carries pollutants such as pesticides, fertilisers, and sediments into freshwater systems. This runoff can cause eutrophication, causing dead zones where aquatic life cannot survive.

Conversely, prolonged droughts reduce water flow in rivers and streams, concentrating pollutants and reducing habitat availability for many species. Droughts also decrease groundwater recharge, affecting the sustainability of aquifers that supply drinking water to millions of people.

Freshwater ecosystems are biodiversity hotspots, supporting a vast array of plant and animal species. These ecosystems provide critical services, including water filtration, flood control, and nutrient cycling. Wetlands, for example, act as natural water filters, trapping sediments and pollutants and improving water quality. They also serve as buffers against floods by absorbing excess rainwater and releasing it slowly, reducing the impact of flooding downstream.

The degradation of freshwater ecosystems has significant implications for human communities. Many people rely on freshwater resources for drinking water, agriculture, and industry. The loss of these ecosystems can lead to water scarcity, reduced agricultural productivity, and increased costs for water treatment and infrastructure repair.

Furthermore, freshwater ecosystems are crucial for recreational activities and tourism, contributing to local economies. The degradation of these environments can reduce their aesthetic and recreational value, impacting tourism and the associated economic benefits.

To protect freshwater ecosystems and ensure the sustainability of water resources, it is essential to mitigate the effects of climate change, by implementing measures to reduce greenhouse gas (GHG) emissions, improve water management practices, and restore degraded ecosystems. Protecting these vital ecosystems is crucial for maintaining biodiversity, supporting human livelihoods, and ensuring the availability of clean water for future generations.

The excessive consumption of water from the water table in California has been linked to the anthropogenic hydrological droughts (where the earth is so dry and water table is so low the capillary reaction no longer lifts water towards the surface). Also, the droughts have been linked to increased intensity of forest fires and therefore carbon emissions of forest fires.

When calculating the embodied carbon of an agricultural product, the impacts of a hydrological drought are not taken into account; therefore, in many cases, the carbon footprint is a significant underestimate. This is an enormous problem.

Climate Change & Glacier Water

Glaciers are critical freshwater reservoirs, especially in regions where they provide a substantial portion of water for rivers and streams. These glacial meltwaters are essential for drinking water, agriculture, and hydropower generation. However, climate change is causing glaciers to retreat at unprecedented rates, posing serious threats to these water resources.

As global temperatures rise, glaciers are melting more rapidly. Initially, this increased meltwater can lead to higher river flows during the summer months, providing temporary relief for water shortages. However, this is a short-term benefit. Over time, as glaciers continue to shrink, the volume of meltwater will decrease, leading to reduced river flows. This reduction can have devastating impacts on communities and ecosystems that rely on consistent water supplies from glacial melt.

The loss of glaciers also affects the seasonal distribution of water. In many regions, glaciers act as natural buffers, releasing water during dry periods and storing it during wet periods. As glaciers diminish, this buffering capacity is lost, leading to more pronounced seasonal variations in water availability. This can exacerbate water scarcity during dry seasons and increase the risk of flooding during wet ones.

Moreover, glaciers are vital for maintaining the health of downstream ecosystems. Many aquatic species rely on the cold, nutrient-rich waters from glaciers. As glacier-fed streams warm, these species may face habitat loss and increased competition, leading to declines in biodiversity.

Climate Change & Groundwater

Groundwater is another crucial component of the global freshwater system, providing nearly half of the world's drinking water and a significant portion of water used for irrigation and industrial processes. Climate change impacts groundwater in several ways, primarily through changes in precipitation patterns and increased evapotranspiration.

Altered precipitation patterns can affect groundwater recharge rates. In some regions, decreased rainfall and prolonged droughts reduce the amount of water infiltrating the ground, leading to lower groundwater levels and thus the depletion of aquifers, which are already being over-exploited in many areas to meet the growing demand for water. Conversely, in regions experiencing increased rainfall, the intensity of precipitation events can lead to rapid runoff, reducing the amount of water that infiltrates the soil and replenishes groundwater supplies. Additionally, heavy rainfall can lead to soil erosion and the contamination of aquifers with pollutants, further compromising groundwater quality.

Increased temperatures also enhance evapotranspiration, the process by which water is transferred from land to the atmosphere through evaporation and plant transpiration. Higher rates of evapotranspiration reduce the amount of water available for groundwater recharge, exacerbating water scarcity.

The depletion of groundwater resources has severe consequences for both human and ecological systems. Many communities, especially in arid and semi-arid regions, rely on groundwater as their primary water source. As groundwater levels decline, wells may run dry, forcing people to seek alternative, often more expensive, water sources. This can lead to increased economic stress and health risks associated with water scarcity.

Groundwater is also essential for maintaining the base flow of rivers and streams during dry periods. As groundwater levels drop, the flow of these surface waters can decrease, affecting aquatic habitats and reducing water availability for downstream users.

Furthermore, water resources are intimately tied to climate change mitigation and adaptation. Changes in precipitation patterns, rising temperatures, and extreme weather events are altering the availability and distribution of water resources, exacerbating droughts, floods, and water scarcity in many regions. Sustainable water management practices, such as rainwater harvesting, water conservation, and integrated watershed management, are crucial for building resilience to climate change and ensuring water security for future generations.

The volume of water in river systems fluctuates with weather systems – for example, in droughts, rivers contain less water and in precipitation events their volume increases; this has always been the case. However, and it is a big however, increasingly severe weather patterns are significantly changing the pace of change in water volume in river systems. For example, in built-up areas, surface runoff occurs more aggressively as concrete does not absorb water so the rate of water being added to a river system is higher. The impact of this is often floods. In drought conditions, the situation is equally severe – for example, when the ground is very dry, water is absorbed more slowly and therefore flash flooding can result. Where deforestation has occurred, the likelihood of landslides in extreme precipitation events also increases.

Water Resources & Human Well-being

Human health, livelihoods, and cultural practices are deeply intertwined with the water resources provided by glaciers, groundwater, freshwater, and marine environments. Glacial meltwater, groundwater, and freshwater sources such as rivers and lakes are vital for supplying clean drinking water, preventing diseases and maintaining overall health. These water sources also support agriculture by irrigating crops, ensuring food security, and sustaining the livelihoods of millions of farmers. Freshwater ecosystems, including wetlands and rivers, provide habitat for diverse species and support fisheries that are crucial for local economies.

Additionally, marine environments, including coral reefs and fisheries, provide crucial food resources and economic opportunities for coastal communities. These water bodies also hold significant cultural and spiritual importance for many indigenous and local communities, who have long-standing traditions and practices centred around them. Water resources often feature prominently in cultural rituals, ceremonies, and social activities, reinforcing community identity and heritage.

Healthy water ecosystems act as natural barriers against extreme weather events, protecting human settlements and infrastructure, thus preserving lives and economic stability. The sustainable management of these resources is critical to ensuring the well-being, prosperity, and cultural continuity of current and future generations.

The Importance of Water Resources

Water resources from glaciers, groundwater, and marine environments are crucial for maintaining ecological balance and supporting human life and progress. These resources provide essential drinking water, are vital for agriculture and industry, and sustain fisheries that many communities rely on for food and income. They are integral to product manufacturing and play a significant role in global trade and economic stability. Additionally, healthy water ecosystems contribute to sustainability by regulating climate, filtering pollutants, and acting as natural barriers against extreme weather events. Therefore, the sustainable management and conservation of water resources are essential for ensuring long-term environmental health, economic prosperity, and social well-being.

Similarly, irrigation significantly impacts global crop yields by enhancing productivity, particularly in regions where rainfall is insufficient. Studies show that irrigation can boost crop yields by substantial margins compared to rainfed agriculture. For instance, a 65-year analysis in the US revealed that irrigation increased corn yields by as much as 270% on average.[5] However, the yield gains from irrigation can vary significantly by crop and region. This highlights the importance of tailored irrigation practices to maximise agricultural productivity and support food security globally, further highlighting the importance of water resources.

In conclusion, caring about water resources and marine resources is not just a moral imperative; it is a pragmatic necessity for safeguarding human health, ensuring food security, conserving biodiversity, and mitigating climate change. By recognising the intrinsic value of water and embracing sustainable management practices, we can forge a more resilient and equitable future for people and the planet alike.

MARINE BIODIVERSITY PROTECTION

Efforts to protect marine biodiversity have shown remarkable success in some regions, highlighting the importance of sustained and well-managed conservation initiatives.

One notable example is the recovery of marine life in the Cabo Pulmo National Marine Park in Mexico. Overfished and degraded by the mid-1990s, the area was designated a national park, and local communities were actively involved in its protection. As a result, the biomass of fish increased by over 460% in less than a decade, showcasing the resilience of marine ecosystems when given a chance to recover.

This success underscores the potential for marine protected areas (MPAs) to restore biodiversity, enhance fisheries, and improve the overall health of ocean ecosystems.

However, not all ocean protection efforts have yielded positive results. For instance, the UK has faced challenges in maintaining clean and healthy marine environments despite various initiatives.

One high-profile example is the banning of plastic straws to protect sea turtles and other marine life. While the straw ban raised awareness about plastic pollution, it has had limited impact compared to the broader issue of microplastics, which continue to pervade marine environments and cause extensive harm to marine species. The focus on plastic straws, while symbolically important, highlights the need for comprehensive strategies addressing all sources of plastic pollution rather than isolated measures.

FRESHWATER ECOSYSTEM PROTECTION

One notable success in freshwater ecosystem protection is the restoration of the Hudson River in New York. Decades of industrial pollution had severely degraded the river's water quality and biodiversity. However, comprehensive clean-up efforts, strict environmental regulations, and community engagement have led to significant improvements. The reintroduction of species like the bald eagle and river otter, along with increased fish populations, showcases the river's ecological recovery.

Another success story is the revival of the Rhine River in Europe. Once heavily polluted by industrial waste, international cooperation and stringent pollution control measures have dramatically improved water quality. The return of salmon to the river after a 50-year absence is testament to the effective restoration efforts that have revitalised aquatic life and enhanced the river's overall health.

In contrast, the protection of glaciers in the Himalayas has faced significant challenges. Despite various initiatives to mitigate climate change and reduce glacier retreat, the region's glaciers continue to shrink at alarming rates. For instance, the Gangotri glacier, one of the largest in the Himalayas and a critical water source for the Ganges River, has been retreating rapidly. Efforts to reduce GHG emissions and promote sustainable practices have not been sufficient to halt or reverse the glacier's decline, highlighting the need for more effective global climate action to protect these vital freshwater resources.

WATER & MARINE RESOURCES REPORTING & GOVERNANCE

Reporting and governance obligations for water and marine resources involves cooperation from many different sectors and encompass a wide array of activities, policies, and stakeholders. These obligations are fundamental pillars of sustainable resource management, serving to monitor, assess, and regulate the use and conservation of these invaluable natural assets.

Water Resources

Starting with water resources, reporting obligations entail comprehensive monitoring and assessment of key indicators such as water quantity, quality, and availability. This involves collecting data from various sources, including gauging stations, water quality monitoring networks, and remote sensing technologies. Parameters such as water levels, flow rates, nutrient concentrations, and pollutant loads are continuously monitored to provide insights into the health and status of water bodies. Additionally, reporting mechanisms extend to the dissemination of information to the public and stakeholders through platforms like water quality reports, environmental assessments, and online databases. Accessible and transparent reporting ensures that communities are informed about the condition of their local water resources, empowering them to participate in decision-making processes and advocate for sustainable water management practices.

Governance obligations for water resources encompass a wide range of policies, laws, and institutions aimed at regulating water use, protecting ecosystems, and ensuring equitable access to water resources. At the national level, governments enact laws and regulations to govern water allocation, pollution control, and water rights. Water management agencies, established at the federal, state, or local level, oversee the implementation of these regulations and coordinate efforts to address water-related challenges. Internationally, transboundary water resources require cooperation and diplomacy among riparian countries to manage shared water bodies effectively. Treaties, agreements, and joint commissions provide frameworks for collaboration on issues such as water allocation, pollution prevention, and ecosystem conservation.

Marine Resources

Turning to marine resources, reporting obligations are similarly focused on monitoring and assessing the status and trends of marine ecosystems, fisheries, and marine pollution. Fisheries management relies on data collection and reporting to track fish stocks, fishing activities, and compliance with regulations. Fishery observers, onboard electronic monitoring systems, and vessel monitoring systems (VMSs) are employed to collect data on catch composition, fishing effort, and bycatch levels. Additionally, reporting mechanisms facilitate the exchange of information among countries and stakeholders through regional fisheries management organisations (RFMOs), which coordinate efforts to conserve and manage shared fish stocks.

Governance obligations for marine resources encompass a broader range of issues, including marine pollution, habitat conservation, and climate change impacts. Countries are obligated to report on measures taken to prevent marine pollution from land-based sources, shipping activities, and offshore oil and gas operations. Initiatives such as the International Maritime Organization's (IMO) *Marine Pollution Prevention Convention* (MARPOL) set standards for vessel pollution control and require member states to report on compliance and enforcement measures. Furthermore, reporting on MPAs and habitat conservation initiatives is essential for tracking progress towards biodiversity conservation goals and preserving critical marine habitats such as coral reefs, mangroves, and seagrass beds.

In conclusion, reporting and governance obligations for water and marine resources are multifaceted and interconnected, spanning multiple scales, sectors, and stakeholders. By ensuring the collection, analysis, and dissemination of accurate and timely information, reporting mechanisms enable evidence-based decision-making, promote transparency and accountability, and facilitate collaboration among governments, institutions, and communities. Moreover, robust governance frameworks provide the foundation for effective resource management, conservation, and sustainable development, ensuring the long-term health and resilience of water and marine ecosystems for current and future generations.

More Work Needed

There is an enormous emphasis on carbon footprints, and, rightly so, However, carbon is only one part of sustainability. We need to see the consumption of water in all industries treated in a similar way to carbon – baseline assessment, reduction roadmap and reporting. If organisations around the world reported on their industrial usage of water *versus* its scarcity as a resource, we would see significant reductions.

Consumer behaviours are directly linked to data. Reporting of calories in food products through a simple traffic light system has changed consumption behaviours in the UK. All foods are reported against some sort of nutrition rating: calories, fat, saturated fat, etc. We also need to see products' consumption of water: imagine reporting "water per 100g of product", perhaps even against some abundance rating in the country of origin. More work is needed.

ESRS-E3 – WATER & MARINE RESOURCES REPORTING OBLIGATIONS

Ingrid De Doncker

ESRS-E3 relates to water and marine resources. This standard is designed to help companies report on their water management and marine resources and contribute to the European *Green Deal*'s ambitions for fresh air, clean water, healthy soil, and biodiversity.

It provides transparency and accountability in the management of water and marine resources, which are essential for the health of our planet and human well-being. It is important for users of the sustainability statement to understand:

- How an organisation affects water and marine resources, in terms of material positive and negative actual or potential impacts;

- The actions it takes, and the result of such actions to prevent or mitigate material actual or potential negative impacts, to protect water and marine resources, also with reference to reduction of water consumption, and to address risks and opportunities;

- Whether, how and to what extent the organisation contributes to the European *Green Deal*'s ambitions for fresh air, clean water, healthy soil and biodiversity, as well as to the sustainability of the blue economy and fisheries sectors, taking account of other related EU directives and the Sustainable Development Goals (SDGs) – specifically, SDG 6 – Clean Water & Sanitation and SDG 14 – Life Below Water;

- The organisation's plans and capacity to adapt its strategy and business model in line with the promotion of sustainable water use based on long-term protection of available water resources, protection of aquatic ecosystems and restoration of freshwater and marine habitats;

- The nature, type and extent of an organisation's material risks and opportunities arising from its own impacts and dependencies on water and marine resources, and how the undertaking manages them; and

- The financial effects on the organisation over the short-, medium- and long-term of material risks and opportunities arising from the undertaking's impacts and dependencies on water and marine resources.

The topic of water and marine resources is closely connected to other environmental subtopics such as climate change, pollution, biodiversity, and the circular economy.

Water & Marine Resources Sub-topics

Under ESRS 1 Article 16, there are two sub-topics and five sub-subtopics to consider. The two topics are:

- **Water:** This standard relates to surface water and groundwater. The use or consumption of water, as well as withdrawals and discharges of water, including the use and sourcing of water, water treatment as a step towards more sustainable sourcing of water, and the prevention and abatement of water pollution are considered. The disclosure requirements on water consumption in own operation's activities, products and services, as well as related information on water withdrawals and water discharges are included;

- **Marine resources**: Reporting covers the extraction and use of resources from the ocean (gravels and deep-sea minerals), seafood products, and other marine resources-related commodities (including other products derived from the ocean, such as seaweed, coral, or other marine organisms).

This Standard should be read in conjunction with ESRS 1 *General Requirements* and the requirements of this section should be read in conjunction with and reported alongside the disclosures required by ESRS 2, *Chapter 4: Impact, Risk & Opportunity Management*.

It is important to understand the *Minimum Disclosure Requirements* (MDRs) in ESRS 2, Chapter 4.2. When an organisation identifies a sustainability matter as material, 34 MDR data points (DPs) for Policies, Actions, Targets, and Metrics (PAT-M) are applicable if the organisation discloses on policies, actions and targets. If it does not provide disclosure on policies, targets or actions, then it needs to disclose the reasons for not doing so, as per the corresponding 10 DPs of ESRS 2 MDR PAT, paragraphs 62 and 81.

ESRS-E3 outlines clearly, in five *Disclosure Requirements* (DRs), the narrative and numeric DPs an organisation should comply with. There are 27 *Shall* DPs, of which 8 are numeric, 17 narrative and 2 semi-narrative, as well as 18 additional *May* DPs. The MDR PAT DPs are to be disclosed under E3-1, E3-2, E3-3 when the sustainability matters are material.

Figure 4.3 shows the structure of the ESRS-E3 DRs and DPs that must be reported, if deemed material by the double materiality assessment.

Figure 4.3: ESRS-E3 Reporting Requirements

ESRS-E3	Water & Marine Resources	
	Water	**Marine resources**
	With the exception of DPs in IRO-1, none of these DPs are applicable if the topic is not material.	
	IMPACT, RISK & OPPORTUNITY MANAGEMENT	
E3-ESRS2-IRO-1	Description of the processes to identify and assess material water and marine resources-related impacts, risks and opportunities.	
ESRS-E3-1	Policies related to water and marine resources.	
ESRS-E3-2	Actions and resources related to water and marine resources.	
	METRICS & TARGETS	
ESRS-E3-3	Targets related to water and marine resources.	
ESRS-E3-4	Metrics related to water consumption.	
ESRS-E3-5	Anticipated financial effects from water and marine resources related impacts, risks and opportunities.	

As always, all standards should be read and applied in conjunction with ESRS 1 *General Requirements* and ESRS 2 *General Disclosures*.

For ESRS-E2, there are 27 *Shall* data points, of which 7 are numeric. There are 18 *May* data points, in addition to the 33 *Minimum Disclosure Requirements* (MDR), which only apply if the high-level topic (in this case, E3) has been deemed material.

Positive Actions

The standard includes some application requirements, such as the use of the LEAP (Locate, Evaluate, Assess, Prepare) approach for materiality assessment, and the consideration of ecological thresholds and entity-specific allocations when setting targets.

By systematically identifying, assessing and managing pollution-related issues this way, companies can make more informed decisions to reduce risks, capitalise on opportunities, and contribute to a sustainable economy with zero pollution.

1   We would like to recognise the valuable collaboration of Dr Robert Moorcroft and Nora Von Xylander (PhD pending) in the creation of this chapter.

2   National Institute of Environmental Health Sciences https://www.niehs.nih.gov/health/topics/agents/algal-blooms, Accessed 31 May 2024.

3   UK Environment Agency https://assets.publishing.service.gov.uk/media/5d4402f5ed915d70645f0a00/Climate_change_and_eutrophication_risk_in_English_rivers__-_summary.pdf , Accessed 31 May 2024.

4   World Resources Institute: https://www.wri.org/initiatives/eutrophication-and-hypoxia/learn, Accessed 31 May 2024.

5   https://cropwatch.unl.edu/2019/gap-growing-between-irrigated-rainfed-crop-yields.

5

BIODIVERSITY & ECOSYSTEMS

Oliver Dauert & Elena Doms

I fell in love with wildlife as a young child. I collected rubber toys, watched Disney movies (especially The Lion King), dressed up for carnival as an elephant seal, etc. The usual stuff.

In my teenage years, I hid my love for nature because it was not cool. But, going to Australia for a year after finishing school helped me realise that I shouldn't hide it. Coming back, I had to choose to study zoology/ecology/marine biology or business.

I decided on business because, for me, companies are the reasons why we are in this ecological mess. So, I needed to understand how some get away with the destruction of nature and how we could use the force of companies to boost biodiversity.

While studying, I lived in six different countries. One of those adventures led me to sleep next to lions in the wilderness of Botswana – just tents, a fire, and no fence. On my way to the bush toilet at night, I realized how sharp my senses were; living in cities had numbed them. How cool would it be if everyone could experience this? The first Wildya spark was born.

I worked my entire career in tech (e-commerce, mobility, travel), so I witnessed the potential of using technology for something good. But I had the constant feeling of not doing enough for nature. Covid-19 brought everything to a halt and, while locked-down, I took the time to reflect on my life and realised that, even though I claimed to be a nature lover, my life did not reflect it at all. I didn't work in the field; I didn't volunteer; I didn't read; I didn't watch documentaries; I had no nature-enthusiastic friends, etc. So I decided to make radical changes in my life.

I took ecology courses, read books, connected with like-minded people, became a field guide and reflected on why we are in this mess. My reflection led me to the observation that the reason for all this destruction and pain is that we humans got disconnected from nature. So I made it my mission to reconnect us all in an awesome way to nature, via Wildya.

Oliver Dauert

I was born and raised in the Arctic, right next to the polar circle. When I was three years old, my parents bought a small piece of land. We grew berries and ate them from the bushes, indulging in sour and delicious cowberries and cloudberries. We pollinated squashes and harvested them for winter. We swam in the ice-cold forest river and ran through the fields collecting wildflowers; and we went to the boreal forests to gather mushrooms, walking on real swamps to reach remote little islands, learning to distinguish edible mushrooms. Although I didn't realise it at the time, my love for nature was born then.

Fifteen years ago, I moved to Belgium and met my husband. His parents live in a house with a small garden, right in the middle of Flanders, one of the most developed and industrialised regions in the world: 20% of the region is already covered in concrete. Yet their garden is abundant with life. My father-in-law has 1,500 plant species: trees, flowers, bushes. They combine so beautifully, no orangerie could compare. There are little ponds and arches full of climbers and flowers. Birds come to feed; pollinators fly around; even rare and protected salamanders come to fetch there and befriend my kids. It's a little island of heaven, surrounded by houses and industry. And this little island is my inspiration and hope: that nature is strong, that nature is plentiful, that nature can restore itself if we just give it a helping hand.

Paul Doms, in his garden in Flanders.

Thanks to my parents and my parents-in-law I know how to grow food and how to create biodiverse spaces. It is definitely thanks to them that I now care about soils. And probably thanks to them that I chose to quit my corporate job to start +EARTH+ with a crazy bold mission to create the largest soil and carbon dioxide (CO2) clean-up through nature. Because let's face it, we often hear that technology will solve all our problems – but I am betting on nature. Nature knows better than us. Nature is circular; nature is restorative; nature is nourishing – and we are nature.

Elena Doms

INTRODUCTION

Nature is all around us, and we depend on it in so many ways, yet most of us learn very little about it in school, university, and other places. Our goal in this chapter is to provide you with the basic knowledge about biodiversity that you need to reduce risk and increase opportunities for your company.

The success of your own business depends on the work of many different departments – each has a role to play. And it is the diversity of roles and responsibilities, and the way they combine together, that produces your current position in the market.

But what would happen if you lost an entire business department? And then another. And then more still – each loss coming faster and faster. Maybe you could keep the lights on for a while without a marketing team, but the number of new customers soon would slow down significantly. Next, if you lost the HR team, over time, your other teams would get unhappier, and no new people would join. And then, after you lose... you see where we are going with this. At some point, your company would not be able to cope with the loss of departments, and it would go bankrupt.

It's a scenario nobody wants to see in their business, yet it's exactly what is currently happening in our natural world. A flourishing natural world is like a successful and thriving company – 'nature as a company' – all the departments work together well to deliver success.

But nature is losing its biodiversity – the equivalent of closing departments in a business – and is tumbling down faster and faster through the inevitable death spiral.

Worse, as businesses, we are the main drivers of this loss. But, as businesses, we also have the power to change this trend, to strengthen these 'departments' by protecting, restoring, and rewilding the natural world.

BIODIVERSITY & ECOSYSTEMS

Let's start directly by clarifying both terms:

- **Biodiversity** refers to the variety of life that exists on Earth;
- **Ecosystems** are units of this life that interact with their non-living environment (water, temperature, etc.).

Without diving into the depths of scientific definitions, you do need to know that biodiversity is not just the diversity of species. Biodiversity is 3 in 1:

- **Species diversity:** The diversity of the different species in the world – elephants, tigers, human, parrots, mosquitos and so on;
- **Genetic diversity**: The diversity of the genetic pool within a species; the more diverse the genetic pool, the more resilient the species. For us humans, this would be our hair colour, eye colour, blood type, etc;
- **Ecosystem diversity**: The diversity of ecosystems: deserts, coral reefs, lakes, and others; we can't just have the Amazon rainforest, we need them all.

Figure 5.1: The Three Types of Biodiversity: The Variety of Life

GENETIC DIVERSITY	SPECIES DIVERSITY	ECOSYSTEM DIVERSITY
Variety of genes and traits available within a species	Variety of species within and ecosystem	Variety of ecosystem and habitat types in an area of land and water

Adapted graphic by Abby Litchfield.

This biodiversity is currently decreasing, which we call biodiversity loss. It is currently happening at alarming levels, as shown in the Planet Boundaries model (described in **Chapter 1: The Customer is the Planet**)

But while alarming, all this may seem quite abstract. Here are seven facts to help you understand the urgency of addressing this challenge right now:

- In the past 50 years, the population of thousands of species has decreased by a staggering 69%;[1]
- 1,000,000 species face extinction in the next few decades due to our actions and inactions;[2]
- These extinction rates are far above (10 to 100 times higher) natural rates, leading us into the sixth mass extinction, and the first that is caused by a single species;[3]
- Nature documentaries usually focus on wild animals (elephants, polar bears, etc.) but wild animals account for just 4% of mammal biomass; us humans (34%) and our livestock (62%) account for the other 96%;[4]
- On average, natural ecosystems have declined by 47% compared to our earliest records;
- Protecting and restoring land and sea areas helps immensely, but only 16% of land and 8% of the sea are currently protected. By 2030, we need to protect and restore 30% of land and sea to stabilise the situation;[5]
- Partnering with Indigenous communities is essential, as they are guardians of 80% of the planet's biodiversity. To succeed, we need to listen to what they have to say, give them a seat at the decision-making table, and provide them with the needed resources so they can keep guarding the majority of biodiversity.[6]

These facts can seem quite daunting, but the good news is that we know the five primary drivers of biodiversity loss, and with your company's help, we can address them and return to the safe space of the planet's boundaries.

Five Key Drivers of Biodiversity Crisis

The five key drivers of biodiversity crisis are (listed by largest relative negative impact):

- **Land/sea-use changes:** The loss of habitat for species due to our expansion of agricultural activities and cities;

- **Direct exploitation:** The extraction of living (fish, trees, etc.) and non-living (minerals, water, etc.) materials to an unsustainable level;
- **Climate change:** Extreme weather events can lead to droughts, floods, wildfires, and coral bleaching events, which are becoming the norm. Additionally, due to climate change, ecosystems will move, but not all species will be able to migrate;
- **Pollution:** Plastic, radioactive material, chemicals, oil, and fertilisers that have devastating effects on nature;
- **Invasive species:** Species brought from one place to another can cause economic and environmental damage. They are a harmful and costly by-product of our global trading, annually costing the economy $423 billion.[7]

As in the other chapters, these direct drivers result from a much bigger picture – indirect drivers – which include:

- **Our values and behaviours:** How we perceive and value nature has immense implications for our actions. Societies with a strong connection to nature have a smaller impact than those that see nature solely as a resource;
- **Demographic and sociocultural:** Continuously increasing population and urbanisation increases the pressure on nature in terms of resources and space;
- **Economical and technological:** Economic growth and technology can have positive and negative effects on biodiversity. Innovations that restore nature (for example, drones for planting trees) are developed daily, as are extractive technologies (for example, deep-sea mining). Economic growth could be used to restore nature at scale, but the current exploitation of nature fuels economic development;
- **Institutions and governance:** Policies, subsidies, penalties, laws, frameworks, and international agreements are all instruments that governments can use to influence biodiversity positively or negatively;
- **Conflicts and epidemics:** In times of crisis, priorities shift, leading to increased pressure on nature through habitat destruction, overexploitation, and resources diverting away from conservation.

And we also need to be conscious of 'shifting baseline syndrome',[8] a potential blind spot (**Figure 5.2**).

The nature you see in your neighbourhood or on your holidays is only a fraction of what our grandparents saw; and they saw only a fraction of what their grandparents saw. With every generation, we get used to a more depleted version of our natural world. We then degrade it even further until, in the near future, none will be left. For most of us, this only becomes evident as our lives progress – when the forest we used to play in as children disappears, or the birds we used to hear in our garden are now mostly silent.

So, while reading the next sections, remember that the baseline of nature we have to return to is not the nature of 2024 but one in which ecosystems are once again healthy, balanced and self-sustaining.

Figure 5.2: Shifting Baseline Syndrome

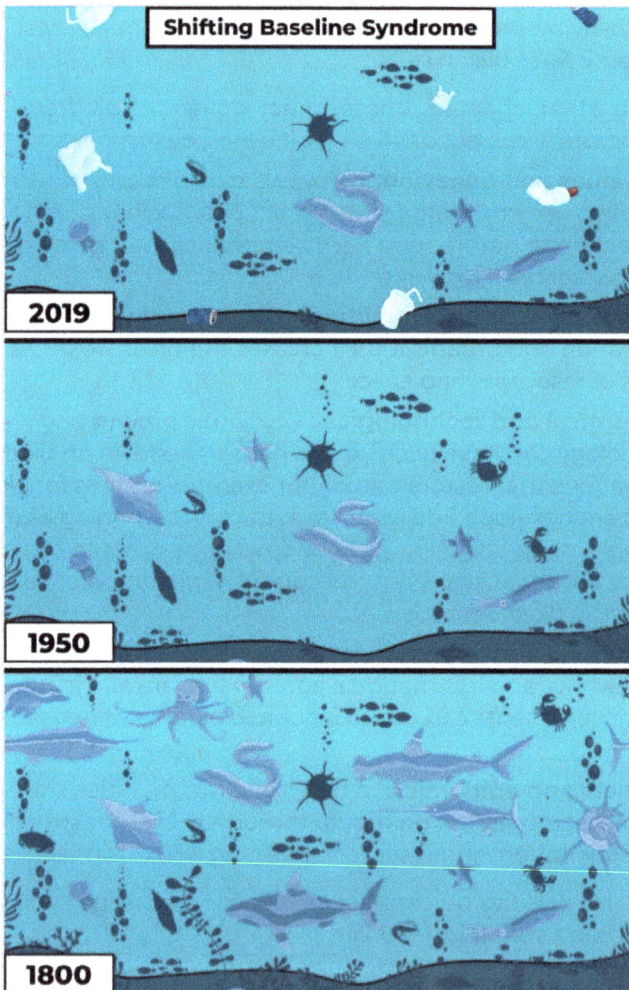

WHY SHOULD WE CARE?

Why should we be that ambitious? Why does all of this matter? Going back to our concept of 'nature as a company', why should we care if the company goes bankrupt?

The problem is that nature not only shapes the economy, it also keeps us alive. Nothing else – no form of technology – could substitute for all the work nature does.

An April 2023 analysis from PwC found that 55% of global GDP, equivalent to an estimated $58 trillion, is moderately or highly dependent on nature. The sectors that currently depend the highest on nature are construction ($4 trillion), agriculture ($2.5 trillion), and food and beverages ($1.4 trillion).[9]

The operations of 85% of the largest companies in the world that make up the S&P 1200 depend significantly on nature. Together, they generate $28.9 trillion and use 22 million hectares of land. Without biodiversity, those companies would struggle to continue their work.[10]

To put this into context, the Covid-19 pandemic (which was caused by the effects of the biodiversity crisis) induced a 3.4% drop in GDP in 2020 and resulted in a loss of $2 trillion.[11] Imagine what would happen if biodiversity collapsed.

All these 'services' that nature currently provides us with, which you use to create your company's revenue and your country's GDP, come free. Nature is just doing what it has done for billions of years. However, the protection, restoration, and rewilding of these ecosystems are not free – no more than running a car is free because you ignore servicing it at the recommended intervals.

To continue benefiting from these services by closing the nature finance gap (the gap between our investment in nature conservation and what's needed to turn around the biodiversity crisis), we need to nearly triple our spending on nature from $200 billion to $542 billion annually. The private sector can accomplish this by repurposing part of the $5 trillion it currently spends on activities that negatively impact nature.

Since companies have been slow to act voluntarily, governments have already begun to take the first steps towards regulations, subsidies, reporting, and other similar measures – such as the European Union's *Corporate Sustainability Reporting Directive* (CSRD) – which will heavily influence your company's activities.[12]

All this sounds quite expensive and might be a hard sell to your company's CFO. But a European Commission study found that every €1 spent on nature returns between €8 and €38 – a healthy payback![13]

Shifting to nature-positive activities could save companies $700 billion annually in costs and provide new business opportunities of $10 trillion annually. Agriculture, infrastructure, food, and energy in particular are sectors that show vast business opportunities. Reducing costs and increasing revenue is the dream of every CFO.[14,15]

But let's be honest. Right now, your company and all other companies benefit from the *status quo*. Currently, companies can externalise all the damage they inflict on nature, while internalising all the profits. Now, is that ethical, and – more important – does it ensure your company's long-term success for the decades to come? We will leave the answer to you. But we will continue to make the case in this chapter that, while investing in nature might cost you money in the short term, it provides you with a habitable, stable planet and sustainable balance sheets for decades to come.

Nature's Contribution to People

'Ecosystem services' is often the better-known term that describes how nature helps people. 'Nature's Contribution to People' (NCP) is a newer, broader idea that examines how nature and people are connected in many ways, including culture and local knowledge. This concept considers the good and bad effects of nature on people's lives. It tries to give a more complete picture of how nature impacts human well-being, going beyond just the services nature provides and capturing a wider range of ways that nature and people interact, including perspectives that might have been overlooked in the past. That's why we have chosen this terminology.

NCPs are split into three overlapping groups and 18 categories. (Except where stated otherwise, the statistics in this section come from the *Global Assessment Report on Biodiversity and Ecosystem Services*,[16] the leading scientific biodiversity report, comparable with the Intergovernmental Panel on Climate Change's report.)

Group 1: Regulating: Providing essential life support to humans

1. **Habitat creation and maintenance:** Eco-systems create and maintain the environmental conditions essential for the survival of species important to humans. Habitat is the base for all biodiversity on earth. Yet only 13% of habitats at sea and 23% on land remain unaltered by humans and can still be called wilderness (and only because they are too remote and 'unproductive' for human activities);

2. **Pollination and dispersal of seeds:** Species help spread pollen among flowers and disperse seeds, larvae, or spores of organisms that benefit or harm humans. Pollinators are responsible for 75% of the global food crop harvest;

3. **Regulation of air quality:** Ecosystems help to regulate the gases in the atmosphere and manage pollution by filtering, breaking down, capturing, or storing harmful substances. Changing the current situation of only 1 in 10 people breathing clean air could extend 3.3 million lives annually;

4. **Regulation of climate:** Ecosystems help regulate the climate and control global warming by affecting greenhouse gas (GHG) emissions. Our land and sea ecosystems are the sole carbon storers, capturing and storing away 60% of human-made emissions;

5. **Regulation of ocean acidification:** Photosynthetic organisms help regulate the amount of CO_2 in the atmosphere, which in turn affects the acidity of seawater. The economic cost of coral reef loss will rise significantly, reaching an estimated $500 billion to $870 billion by 2100;

6. **Regulation of freshwater quantity:** Ecosystems control how much, where, and when water flows on the surface and underground; 75% of all available freshwater is used for our agriculture and livestock;

7. **Regulation of freshwater and coastal water quality:** Ecosystems improve water quality by filtering out particles, pathogens, excess nutrients, and other chemicals. New York City invests $100 million annually to protect its upstate natural water systems, saving billions by avoiding the need for a filtration plant;[17]

8. **Formation, protection and decontamination of soils:** Nature creates and maintains healthy soils by preventing erosion, retaining sediments, preserving soil fertility, and breaking down or storing pollutants. Nature communication focuses largely on what happens above the ground, yet 59% of life is actually found below ground;[18]

9. **Regulation of hazards and extreme events:** Ecosystems help to lessen the effects of these events, reduce their severity, and decrease how often they occur. Coastal ecosystems like mangrove forests and coral reefs protect around 200 million people from storms and tsunamis;[19]

10. **Regulation of detrimental organisms and biological processes:** Ecosystems and organisms help control pests, diseases, predators, competitors, parasites, and other harmful organisms. Intact ecosystems and sufficient habitat avoid the spread of diseases, which would save 700,000 human lives per year.

Group 2: Material: Provide material that we can use to create goods

11. **Energy:** Nature creates fuels from organic materials like biofuel crops, animal waste, firewood, or leftover agricultural products. It is unimaginable for many of us, but two billion people still rely on wood as their primary energy source;

12. **Food and feed:** Nature provides us and our domesticated animals with food in the form of wild or domesticated plants and animals on land or at sea. For 4.3 billion people, 15% of their protein intake comes from fish. In addition, 95% of our food comes from soils, often overlooked and taken for granted; but we will be in trouble if we don't treasure our soil more because it literally feeds us;[20]

13. **Materials and assistance:** Nature produces materials that we can use to create new products. Every year, around 60 billion tons of both renewable and non-renewable resources are taken from the earth globally, almost doubling since 1980;

14. **Medicinal, biochemical, and genetic resources:** Nature allows us to make medicine from organisms and produce genes and genetic information; 70% of our drugs for cancer are derived from nature or inspired by it.

Group 3: Non-material: Spiritual value and inspiration that is hard to quantify

15. **Learning and inspiration:** Nature assists us in gaining knowledge and inspiration, which we can use for art, technology, and other things. Biomimicry helps us innovate: Velcro, less painful needles, airplanes, wind turbines, and many other innovations were inspired by other species;[21]

16. **Physical and psychological experiences:** Nature provides opportunities to improve physical and mental wellbeing by providing places of leisure, relaxation, or healing. Nature-based tourism to protected areas alone generates $600 billion annually;

17. **Supporting identities:** Nature provides a foundation for our religious, spiritual, and social connections, giving people a sense of belonging. Indigenous and traditional communities often live

in areas with rich biodiversity, showing the close connection between cultural and biological diversity;[22]

18. **Maintenance of options:** All this biodiversity keeps our options open for the future well-being of humans. So far, we have categorised 2.16 million species. Research, however, tells us that millions of species are still waiting to be discovered. Because of our actions and inactions, we risk losing these species before we even discover them thereby removing options for future generations.[23]

Note also that nature also has its own intrinsic value and does not exist just to serve us. This point is often overlooked.

To help you understand why and how biodiversity and ecosystems matter to your company, do this exercise: for each service above that your company depends on, score one point. Then see how many points you get. How many NCPs does your company depend on?

After the exercise, you will see that it will be challenging to keep satisfying your stakeholders if you don't start your nature-positive journey. You currently run the risk of being severely impacted if this negative nature trend continues.

It might not happen this quarter or the next, but leading companies like yours are in the long-term game and want to lead the market for the next decades. By picking up this book and reading this chapter, you have taken the first step, but it is crucial that you continue to progress rapidly.

Remember 'nature as a company'? Even the smartest of us have no clue which department's closure will mark the moment of no return – the tipping point that will cause the company to go bankrupt. Unlike companies that can be re-structured or revived, nature doesn't work this way; once bankrupt, it's closed forever. So, it's time to speed up our remedial work.

HOW YOUR COMPANY AFFECTS BIODIVERSITY & ECOSYSTEMS

Before diving into the how, let's address the elephant in the room: why doesn't nature have one universal metric that rules all – like, a ton of carbon? The three key reasons are:

- **Nature:** In nature, everything is interconnected, making it incredibly complex. Biodiversity is 3 in 1; so we can't just look at species diversity; we have to measure genetic diversity and ecosystem diversity, too. Additionally, some species (called keystone species) play a more crucial role in their ecosystems than others. Sea otters, for example, eat sea urchins, thereby protecting kelp forests. Losing species like them have bigger domino effects than others. Temporal changes in ecosystems don't make the job of researchers any easier. Many species are seasonal; they appear in one part of the world in one month only to reappear months later on the other side. Monarch butterflies make their 4,800 kilometre journey from Canada to Mexico every year. Where do we measure them? In Canada? In Mexico? In the US? Last but not least, the local context truly matters in biodiversity research. Every ecosystem functions differently, and even the same species can behave totally differently in other areas. All of this diversity and local specificity makes nature challenging to measure;

- **Poor records:** We are missing crucial historical data that can be used to create an accurate baseline of biodiversity. What have we lost already, without being aware of it? And what sort of influence did that have on biodiversity and our ecosystems today? A stark reminder of this is the passenger pigeon, which used to be abundant, with up to 3 billion birds in 1800, apparently darkening the skies for three days when they moved. They went from billions to extinct in just over 100 years, with the last one dying in 1914. So, when we measure biodiversity today, we often only get a glimpse of what is still left;[24]

- **Money:** Charlie Munger (the former vice chairman of Berkshire Hathaway) used to say, "Show me the incentives, and I will show you the outcome". Humans have had no incentive to measure biodiversity because, until recently, it provided us with everything we needed free of charge. But that's changed. And, in addition, biodiversity research is costly: as you can imagine, it is hard to research blue whales from an office desk.

Yet, there *are* ways to start measuring biodiversity. The three most cited are:

- **Living Planet Index:** The most cited biodiversity index in media (wildlife populations decreased by 69%), it measures the population size changes of 30,000 species over the past 50 years to create an average;[25]

- **Extinction rates:** Extinction occurs normally, but the speed and number of species we lose today are 10 to 100 times higher than the natural rate;[26]

- **Biodiversity Intactness Index (BII):** How much intact biodiversity remains in a certain region, based on the number of species and their population sizes. If the BII is 90% or higher, the area has enough biodiversity to keep the ecosystem healthy and working well; below 90%, ecosystems function less effectively, while a drop to 30% or lower risks the ecosystem collapsing.[27]

But make no mistake. We do have measurements and metrics – Mean Species Abundance, Species Threat Abatement and Restoration Metric, Potentially Disappeared Fraction of Species just to name a few – we just don't have ONE universal metric.

Impact on Species

Your company's activities can influence what species occur in an area and what species become extinct.

Through your logistics, potentially you can transport invasive species without knowing. Rats, aquatic plants (water hyacinth), and snakes (brown tree snake) are all examples of species that have already had vast negative impacts on areas they don't belong in. Rats, for example, have devastating impacts on islands because they eat the eggs and chicks of local bird species that are not adapted to predators, thereby decreasing the species population.[28]

You might also destroy habitat and thereby remove the habitat of some species that can only be found in a particular area. Key biodiversity areas (the most important places in the world for species and their habitats)[29] were defined to reduce this impact, yet research by S&P Global shows that 46% of the biggest companies in the world still have at least one asset in a key biodiversity area – for example, deep-sea mining or the deforestation of an exceptionally biodiverse spot in the tropical rainforest.[30]

Further, the plastic in your products can end up on the surface of the oceans, threatening the survival of sea birds like albatrosses that mistake this plastic for food. This dire mistake is now one of the main causes of their deaths, putting even more pressure on a bird 73% of whose species are threatened with extinction.[31]

Impact on Genetic Diversity

In addition to the pressure on the diversity of species, your company also can severely impact genetic diversity.

One way that can happen is through the overexploitation of a species, thereby reducing its genetic pool. The horseshoe crab's blue blood is the only known source of limulus amebocytelysate, a substance that helps us to make injections (like the Covid-19 vaccine), drugs, and artificial body parts like hips safer. Yet popularity has a price, and with overharvesting, the population of horseshoe crabs could keep shrinking, leading to a smaller genetic pool and potential collapse of the species. Luckily for us, that hasn't happened yet, and the populations and genetic diversity are still intact.[32]

The European bison wasn't as lucky. It became extinct in the wild 100 years ago. Luckily, thanks to conservation and rewilding work, it is making a comeback. But the risk remains because 80% of the genes of the lowland line come from just two founders, making it highly vulnerable to diseases and thereby risking extinction.[33]

Another way your company can affect the genetic pool is by taking too many specimens with specific genetic traits. For example, if your company continuously captures the biggest tuna fish, over time tuna will get smaller because you are taking too much of this particular genetic trait (this is called fisheries-induced evolution).[34]

Impact on Ecosystems

Your company can actively influence the size and condition of ecosystems.

One of the most well-known impacts is pollution. In agriculture, the runoff of fertilisers or animal manure leads to dead zones in the oceans, where there is not enough oxygen for ecosystems to survive. By now, there are more than 400 dead zones, affecting an area the size of the UK (245,000 km^2).[35]

Another example is our destruction of forests (for timber, beef, palm oil), especially tropical forests (the Amazon rainforest) where 95% of global deforestation occurs. These forests are hotspots for biodiversity; their destruction puts enormous pressure on the ecosystems that are in them – and the consequences of losing them would be horrific.[36]

Last but not least, if your company is currently slow in taking action on the climate crisis, your delay will impact ecosystems more. For example, coral bleaching occurs when corals are under too much stress due to high temperatures and start to die off. If temperatures rise above 2°C, we will lose *all* coral, which supports 25% of all marine life.[37,38]

You don't have to wait for biodiversity data and measurements to be perfect to change your business activities. If you look at the five key drivers of biodiversity crisis referenced earlier, you will quickly understand where your company currently puts the biggest pressure on nature. After reading this chapter, your job will be to start taking steps to relieve that pressure. This can easily seem like an overwhelming task, so let's look at what other companies did or didn't do and what consequences they faced.

LIVING IN THE REAL WORLD

We aren't good with nature. For generations, we considered it a free good. But things are changing and, now, nature is making its way into the corporate agenda through both good practices and litigation cases.

Let's dive into the good practices first:

- We often hear about the Amazon rainforest, its biodiversity and importance in regulating climate on Earth. But did you know that it was shaped together with its indigenous people? A study published in 2017 that researched the abundance and distribution of tree species found that the currently dominant species were domesticated by pre-Columbian peoples and used for food and building materials. The Amazon rainforest isn't an untouched pristine forest; it's a result of co-creation and living sustainably with nature for generations;[39]

While big companies talk about value, for us, that whole ecosystem, which is a living thing, is priceless.[40]

Uyunkar Domingo Peas Nampichkai, President of the Board of Directors at the Amazon Sacred Headwaters Alliance (Cuencas Sagradas Amazónicas).

- Brazilian beauty company Natura puts Amazon protection into practice. It sources ingredients for cosmetics from the Amazon rainforest, working together with local farmers and redistributing economic benefits back to their communities. That led to a switch from soybean and cattle farming to harvesting seeds, nuts and berries without destroying the forest. Over two decades, these joint efforts preserved 730,000 hectares.[41] If Natura can do that, so can your company;

- Soil health is becoming increasingly important, especially to companies whose product quality relies on it. LVMH launched the LIFE 360 roadmap with biodiversity as one of its elements and supports the Man & Biosphere programme by UNESCO, forest conservation with Canopy and regenerative agriculture in the wines & spirits sector.[42] In 2022, LVMH created the World Soils

Living Forum, bringing together scientists, NGOs, governments and companies for deep commitment and action to protect and restore soils;[43]

- Apparel brands are pioneering innovations based on nature too. Vivobarefoot designs minimalist footwear, to be as close to barefoot as possible. Why? To regenerate human health and bring people closer to nature. Nature is part of everything it does: products, design, materials, and rewilding projects. Is Vivobarefoot fully regenerative? Not yet, but it's fully transparent on its progress;[44]

- The construction sector is making leaps to be restorative for nature too. C-biotech developed a new approach, by combining construction and agriculture. It works with local farmers to grow restorative plants, like industrial hemp, as rotation crops. Hemp improves soil biodiversity, cleans toxins and helps get better harvests. Hemp biomass is then used to create bio-based construction materials that are circular, healthier to breathe and literally stock carbon in buildings.[45]

Looking for game-changing practices you can implement right away, no matter the industry? Here are the universal ones we really love:

- Putting nature on the board and giving it a vote, like Faith in Nature did.[46] They were first – but your company could follow;

- Calculating impact on nature across scopes 1, 2 and 3 (as we do with emissions) and putting an action plan to be nature-positive across your value chains by 2030, like WSP.[47]

Now, because nature destruction is starting to affect many companies' bottom lines, let's see examples of what shouldn't be done:

- JBS, the world's biggest meat producer, was linked to corruption and food safety scandals in Brazil and already has paid millions of dollars in fines in Brazil and the US. But further new losses may be coming, as it has been accused of buying cattle raised in protected and illegally deforested areas of the Amazon. The State of New York also is suing JBS over greenwashing claims just as the company is trying to get its shares listed on the New York Stock Exchange;[48]

- 3M is one of the largest producers of 'forever chemicals' in the world. Forever chemicals are used to make products non-stick and water-resistant; however, that makes them hard to destroy since they do not decompose in nature and accumulate in human bodies, harming wildlife and our health.[49] 3M has faced legal charges related to the production of forever chemicals and their release into the environment, both in the US and Europe. The company will have to pay over $10.5 billion in charges in the US alone over drinking water contamination. And that's just the beginning![50]

- Toyota had to pay a record fine of $180 million for *Clean Air Act* violations in the US. From 2005 to 2015, the company sold vehicles with defects, causing higher harmful air pollution against the standards for protection of public health and the environment;[51]

- Controversy surrounds oil and gas companies – and the pressure only seems to increase. BP, ExxonMobil, Shell, Chevron and others have faced hundreds of claims over oil spill incidents. BP was fined $29.2 billion in the US alone, mostly after the Deepwater Horizon offshore oil drilling platform in the Gulf of Mexico caught fire in 2010, creating an oil spill of 4 million barrels covering 180,000 square kilometres. That led to the worst sea animals mortality event recorded in the region and a decrease of 50% in some species like bottle-nosed dolphins.[52] While fines for oil spills have become common, other violations are coming to light. In 2023, African communities from South Africa, Mozambique, Uganda and Nigeria gave testimonials against Shell and Total Energies for ecological destruction by oil drilling and displacement of local communities. Reparations are being sought to restore the land and people's health.[53]

If you want to set your company up for success, make it a habit to notice examples of nature restoration and replicate them. Think how you can move beyond just mitigating your business impact on biodiversity to truly restoring it. Because the only way we can regenerate our planet is by building more businesses that are truly regenerative.

WHAT SHOULD WE DO NEXT?

If you are feeling slightly overwhelmed at this stage, don't worry – that's entirely normal. This is a BIG topic!

You started your nature journey by reading this chapter. The Taskforce on Nature-related Financial Disclosures (TNFD), the Science-Based Targets Network (SBTN), and Businesses for Nature are three great institutions that can provide you with a clear blueprint of how you can take your company from where it is now to being one of the leading companies addressing the biodiversity crisis. They can give you a step-by-step guide you can follow in the next weeks, months, and years. So start there.

Your journey towards becoming a regenerative company will not be a sprint, but a marathon. There will be times when you curse it all, but now you understand that just planting trees won't cut it. Unfortunately, our activities have destroyed too much. We need to not only sustain what is still left of nature (sustainability) but also help restore and rewild it (regeneration).

So here are some words of courage and advice:

- **Start today:** There's no time to lose, because tipping points are fast approaching. So, no matter how small or big the action you have in mind, don't postpone it; start today;

- **Knowledge:** Education is always the first step on every journey. Leaving your comfort zone and learning something new is challenging – but you have already taken the hardest step by picking up this book and reading it. It shows that you are curious about how to change from 'business as usual'. If you don't have the knowledge in-house, get experts to consult with you. There are plenty of biodiversity experts who wait to be listened to;

- **Share:** Share this knowledge with someone in your company who could become your ally. Alone, it will almost be impossible to make fundamental and lasting changes;

- **Language:** In this chapter, we tried to make the knowledge accessible to everyone – and you should, too. Speak with your team members in a language everyone can understand. Instead of being alienated, you want them to feel empowered to help you in this bold mission;

- **Focus:** Focus first on those individuals in your company who are already onside and motivated – people who are a friend of nature, have pets, have changed their diet, show sustainable behaviours, etc. Rally them around you and start talking with them about potential activities you can take as a company before you try to convert the ones who don't believe in the importance of change;

- **Leadership:** If you are a C-suite member, that's perfect. Take this topic to the next meeting and make biodiversity an agenda point. If you are not, sooner or later you will need to get the board and C-suite involved. Otherwise, all your activities will be an uphill battle;

- **Levers of change:** You know that the most challenging thing in any company is getting people and departments to change. This work will most likely affect all your departments. The biggest lever of impact is addressing your business model. But you can't always start there. So, look into levers of change. How can you open up people to this topic so they begin to be receptive to making changes? Things that sometimes feel ridiculously small, like starting recycling in the office or having a 5-minute nature keynote, can enable you to spark the change. It is just crucial that you never stop there;

- **Reframe:** This chapter hopefully showed you that this natural crisis is not only a potential cost or pain but also can be a fantastic business opportunity. Rather than fear, use optimism and show your company how positively these changes can influence the bottom line, brand, stakeholder engagement, market leadership, and more;

- **Act:** Constantly ensure you keep moving instead of endlessly debating. Don't look for 100% improvement and the golden bullet. Rather, think about what you can do today and tomorrow to improve things 20% or 30%. If you take your company on this journey and make it even the tiniest bit more regenerative daily, your actions will compound beyond your imagination.

Remember, companies only exist on a sheet of paper. In reality, every company is driven by people: shareholders, board members, customers, and, most importantly, employees. A company is no more than the sum of the daily decisions of all those people. So, if you can convince people that this topic matters, you will change your company.

What If …?

In this chapter, we focused on what currently goes wrong and how we in the business world contribute to it. However, what if we manage to turn this around? What if we achieve a nature-positive future? What if we are the first generation to bend the trend and experience more nature by the end of 2030 than we currently have? And, what if we keep on restoring and rewilding the world to reverse the nature that we have lost so that, by 2050, we live in harmony with nature?[54]

It's ambitious – but precisely what we need. Now what would this nature-positive future mean for you and your company?

Your company will keep flourishing for the decades to come. Instead of increasing costs and risks, many more opportunities will arise – making your shareholders happier than ever. Land productivity will increase, fresh water will keep flowing, etc. Rather than losing nature's contribution to people, your company would benefit even more. Additionally, it would be able to operate in a stabilised climate without extreme weather events. Ecosystems would start to be intact and self-managing because species returned, making them more productive and resilient. You and your key stakeholders, such as investors, customers, and employees, will live happier and healthier lives, thanks to healthier food, leisure time in nature, clean drinking water, etc. Instead of travelling far to experience it, you will have nature right in front of your door, boosting your mental well-being. Imagine again the Covid-19 times and how much you appreciated walking outside; now imagine this happiness x100 because your city will be actually habitable. Last but not least, we would go from the age of extinction to the age of regeneration. Wildlife populations and species would bounce back, ensuring that your children and grandchildren have the pleasure of sharing our planet home with polar bears, elephants, and other animals.

Figure 5.3: The Nature-positive Trend

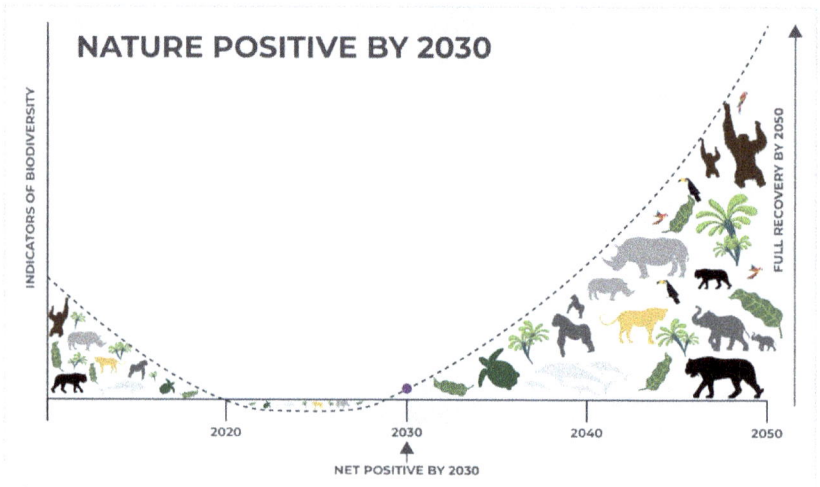

Source: https://www.naturepositive.org/.

This doesn't have to be a dream or theoretical concept. Together, we can build that future, starting today.

Let's return one last time to our story of nature as a company to illustrate what this would mean. Instead of losing crucial employees and departments one after one, the company would be able to do the opposite. The company (nature) would be able to hire the best people available in the market, and old colleagues who were absolute rockstars (species) would return to their former employer. This would result in even more specialised departments (ecosystems) that can produce more and at better quality levels. All while seamlessly communicating with one another to make sure all departments are balanced. Instead of collapsing, the company would regenerate and thrive for decades to come.

Sounds pretty tempting, right? So let's take this nature challenge seriously, because the benefits are tremendous.

Before closing this chapter, we want to leave you with some provocative questions that will further spark your imagination:

- **What if ... we could understand what animals have to say?** The Earth Species Project is already working on using AI to decode what species are talking about, leading us to a future in which we can communicate;[55]

- **What if ... we gave legal rights to nature?** Imagine a river, a mountain, a species, an individual animal or plant having rights. Some already do. New Zealand was the first country to give a river legal rights.[56] Just this year, Pacific indigenous leaders gave whales legal personhood;[57]

- **What if ... nature had a seat on your board?** Usually, board members are senior people, but what if the most senior of all of them, nature (billions of years old), also had a seat? Onboarding nature invites us to get its voice into the boardroom, into our meetings, to be part of our shareholders, etc. Patagonia, Willicroft, and Tony Chocolonely are already doing it;[58]

- **What if ... nature destruction was considered an international crime?** In 2024, Belgium became the first European country to recognise ecocide as an international crime;[59]

- **What if ... we found all the species in this world?** We are still in the dark about how many species we actually share this planet with. Yet new advancements in technology allow us to explore the depths of the oceans or capture and analyse environmental DNA (eDNA). If we could find all the species that exist, what could we learn from them?

- **What if ... we listened to those who still guard and live immersed in nature?** Indigenous people protect 80% of all biodiversity in this world. Throughout the centuries, they managed to value and live in balance with biodiversity. There is probably plenty to learn from them. Amazon Frontlines shares their stories;[60]

- **What if ... we compensated nature for its services?** All the services we identify in this chapter are currently provided free to us by nature. But what if we actually started paying nature for them? Great music stars like London Grammar, Ellie Goulding and others decided this year to start paying music royalties to nature, to thank her for her sounds;[61]

- **What if ... our cities were full of nature?** Currently, our cities are rather grey. But what if they were green, blue, red, or violet? Singapore is using biomimicry to make its skyline resemble a rainforest, Milan has vertical forests, and China creates sponge cities;[62]

- Last and most powerful, **what if ... we are the generation that bends the trend?** The one that only takes what is needed and generates more than destroys? You and your company can be part of making history.

With your help, the future looks wild.

ESRS-E4 – BIODIVERSITY & ECOSYSTEMS REPORTING OBLIGATIONS

Ingrid De Doncker

The terms 'biodiversity' and 'biological diversity' refer to the variability among living organisms from all sources, including terrestrial, freshwater, marine and other aquatic ecosystems, and the ecological complexes of which they are part.

This standard highlights the interconnectedness of environmental issues, showing how biodiversity and ecosystems are linked to other areas like pollution, water resources, and circular economy practices. The reporting requirements relate to the organisation's relationship to terrestrial, freshwater and marine habitats, ecosystems and populations of related fauna and flora species, including diversity within species, between species and of ecosystems and their interrelation with indigenous peoples and other affected communities.

The standard provides transparency for users of the sustainability statement to understand:

- How an organisation affects biodiversity and ecosystems, in terms of material positive and negative, actual and potential impacts, including the extent to which it contributes to the drivers of biodiversity and ecosystem loss and degradation;

- The actions it takes, and the result of such actions to prevent or mitigate material actual or potential negative impacts, to protect and restore biodiversity and ecosystems, and to address risks and opportunities;
- The plans and capacity of an organisation to adapt its strategy and business model in line with:
  - o Respecting planetary boundaries related to biosphere integrity and land-system change;
  - o The vision of the Kunming-Montreal Global Biodiversity Framework and its relevant goals and targets;
  - o Relevant aspects of the EU *Biodiversity Strategy for 2030*;
  - o *Directive 2009/147/EC* of the European Parliament and of the Council and Council *Directive 92/43/EEC* (*EU Birds & Habitats Directives*);
  - o *Directive 2008/56/EC* of the European Parliament and of the Council (*Marine Strategy Framework Directive*);
- The nature, type and extent of an organisation's material risks and opportunities related to biodiversity and ecosystems, and how it manages them;
- The financial effects on the organisation over the short-, medium- and long-term of material risks and opportunities arising from its impacts and dependencies on biodiversity and ecosystems.

Biodiversity & Ecosystems Sub-topics

Under ESRS 1 Article 16, there are four sub-topics to consider. The descriptions of the four sub-topics are expanded a little here for clarity:

- **Direct impact drivers of biodiversity loss** relates to climate change, land-use change, fresh water-use change and sea-use change, direct exploitation, invasive alien species, pollution, etc;
- **The impacts on the state of species** addresses how companies affect the species population size and species global extinction risk. Think about, for example, the impact of oil spills on birds, seabed mining on fish, or agricultural run-off or hazardous chemicals deposits going into rivers. And companies can do good things too;
- **The impacts on the extent and condition of ecosystems** relates to land degradation, desertification, deforestation, and soil sealing. It's about the direct physical changes to the habitats and the living conditions for all species within those ecosystems and, while it is primarily about land, it crosses over to species too;

- **The impacts and dependencies on ecosystem services:** Where #3 relates to the actual ecosystem and the impact a company has on it, this topic relates to the services from the ecosystem, how an organisation's operations rely on and affect the benefits humans gain from ecosystems, such as the provision of water.

This Standard should be read in conjunction with ESRS 1 *General Requirements* and the requirements of this section shall be read in conjunction with the disclosures required by ESRS 2, *Chapter 2: Governance*, *Chapter 3: Strategy* and *Chapter 4: Impact, Risk & Opportunity Management*. The resulting disclosures shall be presented alongside the disclosures required by ESRS 2, except for ESRS 2 SBM-3, for which the company has an option to present the disclosures alongside the topical disclosures. In addition to the requirements in ESRS 2, this Standard also includes the topic-specific Disclosure Requirement E4-1, Transition plan and consideration of biodiversity and ecosystems in strategy and business model.

It is important to understand the *Minimum Disclosure Requirements* (MDRs) in ESRS 2, Chapter 4.2. When an organisation identifies a sustainability matter as material, 34 MDR data points (DPs) for Policies, Actions, Targets, and Metrics (PAT-M) are applicable if the organisation discloses on policies, actions and targets. If it does not provide disclosure on policies, targets or actions, then it needs to disclose the reasons for not doing so, as per the corresponding 10 DPs of ESRS 2 MDR PAT, paragraphs 62 and 81.

ESRS-E4 outlines clearly, in six *Disclosure Requirements (DR)*, the narrative and numeric data DPs an organisation should comply with. There are 54 *Shall* DPs, of which 4 are numeric, 36 narrative and 14 semi-narrative, as well as 65 additional *May* DPs. The MDR PAT DPs are to be disclosed under E4-2, E4-3, E4-4 when the sustainability matters are material.

Figure 5.4 shows the structure of the ESRS-E2 DRs and DPs that must be reported, if deemed material by the double materiality assessment.

Figure 5.4: ESRS-E4 Reporting Requirements

ESRS-E4	Biodiversity & Ecosystems			
	Direct impact drivers of biodiversity loss	The impacts on the state of species	The impacts on the extent and condition of ecosystems	The impacts & dependencies on ecosystem services
	With the exception of DPs in IRO-1, none of these DPs are applicable if the topic is not material.			
	STRATEGY			
ESRS-E4-1	**Transition plan** and consideration of biodiversity and ecosystems in strategy and business model.			
ESRS2-E4-SBM-3	Material impacts, risks and opportunities of biodiversity and ecosystems and their interaction with strategy and business model.			
	IMPACT, RISK & OPPORTUNITY MANAGEMENT			
ESRS2-E4-IRO-1	Description of the processes to identify and assess biodiversity and ecosystems-related impacts, risks, and opportunities.			
ESRS-E4-2	**Policies** related to biodiversity and ecosystems.			
ESRS-E4-3	**Actions** and resources related to biodiversity and ecosystems.			
	METRICS & TARGETS			
ESRS-E4-4	**Targets** related to biodiversity and ecosystems.			
ESRS-E4-5	**Metrics** related to biodiversity and ecosystems change.			
ESRS-E4-6	**Anticipated financial effects** from biodiversity and ecosystems-related impacts, risks and opportunities.			

[1]   https://www.livingplanetindex.org.
[2]   *Global Assessment Report on Biodiversity & Ecosystem Services* https://www.ipbes.net/global-assessment.
[3]   *Global Assessment Report on Biodiversity & Ecosystem Services* https://www.ipbes.net/global-assessment.
[4]   *Biomass Distribution on Earth* https://www.pnas.org/doi/10.1073/pnas.1711842115.
[5]   Protected Planet https://www.protectedplanet.net/en.

6   https://soe.dcceew.gov.au/climate/management/national-and-international-frameworks#-cli-21-figure-21-indigenous-peoples-and-the-environment.
7   https://www.weforum.org/agenda/2023/09/invasive-species-cost-global-economy-billions/.
8   Picture credit: Cameron Shep.
9   https://www3.weforum.org/docs/WEF_New_Nature_Economy_Report_2020.pdf.
10   https://www.spglobal.com/esg/insights/featured/special-editorial/how-the-world-s-largest-companies-depend-on-nature-and-biodiversity.
11   https://www.statista.com/topics/6139/covid-19-impact-on-the-global-economy/#topicOverview.
12   https://www.unep.org/resources/state-finance-nature-2023.
13   https://ec.europa.eu/commission/presscorner/detail/en/qanda_22_3747.
14   https://www.mckinsey.com/capabilities/sustainability/our-insights/nature-in-the-balance-what-companies-can-do-to-restore-natural-capital#/.
15   https://www3.weforum.org/docs/WEF_The_Future_Of_Nature_And_Business_2020.pdf.
16   *Global Assessment Report on Biodiversity & Ecosystem Services* https://www.ipbes.net/global-assessment.
17   WRI https://www.wri.org/insights/cities-can-save-money-investing-natural-infrastructure-water.
18   *Enumerating Soil Biodiversity* https://www.pnas.org/doi/full/10.1073/pnas.2304663120.
19   *The Living Planet Report* https://c402277.ssl.cf1.rackcdn.com/publications/1187/files/original/LPR2018_Full_Report_Spreads.pdf.
20   https://openknowledge.fao.org/home.
21   https://www.learnbiomimicry.com/blog/best-biomimicry-examples.
22   https://www.unep.org/resources/publication/cultural-and-spiritual-values-biodiversity.
23   https://ourworldindata.org/how-many-species-are-there.
24   https://www.scientificamerican.com/article/3-billion-to-zero-what-happened-to-the-passenger-pigeon/.
25   WWF (2022) *The Living Planet Report 2022 – Building a Nature-positive Society*.
26   https://www.science.org/doi/10.1126/sciadv.adh2458.
27   https://www.nhm.ac.uk/our-science/data/biodiversity-indicators/about-the-biodiversity-intactness-index.html.
28   https://zenodo.org/records/11254974.
29   https://www.keybiodiversityareas.org/.
30   https://www.spglobal.com/esg/insights/featured/special-editorial/how-the-world-s-largest-companies-depend-on-nature-and-biodiversity.
31   https://conbio.onlinelibrary.wiley.com/doi/10.1111/conl.12785.
32   https://www.nationalgeographic.com/animals/article/covid-vaccine-needs-horseshoe-crab-blood.
33   https://www.researchgate.net/publication/230144091_Genetic_status_of_European_bison_Bison_bonasus_after_extinction_in_the_wild_and_subsequent_recovery.
34   https://www.science.org/doi/10.1126/science.1245490.
35   https://www.science.org/doi/10.1126/science.1156401.
36   https://ourworldindata.org/deforestation.
37   202206_IPBES GLOBAL REPORT_FULL_DIGITAL_MARCH 2022.pdf.
38   https://www.wri.org/insights/decoding-coral-reefs.
39   https://phys.org/news/2017-03-ancient-peoples-amazon-rainforest.html.

40 https://www.weforum.org/agenda/2024/01/lessons-from-indigenous-leaders-to-protect-the-amazon-rainforest/.

41 https://knowledge.wharton.upenn.edu/article/this-companys-sustainable-partnerships-helped-prevent-amazon-rainforest-deforestation/.

42 https://www.lvmh.com/group/lvmh-commitments/social-environmental-responsibility/life-initiative-lvmh/.

43 https://www.worldlivingsoilsforum.com/en/content/raison-d-etre.

44 https://www.vivobarefoot.com/eu/.

45 www.c-biotech.eu.

46 https://www.faithinnature.co.uk/pages/avotefornature.

47 https://www.wsp.com/-/media/insights/global/image/2023/nature-guidebook---bridging-business-and-nature/wsp_nature_guidebook_.pdf.

48 https://www.politico.com/news/2024/01/28/meat-giant-deforestation-jbs-00137084.

49 https://www.sciencedirect.com/science/article/abs/pii/S0048969723045643?via%3Dihub.

50 https://www.cbsnews.com/minnesota/news/3m-pfas-drinking-water-settlement/.

51 https://www.nytimes.com/2021/01/14/climate/toyota-emissions-fine.html.

52 https://www.offshore-technology.com/features/most-fined-us-oil-gas-companies-bp-occidental-exxonmobil-deepwater-horizon-kerr-mecgee/ https://oceanservice.noaa.gov/news/apr17/dwh-protected-species.html.

53 https://earth.org/the-most-important-climate-litigation-cases-of-2024-and-why-they-matter/.

54 https://www.naturepositive.org.

55 https://www.earthspecies.org.

56 https://www.theguardian.com/world/2017/mar/16/new-zealand-river-granted-same-legal-rights-as-human-being.

57 https://www.teaonews.co.nz/2024/03/28/maori-king-and-other-indigenous-pacific-leaders-sign-up-to-granting-whales-legal-personhood/.

58 https://www.onboardingnature.com.

59 https://www.stopecocide.earth/2024/belgium-becomes-first-european-country-to-recognise-ecocide-as-international-level-crime.

60 https://amazonfrontlines.org.

61 https://www.soundsright.earth.

62 https://wedocs.unep.org/bitstream/handle/20.500.11822/36586/SSRC.pdf?sequence=1&isAllowed=y.

6

MATERIALS & THE CIRCULAR ECONOMY

Marije de Roos,
supported by
Harald Friedl & Elin Bergman

M*y journey into the world of materials and circular economics began on a dark, stormy afternoon when I finally decided to watch a long-recommended documentary – The True Cost – about the fashion industry. I had always loved fashion and had certainly been a fast fashion customer, especially during my studies. There seemed to be a correlation between the number of social events I attended and the growth of my wardrobe. At the time, I was working on my first start-up, which initially planned to generate revenue through affiliate links to various eCommerce websites offering a wide range of clothing. However, something felt off – a gut feeling that I couldn't shake.*

This documentary shook me to my core. It exposed the brutal and inhumane conditions in which our clothes are made in Bangladesh, India, and Pakistan. I realised that I had been feeding the monster. I had 'jokingly' labelled myself a 'fashion culprit' as a twist on the term 'fashion victim'. But the real fashion victims were the workers in the supply chains – from the farmers to the textile dyers to the seamstresses. Every dollar I spent on the joy that fashion brought me was a direct vote for the dire circumstances these garment workers endured.

It dawned on me that fashion is much more than just the clothes we wear. It's a system that impacts every corner of our global society. This is where the circular economy comes in – as a global system in which materials circulate until they eventually return to nature, becoming part of a new life-cycle.

I had first encountered the term 'Circular Economy' in a global supply chain management course, during my Master's in Economics, majoring in International Business, at Copenhagen Business School. But embracing the circular economy was the furthest thing from my mind. I wasn't an environmentalist or an activist. Sure, I would pick up trash on the beach and was conscious about meat consumption, but that was the extent of my environmental awareness.

But, as I dove deeper into ethical fashion and the circular economy, I quickly detected a vast and growing amount of greenwashing, often caused by a lack of knowledge. As a fashion consumer who wanted to wear her values, I began to educate myself in fields like ecology, soil science, material science, microbiology, and green chemistry. I worked tirelessly to uncover the truth behind 'circular fashion'. What I found in the market was not what I wanted to see. This is why I eventually started my own label called Positive Fibers®.

Through this journey, I became known as "The Circular Fashion Detective", a trademark born out of my appreciation for Sherlock Holmes and simply being a pitbull when it comes to getting the facts about fashion in a global circular economy. Hence, since late 2018, I have dedicated myself to scrutinising the fashion industry, exposing greenwashing, and championing true sustainability. To me, circular economics is about managing our household with health as a key pillar of the system's DNA. After all, health equals wealth.

Marije de Roos

INTRODUCTION

Humanity's 21st century challenge is to meet the needs of all within the means of the planet.

Dr Kate Raworth

Humanity's challenge – *per* Kate Raworth – is your company's challenge too. Business can be a force for good if it operates within the planetary boundaries.

The customer is the planet. In business and economic activities, it's essential to consider the impact on the environment and society as a whole. Instead of focusing on short-term profits or the satisfaction of individual consumers, this perspective emphasises the long-term well-being of the planet and all its inhabitants.

In the ever-evolving landscape of modern business, corporate professionals face a pressing imperative: circularity. As the global population grows and resources dwindle, the traditional linear economic model of 'take-make-waste' is becoming increasingly untenable. In Figure 6.1, I have used 'End as Waste' deliberately to emphasise that, while waste can be repurposed or composted to become part of a natural cycle (again), trash generally consists of non-organic matter, often man-made from synthetic polymers.

Figure 6.1: The Linear Economy

TAKE   MAKE   END AS TRASH

Enter the circular economy: an innovative approach that promises not only environmental stewardship but also economic resilience and long-term competitiveness.

At the heart of the circular economy lies the concept of materials management. Materials are the building blocks of industry, essential for the creation of products and the provision of services. We live in a material world, and it is the nature of every material that determines its journey from start to finish. Conventionally, the finish line of all materials is either in landfills or in incinerators. Both destinations are contributors to increasing greenhouse gas (GHGs) emissions.

Businesses should prioritise sustainability, ethical practices, and environmental responsibility in their operations, recognising that the health of the planet ultimately affects everyone, including their customers and workforce.

Figure 6.2: The Circular Economy

Businesses should prioritise sustainability, ethical practices, and environmental responsibility in their operations, recognising that the health of the planet ultimately affects everyone, including their customers and workforce. So:

- What if landfills were obsolete?
- What if no one was left behind?
- What if products did more good than harm to the ecosystem that we humans are all a part of?

The time for positive change is yesterday, but every step forward counts. Now we just need to speed up our pace to get to the finish line of achieving a global system where, paraphrasing Dr Kate Raworth, author of the book *Doughnut Economics*:

We need to meet the needs of all within the means of our planetary boundaries.

Our environment is increasingly contaminated with trash – physical devalued mass created and abandoned by us humans. This ubiquitous presence of trash in our landscapes, oceans, and communities underscores a critical need for re-evaluating our material production and waste management practices. Trash, unlike the natural detritus that seamlessly integrates back into ecosystems, disrupts natural processes, contaminates habitats, and poses significant threats to human health, including your company's workforce.

The challenge is not merely about managing waste (or trash), but transforming our perspective and practices toward materials and their life-cycles.

In their influential book,[1] William McDonough and Michael Braungart propose a transformative approach with their 'Cradle to Cradle®' design philosophy. They argue that in nature, "waste equals food" – everything is reused, repurposed, and re-integrated into the ecosystem without loss of quality.

This biological cycling ensures that nothing is wasted; every output becomes an input for another process, sustaining the balance of natural systems. By mimicking this principle, we can redesign our material world where products are created with their next use in mind, leading to a circular economy. Here, bio-based materials play a crucial role, moving us away from fossil fuel dependency and fostering a sustainable ecosystem.

Circularity is a key component of what makes forests inherently sustainable. And in the same way, circularity is a key component of what makes businesses inherently sustainable.

Hendrith Vanlon Smith, Jr.

Transitioning to a circular economy involves rethinking our material world, integrating principles of sustainability at every stage – from design to end-of-life. Hence, in this chapter, we will dive into the definition of the circular economy on three levels:

- First, we reveal the drivers of a circular economy, followed by the benefits for businesses;
- Next, we discuss common objections, directly followed by corporate success stories;
- Finally, we shine a light on the meaning of the circular economy for the individual, as well as look to future trends.

Standing on the shoulders of giants, we acknowledge the knowledge created by circular economy pioneer professor Walter Stahel, as well as William McDonough and Dr Michael Braungart, and Dr Kate Raworth.

DEFINING THE CIRCULAR ECONOMY

Understanding the circular economy is no easy feat, but it is a crucial step for businesses aiming to thrive in the modern marketplace:

- **The essence of the circular economy**: The circular economy derives its name from the shape of a circle, symbolising a continuous loop (see **Figure 6.2**). In supply chains, 'loop' refers to processes that return to their starting point, promoting sustainability and efficiency. As part of nature's ecosystem, we must consider the global circular economy as a model of sustainable business practices;

- **Defining economy in context**: The word 'economy' comes from the Greek *oikonomia*, meaning household management. Just as we manage our homes, we must manage our planet. The circular economy provides a framework for this management, emphasising sustainability and efficiency over the traditional linear model;

- **The business case for the circular economy**: In a world where the customer is increasingly recognised as the planet, adopting circular economy principles is essential. The circular economy aims to decouple economic growth from resource consumption. Instead of viewing materials as finite inputs to be used and discarded, it recognises their inherent value and seeks to maximise their utility throughout their life-cycle.

The Key Principles of the Circular Economy

The circular economy is a transformative approach to economic development that aims to redefine growth, focusing on positive society-wide benefits. It is underpinned by several key principles that guide its implementation:

- **Design out waste and pollution:** Products and systems are designed from the outset to minimise waste and pollution. This includes using fewer resources, extending product lifespans, and planning for end-of-life recovery;

- **Keep products and materials in use:** Through practices such as recycling, reusing, remanufacturing, and refurbishing, the circular economy aims to keep materials and products in continuous use, maximising their value;

- **Regenerate natural systems:** By returning valuable nutrients to the soil and other ecosystems, the circular economy seeks to enhance natural capital. This principle promotes the use of renewable resources and encourages practices that restore and enhance ecosystems;

- **Rethink business models:** Transitioning from ownership to service-based models, such as leasing or sharing, reduces the need for new products and allows for better resource efficiency and product longevity;

- **Collaborate to create joint value:** Collaboration across sectors and value chains is essential for the circular economy. By working together, businesses, governments, and communities can create solutions that benefit everyone and accelerate the transition;

- **Prioritise renewable energy:** Using renewable energy sources supports the reduction of carbon footprints and aligns with the regenerative principles of the circular economy, promoting sustainable energy practices throughout the lifecycle of products and services.

MATERIALS AS DRIVERS OF THE CIRCULAR ECONOMY

The concept of the circular economy hinges on the innovative management of materials to create a system where resources are perpetually cycled back into the economy, eliminating waste and reducing the need for virgin materials. Unlike the traditional linear economy, which follows a 'take-make-waste' model, the circular economy emphasises closed-loop systems where products and materials are continuously reused, remanufactured, and – if done sustainably – recycled. This paradigm shift is crucial for addressing environmental sustainability and resource scarcity.

The Role of Bio-based Materials

Bio-based materials, derived from renewable biological resources, are pivotal in driving the circular economy. These materials, such as bioplastics, natural fibres, and bio-based chemicals (see the disciplines of Green Chemistry and Synthetic Biology), reduce dependence on fossil fuels and are designed to be biodegradable or easily recyclable.

Scientific studies have shown that bio-based materials can significantly lower carbon footprints compared to their petroleum-based counterparts.[2] For example, polylactic acid (PLA), a bio-based plastic, emits up to 70% less GHGs during production compared to traditional plastics.

Life-cycle Assessment & Sustainability

Life-cycle assessment (LCA) is a crucial tool in evaluating the environmental impact of materials from production to disposal. LCA studies reveal that materials with lower environmental impacts during production, such as bio-based materials, often result in reduced overall environmental burdens.

A comprehensive LCA of biopolymers, for instance, has shown that they generally have lower global warming potential and energy use than conventional polymers, highlighting their suitability for a circular economy.

Design for Disassembly

The design phase plays a critical role in enabling materials to be effectively recovered and reused. Design for disassembly (DfD) ensures that products are created with the end-of-life phase in mind, allowing for easy separation of components and materials. This approach facilitates higher recycling rates and the efficient recovery of valuable materials.

For example, studies in the automotive industry, where DfD principles already are being applied, show significant increases in the recyclability of vehicles, supporting the circular economy framework by keeping materials in circulation.

Advanced Recycling Technologies

Although recycling is not the same as circularity, it can play an important role in enabling a circular economy.

Innovations in recycling technologies are fundamental to material recovery in a circular economy. Chemical recycling, for instance, can break down complex polymers into their monomers, allowing for the production of new, high-quality plastics. Although plastic recycling addresses the limitations of traditional mechanical recycling, today it still comes with the challenge of needing the addition of virgin material derived from oil, which often results in downcycled materials of lower quality. Hence, it's not a circular system, but nonetheless it's important in keeping materials out of landfills and our oceans.

Circular Supply Chains

Creating circular supply chains involves rethinking traditional supply chain models to incorporate material recovery and reuse. This requires collaboration across industries and sectors to establish systems for collecting, sorting, and processing used materials. Case studies in the electronics industry show that implementing circular supply chains can reduce raw material consumption by up to 30%, illustrating the economic and environmental benefits of this approach.

As mentioned in the *Introduction*, it's essential to rethink our material world when transitioning to a circular economy. Whereas conventional supply chains heavily rely on fossil fuels, circular supply chains will prioritise bio-based materials that are renewable, biodegradable, compostable, and non-toxic, ensuring that they can be safely cycled back into the environment or reused in new forms. As with data that goes into an algorithm, the phrase "Garbage In = Garbage Out" applies to supply chains.

The Future of Supply Chains

Bio-based is the way forward. By adopting the paradigm shift away from dependence on fossil fuels, we accelerate the necessary change that respects the planetary boundaries.

In my book *Farm-to-Fashion*, I show how everything that is physically produced comes from materials from various sources. What has caused much of the landfills today is the fact that the source of many of these materials conventionally is crude oil, from which synthetic materials are created that cannot return to nature as a nutrient and hence end up either in an incinerator or in a landfill. Both final destinations contribute to increased GHGs. Thus, the source of the materials that go into the process of making a product ('fashion' originates from the Latin word *factio* meaning 'the act of making') need a big rethink.

Furthermore, by adopting Cradle to Cradle® principles, industries can innovate towards creating products that maintain their value through continuous cycles of use and reuse, rather than contributing to the growing heaps of trash.

BENEFITS FOR BUSINESS

Five Key Benefits for Future-Oriented Businesses

By embracing the principles of circularity, forward-thinking companies can unlock benefits that extend beyond mere environmental considerations and use circularity to future-proof themselves:

- **Benefit 1: Cost savings and reduced material costs:** One of the most compelling benefits of the circular economy is the potential for significant cost savings through reduced material costs. Traditional linear business models rely heavily on the extraction and consumption of finite natural resources, exposing companies to the volatility of raw material prices and supply chain disruptions. In contrast, the circular economy emphasises the efficient use and recovery of materials, minimising the need for virgin resources. By implementing circular strategies such as recycling, remanufacturing, and product life extension, businesses can reduce their dependence on raw materials and capitalise on the cost-effectiveness of recycled inputs. For instance, the automotive industry has embraced circular practices by remanufacturing and reusing components, resulting in substantial cost savings and reduced environmental impact;

- **Benefit 2: Risk mitigation and resilience in a supply-side driven economy**: As the global economy becomes increasingly supply-side driven, with resource scarcity and geopolitical tensions posing threats to traditional supply chains, the circular economy offers businesses a path towards greater resilience and risk mitigation. By decoupling economic growth from finite resource consumption, circular models reduce reliance on vulnerable supply chains and mitigate the risks associated with resource depletion and price volatility. Furthermore, the circular economy promotes local and regional material loops, reducing the need for long-distance transportation and minimising exposure to global supply chain disruptions. This localised approach not only enhances resilience but also fosters economic development and job creation;

- **Benefit 3: Growing demand, new revenue streams, and innovative business models:** The transition towards a circular economy is driving a surge in demand for new products, services, and business models. As consumers become increasingly conscious of their environmental impact, they are seeking out sustainable alternatives and embracing circular practices such as sharing, leasing, and product-as-a-service models. This growing demand presents businesses with opportunities to tap into new revenue streams and explore innovative business models. For example, companies like Philips, Mitsubishi and Michelin have successfully implemented product-as-a-service models, offering lighting, elevators or tyres on a pay-per-use basis. This not only aligns with circular principles but also fosters long-term customer relations and recurring revenue streams;

- **Benefit 4: Enhanced reputation and brand value:** In today's socially and environmentally conscious marketplace, businesses that embrace sustainability and circular practices can reap significant reputational and brand value benefits. Consumers, particularly younger generations, are increasingly making purchasing decisions based on a company's environmental and social responsibility credentials. By adopting circular economy principles, businesses can differentiate themselves from competitors, build trust with stakeholders, and cultivate a positive brand image. This enhanced reputation can translate into increased customer loyalty, attracting top talent, and gaining a competitive edge in the market. Companies like Patagonia and IKEA have successfully leveraged their circular economy initiatives to bolster their brand value and resonate with environmentally-conscious consumers;

- **Benefit 5: Being prepared for emerging compliance and regulatory requirements:** As the urgency of addressing environmental and social challenges intensifies, governments and regulatory bodies are increasingly implementing policies and frameworks that incentivise and mandate sustainable business practices. The circular economy aligns seamlessly with these emerging compliance and regulatory requirements, positioning businesses that embrace circularity as early adopters and leaders in their respective industries. Moreover, the circular economy directly contributes to the environmental, social, and governance (ESG) criteria that are becoming increasingly important for investors, and stakeholders. By integrating circular principles into their operations and reporting, businesses can enhance their ESG performance, access preferential financing opportunities, and attract socially-responsible investments.

As businesses navigate the complexities of the 21st century, embracing the circular economy is becoming no longer merely an option but a 'strategic imperative' for long-term success and resilience.

To effectively manage the transition from a linear to a circular model, companies that are not 'circular natives' should ask themselves these critical questions:

- How can we redesign our products and services to align with circular principles, such as durability, repairability, and recyclability?
- What collaborative partnerships and ecosystems can we establish to facilitate the exchange of materials, resources, and knowledge within the circular economy?
- How can we leverage digital technologies, such as the Internet of Things (IoT) and blockchain, to enable efficient tracking, monitoring, and optimisation of material flows and product life cycles?

By addressing these questions and proactively embracing the circular economy, businesses can position themselves as circular leaders.

OVERCOMING BARRIERS TO CIRCULAR MATERIALS USE

Change is uncomfortable, but to quote the famous Confucius: the only constant is change.

In this section, we address common objections to adopting circular material use in medium to large businesses. First, we address valid concerns followed by what we call a 'hurdle hop'.

Cost Concerns

Switching to circular materials often involves significant initial investment. This can include the cost of new technologies, retooling manufacturing processes, and potentially higher prices for circular materials compared to traditional ones. Corporate professionals might worry about the impact on the company's bottom line, particularly if these costs cannot be immediately passed on to customers.

Hurdle hop #1

Upcoming regulations, such as the European *Green Deal* and various national sustainability initiatives, are expected to impose stricter environmental standards and penalties for non-compliance. Investing now in circular materials can mitigate future costs associated with regulatory fines and help secure financial incentives and subsidies offered for sustainable practices.

Supply Chain Disruption

Integrating circular materials requires a reconfiguration of the entire supply chain, from sourcing to production to logistics. This can disrupt current operations and lead to inefficiencies during the transition period. Concern about the risks of supply chain instability is understandable, as this disruption can affect product availability and customer satisfaction.

Hurdle hop #2

Many governments provide support for businesses transitioning to circular models through grants, tax breaks, and infrastructure investments. Additionally, proactive adaptation to circular materials can position the company ahead of regulatory changes, reducing long-term disruptions and enhancing resilience.

Quality & Performance Issues

There may be concerns that circular materials do not meet the same quality or performance standards as traditional materials. Executives could fear that this might result in inferior products, which could damage the company's reputation and lead to customer dissatisfaction and returns.

Hurdle hop #3

Regulatory standards for circular materials are becoming more stringent, ensuring that they meet high-quality and performance benchmarks. Certification programs and industry standards are evolving to guarantee that circular materials are as reliable as traditional ones, which can alleviate quality concerns.

Supplier Reliability & Scalability

As a decision-maker, you worry about the consistency and volume of supply, which is critical for maintaining production schedules and meeting market demand.

Hurdle hop #4

Governments are increasingly investing in the circular economy, bolstering the development of robust supply chains for circular materials. This support is aimed at ensuring reliability and scalability, thus creating a more stable and predictable supply base for businesses adopting these materials.

Regulatory & Compliance Challenges

Navigating the regulatory landscape for circular materials can be complex, with varying standards and requirements across different regions. Executives might be concerned about ensuring compliance and the potential for increased regulatory scrutiny, which can lead to additional administrative burdens and costs.

Hurdle hop #5

As regulations around circular economy practices become more standardised globally, compliance processes are being streamlined. Governments and industry bodies are providing clear guidelines and support to help businesses transition smoothly, reducing the complexity of regulatory adherence.

Market Readiness & Demand

There may be scepticism about whether the market is ready to fully embrace products made from circular materials. Decision-makers could worry about the potential lack of consumer demand for these products, fearing that customers are not yet willing to pay a premium or change their purchasing habits to favour sustainable options. This uncertainty about market acceptance could make it difficult to justify the investment and operational upheaval required for the transition.

Hurdle hop #6

Consumer (or preferably 'citizen') awareness and demand for sustainable products are growing, driven by environmental concerns and regulatory pressures. Legislation, such as the EU's *Circular Economy Action Plan*, is pushing for greater market adoption of circular products, ensuring that businesses adopting these practices will meet increasing consumer/citizen demand and gain a competitive edge.

Technology & Innovation Limitations

The technology required to efficiently process and use circular materials is still evolving. As a decision-maker, you might be concerned about the maturity and availability of these technologies and whether they can be integrated into existing operations without significant technical challenges or downtime.

Hurdle hop #7
Government and private sectors are investing heavily in research and development for circular economy technologies. Innovations are being accelerated by regulatory mandates and funding opportunities, ensuring that the necessary technologies will be available and increasingly efficient.

Internal Resistance & Culture Change

A shift to circular materials requires a fundamental change in company culture and operations. There might be resistance from employees and management who are accustomed to the current linear supply chain model. Overcoming this resistance and aligning the entire organisation around the new circular economy principles can be a significant hurdle.

Hurdle hop #8
Regulations are creating a clear business case for sustainability, making it imperative for all levels of the organisation to adapt. Training programmes and incentives are being developed to support cultural change, and regulatory pressures can help drive internal alignment towards sustainability goals.

Uncertain Return on Investment

The financial benefits of adopting circular materials may not be immediately apparent. Decision-makers might be wary of committing resources to a strategy with an uncertain return on investment (ROI), especially if the benefits are long-term and difficult to quantify in the short term. This uncertainty can make it challenging to justify the shift to stakeholders and investors.

Hurdle hop #9
Regulations are increasingly incorporating financial incentives for circular economy practices, such as tax benefits, grants, and access to green financing. These measures help improve the ROI of circular materials, providing a clearer financial benefit in both the short and long term.

Complexity in Life-cycle Management

Managing the life-cycle of circular materials involves greater complexity, including the need for robust systems to track materials through production, use, and renewability stages. Corporate decision-makers might be concerned about the additional logistical and managerial challenges this complexity introduces, and whether the company has the necessary expertise and infrastructure to handle it effectively.

Hurdle hop #10
Regulatory frameworks are being designed to support life-cycle management through standardisation and digital tracking systems, such as the EU's Digital Product Passport (DPP). These initiatives aim to simplify the tracking and management of materials throughout their life-cycle, reducing the associated complexity.

Partnership & Collaboration Challenges

Implementing a circular economy model often requires collaboration with various stakeholders, including suppliers, recyclers, composting enablers, and even competitors. You might be apprehensive about the complexities of forming and maintaining these partnerships, especially if they involve sharing sensitive information or aligning on common goals and standards.

Hurdle hop #11
Regulatory bodies are encouraging – and sometimes mandating – collaborative efforts across industries through frameworks and platforms that facilitate partnerships. Public-private partnerships and industry consortia are being promoted to streamline collaboration efforts, making it easier for companies to work together towards common sustainability goals.

CASE STUDIES OF CORPORATE SUCCESSES

Rolls-Royce 'Power-by-the-Hour' Product-as-a-Service Business Model

'Power-by-the-Hour®' is a Rolls-Royce trademark that was invented in 1962 as a complete engine and accessory replacement service, offered on a fixed-cost-per-flying-hour basis. This aligned the interests of the manufacturer and operator, who only paid for engines that performed well. High quality and longevity is therefore the highest focus for the company.

Rolls-Royce CorporateCare®, launched in 2002, added a range of additional features, including engine health monitoring, which tracks on-wing performance using onboard sensors; lease engine access to replace an operator's engine during off-wing maintenance, thereby minimising downtime; and a global network of authorised maintenance centres to ensure that world-class support is readily available to customers whenever required. The service allows operators to lower risk related to unscheduled maintenance events and make maintenance costs planned and predictable.

As a result of this strategy, Rolls-Royce has a broad customer base comprising more than 500 airlines, 4,000 corporate and utility aircraft and helicopter operators, 160 armed forces, more than 4,000 marine customers, including 70 navies, and energy customers in more than 80 countries. This business now accounts for 70% of Rolls-Royce's revenue, which in 2023 was $20.5 billion.

Foxway – A Circular IT Unicorn

Foxway is a Swedish company focused on helping large organisations, the public sector and resellers of consumer electronics to become more circular in the way they think and act. It provides its partners and customers with services that help them to manage mobile phones, computers and other tech devices in a way that is both cost-efficient and sustainable.

The services Foxway offer are:

- **Life-cycle:** Tech devices, such as computers and mobiles, as a service to partners and customers. Foxway handles repairs, replacement of new products, returns, invoicing, etc. during the period of the agreement. Since it takes back the products that it manages, Foxway can give the products more than one life;

- **Recovery:** A range of services to take back used devices, so the current users get a smooth transition when it is time to upgrade. When the products come back to Foxway, it ensures the safe deletion of data before repair and refurbishment. Foxway also offers buyout solutions for overstock;

- **Remarketing:** Used, unsold or returned devices are given another life to new users all around the world. These remarketing services provide circularity and value, both for the end-users as well as for their partners.

With circularity as its core business model, in 2022 Foxway sourced, financed, and refurbished more than 1.5 million devices annually in the circular flow, avoiding 120,948 tons of carbon dioxide equivalent (CO_2e) emissions, and reported over SEK7.6 billion in gross revenue.

Foxway was founded in 2009 and now has offices in Europe, with a presence in Asia and the US. Nordic Capital acquired a majority share in Foxway in 2023 since, to quote Joakim Andreasson, Managing Director, Nordic Capital:

> *Foxway will be in a strong position to help accelerate an industry-wide sustainable transformation.*

Successful Circular Fashion Companies

Secondhand fashion company Vinted aims to make fashion more accessible, affordable, and environmentally-friendly by extending the life-cycle of clothing items. The company had a revenue of €596.3 million in 2023, growing 65% compared to the previous year.

By promoting the resale of luxury fashion, Vestiaire Collective contributes to a circular economy. It extends the lifespan of fashion items, reducing waste and environmental impact. Vestiaire Collective had a gross merchandise value (GMV) of $410.3 million in 2023 and reported a combined 90% environmental impact saving across GHG emissions, air pollution and other metrics.

Circular Packaging Solutions

Apeel Sciences develops plant-based coatings for fresh produce, extending shelf life and reducing food waste. This innovative approach has garnered significant investment, making it a circular unicorn. In 2023, Apeel made $71.9 million in revenue.

Disruptive Packaging is revolutionising the industry with its innovative product called Unicor®, which replaces conventional waxed cardboard and polystyrene packaging with calcium carbonate. It is 100% recyclable and supports a closed-loop circular economy. In 2023, Disruptive Packaging generated approximately $40.7 million in revenue.

THE CIRCULAR ECONOMY & YOU

Reshaping Consumerism for a Sustainable Future

The rise of the circular economy is not only a new opportunity for businesses, it also has potential to transform our lives as consumers. More and more people asking themselves: How does it affect me and how can I be more circular?

Here are four key considerations that are relevant for your life:

- **Conscious consumption as the new normal:** The rise of the circular economy is reshaping consumerism, opening the door into a new era of mindful and sustainable purchasing decisions, when we step into our responsibility to the planet and future generations. Gone are the days of mindless overconsumption and disposable products; instead, we can embrace a 'buy less, consume better' mentality, prioritising quality over quantity. This shift is also driven by an increasing availability of circular products and purchasing options. By opting for durable, long-lasting products and services, we can reduce waste and minimise our carbon footprint. Moreover, conscious consumers are increasingly seeking out brands and companies that prioritise sustainability and ethical practices. We are part of the solution;

- **The 2020s – a new era of reuse and repair:** One of the core principles of the circular economy is extending the life of products through reuse, repair, and refurbishment. This 'reuse and repair' revolution enables us to keep products in longer use. Accessible repair services, DIY repair resources, and the growing 'right to repair' movement are empowering consumers to take an active role in prolonging the lifespan of their possessions;

- **Embracing the sharing economy:** The circular economy is also driving the growth of the sharing economy, Circularity prioritises access to products and services over ownership. This transition from ownership to access-based models is facilitated by the rise of product-as-a-service and collaborative consumption platforms. This not only has environmental benefits but also promotes social connections and fosters a sense of community. 'Everything-as-a-service' solutions will experience increased demand, especially in sectors such as mobility and construction;

- **The circular lifestyle:** Ultimately, the circular economy is not just about changing our consumption patterns but about embracing a holistic circular lifestyle. This involves integrating circular principles into our daily lives, from the way we consume and dispose of products to the way we interact with our communities. Education and community engagement play a crucial role in driving this change. By raising awareness about the benefits of a circular economy and fostering a sense of collective responsibility, we can empower individuals to make more sustainable choices. The personal and collective benefits of a circular economy extend beyond environmental sustainability, promoting social cohesion, economic resilience, and overall well-being.

The transition towards a circular economy represents the dawn of a new era of healthy consumerism. As consumers, we hold the power to shape a sustainable future. The circular economy is not just a trend; it is a paradigm shift that empowers us to reshape consumerism and our relationship with the planet.

FUTURE TRENDS

The concept of the circular economy is quickly becoming mainstream. The coming years will encompass massive technology changes where, for example, AI and self-driving vehicles will make logistics cheap enough to make the sharing economy happen on a global scale. This will make circular products shift from low quality and fast discarded to products that last and increase in value over time. This will also kickstart a trend in less, and more flexible, ownership.

Flexible living also will become a larger trend. Why buy an apartment or house that needs maintenance when you can work remotely and move and explore new places while you work? Many of the buildings we live in will be old re-furbished buildings and the new houses we do build will prioritise sustainability, adaptability, and community well-being. They will be efficient, resource-conscious, and exist in harmony with nature.

We will make buildings in line with circular design principles:

- **Energy efficiency:** Circular buildings will not only maximise energy efficiency by using materials with high thermal insulation capacity, smart design also will use biomimicry solutions to heat and cool the buildings when needed and take advantage of natural light, reducing the need for artificial lighting;

- **Renewable energy integration:** Buildings will incorporate renewable energy systems such as solar panels, wind turbines, and geothermal heat pumps to generate their own energy and contribute to the grid when possible;

- **Modularity and adaptability:** Circular buildings will be designed for adaptability. Modular components will allow for easy reconfiguration, expansion, or repurposing without excessive demolition or waste. They also will be flexible in adapting for lifestyle changes: if you are alone, you need less space; if you have children, then you need more. Inner walls will be more easily moved and the spaces adapted for the residents' needs;

- **Biophilic design:** Circular buildings will prioritise human well-being by integrating nature into the design. Green roofs, indoor plants, and natural materials will enhance occupants' health and productivity;

- **Recycled and upcycled materials:** The buildings will use recycled and upcycled materials wherever possible. Reclaimed wood, recycled steel, and repurposed glass will reduce the demand for virgin resources;

- **Biodegradable, bio-based and living materials:** Builders will opt for materials that decompose naturally, minimising waste and allergies. Biodegradable plastics, hempcrete, and mycelium-based materials are examples. Buildings might also feature living materials like algae-based panels, which absorb carbon dioxide (CO_2) and release oxygen. These materials can also be grown on-site;

- **Circular concrete:** Innovations in concrete production will reduce its environmental impact. Circular concrete may incorporate recycled aggregates, carbon capture, and alternative binders;

- **Prefabrication and off-site construction:** Circular buildings will increasingly use prefabricated components manufactured off-site. This reduces construction waste and speeds up the building process, as well as being energy-efficient;

- **Zero-waste facilities and on-site recycling:** Circular buildings will integrate waste reduction strategies. On-site recycling facilities will process materials like plastics, glass, and metals. Biodigesters may convert organic waste into energy or compost, closing the loop within the building itself. The buildings also will recycle fresh water and sewage in order to put it back in to use and close the food-cycle loops;

- **Community and collaboration:** Circular buildings will be part of circular neighbourhoods and communities where they share resources, such as vehicles and tools, community gardens, and collaborative spaces;

- **Life-cycle thinking:** Circular buildings will be designed with end-of-life considerations. Demolition won't mean destruction; instead, materials will be disassembled and reused elsewhere. Life-cycle assessments will guide material choices, ensuring that the environmental impact is minimised throughout the building's existence.

Other future trends connected to the circular economy are:

- **Circularity merges with geopolitics:** As global challenges like climate change and wars intensify, material and resource sustainability will become a key geopolitical issue. Countries and regions will collaborate to drive circular practices and reduce environmental impact, as well as helping each other become more resilient to change;

- **EU as a regulator:** The EU is already taking a leading role in shaping circular economy policies. More regulations and incentives to promote circular practices across industries are coming in the future that will impact companies' decisions and value chains globally;

- **Tracking, tracing, and transparency:** Technologies like blockchain, DPPs and IoT will enhance supply chain transparency. Consumers and businesses will demand more information about product origins, materials, and recycling processes in order to choose what to purchase;

- **Advancements despite setbacks:** Despite challenges, such as the high cost of changing business models and re-designing products and services, the circular economy will continue to advance. The scarcity and higher cost of materials, as well as new innovations in materials, recycling, and business models will drive progress;

- **Ownership faces competition:** Ownership models will evolve to enable circularity. Sharing, renting, and subscription services will compete with traditional ownership, reducing resource consumption;

- **AI speeds up transition:** Artificial intelligence (AI) will play a crucial role in optimising circular processes. Predictive analytics, automation, and data-driven decisions will drive efficiency;

- **Consumer demand for sustainable comfort:** Consumers will seek products and services that balance sustainability with comfort. Brands that prioritise both will thrive.

Conclusion

The future business landscape will be dominated by companies that can innovate within the circular economy framework. Companies that prioritise sustainability, resource efficiency, and collaboration will lead the way. Embracing the circular economy is not just an environmental imperative but a strategic business decision that can drive growth, reduce costs, and enhance corporate reputation.

Seeing the forests for the trees in the context of the circular economy means recognising the broader benefits of sustainable practices. By understanding and implementing the principles of the circular economy, businesses can achieve long-term success and contribute to a healthier planet.

ESRS-E5 – RESOURCES & THE CIRCULAR ECONOMY REPORTING OBLIGATIONS

Ingrid De Doncker

ESRS-E5 details the reporting requirements for resource use and the circular economy. It provide clarity and transparency for users of the sustainability statement to understand:

- How an organisation affects resource use, including resource efficiency, avoiding the depletion of resources and the sustainable sourcing and use of renewable resources in terms of material positive and negative actual or potential impacts;
- Any actions taken, and the result of such actions, to prevent or mitigate actual or potential negative impacts arising from resource use, including measures to help decoupling the organisation's economic growth from the use of materials, and to address risks and opportunities;
- The organisation's plans and capacity to adapt its strategy and business model in line with circular economy principles including, but not limited to, minimising waste, maintaining the value of products, materials and other resources at their highest value and enhancing their efficient use in production and consumption;
- The nature, type and extent of an organisation's material risks and opportunities related to their impacts and dependencies, arising

from resource use and circular economy, and how the organisation manages them; and

- The financial effects on the organisation over the short-, medium- and long-term of material risks and opportunities arising from its own impacts and dependencies on resource use and circular economy.

Resources & Circular Economy Sub-topics

Under ESRS 1 Article 16, there are three sub-topics to consider. The wording is unclear sometimes so the descriptions are expanded here a little for clarity:

- **Resources inflows** includes the circularity of material resource inflows, and considers renewable and non-renewable resources. It represent the resources a company takes in from external sources to enable its operational resource use and value creation activities. This covers raw materials, components used to manufacture products, packaging materials, water use, energy resources like fuels, electricity, equipment and machinery used, etc. It covers the full lifecycle from sourcing and procurement of the resources as inflows, through their use and transformation within the company's processes, to the eventual outflow;

- **Resource outflows related to products and services** include the final products and goods produced and sold to customers, any packaging materials used for those products, waste, emissions, or by-products generated during the production and delivery of those products and services. This includes also the information on products and materials;

- **Waste** is any unwanted or unusable material that is disposed of after its initial use. It includes items or substances that are left over, defective, or no longer needed and are intended to be thrown away or discharged. The different types of waste that companies need to disclose information on include hazardous waste, non-hazardous waste and generated radioactive waste, along with how much is diverted for recovery versus directed to disposal through different treatment methods like recycling, incineration, landfill, etc.

This Standard should be read in conjunction with ESRS 1 *General Requirements* and ESRS 2 *General Disclosures*. The requirements of this section should be read in conjunction with, and reported alongside, the disclosures required by ESRS 2, *Chapter 4: Impact, Risk & Opportunity Management*.

It is important to understand the *Minimum Disclosure Requirements* (MDRs) in ESRS 2, Chapter 4.2. When an organisation identifies a sustainability matter as material, 34 MDR data points (DPs) for Policies, Actions, Targets, and Metrics (PAT-M) are applicable if the organisation discloses on policies, actions and targets. If it does not provide disclosure on policies, targets or actions, then it needs to disclose the reasons for not doing so, as per the corresponding 10 DPs of ESRS 2 MDR PAT, paragraphs 62 and 81.

ESRS-E5 outlines clearly, in six *Disclosure Requirements* (DRs), the narrative and numeric data DPs an organisation should comply with. There are 42 *Shall* DPs, of which 15 are numeric, 24 narrative and 3 semi-narrative, as well as 19 additional *May* DPs. The MDR PAT DPs are to be disclosed under E5-1, E5-2, E5-3 when the sustainability matters are material. **Figure 6.3** shows the structure of the ESRS-E5 DRs and DPs that must be reported, if deemed material by the double materiality assessment.

Figure 6.3: ESRS-E5 Reporting Requirements

ESRS-E4	Resource Use & Circular Economy		
	Resources inflows, including resources use	**Resource outflows related to products and services**	**Waste**
	With the exception of DPs in IRO-1, none of these DPs are applicable if the topic is not material.		
	IMPACT, RISK & OPPORTUNITY MANAGEMENT		
ESRS2-E5-IRO-1	Description of the processes to identify and assess material use and circular economy-related impacts, risks, opportunities.		
ESRS-E5-1	**Policies** related to resource use and circular economy.		
ESRS-E5-2	**Actions** and resources related to resource use and circular economy.		
	METRICS & TARGETS		
ESRS-E5-4	**Targets** related to resource use and circular economy.		
ESRS-E5-4	**Resource inflows.**		
ESRS-E5-5	**Resource outflows.**		
ESRS-E5-6	**Anticipated financial effects** from resource use and circular economy-related impacts, risks and opportunities.		

Targets & Actions

Companies should set specific targets aligned with waste reduction and circular economy strategies across their operations and value chains, such as:

- The increase of circular product design (including, for instance, design for durability, dismantling, reparability, recyclability, etc);
- The increase of circular material use rate;
- The minimisation of primary raw material;
- Sustainable sourcing and use (in line with the cascading principle) of renewable resources;
- Waste management, including preparation for proper treatment;
- Other matters related to resource use or circular economy.

Some key strategies and actions that companies can take to reduce waste include:

- **Applying circular design principles:**
  - o Designing products for durability, repairability, refurbishing, remanufacturing, and recyclability to extend product life and enable circularity;
  - o Optimising product use through sharing economy and product-as-a-service business models;
- **Implementing circular business practices:**
  - o Value retention actions like maintenance, repair, refurbishing, remanufacturing, component harvesting, and reverse logistics;
  - o Value maximisation through product-service systems and sharing models;
  - o End-of-life actions focused on recycling, upcycling, and extended producer responsibility schemes;
  - o Industrial symbiosis and other systems efficiency actions;
- **Waste prevention in the value chain:** Taking actions to prevent waste generation upstream and downstream in the company's value chain;
- **Optimising waste management:**
  - o Following the waste hierarchy principles of prevention, preparation for reuse, recycling, other recovery (for example, energy recovery), and disposal as the last resort;

- o   Improving waste sorting, collection and treatment processes;
- **Increasing resource efficiency:**
  - o   Using materials, water and other resources more efficiently in production processes to reduce waste;
  - o   Increasing use of recycled/secondary raw materials and renewable resources;
- **Eco-design and circular product development**: Applying the 9R principles - refuse, rethink, reduce, reuse, repair, refurbish, remanufacture, repurpose, recycle in product design.

---

[1]   *Cradle to Cradle; Remaking the Way We Make Things*, William McDonough & Michael Braungart (Vintage Publishing, 2022).

[2]   https://www.mdpi.com/2073-4360/13/11/1854.

7

OWN WORKFORCE & WORKERS IN THE VALUE CHAIN

Anna Triponel[1]

For as long as I can remember, I've felt that my reason for being on this planet was to advocate for a fairer, more equitable and more peaceful world. In law school, I organised a trip to West Africa that left me with a strong sense that there are some basic fundamental human rights that all people should have – irrespective of where they were born and that, equally, companies have significant potential in helping ensure that those that they touch – whether as workers, contractors, customers, or neighbouring community members – have their rights respected.

This set me on a mission to transform the field and to shape what human rights meant for companies – both in theory and in practice. During my time as a corporate lawyer practising in New York, as well as an international lawyer in Africa and a consultant at Harvard, I helped shape the consensus of what can reasonably be expected of companies when it comes to human rights. Developed over six years, and endorsed by the United Nations (UN) in 2011, this consensus has since become the backbone for the EU's Corporate Sustainability Due Diligence Directive (CSDDD) – as well as other similar laws. And during my time at Shift, I travelled extensively to help shape the consensus of expectations of companies when it comes to human rights reporting, which in turn has fed into the EU's Corporate Sustainability Reporting Directive (CSRD).

I have been working in partnership with companies to help drive them toward these expectations of due diligence and resulting reporting ever since. Working with hundreds of companies – from pioneering multinationals to family-owned suppliers on the ground worldwide – over the years, I have seen the sheer complexity of human rights for business in practice. The world is a messy place, and is becoming increasingly complex to navigate. Laws may not be protective, or enforced – or they may even run counter to human rights respect. Spaces for worker and community voice are increasingly constrained, and democracies are backsliding. Significant profits can be made by relying on human rights impacts, such as forced labour and child labour. Some impacts are endemic to a sector or context, such as sexual harassment and discrimination. And, above all, we are in the midst of a climate crisis that will heighten all of the human rights risks and impacts faced by companies – and lead to new ones by virtue of how companies are transforming their business models to meet climate and sustainability commitments, and to adapt to the effects of a rapidly warming planet.

I always ask business leaders I work with: "Do you want your company to be here in 50 years' time?" The answer always is "Yes". In that case, let us fully capitalise on existing and upcoming laws to better understand risks and impacts, *and make well-informed decisions. This, in turn, will position companies to drive innovation, foster stakeholder trust, and position themselves as responsible corporate citizens in a rapidly evolving global landscape. I have seen first-hand how recognising the reality of human rights impacts and risks, as well as the interconnectedness between human rights, climate and environmental sustainability, positions companies for success. The combination of the CSRD and the CSDDD will be pivotal for companies as they progress into the future.*

Anna Triponel

INTRODUCTION

As the planet warms up, and as companies transition toward a net zero future – while adapting to a warmer planet – we are likely to see a growing number of adverse impacts on people, including workers in companies' own workforce, as well as workers in their value chain.

For instance, we are seeing growing pressures on farmer livelihoods due to the impact of extreme weather events and rising temperatures on crop yields – coupled with the financial costs of adapting to regenerative agriculture. We are seeing growing health impacts on workers, resulting from increased exposure to heat stress. And we are seeing pressures on working conditions increase – for instance, of waste pickers in the recycled plastics supply chain.[2]

In parallel, we are also seeing that a number of adverse impacts in company operations and value chains are worsening. For instance, forced labour has increased over the past 10 years – despite significant efforts by companies to tackle it. Other impacts on workers in company operations and value chains are endemic to the operating context they are working in and sourcing from, and can be challenging to identify and address. In addition, as the climate crisis deepens, we are seeing increased pressures on operating contexts, including growing conflict, backsliding in democracies, and growing crackdowns on voices of workers as well as environmental and human rights defenders, which in turn increase the severity and likelihood of impacts on people.

This growth in severity and likelihood of impacts on people in company operations and value chain matter – for people, planet and business. Impacts on workers can lead to a wide range of consequences, ranging from life-altering injuries and deaths, restrictions on freedoms and a lack of lived potential. Impacts on workers also can contribute to workers opposing the necessary climate and environmental transition, for fear of further impacts, which in turn delays or jeopardises the transition. And impacts on workers can translate into significant financial costs for companies, ranging from more costly operations, fines, lawsuits, campaigns that taint company reputations, divestment from investors, and the application of import bans halting goods at borders.

It is this recognition of the growth in complexity of the contexts within which companies are operating, coupled with the growth in importance of respecting the rights of workers in company operations and value chains as the EU transitions in alignment with the *European Green Deal*, that forms the backbone of *European Sustainability Reporting Standards* (ESRS) ESRS-S1 and ESRS-S2 that underpin the CSRD.

The EU has recognised that it will not achieve its policy objective of "no person and no place left behind" embedded in its *European Green Deal* if it does not expect companies to take pro-active and meaningful steps to respect the human rights of workers in their operations and value chain, and to report on these steps (ESRS-S1 and ESRS-S2, respectively).

The CSRD forms part of a larger package of measures for companies, intended to ensure that companies respect people's rights as they transition to net zero and take steps toward nature positive. The EU's CSDDD, another part of this package, is a game-changer for companies, since it expects companies legally to conduct sustainability due diligence – including human rights due diligence (HRDD) – in a way that is aligned with the *UN Guiding Principles on Business & Human Rights* (the *UN Guiding Principles* – UNGPs). This obligation to conduct HRDD was previously (primarily) an expectation in the realm of soft law and, until the CSDDD, was not a legal obligation of companies.

The CSRD then acts as a complement to the CSDDD, providing a mechanism for companies to report on their HRDD efforts. In other words, the CSDDD provides the expectations of what to *do*, while the CSRD provides the expectations of what to *say*. The EU itself creates this connection, by noting that companies subject to the CSDDD satisfy their communication expectations by following the CSRD. And both legal instruments are grounded in the soft law that shape companies' expectations in the field of human rights, the UNGPs. Therefore, the reporting obligations of the CSRD are to be read alongside the due diligence obligations of the CSDDD, with both to be read alongside the soft law that shaped them.

This chapter delves into the reporting expectations of the CSRD, and provides further colour on why these reporting expectations are articulated the way they are, and what they are intended to surface. Although the reporting obligations under the CSRD may appear extensive at first, if they are approached with an open mind with the intent to strengthen the company's relevant due diligence processes in light of the operating contexts the company is operating in and sourcing from, they carry significant opportunity in equipping companies for the growth in complexity of the world they are operating in.

In addition, the expectations are not new, since they are grounded in the soft law of business and human rights that a number of companies have already been implementing since 2011. Understanding the soft law that shaped these due diligence and reporting obligations, and why they are articulated the way they are, will help companies harness this opportunity ahead.

THE ORIGINS OF ESRS-S1 & ESRS-S2

Expectations of Companies to Respect Human Rights

Until 2011, it was unclear what could be expected of companies when it came to human rights. Human rights – civil, political, economic, social and cultural rights that all human beings should enjoy – were a matter for States.

States – in the United Nations General Assembly – first adopted the *Universal Declaration of Human Rights* (UDHR) in 1948, three years after the end of the World War II. The UDHR was a milestone document: it set out, for the first time, fundamental human rights to be universally protected – irrespective of whether States had granted these rights under national law. In other words, this was the first time we had articulated certain rights that were inalienable, which means that the general rule is that they cannot be taken away. Human rights are viewed as universal, which means that we are all equally entitled to our human rights. And human rights are indivisible and interdependent, which means that the rights don't operate in a silo. They work together: having certain rights protected helps us have other rights protected as well.

This declaration was followed by further international conventions and treaties that are binding on States under international law. For instance, the *International Covenant on Civil & Political Rights* (ICCPR) and the *International Covenant on Economic, Social & Cultural Rights* (ICESCR) of 1966 enshrine the rights contained in the UDHR into international law. Alongside the UDHR, these two covenants are known as the *International Bill of Human Rights*. By becoming parties to these international treaties, States assume obligations and duties under international law to respect, protect and fulfil human rights.

States also have obligations and duties under International Labour Organization (ILO) Conventions that focus on one group of human rights: labour rights that are provided to workers. In particular, the ILO's *Declaration on Fundamental Principles & Rights at Work*, adopted by the member states in 1998, identified fundamental Conventions that are binding on all States, and that cover freedom of association and the effective recognition of the right to collective bargaining; the elimination of all forms of forced or compulsory labour; the effective abolition of child labour; and the elimination of discrimination in respect of employment and occupation. (This was revised in 2022 to include a safe and healthy working environment.)

Specifically, the obligation to protect under international law requires States to protect individuals and groups against human rights violations – including by companies. This, in turn, has led to a number of national human rights-related laws seeking to enshrine international human rights law into national laws that apply to companies. Until 2011, this was the core expectation of companies: to comply with national laws related to human rights, irrespective of whether these national laws aligned with internationally recognised human rights standards, or not.

This changed on 16 June 2011. On that date, the UN Human Rights Council unanimously endorsed the UNGPs.[3] For the first time ever, the UNGPs described what international human rights meant for companies. Based on an extensive six-year consultation process with stakeholders globally, then UN Special Representative of the Secretary-General on Human Rights & Transnational Corporations & Other Business Enterprises, John Ruggie, forged an international consensus with regard to the connection between human rights and business.

This consensus was as follows: Companies are not expected to take on the same duties as States. They do not have an obligation to fulfil human rights: they are not expected to take positive actions to facilitate the enjoyment of human rights. Neither do they have an obligation to protect individuals and groups against violations of human rights. At the same time, they *do* have a responsibility: to respect human rights.

Companies' responsibility to respect human rights means that they should avoid infringing on the human rights of others, and should address adverse human rights impacts with which they are involved. The human rights that companies are expected to respect under this international consensus are internationally recognised human rights, which may differ from those human rights States have articulated under national laws. These internationally recognised human rights are – at a minimum – those contained in the *International Bill of Human Rights*, as well as the principles concerning fundamental rights set out in the ILO's *Declaration on Fundamental Principles & Rights at Work* described above. There are a number of other human rights in other treaties and conventions that also can be captured within a company's responsibility to respect rights.

This international consensus also found that the responsibility to respect human rights extends to the company's full value chain. It captures a responsibility to respect the human rights of the company's own workforce – but also to take steps to ensure that the rights of workers in its value chain are also respected, alongside other people who may be impacted by the company's operations and value chain (for example, neighbouring communities and end-users). The CSRD, and accompanying ESRS, seek to ensure that companies are looking at this full value chain scope, by providing for reporting on four groups within its social reporting: own workforce and value chain workers (which is the focus of this chapter and also ESRS-S1 and ESRS-S2), as well as affected communities, consumers and end-users (which are the focus of ESRS-S3 and ESRS-S4, covered by other chapters).

The soft law consensus on business and human rights expects companies to look at the risks of impacts on people's human rights, and to prioritise those impacts for action based on their severity to people. What matters is the severity of impacts, from the perspective of the people impacted. This was different from prior prioritisation processes where impacts on people were prioritised based on how they were likely to lead to impacts on the business (for example, a lawsuit, a blockage, or a boycott). The UNGPs made clear that impacts on people matter – irrespective of whether these impacts also translate into costs to the business. At the same time, the work around the UNGPs also surfaced that most severe human rights impacts also translate into financial risks to the business – with some financial risks manifesting over the short-term, and some manifesting more over the longer-term. (This helps explain why we landed on the double materiality concept within the CSRD – more on this below).

To fully comprehend the reporting obligations set forth in the CSRD and accompanying ESRS (as well as the due diligence obligations contained in the CSDDD), it's particularly helpful to come back to the foundations of these expectations. The UNGPs set out the policies and processes that are expected of companies for them to be able to 'know and show' that they are indeed respecting human rights.

There are four expectations of policies and processes:

- **A policy:** A company is expected to have a policy commitment that expresses the company's commitment to meet its responsibility to respect human rights;

- **Embedding of policy:** A company is expected to reflect this human rights policy commitment in operational policies and procedures necessary to embed it throughout the company;

- **Human rights due diligence:** A company is expected to conduct meaningful HRDD, which entails:

  - *Identify and assess:* Identifying and assessing their actual and potential negative impacts on people, and prioritising them for action based on their severity;

  - *Engage:* Engaging directly with potentially affected stakeholders or their proxies to understand the human rights impacts from their perspective through HRDD;

  - *Integrate and act:* Integrating the findings and taking action to prevent or mitigate potential impacts, and play a role to effectively remediate them when they have arisen;

  - *Track:* Tracking the effectiveness of actions taken;

  - *Communicate:* Communicating how the company is addressing the impacts;

- **Remedy processes:** A company is expected to implement processes to provide or enable effective remedy to those harmed, if the company causes or contributes to a negative impact.

A soft law expectation signals the expectations of the international community when it comes to companies. It shapes, in turn, other expectations of companies – for instance, the Organisation for Economic Co-operation & Development's (OECD) *Guidelines for Multinational Enterprises* were revised to reflect the same human rights expectation. As a soft law expectation endorsed by the UN Human Rights Council, these policies and processes are intended to be put in place by all companies globally, irrespective of where they operate, their size, sector, operational context, ownership and structure. At the same time, soft law expectations by themselves are not legally binding on companies. They shape drivers of company behaviour and performance – including laws that are legally binding, as is the case here with the CSDDD and CSRD.

The Early Days of Double Materiality for Human Rights Reporting

Shortly following the endorsement of the UNGPs, work started to further refine what it would mean to report on human rights. Indeed, the UNGPs expect companies to communicate about their HRDD to individuals or groups who may be impacted, as well as to other relevant stakeholders, including investors. Communication itself can take a variety of forms beyond formal reporting, including in-person meetings and online dialogues. Formal reporting by companies is expected where risks of severe human rights impacts exist, and should cover topics and indicators concerning how companies identify and address adverse impacts on human rights.

In 2012, two organisations – Shift (a leading centre of expertise on UNGPs) and Mazars (an audit, accountancy and advisory firm) – undertook a multi-stakeholder consultative process to answer the question: What does good human rights reporting look like? This process, called the Human Rights Reporting & Assurance Frameworks Initiative (RAFI), took place over the course of 2012 to 2015, with inputs from a range of companies, auditors and assessors, and end-users of reports (including investors, civil society organisations and trade unions). It also benefited from input from a range of reporting organisations on the initiative's steering body, including from the Global Reporting Initiative (GRI) and the International Integrated Reporting Committee (IIRC).[4]

These conversations, held in a number of locations worldwide over the course of three years, surfaced a key challenge in human rights reporting: it tended to be disconnected from a company's HRDD. In other words, social reporting tended to cover topics that were distinct from those areas a company was managing through its HRDD under the UNGPs. This meant that issues resulting from companies' HRDD were not necessarily benefiting from senior-level attention being paid to those areas included in the company's formal reporting, and human rights colleagues needed to spend additional time to gather information to communicate on HRDD, alongside the time spent to gather information on social reporting. This also meant that the end-users of the report were not benefiting from the information that matters: information on where the company may impact people in the most severe way, and what the company can do about this.

The move to 'salience' in human rights reporting, which in turn forms the foundation for the double materiality contained in the CSRD, was the response to this challenge. Salience as an entry point for determining what to report on in the area of social and human rights reporting was captured in one of the outputs of RAFI: the *UN Guiding Principles Reporting Framework* released in 2015.[5] Salience signalled a move away from reporting human rights information because it can translate into financial implications for the business (financial materiality), as well as a move away from reporting human rights information because it is viewed as important for certain stakeholders.

Salience was about aligning a company's reporting on human rights with its HRDD. Since HRDD prioritises human rights issues based on their severity to people, reporting due diligence efforts should focus on a company's salient human rights issues (which are the human rights at risk of the most severe negative impact through the company's activities and business relationships).[6] The application of the UNGPs, and the *Reporting Framework*, has led a number of companies over the years to report on their HRDD efforts, using their most salient human rights issues as their entry point. The double materiality captured in the CSRD builds on these developments.

The CSRD specifically entails the premise of reporting based on impacts on people – irrespective of the financial implications of the impact, or what people say about them – into its first prong of double materiality. The CSRD calls for impact materiality ('inside out' materiality), which calls for information related to impacts on people and the environment resulting from a company's activities and business relationships. In parallel, the CSRD acknowledges that there may be some human rights issues that may matter to investors, but may not be the company's salient human rights issues. Therefore, it also calls for financial materiality ('outside in' materiality), which entails reporting on human rights-related risks or opportunities that influence the company's development, financial position, financial performance, cash flows, access to finance or cost of capital.

This is the first time that both aspects are requested together, and the ESRS recognises the dynamic nature of this materiality: both are interconnected – for instance, an impact on people or the environment can become financially material over time. To this end, Shift describes the approach to take to double materiality in this context of social and human rights matters: the key starting point is impact materiality – with the first step of assessing material impacts mirroring the first step of human rights due diligence.[7] These material impacts then set the basis for the financial materiality assessment.

The Resulting ESRS-S1 & ESRS-S2

As described above, a company's responsibility to respect human rights extends to workers beyond its own workforce to capture workers in its value chain, as well as other potentially affected stakeholder groups, such as neighbouring communities, consumers and end-users. Therefore, the social parts of the ESRS seek to help a company to consider all of the people whose rights could be impacted in its value chain, and prioritise on this basis.

Specifically, the ESRS expect companies to conduct a double materiality assessment to identify its material impacts on and/or material risks and opportunities related to their own workforce and value chain workers (as laid out in ESRS 2 *General Disclosures*). With impact materiality based on impacts on people, the CSRD's ESRS-S1 – *Own Workforce* supports a company in reporting how it is meeting its responsibility to respect human rights (and meets corresponding CSDDD) when it comes to the human rights of its workforce. And the CSRD's ESRS-S2 – *Workers in the Value Chain* – does the same thing with regard to workers in the company's value chain, which covers in the company's upstream or downstream value chain. **Figure 7.1** shows the workers in scope for both standards.

ESRS-S1 (S1-6 and S1-7) specifically calls for disclosure of the specific characteristics of the workforce when it comes to both employees and non-employees in order to provide insight into the company's approach to employment, and to provide contextual information that supports an understanding of the information reported in other disclosures.

There is a strong connection between ESRS-S1 and ESRS-S2. Each specifically provides that reporting under the standards needs to be consistent, coherent and (where relevant) clearly linked with reporting on the other standard, in order to ensure effective reporting. Both standards relate to the kinds of material risks and impacts faced by workers – with some workers being in the company's own operations, and some being in the company's value chain. The social factors, including human rights, relevant to a company's own workforce (ESRS-S1) are the same as those for workers in their value chain (ESRS-S2 – which also references water and sanitation) – see **Figure 7.2**.

The ESRS make clear that these are matters that the company is expected to consider in its materiality assessment undertaken (when following ESRS 1 Chapter 3 and ESRS 2 IRO-1) related to workforce and value chain workers and, as appropriate, to disclose as material impacts, risks and opportunities within the scope of the ESRS.

Figure 7.1: Workers in Scope – ESRS-S1 & ESRS-S2

	Category of workers	Examples according to ESRS-S1 & ESRS-S2
S1	Own workforce: Direct employees (people who are in an employment relationship with the company); Non-employees (self-employed workers and workers provided by third-party agencies).	Non-employees who are self-employed workers: • Contractors hired by the company to perform work that would otherwise be • carried out by an employee; • Contractors hired by the company to perform work in a public area (for example, on a road or street); • Contractors hired by the company to deliver the work/service directly at the workplace of a client of the company. Non-employees who are workers provided by third-party agencies: • People who fill in for employees who are temporarily absent (due to illness, holiday, • parental leave, etc.); • People performing work additional to regular employees; • People who are dispatched temporarily from another EU member state to work for the company ('posted workers').
S2	Value chain workers: all workers in the company's upstream and downstream value chain who are or can be materially impacted by the company, including impacts that are connected with the company's own operations and value chain, including through its products or services, as well as through its business relationships.	• Workers working on the company's site who are not part of the company's own workforce; • Workers of outsourced services working in the workplace of the company (for example, third party catering or security workers); • Workers of a supplier contracted by the company who work on the supplier's premises using the supplier's work methods; • Workers of an equipment supplier to the company who, at a workplace controlled by the company, perform regular maintenance on the supplier's equipment; • Workers working for entities in the company's upstream value chain (those involved in the extraction of metals or minerals or harvesting of commodities, in refining, manufacturing or other forms of processing); • Workers working for entities in the company's downstream value chain which purchases goods or services from the company (for example, those involved in the activities of logistics or distribution providers, franchisees, retailers); • Workers working in the operations of a joint venture or special purpose vehicle involving the company.

Figure 7.2: Social & Human Rights Matters Identified in ESRS-S1 & ESRS-S2

Working Conditions	Equal treatment and opportunities for all	Other work-related rights
• Secure employment • Working time • Adequate wages • Social dialogue • Freedom of association • Collective bargaining • Work-life balance • Health and safety	• Gender equality and equal pay for work of equal value • Training and skills development • Employment and inclusion of persons with disabilities • Measures against violence and harassment in the workplace • Diversity	• Child labour • Forced labour • Adequate housing • Privacy • Water and sanitation (S2 only)

Although the list is the same, these issues are likely to manifest differently for companies, depending on where they take place in the value chain. Human rights impacts vary depending on a range of factors. In particular, their severity is often connected to the pre-existing vulnerability of a worker, or group of workers (for example, connected to their status as migrant workers, or as low-income workers, or as women). Their likelihood is often connected to the operating context and whether laws that protect workers are in place and enforced, as well as the type of business activity being conducted and the type of business relationship conducting it. The strength of a company's existing mitigation measures also play a role in determining likelihood. This in turn means that although the issues listed are the same, they will manifest differently for companies, depending on what they do, with whom and in which countries. In practice, therefore, the issues found resulting from ESRS-S1 and ESRS-S2 are likely to be different for different companies, although some may apply in both contexts.

Reviewing existing human rights reports following the *UNGP Reporting Framework*, and getting a clearer sense of where the human rights issues are being reported on for the workforce, and when they are being reported on for the value chain workers, can help companies better understand existing human rights reporting and how the issues differ, between ESRS-S1 and ESRS-S2. It can be particularly valuable to consider reports from companies operating in the same or similar sectors, although, as further described below, each company will have its own unique set of risks depending on its own strategy, business model and value chain.

The standards that human rights impacts are assessed against in the ESRS are those contained in international and European human rights instruments and conventions; they are the same ones as expected under the UNGPs (with specific reference to EU-related human rights laws as well).

STRATEGY

Strategy, Business Model & Value Chain

A company's strategy, its business model, and its resulting value chain will play a central part in informing the company's material impacts, risks and opportunities. How the company runs its business, the people the company relies on, the direction of travel for the business, and sourcing decisions all will influence the kinds of human rights-related impacts, risks and opportunities for the company.

The ESRS recognise this in ESRS 2 on Strategy & Business Model (SBM), which specifically requests information related to the elements of the company's strategy that relate to or affect sustainability matters, its business model and its value chain (ESRS 2 SBM-1).

The Interests & Views of Stakeholders

At the same time, a company may not know itself how its strategy, business model, and value chain lends itself to material human rights risks and impacts. To respond to this, ESRS 2 on Strategy (ESRS 2 SBM-2) requests companies to report on how the interests and views of the company's stakeholders are taken into account by the company's strategy and business model.

When it comes to human rights, ESRS-S1 and ESRS-S2 seek to incentivise companies to gather views and perspectives from those stakeholders who could be impacted themselves – the workforce and value chain workers – by requesting companies to disclose how the interests, views, and rights of people in their own workforce and value chain inform their strategy and business model. ESRS-S1 and ESRS-S2 note that a company's own workforce, and its value chain workers, are key groups of affected stakeholders, and acknowledges the feasibility aspect by recognising that, when it comes to own workforce, the views of workers' representatives may be particularly helpful to consider. This process of gathering inputs and views can be integrated into the company's engagement processes undertaken as part of its due diligence (and reported on further in S1-2 and S2-2).

Material Impacts, Risks & Opportunities & their Interaction with Strategy & Business Model

ESRS 2 further requests companies to report the outcome of the company's assessment of material impacts, risks and opportunities, including how they inform its strategy and business model (ESRS 2 SBM-3). The purpose here is to understand how the company's material impacts, risks and opportunities related to its workforce, as well as its value chain workers, originate from the company's strategy and business model, as well as whether they trigger any adaptation to the company's strategy and business model.

Examples provided by the ESRS include impacts that may relate to the company's:

- Value proposition (such as providing lowest cost products or services, or high-speed delivery, in ways that put pressure on labour rights in its operations, or the upstream and downstream value chains);
- Cost structure and revenue model (for example, shifting inventory risk to suppliers, with knock-on effects on the labour rights of their workers);
- Value chain (such as relying on commodities of unclear provenance, without visibility on impacts on workers).

Work conducted by Shift on the business model red flags, organised precisely around the value proposition, the cost structure and revenue model, and the value chain, can be a particularly helpful tool to review to gain a better understanding of the kinds of areas to look out for.[8]

In the spirit of double materiality, the ESRS also request companies to delve into where the impacts on the company's workforce and value chain workers that originate in the strategy or business model bring material risks to the company. The ESRS provide examples, including:

- A global pandemic leading to severe worker health impacts, leading in turn to major disruptions to production and distribution;

- Instances of forced labour leading to severe impacts on workers, leading in turn to the confiscation of imported goods that are suspected of being made with forced labour under import bans;
- Suppliers under extreme price pressure sub-contract production, leading to poor working conditions and lower quality products;
- Reliance on low skilled, low-paid workers with minimal protections leading to impacts on the workers, as well as media backlash and consumer preferences moving to more ethically sourced or sustainable goods.

In this disclosure, the ESRS specifically request a brief description of the types of employees and non-employees in the company's workforce, as well as the types of value chain workers who are at risk of material impacts and risks. This is a way of ensuring that companies have tailored their due diligence to specific workers rather than blanket categories of workers. Both ESRS-S1 and ESRS-S2 also request information on whether and how the company has developed an understanding of how people with particular characteristics, those working in particular contexts, or those undertaking particular activities may be at greater risk of harm (for example, trade unionists, migrant workers, home workers, women or young workers).

ESRS-S1 and ESRS-S2 also request information on the systemic nature of human rights risks and impacts. Companies are expected to disclose whether the material negative impacts reported on are widespread or systemic in contexts where the company operates (or has sourcing or other business relationships for value chain workers). (There is also a specific emphasis on child labour and forced labour or compulsory labour in both ESRS-S1 and ESRS-S2, with a request for companies to report on types of operations, geographies and commodities for which there is a significant risk of these issues arising.)

Of particular note, there is a specific emphasis on just transition-related disclosures on the part of companies. When it comes to own workforce, ESRS-S1 requests information on any material impacts on the company's workforce that may arise from transition plans for reducing negative impacts on the environment and achieving greener and climate-neutral operations. This includes information on the impacts on own workforce caused by the company's plans and actions to reduce carbon emissions in line with international agreements – which is viewed as referring to the *Paris Agreement*, even if not explicitly referenced. ESRS-S1 specifically provides that impacts, risks and opportunities include restructuring and employment loss, as well as opportunities arising from job creation and reskilling or upskilling.

Similarly, when it comes to value chain workers, ESRS-S2 requests that companies consider the impacts on value chain workers that may arise from the transition to greener and climate-neutral operations. Potential impacts referenced include impacts associated with innovation and restructuring, closure of mines, increased mining of minerals needed for the transition to a sustainable economy, and solar panel production.

Just transition also is referenced when it comes to material positive impacts: companies are asked, in the case of material positive impacts, to include a brief description of the activities that result in the positive impacts (for example, updated purchasing practices, capacity-building to supply chain workers), including providing opportunities for the workforce such as job creation and upskilling in the context of a just transition, and the types of value chain workers that are positively affected or could be positively affected; the company also may disclose whether the positive impacts occur in specific countries or regions.

POLICIES

Why This Matters

Soft law in the field of business and human rights (UNGP 16) expects companies to have a statement of policy through which the company expresses its commitment to respect human rights. Human rights policies are a key grounding for a company's HRDD efforts. It will be a challenge for a company to pay serious attention to its human rights impacts, risks and opportunities, where senior leadership has not articulated the importance of human rights to the company. The 'tone from the top' set by senior leadership in a human rights policy paves the way for meaningful HRDD, which in turn paves the way for meaningful reporting on the outcomes of such due diligence.

We see that, in practice, a human rights policy serves multiple purposes. It:

- Signals the importance of human rights for the company's top leadership;
- Educates senior leadership on what human rights mean in practice for the company;

- Helps the company benefit from internal and external knowledge and expertise;
- Helps the company connect its human rights-related policies to other related policies (for example, health and safety; diversity, equity and inclusion; harassment and violence), as well as to other sustainability policies (for example, climate or nature);
- Provides the foundation for measures that seek to embed the commitment into the company (for example, governance structures, training, incentives);
- Provides the foundation for the company's HRDD efforts;
- Helps protect employees and other workers who seek to live up to the company's human rights commitment.

CSDDD (Article 7) enshrines UNGP 16 into EU law, and expects companies to have a policy in place that contains a description of the company's approach to due diligence developed in prior consultation with the company's employees and their representatives.

Resulting Reporting

ESRS-S1 and ESRS-S2 (*Disclosure Requirements* S1-1 and S2-1) request companies to disclose information on their human rights policies. There also may be specific policies that cover material impacts, risks and opportunities related to the company's own workforce and value chain workers to report on – including, for instance, a supplier code of conduct that applies for value chain workers.

Specifically, ESRS-S1 and ESRS-S2 request that companies disclose whether and how their policies are aligned with the UNGPs. This means that, at a minimum, the human rights policy commitment reported on needs to:

- Commit to respecting all internationally recognised human rights;
- Apply the commitment to respect human rights to impacts the company may cause or contribute to, as well as impacts that are directly linked to the company's operations, products or services by its business relationships;
- Be approved at the most senior level of the company;
- Be informed by relevant internal and/or external expertise;
- Provide for the company's human rights expectations of personnel, business partners and other parties directly linked to its operations, products or services;

- Be publicly available and communicated internally and externally to all personnel, business partners and other relevant parties.

According to ESRS, the disclosure on the human rights policy also can specify:

- Whether the company has specific policies to manage specific material impacts, risks and opportunities related to its own workforce, or whether these are in an overarching policy (for example, related to trafficking in human beings; forced labour or compulsory labour; child labour; non-discrimination; health and safety);

- The company's approach to HRDD. This is also an expectation of the CSDDD. Two areas of due diligence to provide particular attention to reporting on, according to ESRS-S1 and ESRS-S2, are stakeholder engagement (whether the policies provide for engagement with people in the company's own workforce and value chain workers) and remedy (whether the policies provide for measures to provide and/or enable remedy for human rights impacts);

- Whether the provisions of the policies are fully in line with ILO standards;

- Whether the provisions of the policies are aligned with internal business policies – for instance, related to responsible sourcing;

- The company's approach to specific groups, and whether the policies cover specific groups within the company's own workforce or all of its own workforce, and specific groups of value chain workers, or all value chain workers;

- The company's approach to inter-connecting its human rights approach to other sustainability topics, and in particular its approach to implementing a just transition. The *Application Requirements* for this disclosure specifically reference the disclosure of the company's commitment to prevent or mitigate the risks and negative impacts on people in its own workforce of reducing carbon emissions and transitioning to greener and climate-neutral operations, as well as to provide opportunities for the workforce such as job creation and upskilling, including explicit commitments to a just transition.

SELECTED ASPECTS OF HUMAN RIGHTS DUE DILIGENCE

As discussed above, HRDD captures a number of components:

- **Identify and assess:** Identifying and assessing their actual and potential negative impacts on people, and prioritising them for action based on their severity;
- **Engage:** Engaging directly with potentially affected stakeholders or their proxies to understand the human rights impacts from their perspective through human rights due diligence;
- **Integrate and act:** Integrating the findings and taking action to prevent or mitigate potential impacts, and play a role to effectively remediate them when they have arisen;
- **Track:** Tracking the effectiveness of actions taken;
- **Communicate:** Communicating how the company is addressing the impacts.

The first step of identifying and assessing companies' actual and potential negative impacts on people, and prioritising them for action based on their severity is captured in the impact materiality process. And the final step of communicating on a company's HRDD measures is captured in the reporting that results from applying the CSRD.

ESRS-S1 and ESRS-S2, therefore, delve into the remaining steps of HRDD, namely engage, integrate and act (including remediation), and tracking. We go through these in turn.

Worker Engagement

Why it matters

Soft law in the field of business and human rights (UNGP 18) expects companies to undertake meaningful consultation with potentially affected groups and other relevant stakeholders to better understand their human rights risks and impacts. This stakeholder engagement plays a role throughout human rights due diligence, not only to help inform the company's list of salient human rights issues, but also to inform what the company should be doing about them, how they can best remediate them, and how they can measure the effectiveness of their actions.

The UNGPs specifically call for direct engagement with potentially affected stakeholders – for example, workers and their representatives. Engagement with reasonable alternatives (for example, credible independent experts or civil society organisations) can happen in situations where this direct consultation is not possible. The UNGPs also place a specific emphasis on considering how to bring in perspectives from groups or populations that may be at heightened risk of vulnerability or marginalisation – those who are more vulnerable to impacts, and who can be overlooked for company engagement efforts.

Stakeholder engagement is at the cornerstone of HRDD because it helps the company identify human rights impacts, risks and opportunities that it may not have considered, from the people's perspective rather than from the company's. In other words, it helps ensure that the company is not making assumptions about the impacts – or, at the very least, testing its assumptions with those the assumptions are being made about.

Engaging with workers and their representatives on HRDD also helps the company:

- Hear from stakeholders who may be at heightened risk of vulnerability or marginalisation, and who the company is less accustomed to hearing from;
- Evaluate the materiality of impacts and risks from the perspectives of the people who can be impacted;
- Strengthen relationships with those the company may impact, including its workforce;
- Hear about issues, concerns, risks, impacts and opportunities on a pro-active and forward-looking basis;
- Benefit from suggestions of actions to prevent, mitigate and remediate the impacts that it may not have considered itself, from the people who may be impacted themselves;
- Identify helpful indicators and metrics that can be used to track the effectiveness of due diligence actions taken;
- Understand what meaningful communication on HRDD could look like, from the perspective of those the communication is intended for.

At the same time, stakeholder engagement can only achieve these purposes if it is done in the right way. Meaningful stakeholder engagement entails engaging with the right stakeholders, about the right issues, in the right way, at the right time and acting on the results of the engagement. ESRS *Disclosure Requirements* S1-2 and S2-2 seeks to place particular emphasis on these components of meaningful stakeholder engagement, to ensure that the engagement being reported on is valuable to a company's human rights approach.

Resulting reporting

ESRS *Disclosure Requirements* S1-2 and S2-2 specifically ask for information on the company's processes for engaging with its own workforce and workers' representatives (S1), as well as its value chain workers and their legitimate representatives or credible proxies (S2) about material, actual and potential, positive and / or negative impacts that affect or are likely to affect them. There are a number of expectations of reporting intended to help readers of the information understand whether the stakeholder engagement conducted was meaningful – beyond the fact that it happened.

Companies are asked to consider the following (with a mirroring of expectations across S1 and S2, with slight amends to reflect that direct engagement may not be possible in the value chain, and that the scope of Global Framework Agreements will differ when it comes to value chain workers):

- **Who?** For S1, whether direct engagement occurs with people in the company's own workforce and workers' representatives.

  For S2, in addition to direct engagement with value chain workers and their legitimate representatives, S2 also provides for the possibility of engagement with credible proxies. This is to reflect the fact that, in practice, companies at first may engage with local worker organisations, civil society organisations and experts to better understand the perspectives of value chain workers in specific settings. Direct engagement with value chain workers is possible, and does take place, for higher-risk settings – for instance, through human rights impact assessments or other similar assessments. This direct engagement implies a relationship has been built with the relevant supplier, to enable them to open their workplaces to the engagement – in a way that ensures the engagement can be meaningful (for example, without coaching workers about what to say during the engagement).

  In both cases of engagement, the company is asked to discuss any steps it takes to gain insight into the perspectives of workers who may be particularly vulnerable to impacts and / or marginalised (for example, women, migrants, people with disabilities);

- **How?** The stage(s) at which engagement occurs within HRDD, the type of engagement (for example, participation consultation and/or information) and frequency of the engagement.

S1 provides that this can include information on how the company has tailored its engagement to be fit-for-purpose for the stakeholders, such as how it considers potential barriers to engagement with people (for example, language and cultural differences, gender and power imbalances, divisions within a group) and how it provides information that is understandable and accessible through appropriate communication channels. This is particularly important to pay attention to, as not all engagement is equal. Taking active steps to ensure that the engagement works for those being engaged with helps ensure that the company gains the most helpful information possible, while helping ensure that engagement does not lead to unintended consequences of leading to frustrations amongst those engaged with;

- **Where?** For S1, whether engagement activities take place at the organisational level or at a lower level, such as at the site or project level, and, in the latter case, how information from engagement activities is centralised.

- **About what?** Whether the engagement is related to the company's HRDD, including material, actual and potential, positive and / or negative impacts that affect or are likely to affect those engaged with.

  The *Application Requirements* for S1 specifically request companies to consider how they engage with people in their workforce and workers' representatives on just transition-related impacts – impacts on their own workforce that may arise from reducing carbon emissions and transitioning to greener and climate-neutral operations, in particular restructuring, employment loss or creation, training and up/reskilling, gender and social equity, and health and safety.

- **To what end?** Whether and how the perspectives of its own workforce inform the company's decisions or activities aimed at managing the actual and potential impacts on its own workforce – and for own workforce, how people are informed about the way in which their feedback has influenced the company's decision-making. In this regard, the standards note that the company may provide examples of how the perspectives of workers have informed specific decisions or activities. This expectation is to help avoid engagement happening without any bearing on the impacts identified or resulting actions. Engagement is only meaningful where it takes place on the premise that it will feed into the company's decision-making;

- **Whose responsibility, and which resources?** The function and the most senior role within the company that has operational responsibility for ensuring that this engagement happens, and that the results inform the company's approach – as well as the resources (for example, financial or human resources) allocated to engagement. This expectation is in recognition of the fact that actions happen when they become someone's job, preferably at a senior-level, and when that person (and his / her team) has resources to undertake them;

- **Any related agreement?** Whether the company has a Global Framework Agreement or another agreement with workers' representatives related to the respect of human rights of its own workforce or another agreement with global union federations related to the rights of value chain workers. If so, how the agreement enables the company to gain insight into the workers' perspectives;

- **Effectiveness?** How the company assesses the effectiveness of its engagement with its workforce.

The CSDDD (Article 13) also expects companies to carry out meaningful engagement with stakeholders. The law provides for occasions where this engagement is needed throughout due diligence (when assessing risks and impacts, when acting on them – and, in particular, when deciding to terminate or suspend a business relationship as well as when remediating, and when developing indicators). Companies are further asked to identify and address barriers to engagement and ensure that those engaged with are not the subject of retaliation or retribution.

Remedy & Grievance Mechanisms

Why it matters

The UNGPs recognise that – even with HRDD processes in place – material impacts can still happen. There may be impacts that companies have been unable to prevent, or have not foreseen. Remedy is relevant where a risk has materialised, and becomes an impact. Remedy is at the heart of human rights: when an impact has occurred, how it is put right? The concept of remedy aims to restore individuals or groups whose rights have been impacted by a company's activities to the situation they would have been in had the impact not occurred. Where this is not possible, remedy can involve compensation or other forms of remedy that seek to make amends for the impact.

Soft law in the field of business and human rights (UNGP 22) expects companies to engage in remediation, by themselves or in cooperation with other actors, when impacts have occurred. Soft law contained in the UNGPs clarifies that there are three ways in which a company can be connected to material risks and impacts:

- Cause;
- Contribute;
- Direct linkage.

How a company is connected, in turn, shapes the resulting expectations of that company when it comes to actions to prevent and mitigate (the next disclosure requirement), as well as to remediate (this disclosure requirement).

Imagine a situation where excessive overtime and poor working conditions have arisen at the workplace of a supplier. The role for a buying company when it comes to supporting the remediation of these impacts will not be the same for a buyer that consistently changes its delivery dates on orders at the last minute, without providing additional payment to suppliers, in a context where these poor working conditions impacts are well known (a likely situation of 'contribution'), as for a company that finds these issues in its value chain, but has not taken action to incentivise or facilitate the impacts (a likely situation of 'direct linkage').

The three modes of involvement – cause, contribute and direct linkage – also are reflected in the CSDDD. The Directive uses the same expected actions for the three modes of involvement that exist in the UNGPs, but the text has captured these three modes with terminology related to 'causing'. This is to avoid confusion with existing legal terms in national legal systems, while covering the same causal relations as described in the UNGPs.

These three modes of involvement contained in the UNGPs also are referenced in ESRS-S1 and ESRS-S2. Therefore, it will be helpful for companies to build their understanding of these three modes of involvement, and the resulting expected actions – since they are now being asked to report on these resulting actions under S1-3 and S2-3 related to remediation, and S1-4 and S2-4 related to actions (see **Figure 7.3**).

These expected actions are also contained in the CSDDD. Of particular note, CSDDD also contains the expectation of playing a role in the remedy eco-system in situations of direct linkage. The text provides that a company may provide voluntary remediation and may use its ability to influence the business partner that is causing the adverse impact to provide remediation.

Figure 7.3: Modes of Involvement & Related Expected Actions

Mode of involvement	Explanation	Expectation of action	Expectation of remedy
Cause Under CSDDD: the company causes by itself	When the company's actions or omissions on their own are sufficient to cause a material impact.	Take the necessary steps to cease or prevent the impact.	Remedy the impact.
Contribution Under CSDDD: the company causes jointly with subsidiaries or business partners	When the company contributes to an impact through its own activities (whether these are actions or omissions), including by incentivising or facilitating other entities to contribute to impacts.	Take the necessary steps to cease or prevent its contribution to the impact. Build and use leverage to mitigate any remaining impact to the greatest extent possible.	Remedy impacts to the extent of its contribution. Build and use leverage to ensure that the other responsible parties play a role in remedy too. This is echoed in CSDDD.
Direct linkage Under CSDDD: the adverse impact is caused only by the company's business partner in its chain of activities	When an impact is directly linked to a company's operations, products or service through a business relationship.	Build and use leverage to seek to prevent the impact from continuing or recurring.	Although not expected to contribute to remedy, one of the most effective ways to build and use leverage is to play a role in enabling remedy to happen, thereby playing a role in the 'remedy eco-system'.

Factors that can help companies understand whether they would be viewed as having contributed to, or viewed as being directly linked to, an impact include:

- The quality of the company's HRDD process;
- The degree to which an activity increased the risk of an impact occurring, by incentivising or facilitating it; and
- The effectiveness of mitigating measures in reducing the risk of impacts occurring.[9]

In particular, whether the company knew or should have known about the risks of impacts plays a role in determining the adequacy of a company's HRDD, and therefore which mode of involvement applies.

Determining whether a company has contributed to, or is directly linked to, impacts is not a static assessment. Companies can move along a continuum of involvement in impacts (from direct linkage to contribution, and *vice versa*), depending on the context and the actions taken or omissions made by the company at different moments in time.

Operational-level grievance mechanisms (OGMs) for those potentially impacted by the company's activities can be one effective means of enabling remediation – provided they *are* effective. In addition to helping support the provision of remedy where a company causes or contributes to negative impacts, grievance mechanisms also help inform a company's HRDD.

OGMs enable companies to hear directly from workers, including those who are most vulnerable – this is more resource-efficient than other methods for gathering issues, such as audits, assessments and certifications. In addition, OGMs help companies:

- Provide, contribute to or enable remedy for impacts that have arisen;
- Hear about and address issues before they escalate into material risks and impacts;
- Receive valuable input on how the company is perceived and the effectiveness of its actions and decisions;
- Improve on a continuous basis where complaints point to weaknesses in company policies, processes and practices;
- Identify patterns and trends over time;
- Demonstrate that it cares about the concerns of affected stakeholders and is committed to hearing and addressing them.

At the same time, practice in OGMs has shown that it can be a particular challenge for companies to design and operate OGMs that actually work for the intended users. There is an imbalance of power between those creating the OGM and those using it, and the operating context may not lend itself well to the use of an OGM. Well-documented challenges include OGMs that:

- May exist in practice but are not used (for example, for fear of retaliation, lack of confidence that actions will arise, lack of trust in the back-end);
- Are used for minor issues but are not used for the most important issues;
- Are not accessible to stakeholders, especially those that are illiterate, vulnerable, and marginalised;
- Do not protect the confidentiality of stakeholders;
- Do not provide meaningful remedy.

To help ensure that OGMs can be a helpful tool for due diligence and remedying impacts, the soft law expectations provide for criteria (known as the 'effectiveness criteria') that companies are expected to consider as they create their OGMs (**Figure 7.4**).

Under CSDDD (Article 9), companies also need to create a complaints procedure to enable persons to submit complaints related to impacts. This procedure needs to be fair, publicly available, accessible, predictable and transparent, and the directive specifically references the UNGPs effectiveness criteria.

Resulting reporting

Disclosure Requirements S1-3 and S2-3 specifically ask for information on:

- The processes the company has in place to provide for, or cooperate in, the remediation of negative impacts on people in its workforce, as well as on value chain workers that the company is connected with;
- Channels available to its workforce and value chain workers to raise concerns and have them addressed.

The disclosure expectation reiterates the soft law expectations related to the company's approach to and processes for providing or contributing to remedy where it has caused or contributed to a material negative impact on people in its own workforce. Companies are asked to consider whether and how people that may be affected are able to access channels at the level of the company they are employed by, or contracted to work for, in relation to each material impact. A similar consideration is included for own value chain workers in the *Application Requirements*.

Figure 7.4: Effectiveness Criteria & Guiding Questions

Effectiveness criteria	Description (from UNGP 31)	Guiding questions provided by ESRS-S1 (in its *Application Requirements*)
1. Legitimate	Enabling trust from the stakeholder groups for whose use they are intended, and being accountable for the fair conduct of grievance processes.	Do the channels have legitimacy by providing appropriate accountability for their fair conduct and building stakeholder trust?
2. Accessible	Being known to all stakeholder groups for whose use they are intended, and providing adequate assistance for those who may face particular barriers to access.	Are the channels known and accessible to stakeholders?
3. Predictable	Providing a clear and known procedure with an indicative time frame for each stage, and clarity on the types of process and outcome available and means of monitoring implementation.	Do the channels have clear and known procedures, with indicative timeframes?
4. Equitable	Seeking to ensure that aggrieved parties have reasonable access to sources of information, advice and expertise necessary to engage in a grievance process on fair, informed and respectful terms.	Do the channels ensure reasonable access for stakeholders to sources of information, advice and expertise?
5. Transparent	Keeping parties to a grievance informed about its progress, and providing sufficient information about the mechanism's performance to build confidence in its effectiveness and meet any public interest at stake.	Do the channels offer transparency by providing sufficient information both to complainants and, where applicable, to meet any public interest?

Effectiveness criteria	Description (from UNGP 31)	Guiding questions provided by ESRS-S1 (in its *Application Requirements*)
6. Rights-compatible	Ensuring that outcomes and remedies accord with internationally recognised human rights.	Do outcomes achieved through the channels accord with internationally recognised human rights?
7. A source of continuous learning	Drawing on relevant measures to identify lessons for improving the mechanism and preventing future grievances and harm.	Does the company identify insights from the channels that support continuous learning in both improving the channels and preventing future impacts?
8. Dialogue and engagement	Consulting the stakeholder groups for whose use they are intended on their design and performance, and focusing on dialogue as the means to address and resolve grievances.	Does the company focus on dialogue with complainants as the means to reach agreed solutions, rather than seeking to unilaterally determine the outcome?

There is a focus on effectiveness of remedy: the reporting includes whether and how the company assesses that the remedy provided is effective, as well as the effectiveness of channels used, including through the involvement of stakeholders who are intended users. In explaining whether and how the company knows that workers are aware of and trust any of these channels, the *Application Requirement* provides that the company may provide relevant and reliable data about the effectiveness of these channels from the perspective of the people concerned. Examples of sources of information are surveys of people in the workforce that have used such channels and their levels of satisfaction with the process and outcomes. This also includes disclosure on whether the company has policies in place regarding the protection of individuals that use the mechanisms against retaliation.

In describing the effectiveness of channels for its own workforce and workers' representatives to raise concerns, the *Application Requirements* specifically reference the UNGP effectiveness criteria, and provides probing questions (referenced above).

Taking Action on Material Impacts & the Effectiveness of Those Actions

Why it matters

Soft law in the field of business and human rights (UNGP 19) expects companies to take appropriate action to prevent and mitigate adverse human rights impacts. These prevention and mitigation efforts are forward-looking – focused on attempting to stop risks from becoming impacts. Where risks have become actual impacts, then the focus turns to remediation, as referenced above.

Where a company causes or may cause an adverse human rights impact, it should take the necessary steps to cease or prevent the impact. At the same time, the UNGPs recognise that, in situations of contribution and direct linkage, there will be instances where a third party is, or third parties are, involved in the human rights impacts. In these cases, a company's leverage (its influence) over those third parties to get them to change their behaviour – and its ability to increase leverage, where necessary – becomes crucial. This is echoed in the CSDDD. **Figure 7.4** helps explain how the use of leverage is relevant for acting on certain impacts.

Resulting reporting

Disclosure Requirements S1-4 and S2-4 call on a company to disclose the action plans and resources to manage its material impacts, risks, and opportunities related to its own workforce, as well as related to its value chain workers. This echoes the expectations of soft law, as the expectations of disclosure relate to actions taken, planned or underway to prevent or mitigate material negative impacts – as well as actions to provide or enable remedy in relation to an actual material impact.

Companies are specifically asked to describe the processes through which they identify what action is needed and appropriate in response to particular actual or potential negative impacts on their workforce and value chain workers. The distinct actions, depending on the mode of involvement, will help feed into this articulation of the appropriate resulting actions. The *Application Requirements* specifically describe that the appropriate action taken by the company can vary, according to whether the company causes or contributes to a material impact, or whether it is involved because the impact is directly linked to its operations, products or services by a business relationship.

In light of the importance of leverage in two modes of involvement (contribution and direct linkage), the *Application Requirements* also provide that a company may disclose whether and how it seeks to use its leverage in its business relationships to manage those impacts. The company also may refer to the use of commercial leverage (for example, enforcing contractual requirements with business relationships or implementing incentives), as well as other forms of leverage within the relationship (such as providing training or capacity-building on workers' rights) or collaborative leverage with peers or other actors (such as initiatives aimed at responsible recruitment or ensuring workers receive an adequate wage).

This echoes the prevailing guidance around use of leverage, which includes many forms – one-on-one with business partners, as well as with other stakeholders (other buyers, for instance, or with a civil society organisation), as well as with a range of stakeholders, including governments where helpful, as part of multi-stakeholder leverage. In light of growing scrutiny on the effectiveness of industry and multi-stakeholder initiatives, the *Application Requirements* specifically provide that the company may disclose how the initiative, and its own involvement in the initiative, is aiming to address the material impact concerned. It may report (under the next disclosure requirement ESRS-S1-5 or ESRS-S2-5) the relevant targets set by the initiative and progress towards them.

Of particular note, there is an emphasis on purchasing practices in ESRS-S1-4 and ESRS-S2-4. Companies are asked to disclose whether and how they ensure that their own practices do not cause or contribute to material negative impacts on their own workforce, including, where relevant, their practices in relation to procurement, sales and data use. The same applies for value chain workers, with companies asked to disclose whether and how they take action to avoid causing or contributing to material negative impacts on value chain workers through their own practices. This may include disclosing what approach is taken when tensions arise between the prevention or mitigation of material negative impacts and other business pressures. The ESRS also specifically point to whether the company has taken any internal actions to address specific material negative impacts, including any action in relation to its own purchasing practices.

This emphasis on purchasing practices is also included in the CSDDD, which includes a consideration for companies to adapt their own business plans, overall strategies and operations, including purchasing practices, design and distribution practices.

There is also an emphasis on the resources allocated to the management of the company's material impacts, with a request for disclosure of the allocated resources, which may include an explanation of which internal functions are involved in managing the impacts and what types of action they take to address the impacts.

There is a focus on responsible disengagement in both ESRS. Companies are asked to disclose whether and how they consider actual and potential impacts on their own workforce and value chain workers in decisions to terminate business relationships, as well as and whether and how they seek to address any negative impacts that may result from termination. This can include examples.

There is also a focus on just transition. Specifically, when it comes to own workforce, the *Application Requirements* provides that, if the company has taken measures to mitigate negative impacts on its own workforce that arise from the transition to a greener, climate-neutral economy, such as training and reskilling, employment guarantees, and in the case of downscaling or mass dismissal, measures such as job counselling, coaching, intra-company placements and early retirement plans, the company shall disclose those measures. This includes measures to comply with prevailing regulation. The company also may highlight present and / or expected external developments that influence whether dependencies turn into risks. This includes consideration of impacts that may arise from the transition to greener and climate-neutral operations.

Finally, although this disclosure requirement relates to action, it also includes a component of tracking effectiveness. Companies are asked to describe how they track and assess the effectiveness of the actions and initiatives undertaken related to the material impacts related to their workforce and value chain workers. This is intended to help readers of the report understand the connection between actions taken by the company, and the effective management of impacts. Examples provided include data showing a decrease in the number of incidents identified (for workforce), and survey feedback from the suppliers' workers showing that working conditions have improved since the time the company began working with those suppliers (for value chain workers). Stakeholder feedback, impact assessments, and the outcomes of grievance mechanisms are viewed as particularly helpful tools for assessing effectiveness in this field.

Targets

Why it matters

Soft law in the field of business and human rights (UNGP 20) expects companies to track the effectiveness of their response to adverse human rights risks and impacts. This tracking helps companies know whether their human rights policies are being implemented optimally and whether they have responded effectively to the identified human rights impacts. This helps in turn drive continuous improvement. The UNGPs expect tracking to be based on appropriate qualitative and quantitative indicators, and to draw on feedback from both internal and external sources, including affected stakeholders. Similarly, under CSDDD, companies are expected to monitor the implementation, adequacy and effectiveness of their due diligence measures. They can do this periodically, and every 12 months.

Resulting reporting

The objective of the *Disclosure Requirements* S1-5 and S2-5 are to enable an understanding of the extent to which the company is using outcome-oriented targets to drive and measure its progress in addressing its material negative impacts and/or advancing positive impacts on its own workforce and value chain workers, and/or in managing material risks and opportunities related to its workforce and value chain workers.

The disclosure includes the process undertaken for setting the targets for the workforce. For own workforce (S1), this includes whether and how the company engaged directly with its own workforce or workers' representatives in setting the targets, tracking the company's performance against them and identifying any lessons or improvements as a result of the company's performance. For value chain workers (S2), the focus is on engagement with workers in the value chain, their legitimate representatives or credible proxies. In this way, the resulting disclosure brings in an emphasis of stakeholder engagement – as provided for in the soft law's expectation of stakeholder engagement through the process of HRDD. There is a specific focus on effectiveness of tracking, with a reference to time-bound targets and outcome-oriented targets.

The *Application Requirements* provide specific guidance on this point. The company may disclose the intended outcomes to be achieved in the lives of a certain number of people in its own workforce (S1), or in the lives of value chain workers (S2), being as specific as possible. The company also may disclose the standards or commitments which the targets are based on (for instance codes of conduct, sourcing policies, global frameworks, or industry codes). The company can also distinguish between short-, medium- and long-term targets.

The ESRS acknowledge that targets related to impacts at times may be the same as targets related to risks and opportunities, in light of the strong connection between impact materiality and financial materiality. For instance, the *Application Requirements* provide the illustration of a target related to living / adequate wage, which could both reduce impacts on people, while also reducing associated risks in terms of the quality and reliability of their output:

AR 51. The undertaking may also distinguish between short-, medium- and long-term targets covering the same policy commitment. For example, the undertaking may have a long-term target to achieve an 80% reduction in health and safety incidents affecting its delivery drivers by 2030 and a near-term target to reduce the overtime hours of delivery drivers by x% while maintaining their income by 2024.

THEMES & ISSUES

ESRS-S1 and ESRS-S2 delve into a number of social and human rights matters, grouped into three categories:

- Working conditions;
- Equal treatment and opportunities for all;
- Other work-related rights.

Companies are expected to consider these matters in their materiality assessments. This is viewed as a non-exhaustive list, and although ESRS-S1 includes some specific disclosures on some of these more detailed topics, equally this does not mean that other social and human rights standards are not to be considered. The following provides some further context on the social and human rights topics referenced in ESRS-S1 and ESRS-S2, and why they merit consideration by companies in their materiality assessment – both for impact materiality, as well as financial materiality reasons.

Working Conditions

Secure employment

The ILO defines secure employment as "protection against disruptions in worker income resulting from job loss". It can be ensured by providing secure and official contracts at the time of hiring, as well as fair treatment for protecting workers' income security and hours – while allowing organisations to adapt to the changing market and economy.[10]

Secure employment is declining. For instance, a survey of over 6,000 US workers conducted by the *Harvard Business Review* found that "historically, job security – and the predictable income, attractive benefits, peace of mind, and career progression it represents – has been one of the main attractions of traditional full-time employment".[11] The study finds that, in recent years, many do not feel secure in their roles due to declining payroll, mass layoffs and a decrease in job quality.

Secure employment is more at risk where companies rely on certain types of contracts for their workforce, that do not give the protection of employment contracts. For instance, there has been significant scrutiny of zero hour contracts, which tend to lead to both contractual and financial insecurity.[12] Secure employment is more at risk where companies have these contracts in their value chain. It is also more at risk where companies rely on the informal economy in their business. Informal workers often lack social protections, reducing job security. In 2022, the ILO reported that 58% of workers (roughly 2 billion people) were informal.[13] During the Covid-19 pandemic, this group was disproportionately affected by job loss.

Providing secure employment helps avoid a number of impacts on workers – including overload, precarious working conditions, and strains on physical and mental health. When workers experience instability in the number of hours they work, they are more vulnerable to suffering from worsened health-related outcomes, like increased stress and fatigue, poor sleep quality, and difficulty in accessing medical care. They may also experience difficulty in accessing consistent childcare, continuing education, maintaining family relationships, and having predictable earnings.[14] Not providing secure employment can also be costly to the business, in the form of reduced productivity, high turnover, loss of knowledge and expertise, and higher recruitment costs.

Working time

Working time is governed by ILO standards, which provide for 48 hours per week and a standard working day of eight hours maximum, with limited overtime allowed. Workers are also entitled to at least 24 hours of rest every seven days, and three weeks' paid leave each year.

In 2021, the World Health Organization (WHO) and the ILO published a landmark study on working hours, finding that the number of people working long hours (55 hours or more per week) is increasing and stands at 479 million people, which is 9% of the global population.[15] The study found that long working hours led to 745,000 deaths from stroke and ischemic heart disease in 2016 – up 29% since 2000. It concludes that working long hours is responsible for about one-third of the total estimated work-related burden of disease.

Working excessive working hours will be even more detrimental to workers' health as the planet warms up. In 2024, Climate Rights International published a report highlighting the risks and impacts of rising global temperatures on workers and reported that, from 2018 to 2022, on average there were 86 days of life-threatening high temperatures annually[16] – especially relevant for certain workers, such as agricultural workers, who have long hours outside. Impacts on worker health in turn have impacts on companies, including lower quality of resulting products, diminished productivity, and impact on worker morale and engagement.

Social protection
The ILO defines social protection as "benefits to individuals on the basis of risks faced across the life cycle (for example, unemployment, disability, maternity, etc.) and to those suffering general poverty and social exclusion".[17] The ILO further finds that, as of 2020, the global population covered by at least one social protection was 46.9% – leaving close to 4.1 billion people without protection.[18]

The importance of social protection in the workplace has become all the more apparent in the aftermath of the Covid-19 pandemic, which exposed on a global scale the vulnerabilities present in the workforce and across regions. In the words of the ILO, the vulnerabilities exacerbated and created "high levels of economic insecurity, persistent poverty, rising inequality, extensive informality and a fragile social contract".[19] Traditionally, vulnerable groups, such as migrants, women and young people, also faced disproportionate challenges, as these groups are more likely to take on informal work, and therefore experience less protection.[20]

Lack of effective social protections can greatly impact workers in several ways. In addition to financial insecurity and increased poverty, it can lead to workers neglecting their health, stress and mental health issues, and increased social inequality. This, in turn, can be passed down to future generations, perpetuating cycles of poverty and limited opportunities. These impacts on workers can also impact companies – for instance, leading to reduced productivity, increased absenteeism and higher turnover rates.

Adequate wages
Living wage is defined by the Global Living Wage Coalition as: "the remuneration received for a standard workweek by a worker in a particular place sufficient to afford a decent standard of living for the worker and her or his family".[21]

Living wage tends to be higher than a minimum wage. Even so, the ILO has found that the number of workers and families earning less than the minimum wage is growing.[22] The ILO reports on workers in extreme poverty (earning less than $2.15 per day per person in purchasing power parity (PPP) terms) and in poverty (less than $3.65 per day per person). In 2023, the number of workers in extreme poverty increased by 1 million, and those in moderate poverty increased by around 8.4 million. Although the majority of G20 countries have seen their employment growth increase, workers' wages have decreased.[23] The rise in inflation has exacerbated the issue, with wages unable to match the cost of living due to increases in the cost of basic needs, which puts a living wage out of reach. The Living Wage Foundation has found that part-time workers, contract workers, minority workers, and women in particular need pay increases to achieve a living wage.[24]

Adequate wages enable workers and their families to achieve a secure and decent standard of living. With adequate wages they can meet their basic needs, such as food, housing, healthcare, education, transport and clothing. In addition, studies have shown that greater economic security for workers contributes to higher productivity and morale within companies, which in turn results in lower worker turnover and higher revenues and profit.[25]

Disclosure Requirement S1-10 focuses on adequate wages, specifically whether employees are paid an adequate wage in line with applicable benchmarks and, if they are not all paid an adequate wage, the countries and percentage of employees concerned. Practice by leading companies is to commit to paying a living wage, and to find ways in which to support their suppliers in meeting living wage over time. The *Application Requirements* acknowledge this direction of travel by referencing benchmarks that meet the criteria set out by the Sustainable Trade Initiative IDH (*Roadmap on Living Wages: A Platform to Secure Living Wages in Supply Chains*), including applicable benchmarks aligned with the Anker methodology, or provided by the Wage Indicator Foundation or Fair Wage Network.[26]

Collective bargaining, social dialogue, and freedom of association

The ILO defines collective bargaining as "a key means through which employers and their organizations and trade unions can establish fair wages and working conditions. It also provides the basis for sound labour relations. Typical issues on the bargaining agenda include wages, working time, training, occupational health and safety and equal treatment".[27]

The ILO finds that social dialogue includes four components:

- "Negotiation, consultation and information exchange between and among governments, employers' and workers' organizations";
- "Collective bargaining between employers / employers' organizations and workers' organizations";

- "Dispute prevention and resolution";
- "Other approaches such as workplace cooperation, international framework agreements and social dialogue in the context of regional economic communities".[28]

In 2023, the International Trade Union Confederation (ITUC) found that "87% of countries violated the right to strike, while 79% violated the right to collective bargaining".[29] The ITUC further found that, since 2014, every region of the world has experienced a decline in performance on fundamental workers' rights, with a particular focus on a decline in the right to freedom of association, right to strike and collective bargaining.[30]

When it comes to freedom of association, the ILO finds that the "right of workers and employers to form and join organizations of their own choosing is an integral part of a free and open society".[31]

Freedom of association and the right to collective bargaining are together considered an 'enabling right' because they provide workers with the capability to come together to organise, express, and pursue their joint interests, which in turn facilitates the exercise of other rights and enhances their overall effectiveness. In other words, without freedom of association and the right to collective bargaining, it is likely that a range of other rights will be impacted – and therefore material for companies. Providing freedom of association and the right to collective bargaining is also found to have a number of other business benefits, including a greater involvement of workers in decision-making, a greater likelihood of reaching sustainability targets and a more committed and motivated workforce.[32]

Work-life balance

The ILO defines work-life balance as "paid work that allows workers to meet their material needs and fulfil their personal lives at the same time".[33] Therefore, this aspect of work-life balance is closely connected to the aspect of the number of hours of work (working time). It also relates to how these hours are organised, such as work schedules.[34] For instance, unpredictable and inflexible working arrangements can impact workers' health and well-being and lead to unhealthy work-life balance.

A lack of a work-life balance can impact people in a number of ways. Poor work-life balance can lead to severe mental and physical health issues, such as stress, impaired sleep and memory, depression, heavy drinking, diabetes, and heart disease.[35] The WHO has classified 'burnout' as an occupational phenomenon caused by unmanaged workplace stress, which manifests as feeling tired and depleted at work, feeling negative towards work, and reduced efficacy at work.[36]

Poor work-life balance also affects a company's bottom line. Exhausted and overwhelmed workers lead to higher rates of absenteeism and employee turnover, as well as rising health insurance costs for businesses. A lack of sleep and rest also reduces productivity.[37] Conversely, companies that implement work-life balance policies benefit from improved retention of employees and recruitment, lower rates of absenteeism and higher productivity.[38] In addition, a study has found that better work-life balance policies can facilitate improved diversity outcomes in the workforce.[39]

The *Disclosure Requirement* S1-15 focuses on one dimension of work-life balance: the extent to which workers can take family-related leave in a gender-equitable manner. As described above, there may be other aspects of work-life balance that companies can disclose, for impact materiality, or financial materiality, or both.

Health & safety

The ILO defines 'health' in a work context as not only the absence of disease or infirmity, but also the physical and mental elements that can affect health related to safety at work.[40] Impacts can include risks to physical safety, biological hazards, chemicals and hazardous substances and ergonomic and psychosocial hazards.[41] The ILO requires the implementation of health and safety policies in the workplace, including action to ensure these policies are effective and improve working conditions.[42] The primary principle is prevention of accidents and injuries in the workplace by minimising hazards in the workplace as much as is reasonably possible.[43]

The ILO has estimated that every year around 3 million people die of work-related injury or disease, and that 395 million face non-fatal injuries.[44] Certain sectors, such as agriculture, forestry and fishing, mining, construction, and manufacturing, are more hazardous to workers: 200,000 fatal injuries occur across these sectors every year, representing 60% of all fatal occupational injuries.[45] In addition, workers in non-standard employment, including informal work, platform-based work and homework, may face higher health and safety risks due to a lack of protection.[46]

In terms of mental health, the WHO reports that poor working conditions, like discrimination and inequality, excessive work, limited job control and job insecurity, can pose a risk to the mental health of workers.[47]

Some health and safety-related impacts are evolving due to global factors. For example, in light of rising temperatures across the globe, heat stress is a significant risk to workers' health, especially those working in manual labour-heavy professions like warehousing and construction.[48] Heat stress can cause serious illness or death.[49] The risk of heat stress is projected to continue to rise as climate change intensifies, with the most immediate and severe risks to workers in already heat-stressed places. This is also significant for business. The ILO predicts that, by 2030, the impacts of heat stress could result in a productivity loss of at minimum 2.2% of total working hours worldwide, equivalent to 80 million full-time jobs.[50]

For business, lost hours of work due to accidents and injuries can lower productivity, lead to litigation or regulatory fines, increase insurance costs or even temporarily halt business activities. Mental health impacts also can affect individual worker productivity and can increase absenteeism and turnover.

Equal Treatment & Opportunities for All

Gender equality & equal pay for work of equal value
Fair wages and equal remuneration (and the broader concept of equality and non-discrimination) is a fundamental human right recognised in international human rights law.[51] In short, workers – irrespective of their sex/gender – should be paid the same for identical tasks and for different work considered of equal value.

The ILO found in 2022 that the gender pay gap currently stands at 20%, which means that women are earning 80% of what men do for work of equal value.[52] The cumulative effect of pay disparities "has real, daily negative consequences for women, their families, and society, especially during crises".[53] The World Economic Forum (WEF) has recently estimated that, at the current rate of progress, it will take 134 years (five generations) to close the global gender gap and 152 years to close the gap in women's economic participation.[54] Pay gaps are exacerbated by inequity that is present in higher-paying roles. For example, women account for 42% of the global workforce and only 31.7% of senior leaders. They also make up only 28.8% of the science, technology, engineering, and mathematics (STEM) workforce.[55]

Pay equity, between genders and workers, matters because pay inequity breeds injustice and entrenches poverty. Tackling pay inequity helps companies comply with laws and regulations on pay equity and avoid legal disputes and penalties. It also helps companies create a more positive work environment, where employees feel valued, motivated and productive, which can improve worker retention. In turn, businesses save on costs associated with hiring and training new employees and improve their bottom line.[56]

Training & skills development
Both the UDHR and the ICESCR recognise that, as part of the right to education, technical and professional education should be made available

to everyone.[57] The UN Committee on Economic, Social & Cultural Rights also links skills development to the right to equal opportunity for promotion (a component of decent work). Obstacles to promotion should be removed, including through opportunities for training.[58]

The importance of skills and training will grow as the world shifts towards what the ILO calls the "future of work" — namely, "transformative change in the world of work, driven by technological innovations, demographic shifts, environmental and climate change, and globalization, as well as at a time of persistent inequalities".[59] These trends are expected to transform over 1.1 billion jobs in the next decade.[60] However, around 450 million young people (7 in 10) are economically disengaged due to a lack of adequate skills to find work in the labour market.[61] In addition, women tend to face higher barriers to gaining the skills needed for the future of work; the WEF has found that gender gaps are more likely in fields that require technical skills in areas like cloud computing, data and AI, and engineering.[62]

Improving workers' access to professional growth opportunities can increase the retention of employees, improve workers' productivity and engagement, and enhance workers' leadership capabilities.[63] In addition, for companies to adapt to a changing economy requires that workers have the skills to make the transition. Closing the skills gap could lead to the global economy gaining an estimated US$6.5 trillion in the next seven years (5% to 6% of GDP).[64]

Employment & inclusion of persons with disabilities

The UN *Convention on the Rights of Persons with Disabilities* (CRPD) recognises the equality of all people, including the right of persons with disabilities to work on an equal basis with others.[65] The ILO also provides for specific vocational interventions to allow persons with disabilities to have equal access to the job market.[66]

In 2016, the ILO reported that people with disabilities account for close to 15% of the world's population, and 80% are of working age.[67] In 2019, the OECD found that the employment rate for persons with disabilities in 32 OECD countries was 27% lower than for people without disability. This gap tends to be worse for women with disabilities.[68] The ILO has reported that those with disabilities face obstacles to equal opportunities in the world of work, due to social attitudes and physical and informational barriers. In comparison to people without disabilities, employment and economic gaps can put persons with disabilities at greater risk of insufficient social protection, which is necessary to reduce extreme poverty.[69]

Studies of persons with disabilities in the workforce have shown that equal opportunity to work is a source of identity, and provides feelings of normality, opportunities for socialisation and financial support.[70] Inclusion of persons with disability in the workplace has benefits for business. According to a study of 140 US companies, workplaces with better inclusion of persons with disabilities on average had 28% higher revenue, two times more net income, and 30% higher economic profit margins. They also can experience better recruitment and retention of employees and reputational benefits.[71]

Measures against violence & harassment in the workplace
The ILO recognises the right of everyone to a workplace free from violence and harassment.[72] It defines violence and harassment as "unacceptable behaviours, practices or threats that are intended to or can result in physical, psychological, sexual or economic harm".[73] Gender-based violence and harassment (GBVH) is included in this definition.[74]

More than one in five people (almost 23%) have experienced violence and harassment at work, whether physical, psychological or sexual, according to a study of 121 countries.[75] This can cause negative impacts on workers' physical and mental health, well-being, dignity and self-esteem.[76] It also increases the risk of physical health issues, such as musculoskeletal disorders and cardiovascular diseases.[77]

At the same time, workplace violence and harassment are bad for businesses because they can increase absenteeism and staff turnover; increase recruitment, onboarding and training costs; reduce morale, performance and productivity; damage a company's reputation; and increase insurance premiums for business.[78]

Diversity
All people have the right to equality and non-discrimination, including enjoying other rights set out by international human rights conventions.[79] Diversity can manifest in many different ways in the workforce. The ILO acknowledges the importance of diversity in workplaces, across gender, ethnicity, race, Indigenous status, disability, HIV status, sexual orientation and gender identity.[80] In some contexts, other factors can also result in discrimination, like age and religion.

Discrimination can lead to negative physical and mental health outcomes. For example, one study found that people who face discrimination in the workplace have a higher risk of developing high blood pressure than adults who reported less discrimination at work.[81] In addition, a survey of US workers found that workplace discrimination can affect employees' perceptions of the company culture, available opportunities and co-workers' intentions. It can also impact feelings of psychological safety and belonging and may negatively impact their ability to perform at work.[82]

Intersectionality (how multiple forms of inequality exacerbate one another) means that different groups may experience different levels of discrimination in the workplace.[83] For example, the experiences of racism and sexism can intersect for women of colour, Indigenous women, migrant women and other marginalised groups.[84] In Brazil, the pay gap between white men and white women in 2019 was 26%, but 56% between white men and Black women.[85] In the aforementioned survey of US workers, Black and Hispanic workers reported higher levels of discrimination and had lower levels of workplace well-being compared to other colleagues, demonstrating that discrimination does not impact all people equally.[86]

For companies, having a more diverse workforce and acknowledging the complexities brought by intersectionality can increase employee satisfaction, retention and recruitment; can decrease absenteeism and turnover; and result in higher productivity and innovative thinking.[87] Conversely, not addressing the issue of discrimination in the workplace can lead to legal risk, reputational and brand risk, and financial risk and pressure from investors.

Other Work-related Rights

Child labour

The ILO conventions *Minimum Age Convention No. 138* and the *Worst Forms of Child Labour Convention No. 182* outline definitions of child labour.[88] Child labour is work that is mentally, physically, socially or morally dangerous and harmful to children. It also refers to work that interferes with children's schooling by depriving them of the opportunity to attend school, obliging them to leave school prematurely, or requiring them to attempt to combine school attendance with excessively long and heavy work.[89] Whether work can be called child labour depends on a range of factors, including the child's age, the type of work, the hours worked, the conditions under which the work takes place and individual countries' objectives.

As of 2021, UNICEF and the ILO report that globally 160 million children (1 in 10) are involved in child labour.[90] This is more extreme in low-income countries; as of 2023, UNICEF data shows that 1 in 5 children in the world's poorest countries are in child labour.[91] The ILO-UNICEF global estimates shows that from 2016 to 2020, the number of children engaged in child labour rose by more than 8 million.[92] Global shocks like the Covid-19 pandemic have increased the number of children in child labour.[93] Child labour also needs to be accounted for in a just transition. As climate change intensifies, child labour is expected to grow.[94] In addition, children also are increasingly found in renewable energy supply chains, according to research by the US Department of Labor's International Labor Affairs Bureau.[95]

Child labour not only jeopardises the mental and physical health of the child, but many children engaged in child labour are unable to complete their schooling, and as a result are more likely to be illiterate, greatly decreasing their chances of finding decent work.[96] In other words, the impacts continue throughout their lifetime. Certain factors like access to decent work opportunities, the right to collective bargaining and poverty also increase the likelihood of child labour, demonstrating the complexity and systemic nature of the issue.[97]

While child labour can be very difficult to detect in the value chain because of its hidden nature, it poses risks in the private sector. Child labour is found in every country and across all sectors, with 70% of children in child labour in agriculture, 19.7% in services and 10.3% in industry.[98] Instances of child labour in a company's own operations or supply chain can impact brand reputation, increase legal risk, increase investor pressure and the likelihood of divestment, and can disrupt operations if a company terminates supplier contracts.

Forced labour
The ILO defines forced labour as "all work or service which is exacted from any person under the threat of a penalty and for which the person has not offered himself or herself voluntarily".[99] In short, forced labour refers to situations where employers take advantage of workers' vulnerability using deception, threats and abuse of power. The ILO lists 11 indicators of forced labour: abuse of vulnerability; deception; restriction of movement; isolation; physical and sexual violence; intimidation and threats; retention of identity documents; withholding of wages; debt bondage; abusive working and living conditions; and excessive overtime. Often victims of forced labour are subject to a combination of aspects of these indicators, but not all of these indicators need to be in place for forced labour to occur.[100]

The ILO has found that the private sector gains from forced labour by nearly US$10,000 profit per victim, a total of US$236 billion generated from forced labour annually.[101] Profits from forced labour are highest in industry (mining and quarrying, manufacturing, construction and utilities), and in services (wholesale and trade, accommodation and food service activities, art and entertainment, personal services, administrative and support services, education, health and social services, and transport and storage).[102]

The ILO reports that compounding global crises, especially climate change, the Covid-19 pandemic and armed conflict, are increasing the risk of forced labour. These crises are increasing the risks of forced labour through disruptions to stable employment and education, increases in informal employment, increases in extreme poverty and forced migration, and an increase in rates of gender-based violence.[103] At the same time, certain groups of people – such as children, people living in poverty, migrant and refugee workers – are disproportionately impacted by forced labour due to inherent vulnerabilities.[104] For instance, migrant workers are at higher risk of forced labour exploitation because they are targeted for their lack of language skills and support networks, as well as their reliance on employers for accommodation, food and legal right to remain in the country.[105]

Victims of forced labour often face psychological and physical consequences like depression, post-traumatic stress disorder and other anxiety disorders, thoughts of suicide and disabling physical pain.[106]

Businesses with instances of forced labour are subject to increased risks of legal action, regulatory consequences like fines and loss of permits, sanctions, and operational risks if they choose to disengage from suppliers where forced labour has been identified. Import bans halting goods at borders when they have been made in situations of forced labour are a particularly important business risk. Companies also face reputational risks, investor pressure and risks of divestment.[107]

Adequate housing

The right to adequate housing includes freedom from forced eviction and destruction of home; freedom from arbitrary interference of one's family, privacy and home; and the autonomy to choose where to live, one's home and the ability to move.[108] It also entails security of tenure; restitution for housing, land and property; equal and non-discriminatory access to adequate housing; and participation in housing-related decision-making at national and community levels.[109] Adequate housing is considered a component of the right to an adequate standard of living.[110] In addition, a lack of adequate housing can undermine other human rights, like the right to water and sanitation, food security, access to education and access to healthcare.[111]

Housing affordability has been impacted by a series of financial crises and other shocks like the Covid-19 pandemic. The private sector, especially financial actors, are exacerbating this through investments in housing and real estate. The increasing 'financialisation' of housing, coupled with rising inflation, also has decreased affordability, availability and quality of housing. Discrimination in housing and spatial segregation have reduced access to public services, education and transportation for vulnerable groups like women, religious and ethnic minorities, Indigenous Peoples, persons with disabilities, migrants and refugees.[112] Further, paying wages that do not match the cost of living can make access to housing even more difficult for workers.[113]

For workers, a lack of stable, affordable and secure housing can have impacts on their physical and mental health.[114] For companies, inadequate housing can have impacts on productivity and absenteeism. A review of data in the US showed that housing that is far from public transportation and economic centres can prevent workers from coming to work on time.[115] This can be exacerbated by the physical risks posed by climate change. For example, a study determined that the apparel sector has suffered economic impacts because garment sector workers living in flood-prone areas are unable to get to work after storms.[116] By providing access to adequate housing, facilitating the creation of housing near their business or improving local neighbourhoods, companies may be able to address a skilled labour shortage and improve employee retention.[117]

Water & sanitation
In 2010, the UN General Assembly recognised the right to safe and clean drinking water and sanitation as a human right "that is essential for the full enjoyment of life and all human rights".[118] Since 2015, both the UN Human Rights Council and the UN General Assembly have recognised the right to safe drinking water and the right to sanitation as distinct human rights (although closely related).[119] There are five criteria for the right to water: availability, accessibility, affordability, acceptability and quality and safety.[120]

As of 2024, an estimated 2 billion people lack access to safe and clean water, sanitation and hygiene services.[121] In 2023, the World Resources Institute reported that 25 countries, home to a quarter of the world's population, face extremely high water stress each year; this means that they use up nearly their entire available water supply.[122] In addition, at least half of the world's population lives under highly water-stressed conditions for at least one month each year.[123] The Intergovernmental Panel on Climate Change (IPCC) reports that water scarcity disproportionately impacts people in poverty, women, children, Indigenous Peoples and the elderly, especially in low-income countries, small island states and mountain regions.[124]

Water availability and accessibility is being impacted by crises like climate change, biodiversity loss and armed conflict.[125] Economic activities are also driving water stress. Since 1960, global demand for water has doubled, spurred by a growing population and the industrialisation of agriculture, livestock, energy production, mining and manufacturing.[126]

Water insecurity can impact workers' overall physical and mental health, standard of living and household costs.[127] It can also impact food security and malnutrition.[128] Water scarcity is also likely to have economic impacts for business. For example, the IPCC has estimated that extreme droughts impacting the agricultural sector are likelier with each degree of global warming above the 1.5°C limit set by the *Paris Agreement*.[129]

Addressing water insecurity can bring benefits for business. For instance, a 2018 to 2022 study by WaterAid, Diageo, Gap Inc, HSBC, Twinings and Ekaterra found that, when businesses provided workers along the full value chain with improved water and sanitation, workers' health and well-being improved, medical and sick pay costs decreased, and staff motivation and productivity increased.[130]

Privacy

The right to privacy is protected in the ICCPR.[131] The right to privacy underlies other human rights, like freedom of expression, freedom of association and assembly, and enjoyment of economic and social rights. The Office of the United Nations High Commissioner for Human Rights (OHCHR) states that interference with the right to privacy can disproportionately impact certain groups, thereby worsening inequality and discrimination.[132]

According to the ILO, impacts on the right to privacy in the workplace can manifest as improper collection and storage of workers' personal data.[133] Another way companies can impact their workers' right to privacy is through surveillance, such as monitoring their computer activity, productivity, calls and outputs. This can have indirect effects on other human rights in the workplace, such as setting and tracking high productivity targets that decrease rest time, reduce workers' ability to take breaks and increase the risk of accidents. One review of data on workplace surveillance found that it can also increase the potential for discrimination against workers; have a chilling effect on worker organising and collective bargaining; and worsen work-life balance by making it harder for workers to disconnect from their jobs and sign out of employer surveillance apps.[134]

Workers have reported that being constantly monitored in the workplace is having a negative impact on their mental health and their physical health. A study of US workers determined that 56% of workers who experience monitoring by their employer typically feel tense or stressed out at work.[135] This can impact worker productivity, increase dissatisfaction at work and increase illness and absenteeism. Another study found that increased digital tracking of employees actually increased "deviance" like intentionally working more slowly and stealing office supplies.[136] In addition, companies that do not respect the right to privacy can face legal risk if they are noncompliant with regulations protecting worker data.[137]

CONCLUSION

The upcoming EU CSDDD that expects companies to conduct environmental and human rights due diligence will start to set the bar for all companies – in the EU and beyond – as to how to navigate the increasingly complex world companies are operating in. Companies are expected to conduct meaningful due diligence that seeks to prevent and mitigate impacts on people, bring impacts to an end (where they exist), minimise the extent of impacts (where there are impacts that cannot be brought to an end), and remediate these impacts.

The EU CSRD provides a significant opportunity for companies to report on how they are conducting due diligence on their human rights risks and impacts. This matters – both for people, but also for the business. The connection between impact materiality and financial materiality has never been stronger, as impacts on people increasingly result in a wide range of business impacts across the board – financial, legal, compliance, operational, reputational and beyond.

By effectively identifying, assessing, and mitigating their risks and impacts on people, businesses will enhance their resilience, competitiveness, and long-term sustainability in an ever-evolving business landscape and a rapidly warming planet. The CSRD presents itself as an invaluable tool for companies aspiring to play a part in a successful future – provided they apply it effectively and meaningfully, with full knowledge of the world that they are operating in.

ESRS-S1 – OWN WORKFORCE & ESRS-S2 – WORKERS IN THE VALUE CHAIN REPORTING OBLIGATIONS

Ingrid De Doncker

Reporting for ESRS-S1 – Own Workforce

The ESRS-S1 standard covers an organisation's own workforce, which is understood to include both people who are in an employment relationship with the organisation ('employees') and non-employees, who are either people with contracts with the organisation to supply labour ('self-employed people') or people provided by the organisation primarily engaged in 'employment activities' (NACE Code N78).

The standard provides disclosure transparency to enable users of the sustainability statement to understand the organisation's material impacts on its own workforce, as well as related material risks and opportunities, including:

- How the organisation affects its own workforce, in terms of material positive and negative actual or potential impacts;
- Any actions taken, and the result of such actions, to prevent, mitigate or remediate actual or potential negative impacts, and to address risks and opportunities;
- The nature, type and extent of the organisation's material risks and opportunities related to its impacts and dependencies on its own workforce, and how it manages them; and
- The financial effects on the organisation over the short-, medium- and long-term of material risks and opportunities arising from its impacts and dependencies on its own workforce.

Under ESRS-S1, there are three sub-topics to consider. These sub-topics include various aspects of workforce management, promoting fair, safe, and inclusive working environments, and have been extensively covered in this chapter:

- Working conditions;
- Equal treatment and opportunities for all;
- Other work-related rights.

This Standard shall be read in conjunction with ESRS 1 *General Requirements* and ESRS 2 *General Disclosures*. This Standard shall be read in conjunction with ESRS-S2: *Workers in the Value Chain*, ESRS-S3: *Affected Communities* and ESRS-S4: *Consumers & End-users*. The reporting under this Standard shall be consistent, coherent and, where relevant, clearly linked with reporting on the organisation's own workforce under ESRS-S2, in order to ensure effective reporting. The requirements of this section should be read in conjunction with the disclosures required by ESRS 2 on Strategy & Business Model (SBM). The resulting disclosures shall be presented alongside the disclosures required by ESRS 2, except for ESRS 2 SBM-3, for which the undertaking has an option to present the disclosures alongside the topical disclosure.

It is important to understand the *Minimum Disclosure Requirements* (MDRs) in ESRS 2, Chapter 4.2. When an organisation identifies a sustainability matter as material, 34 MDR data points

(DPs) for Policies, Actions, Targets, and Metrics (PAT-M) are applicable if the organisation discloses on policies, actions and targets. If it does not provide disclosure on policies, targets or actions, then it needs to disclose the reasons for not doing so, as per the corresponding 10 DPs of ESRS 2 MDR PAT, paragraphs 62 and 81.

ESRS-S1 outlines clearly, in 17 *Disclosure Requirements* (DRs), the narrative and numeric DPs an organisation should comply with. For ESRS-S1, there are 127 *Shall* DPs, of which 44 are numeric, 61 are narrative and 22 are semi-narrative, as well as an additional 55 *May* DPs. The MDR PAT DPs are to be disclosed under S1-1, S1-4, S1-5 when the sustainability matters are material.

Figure 7.5: ESRS-S1 Reporting Requirements

ESRS-S1	Own Workforce		
	Working conditions	Equal treatment and opportunities for all	Other worker related rights
	All below are subject to materiality for each of the sub-topics.		
	STRATEGY		
ESRS2-S1-SBM-2	**interest and views of stakeholders.**		
ESRS2-S1-SBM-3	**Material impacts**, risks and opportunities and their interaction with strategy and business model.		
	IMPACTS, RISKS & OPPORTUNITIES MANAGEMENT		
ESRS-S1-1	**Policies** related to consumers and end-users.		
ESRS-S1-2	**Processes** for engaging with consumers and end-users about impacts.		
ESRS-S1-3	**Processes** to remediate negative impacts and channels for consumers and end-users to raise concerns.		
ESRS-S1-4	**Taking action** on material impacts on consumers and end-users, and approaches to mitigating material risks and pursuing material opportunities related to consumers and end-users, and effectiveness of those actions.		
	METRICS & TARGETS		
ESRS-S1-5	**Targets** related to managing material negative impacts, advancing positive impacts, and managing material risks and opportunities.		

ESRS-S1-6	Characteristics of the undertaking's employees.
ESRS-S1-7	Characteristics of non-employee workers in the undertaking's own workforce.
ESRS-S1-8	Collective bargaining coverage and social dialogue.
ESRS-S1-9	Diversity metrics.
ESRS-S1-10	Adequate wages.
ESRS-S1-11	Social protection.
ESRS-S1-12	Persons with disabilities.
ESRS-S1-13	Training and skills development metrics.
ESRS-S1-14	Health and safety metrics.
ESRS-S1-15	Work-life balance metrics.
ESRS-S1-16	Compensation metrics (pay gap and total compensation).
ESRS-S1-17	Incidents, complaints, and severe human rights impacts.

Reporting for ESRS-S2 – Workers in the Value Chain

ESRS-S2 is similar to ESRS-S1 from a reporting perspective.

The ESRS-S2 *Workers in the Value Chain* standard covers all workers in the organisation's upstream and downstream value chain who are or can be materially impacted by the organisation, including impacts that are connected with the organisation's own operations and value chain, including through its products or services, as well as through its business relationships. This includes all workers who are not included in the scope of 'own workforce'.

This standard shines a light on the often-overlooked workers in the value chain, aiming to hear their voices and protect their rights. There are three sub-topics to consider, which ensure:

- Working conditions;
- Equal treatment and opportunities for all;
- Other work-related rights.

Figure 7.6: ESRS-S2 Reporting Requirements

ESRS-S2	Workers in the Value Chain		
	Working conditions	Equal treatment and opportunities for all	Other worker related rights
	All below are subject to materiality for each of the sub-topics.		
	STRATEGY		
ESRS2-S2-SBM-2	**Interests and views of stakeholders.**		
ESRS2-S2-SBM-3	**Material impacts**, risks and opportunities and their interaction with strategy and business model.		
	IMPACTS, RISKS & OPPORTUNITIES MANAGEMENT		
ESRS-S2-1	**Policies** related to value chain workers.		
ESRS-S2-2	**Processes** for engaging with value chain workers about impacts.		
ESRS-S2-3	**Processes** to remediate negative impacts and channels for value chain workers to raise concerns.		
ESRS-S2-4	**Taking action** on material impacts on value chain workers, and approaches to mitigating material risks and pursuing material opportunities related to value chain workers, and effectiveness of those actions.		
	METRICS & TARGETS		
ESRS-S2-5	**Targets** related to managing material negative impacts, advancing positive impacts, and managing material risks and opportunities.		

This Standard shall be read in conjunction with ESRS 1 *General Disclosures*, and ESRS 2 *General Requirements*, as well as ESRS-S1, ESRS-S3: *Affected Communities* and ESRS-S4: *Consumers & End-users*. The reporting under this Standard shall be consistent, coherent and, where relevant, clearly linked with reporting on the organisation's own workforce under ESRS-S1, in order to ensure effective reporting. The requirements of this section should be read in conjunction with the disclosures required by ESRS 2 on SBM. The resulting disclosures shall be presented alongside the disclosures required by ESRS 2, except for SBM-3 Material impacts, risks and opportunities and their interaction with SBM, for which the organisation has an option to present the disclosures alongside the topical disclosure.

It is important to understand the *Minimum Disclosure Requirements* (MDRs) in ESRS 2, Chapter 4.2. When an organisation identifies a sustainability matter as material, 34 MDR data points (DPs) for Policies, Actions, Targets, and Metrics (PAT-M) are applicable if the organisation discloses on policies, actions and targets. If it does not provide disclosure on policies, targets or actions, then it needs to disclose the reasons for not doing so, as per the corresponding 10 DPs of ESRS 2 MDR PAT, paragraphs 62 and 81.

ESRS-S2 outlines clearly, in five *Disclosure Requirements* (DRs), the narrative and numeric DPs an organisation should comply with. For ESRS-S2, there are 47 *Shall* DPs, of which 40 are narrative and 7 are semi-narrative, as well as an additional 18 *May* DPs. The MDR PAT DPs are to be disclosed under S2-1, S2-4, S2-5 when the sustainability matters are material.

---

[1]   Anna expresses her gratitude to the team members at Human Level for their unwavering support and dedication to the endeavour of supporting companies to place human rights at the core of their business. She also extends her appreciation to Human Level's clients and partners for their persistent efforts in driving forward impactful human rights due diligence and reporting. Special appreciation is extended to Jodie Tang, Maddie Wolberg and Sophia Colvin for their valuable assistance with this article.

[2]   For an overview of the recent reported human rights instances, see Human Level Content Hub at https://www.wearehumanlevel.com/content-hub.

[3]   https://www.ohchr.org/sites/default/files/documents/publications/guidingprinciplesbusinesshr_en.pdf.

[4]   For further information on the Reporting & Assurance Frameworks Initiative, see https://shiftproject.org/resource/human-rights-reporting-and-assurance-frameworks-initiative/.

[5]   https://www.ungpreporting.org.

[6]   https://www.ungpreporting.org/resources/salient-human-rights-issues/.

[7]   https://shiftproject.org/wp-content/uploads/2023/08/Double-materiality-what-you-need-to-know.pdf.

[8]   https://shiftproject.org/resource/business-model-red-flags/red-flags-about/#:~:text=Shift%27s%20Business%20Model%20Red%20Flags,identificati on%20of%20additional%20red%20flags.

[9]   For more on this, see *Dutch Banking Sector Agreement, Discussion Paper*, Working Group on Enabling Remediation (2019), https://www.imvoconvenanten.nl/-/media/imvo/files/banking/paper-enabling-remediation.pdf; UN OHCHR, *Remedy in Development Finance*, https://www.ohchr.org/sites/default/files/2022-02/Remedy-in-Development.pdf;

and UN OHCHR, *BankTrack response*, https://www.ohchr.org/sites/default/files/Documents/Issues/Business/InterpretationGuiding-Principles.pdf.

10 https://www.ilo.org/topics/employment-security.

11 https://hbr.org/2022/03/workers-dont-feel-like-a-9-to-5-job-is-a-safe-bet-anymore.

12 https://www.lancaster.ac.uk/media/lancaster-university/content-assets/documents/lums/work-foundation/reports/ZeroChoices.pdf.

13 https://ilostat.ilo.org/blog/assessing-the-current-state-of-the-global-labour-market-implications-for-achieving-the-global-goals/.

14 https://blogs.lse.ac.uk/usappblog/2019/06/12/low-wage-workers-experience-more-volatility-in-hours-worked-but-increased-worker-power-can-help-to-narrow-the-gap/.

15 https://www.who.int/news/item/17-05-2021-long-working-hours-increasing-deaths-from-heart-disease-and-stroke-who-ilo.

16 https://cri.org/reports/i-cant-cool/.

17 https://www.ilo.org/topics/social-protection#:~:text=Social%20protection%2C%20or%20social%20security,general%20poverty%20and%20social%20exclusion.

18 https://www.ilo.org/publications/world-social-protection-report-2020-22-social-protection-crossroads-pursuit.

19 https://www.ilo.org/publications/world-social-protection-report-2020-22-social-protection-crossroads-pursuit.

20 https://www.ilo.org/publications/flagship-reports/world-employment-and-social-outlook-trends-2024#:~:text=The%20report%20reveals%20a%20complex,rates%20in%20lower%2Dincome%20nations.

21 https://www.ilo.org/resource/brief/setting-adequate-wages-question-living-wages.

22 https://www.ilo.org/publications/flagship-reports/world-employment-and-social-outlook-trends-2024#:~:text=The%20report%20reveals%20a%20complex,rates%20in%20lower%2Dincome%20nations.

23 https://www.ituc-csi.org/IMG/pdf/ituc_global_survey_on_minimum_living_wages_2024_en.pdf.

24 https://livingwage.org.uk/twenty-years-living-wage-employer-experience.

25 https://www.ilo.org/publications/flagship-reports/world-employment-and-social-outlook-trends-2024#:~:text=The%20report%20reveals%20a%20complex,rates%20in%20lower%2Dincome%20nations.

26 https://www.idhsustainabletrade.com/living-wage-platform/.

27 https://www.ilo.org/topics/collective-bargaining-and-labour-relations.

28 https://www.ilo.org/topics/social-dialogue-and-tripartism.

29 https://www.ituc-csi.org/IMG/pdf/for_democracy_-_political_brief_en.pdf.

30 https://www.ituc-csi.org/IMG/pdf/2024_ituc_global_rights_index_en.pdf.

31 https://www.ilo.org/topics/freedom-association.

32 https://www.theglobaldeal.com/resources/The%20Business%20Case%20for%20Social%20Dialogue_FINAL.pdf.

33 https://www.ilo.org/publications/working-time-and-work-life-balance-around-world.

34 https://www.ilo.org/publications/working-time-and-work-life-balance-around-world.

35 https://hbr.org/2015/08/the-research-is-clear-long-hours-backfire-for-people-and-for-companies; https://www.ncbi.nlm.nih.gov/pmc/articles/PMC6617405/.

36 https://www.who.int/standards/classifications/frequently-asked-questions/burn-out-an-occupational-phenomenon.

37 https://hbr.org/2015/08/the-research-is-clear-long-hours-backfire-for-people-and-for-companies.
38 https://www.ilo.org/publications/working-time-and-work-life-balance-around-world.
39 https://hbr.org/2022/09/the-surprising-benefits-of-work-life-support.
40 https://normlex.ilo.org/dyn/normlex/en/f?p=NORMLEXPUB:12100:0::NO::P12100_ILO_CODE:C155.
41 https://www.ilo.org/publications/call-safer-and-healthier-working-environments.
42 https://normlex.ilo.org/dyn/normlex/en/f?p=NORMLEXPUB:12100:0::NO::P12100_ILO_CODE:C155.
43 https://www.ilo.org/media/364861/download.
44 https://www.ilo.org/publications/call-safer-and-healthier-working-environments.
45 https://www.ilo.org/publications/call-safer-and-healthier-working-environments.
46 https://www.ilo.org/publications/call-safer-and-healthier-working-environments.
47 https://www.who.int/news-room/fact-sheets/detail/mental-health-at-work.
48 https://www.hrw.org/news/2022/07/21/protecting-people-extreme-heat.
49 https://www.ilo.org/wcmsp5/groups/public/---dgreports/---dcomm/---publ/documents/publication/wcms_711919.pdf.
50 https://www.ilo.org/wcmsp5/groups/public/---dgreports/---dcomm/---publ/documents/publication/wcms_711919.pdf.
51 Refer to the *International Bill of Rights*, which includes the UDHR, the ICESCR and the ICCPR. See UDHR, Articles 2, 7 & 23; ICCPR, Article 3; and ICESCR, Articles 3 & 7.
52 https://www.ilo.org/publications/pay-transparency-legislation-implications-employers-and-workers.
53 https://www.unwomen.org/en/news/stories/2020/9/explainer-everything-you-need-to-know-about-equal-pay.
54 https://www3.weforum.org/docs/WEF_GGGR_2024.pdf.
55 https://www3.weforum.org/docs/WEF_GGGR_2024.pdf.
56 https://www.forbes.com/advisor/business/pay-equity/.
57 UDHR, Article 26, and ICESCR, Article 13.
58 https://docstore.ohchr.org/SelfServices/FilesHandler.ashx?enc=4slQ6QSmlBEDzFEovLCuW1a0Szab0oXTdImnsJZZVQfoUYY19kME5pOqRbao%2BukB1Kzn1MMnQL24FFvtIIdk%2F%2FR%2FF0GthE%2BTiGSATb%2BUa3WMs0%2F%2BfVfQFg02%2BY%2FTVuqU.
59 https://www.ilo.org/resource/ilc/108/ilo-centenary-declaration-future-work.
60 https://www.worldbank.org/en/topic/skillsdevelopment.
61 https://www.worldbank.org/en/topic/skillsdevelopment.
62 https://es.weforum.org/publications/global-gender-gap-report-2021/in-full/gggr2-gender-gaps-in-jobs-of-tomorrow/.
63 https://www.forbes.com/sites/forbeshumanresourcescouncil/2023/06/13/creating-a-culture-of-training-and-development-in-the-workplace/.
64 https://www.worldbank.org/en/topic/skillsdevelopment.
65 CRPD, Article 27, https://www.ohchr.org/en/instruments-mechanisms/instruments/convention-rights-persons-disabilities.
66 https://normlex.ilo.org/dyn/normlex/en/f?p=NORMLEXPUB:12100:0::NO::P12100_INSTRUMENT_ID:312304.
67 https://www.ilo.org/resource/disability-and-work.

68   https://www.oecd.org/en/publications/disability-work-and-inclusion_1eaa5e9c-en.html.

69   https://www.ilo.org/resource/disability-and-work.

70   https://www.nature.com/articles/s41599-021-00707-y.

71   https://www.accenture.com/content/dam/accenture/final/a-com-migration/pdf/pdf-89/accenture-disability-inclusion-research-report.pdf.

72   https://normlex.ilo.org/dyn/normlex/en/f?p=NORMLEXPUB:12100:0::NO::P12100_ILO_CODE:C190.

73   Article 1(a) of https://normlex.ilo.org/dyn/normlex/en/f?p=NORMLEXPUB:12100:0::NO::P12100_ILO_CODE:C190.

74   See *Convention on the Elimination of All Forms of Discrimination Against Women*.

75   https://www.ilo.org/publications/major-publications/experiences-violence-and-harassment-work-global-first-survey.

76   ILO: *Safe & Healthy Working Environments Free from Violence & Harassment: The Report at a Glance*.

77   ILO: *Safe & Healthy Working Environments Free from Violence & Harassment: The Report at a Glance*.

78   ILO: *Safe & Healthy Working Environments Free from Violence & Harassment: The Report at a Glance*.

79   https://unglobalcompact.org/take-action/action/dei.

80   https://webapps.ilo.org/wcmsp5/groups/public/---ed_dialogue/---act_emp/documents/publication/wcms_841348.pdf.

81   https://www.ahajournals.org/doi/10.1161/JAHA.122.027374.

82   https://www.gallup.com/workplace/349865/understanding-effects-discrimination-workplace.aspx.

83   https://www.weps.org/sites/default/files/2021-09/WEPs%20GUIDANCE%20%20Anti-Discrimination%20FINAL %20FINAL.pdf.

84   https://www.ilo.org/publications/equality-work-continuing-challenge-global-report-under-follow-ilo.

85   https://biblioteca.ibge.gov.br/visualizacao/livros/liv101678.pdf in https://www.weps.org/sites/default/files/2021-09/WEPs%20GUIDANCE%20%20Anti-Discrimination%20FINAL %20FINAL.pdf.

86   https://www.gallup.com/workplace/349865/understanding-effects-discrimination-workplace.aspx.

87   https://www.catalyst.org/research/why-diversity-and-inclusion-matter/.

88   https://normlex.ilo.org/dyn/normlex/en/f?p=NORMLEXPUB:12100:0::NO::P12100_ilo_code:C138; https://normlex.ilo.org/dyn/normlex/en/f?p=NORMLEXPUB:12100:0::NO::P12100_ILO_CODE:C182.

89   https://www.ilo.org/international-programme-elimination-child-labour-ipec/what-child-labour#:~:text=The%20term%20"child%20labour"%20is,harmful%20to%20children%3B%20and%2For.

90   https://data.unicef.org/resources/child-labour-2020-global-estimates-trends-and-the-road-forward/.

91   https://data.unicef.org/topic/child-protection/child-labour/.

92   https://www.ilo.org/publications/major-publications/child-labour-global-estimates-2020-trends-and-road-forward.

93   https://data.unicef.org/resources/covid-19-and-child-labour-a-time-of-crisis-a-time-to-act/.

94   https://www.ilo.org/publications/issue-paper-child-labour-and-climate-change.

95   https://www.dol.gov/sites/dolgov/files/ILAB/child_labor_reports/ tda2022/2022-Findings-on-the-Worst-Forms-of-Child-Labor.pdf.

96   https://unglobalcompact.org/what-is-gc/mission/principles/principle-5.

97   https://www.ilo.org/sites/default/files/wcmsp5/groups/public/@ed_norm/
     @ipec/documents/publication/wcms_653987.pdf.
98   https://www.ilo.org/publications/major-publications/child-labour-global-
     estimates-2020-trends-and-road-forward.
99   https://normlex.ilo.org/dyn/normlex/en/f?p=NORMLEXPUB:12100:::NO:
     12100:P12100_ILO_CODE:C029:NO.
100 https://www.ilo.org/wcmsp5/groups/public/---ed_norm/---
     declaration/documents/publication/wcms_203832.pdf.
101 https://www.ilo.org/sites/default/files/wcmsp5/groups/public/@ed_norm/
     @ipec/documents/publication/wcms_918034.pdf.
102 https://www.ilo.org/sites/default/files/wcmsp5/groups/public/@ed_norm/
     @ipec/documents/publication/wcms_918034.pdf.
103 https://www.ilo.org/publications/major-publications/global-estimates-
     modern-slavery-forced-labour-and-forced-marriage.
104 https://www.ilo.org/publications/major-publications/global-estimates-
     modern-slavery-forced-labour-and-forced-marriage.
105 https://www.ilo.org/sites/default/files/wcmsp5/groups/public/@ed_norm/
     @ipec/documents/publication/wcms_854733.pdf.
106 https://apps.who.int/iris/bitstream/handle/10665/77394/WHO_RHR_12.
     42_eng.pdf;sequence=1.
107 https://flbusiness.network/wp-content/uploads/2021/09/ilo-gbnfl_global-
     brief_why-and-how-businesses-want-to-eradicate-forced-labour.pdf;
     https://www.ilo.org/publications/can-better-working-conditions-improve-
     performance-smes-international-0.
108 https://www.ohchr.org/sites/default/files/Documents/Publications/
     FS21_rev_1_Housing_en.pdf.
109 https://www.ohchr.org/sites/default/files/Documents/Publications/
     FS21_rev_1_Housing_en.pdf.
110 https://www.ohchr.org/sites/default/files/Documents/Publications/
     FS21_rev_1_Housing_en.pdf.
111 https://www.ohchr.org/sites/default/files/Documents/Publications/
     FS21_rev_1_Housing_en.pdf.
112 https://www.ohchr.org/en/special-procedures/sr-housing/human-right-
     adequate-housing.
113 https://www.ohchr.org/sites/default/files/wcmsp5/groups/public/@ed_
     protect/@protrav/@travail/documents/publication/wcms_862569.pdf.
114 https://www.ncbi.nlm.nih.gov/pmc/articles/PMC7525583/.
115 https://www.urban.org/features/too-far-jobs-spatial-mismatch-and-hourly-
     workers.
116 https://www.ilr.cornell.edu/sites/default/files-d8/2023-
     09/Higher%20Ground%20Report%201%20FINAL.pdf.
117 https://www.weforum.org/agenda/2020/01/closing-the-housing-gap-how-
     industry-can-help/.
118 UN General Assembly, A/RES/64/292; https://undocs.org/A/RES/64/292.
119 https://www.ohchr.org/en/water-and-sanitation/about-water-and-
     sanitation#:~:text=OHCHR%20and%20the%20rights%20to%20water%20and%
     20sanitation,-Overview&text=International%20human%20rights%20law
     %20obliges,prioritizing%20those%20most%20in%20need.
120 https://www.ohchr.org/en/water-and-sanitation/about-water-and-
     sanitation#:~:text=OHCHR%20and%20the%20rights%20to%20water%20and%
     20sanitation,-Overview&text=International%20human%20rights%20law
     %20obliges,prioritizing%20those%20most%20in%20need.

121 https://www.unops.org/news-and-stories/news/developing-inclusive-water-sanitation-and-hygiene-infrastructure.

122 https://www.wri.org/insights/highest-water-stressed-countries.

123 https://www.wri.org/insights/highest-water-stressed-countries.

124 https://www.ipcc.ch/report/ar6/wg2/downloads/outreach/IPCC_AR6 _WGII_FactSheet_FoodAndWater.pdf.

125 https://www.ipcc.ch/report/ar6/wg2/downloads/outreach/IPCC_AR6 _WGII_FactSheet_FoodAndWater.pdf; https://www.cfr.org/backgrounder/ water-stress-global-problem-thats-getting-worse.

126 https://www.wri.org/insights/highest-water-stressed-countries.

127 https://www.digdeep.org/draining.

128 https://www.ipcc.ch/report/ar6/wg2/downloads/outreach/IPCC_AR6 _WGII_FactSheet_FoodAndWater.pdf.

129 https://www.ipcc.ch/report/ar6/wg2/downloads/outreach/IPCC_AR6 _WGII_FactSheet_FoodAndWater.pdf.

130 https://washmatters.wateraid.org/projects/boosting-business-why-investing-water-sanitation-hygiene-pays-off.

131 ICCPR, Article 17: https://www.ohchr.org/en/instruments-mechanisms/instruments/international-covenant-civil-and-political-rights.

132 https://www.ohchr.org/en/privacy-in-the-digital-age/international-standards.

133 https://www.ilo.org/resource/protection-workers-personal-data.

134 https://ssir.org/articles/entry/the_long_shadow_of_workplace_surveillance.

135 https://www.apa.org/topics/healthy-workplaces/employee-electronic-monitoring.

136 https://journals.sagepub.com/doi/10.1177/01492063211053224.

137 https://www.reuters.com/legal/legalindustry/ai-employee-privacy-important-considerations-employers-2023-09-29/.

8

AFFECTED COMMUNITIES

Donal Daly & Minou Schillings
with stories from
Joy Njeri & Kowawa Kapukaja
Apurinã
(with Tiago Paes Vilas Boas)

W e did not expect this chapter to start this way. We had planned that John (not his real name), our friend and sustainable development advocate and climate warrior, would be the main contributor, and that Donal Daly, author of **Chapter 1: The Customer is the Planet**, and Minou Schillings, author of **Chapter 11: What If…?**, would support him.

Then, earlier this year, in a country distant from us, a military conflict devastated John's family, some of whom were environmental and human rights activists and targets of the right-wing actors in their home country. John's world fell apart.

John's story, or more particularly that of John's extended family, was to be told later in this chapter, as one shockingly real example of what being part of an Affected Community means. However, we have been asked not to share any details that could possibly identify John or his family since they fear for their lives. Such is the wanton greed, ruthlessness, and inhumanity of those who pillage and plunder our planet in pursuit of power and profit.

For now, guided by John's wisdom and counsel from afar, Minou and Donal, supported by Tiago, Joy, Kowawa and others, have taken on the task. Our hope is that we can expand your understanding of who is affected by the environmental, societal, and economic challenges that are happening in our world, and explore what we can do, together and apart, to do no further harm to these Affected Communities, and indeed go further to improve their circumstances.

We would like to dedicate this chapter to John and his family.

Donal Daly & Minou Schillings

WHO IS AFFECTED?

Unfortunately John's story is not an isolated one. There are many other examples of environmental activists who stand up for us and suffer personal hardship as a result of their actions. They fight for the protection of our oceans, advocate in opposition to deforestation, protest against new oil and gas extraction, publicise the damage done by mining for rare materials, and expose labour abuses in the fashion industry. As a consequence, they are targeted by powerful political, economic, and sometimes military interests; sometimes, they even are killed for their actions.

But it is not just activists who are affected. It is *every one* of us. Eight billion people today are affected by climate change and social upheaval. And then, of course, there is nature and the animals, the world's flora and fauna, from soil to sky – nothing is impervious to the footprints of our recent past that press down on us now.

Since you have got this far in the book, you know that the planet and its people are under severe stress. Through our collective action – typified by the consumption habits of the 'Western world', the 'developed world', or the 'Global North', or whichever sobriquet you want to use – life on the planet has become more perilous. And we are all, each and every one of us, affected by it. Each one of us is part of an Affected Community.

Our first definition of Affected Communities was:

Groups of people or communities that are impacted by the activities of individuals, companies, or nations. This impact can be direct or indirect, positive or negative, and may include environmental, social, and economic aspects.

But then, as we thought about how we are wholly interdependent with the natural world of land, oceans, and animals, we should extend our definition to explicitly call out that symbiosis.

Our revised definition of Affected Communities is:

Groups of people or communities or the ecosystems that they inhabit – the land, sea and animals – that are impacted by the activities of other individuals, companies, or nations. This impact can be direct or indirect, positive or negative, and may include environmental, social, and economic aspects.

Perspective Matters

Living as we are on a planet with limited resources, every action we take either depletes the planet's remaining resources, or augments the planet's reserves. Someone is affected: sometimes individuals, sometimes communities, and sometimes whole countries. When we use more than our fair share of something, then it means there is not a fair share left for others.

The 'Tragedy of the Commons'[1] – a concept that explains how individuals acting independently and rationally according to their self-interest behave contrary to the best interests of the whole group by depleting a common resource – remains a fundamental principle in environmental science, economics, and political science, reflecting the complexity of human-environment interactions. It challenges us to find a balance between liberty and sustainability for the survival of our commons. The solution, the originator of the concept, George Hardin, suggested, lies in mutual coercion, mutually agreed upon by the majority of the people affected.

When our community is the planet and all its inhabitants, then it is clear to see the tension between personal benefits, or protectionist benefits pursued by avaricious nations or regions, and enduring environmental stewardship. Many would say that capitalism, or consumerism *per se* is in direct conflict with the common good.

In simple terms, we know that we use resources for everything that we do: every mile we drive, kettle we boil, bottle of water we drink, road we pave, building we construct, shower we take, meal we eat, and every item of clothing, sporting goods, or electronic equipment that we buy. When we use these resources, there is less left for others. Someone is affected:

- When we pay €5 for a T-shirt, somewhere along the way, at some point in the supply chain, someone was exploited;
- When an oil company extracts oil in the Niger Delta, we should not be surprised that whole communities are impacted;
- When industrial companies' chemical effluent poisons rivers and land, water sources are contaminated and food can't be grown on the land.

As temperatures rise, as a consequence of anthropogenic emissions, parts of the world become uninhabitable, people lose their homes and livelihoods, and climate refugees seek new places to call home. Sustained extreme heat brings droughts that threaten food supplies. People go hungry, marine life dies and, with it, segments of the fishing industry. Everyone is affected.

Increased climate-based migration, climate injustice and growing inequity creates swathes of disaffected communities with few resources and little to lose, the perfect cocktail for civil unrest. More people are affected.

None of this is simple. Using the United Nations Sustainable Development Goals (SDGs) as a framework for thinking illustrates the inherent conflicts. There is a grand compromise at the core of sustainable development between those who prioritise the environment, those who prioritise social development, and those who prioritise economic development. This tension is at the heart of sustainability and can seem to be intractable. But, to deliver a just world, or at least the most just that we can muster, all perspectives need to be considered when we are considering who is affected.

In isolation, the pursuit of SDG 2: Zero Hunger seems inarguable. No one can argue that zero hunger is not a laudable goal. The urgent need to combat such a basic human problem as sufficient and nutritious food supply is by far one of the top priorities of the SDGs. But, for example, to espouse a singular focus on agricultural productivity to maximise the food output, without reference to the impact on land, or restraints or constraints with respect to the use of land or water resources, conflicts directly with SDG 15: Life on Land. Damage done to land from agricultural productivity measures, such as chemical interventions and poorly governed agricultural effluent management, bring into focus the potentially opposing objectives of the two SDGs.

Donal was a speaker at a conference in Ireland in late 2023 on the topic of doing business in Asia. Fellow speakers at the conference – discussing 'Global Transformation to a Climate Resilient World' – were the Ambassadors to Ireland of China, Indonesia, Pakistan and United Arab Emirates, who spoke about their country's climate resilience, adaptation and mitigation – couched, as you might expect, in very diplomatic language.

A follow-up question – "Is there any resistance from the citizens in your country to actions to prevent or respond to climate change?" – brought a moment of truth. The answer from Her Excellency Aisha Farooqui, Ambassador of Pakistan, was striking both in its clarity and because of her calm and measured delivery. "No resistance", she said. "The resistance was all washed away last year. We are now focused on food security".

Ambassador Farooqui was referring to the floods that happened in Pakistan in 2022, where one-third of the country was underwater and 1,739 people died. The monsoon season in Pakistan, which typically brings heavy rainfall, saw record-breaking levels of rain in 2022:[2] June saw rains 67% above normal levels, and the country had received nearly three times its average 30-year rainfall by August of that year.

In October 2023, Pakistan's health system was on the verge of collapse from an alarming surge in waterborne ailments, including diarrhoea, drug-resistant typhoid and cholera, and diseases like malaria and dengue. At that time, it was estimated between 30,000 to 50,000 people in Pakistan, mostly children, lost their lives due to diarrhoea caused by consuming contaminated water and food. Pakistan has also witnessed a massive surge in malaria cases. And last year 6,000 dengue cases were reported in the month of January, while in 2024 Pakistan has seen around 124,000 cases.

Climate change is believed to have played a significant role in the severity of the floods. Rising global temperatures are linked to more frequent, and intense, droughts and floods. Pakistan, which is responsible for less than 1% of global greenhouse gas (GHG) emissions, is now one of the countries most affected by extreme weather events. The pattern has been repeated in Libya in 2023 and Kenya (see below) and Brazil in 2024, where many lives were lost and many more destroyed. This is real climate injustice, an extreme example of the Tragedy of the Commons.

AFFECTED COMMUNITIES IN AFRICA: A CALL FOR RESPONSIBLE ENGAGEMENT

Joy Njeri

My motherland, Kenya, is a land of vivid contrasts. One day, you are met by an infinite tapestry of ochre and emerald stretching across the savannah, bursting with life. The next day, you could find yourself in the heart of Nairobi, a vibrant city with buildings that reach to the sky. However, beneath this colourful surface lurks a traumatic past that weighs heavily on our hearts.

A Nation Drowning

The relentless rains of 2024 submerged Kenya in water. Brutal statistics paint a bleak picture: over 306,000 people displaced, 315 killed, nearly 2,000 schools destroyed, and more than 41,000 acres of farmland ravaged. But behind the statistics are stories of fear, loss, and a desperate struggle for survival:

- *Amina's rooftop refuge:* The deluge terrified Amina, a mother of three, who lives in Nairobi's Mukuru kwa Reuben slum. "The water roared in", she said, her voice trembling, "We scrambled to the roof and clung for hours until rescuers arrived". Amina lost everything, including the humble possessions that had served as the foundation of her family's life. Her story resonates with countless others, whose homes have been transformed into islands in the midst of a raging sea;[3,4]

- *Stranded on flooded highways:* The chaos extended beyond informal settlements. An Uber driver in Nairobi, Kelvin Mwangi, described the city as paralysed. "The roads are like rivers, clogging everything", he lamented. "I could not even contact my family, let alone navigate the submerged highways". Kelvin's experience exemplifies the floods' devastating ripple effect, which disrupted livelihoods and severed vital connections;[5]

- *Communities submerged:* Beyond Nairobi, the Mathare slum witnessed scenes of heartbreaking desperation. Floodwaters transformed streets into canals, submerging homes and forcing residents to seek shelter on rooftops. Entire neighbourhoods were isolated and deprived of basic necessities. The image of a community huddled precariously above a watery abyss serves as a stark reminder of the vulnerabilities caused by insufficient infrastructure and poor drainage systems;[6]

- *Mai Mahiu market, a vital centre, was lost:* When a mudslide caused by the relentless rain ripped through the community, shops and stalls could not withstand nature's fury, collapsing under the weight of mud. This critical economic centre, a source of income for countless families, was destroyed. Eyewitness accounts described a scene of complete devastation, with the screams of the injured and the cries of the bereaved blending with the roar of the mudslide.[7]

These stories from Kenya are only a microcosm of a larger global phenomenon. Climate change casts a long shadow over the planet, from rising sea levels endangering island nations to wildfires ravaging vast ecosystems. We are all interconnected. The destruction of one part of the world, whether through the destruction of forests or the extraction of natural resources, weakens us all. A Kenyan farmer may find the idyllic beaches of a distant island irrelevant, but rising sea levels threaten both of their futures.

The Kenyan floods of 2024 serve as a stark reminder that climate change is the great equaliser. It makes no distinctions based on wealth, status, or geographical location. The consequences of years of neglect and unsustainable practices are now upon us. Kenya's story is a powerful wake-up call, urging us to accept our collective responsibility for our planet's health.

Amina, clinging to her rooftop refuge, is more than just a Kenyan mother grieving her loss. She represents humanity, demonstrating the frailty of our existence and the urgent need for action.

A Nation Scarred: A Story of Loss

The post-election violence of 2007 is still a vivid memory. Seeing the damage first-hand made an indelible impression. Families were ripped apart, homes were turned to burning ruins, and livelihoods were destroyed in an instant. I worked with the victims – people who had lost everything.

One anecdote that will always stay with me is about a wealthy businessman in his 60s. He had constructed a secure life and was about to 'transmit the torch' to his children. Political turmoil stripped him naked. Displaced and heartbroken, he tried to rebuild through a modest business. The weight of loss, however, proved too much. He died from excessive blood pressure shortly after our last discussion. His story is only one of many tragedies.

Here are two more:

- *The Kiambaa church massacre was an especially terrible occurrence. Hundreds of people (mainly women and children) sought safety in a church in Kiambaa, Eldoret, as violence escalated. In a brutal act of cruelty, a crowd set fire to the church. Over 30 people died, while others were severely burned, their screams echoing throughout the night. The massacre became a horrific metaphor for the indiscriminate nature of violence, transforming a sanctuary into a fiery tomb. This act became a symbol of the violence and ethnic targeting that took place throughout the uprising;[8,9]*

- *Another story is of a young man named Moses, whose brother was almost killed during the post-election turmoil. When Moses was 11 years old, his brother was caught up in the violence that erupted following the disputed 2007 Kenyan elections. Fortunately, Moses' sibling survived, but the incident had a lasting influence on him and his family.[10]*

These tales reflect the human toll and catastrophic repercussions of Kenya's post-election violence in 2007 and 2008. The violence claimed over 1,200 lives, injured others, and displaced over 300,000 people.[11] Addressing the underlying causes and ensuring accountability remain significant challenges for Kenya.

This is only one of innumerable tragedies, a harsh reminder of the human cost of political instability caused by resource mismanagement.

A Broken System & a Nation's Song of Hope

The recent unrest in Kenya exposes a deep-seated issue: the complex interplay of political instability, resource mismanagement, and economic hardship. This phenomenon, known as the 'resource curse', is well-documented, with resource wealth fuelling corruption and conflict instead of development.[12]

In June 2024, a financial bill triggered economic anxieties in Kenya and became the catalyst for a new movement. The young generation, armed with social media and a burning sense of justice, took to the streets. Their actions embody the spirit of Article 1 of the Kenyan Constitution:

> *The sovereign power of the Republic of Kenya belongs to the people of Kenya, and shall be exercised by them either directly or through their representatives in accordance with this Constitution. (Constitution of Kenya 2010, Article 1)*

Their voices resonate with a bitter truth: leaders entrusted with the stewardship of the nation's wealth have fallen short. As the iconic Nigerian novelist Chinua Achebe lamented, "We were not incapable of building, but building to enrich ourselves – and not for a long vision or a common good". The irony is stark – Kenya, a land overflowing with natural resources, coexists with widespread poverty.

The young generation understands this. They see the exploitation of resources and the funnelling of wealth into the pockets of a privileged few, both within Kenya and abroad. They recognise the neocolonial trap – a system where Africa's riches fuel the prosperity of others, while leaving its own people impoverished. This economic discontent, as reported by The Economist, has led to a concerning situation:

> *Companies are leaving the country, healthcare access is dwindling, and poverty deepens.*

However, amidst this hardship, a new song is rising in Kenya. It's a song of hope, sung by a generation demanding change. They envision a future where abundant resources empower the nation, creating a more equitable society. This resonates with Nelson Mandela's powerful words:

> *Poverty is not an accident. Like slavery and apartheid, it is man-made and can be removed by actions of human beings.*

The youth of Kenya are not just singing a song; they are calling for a global shift. They urge a move from exploitation to collaboration and mutual benefit. Their call is for responsible leadership, where resource wealth empowers the nation, not enriches a select few. Only then can we create a world where the abundance of the earth is enjoyed by all.

Why Businesses Should Care?

Instability in Africa has a ripple effect impacting businesses worldwide. Increased immigration, a consequence of poverty and conflict, can strain labour markets in other regions. We are all interconnected in the global economy. "Consumers are demanding more ethical and sustainable practices from the companies they support" – this has been said a lot in the business media, expressing the importance of responsible sourcing in Africa. Businesses that turn a blind eye to the social and environmental impact of their supply chains contribute to the problem.

But Western businesses can play a crucial role in fostering positive change. Here's how they can move beyond extraction and contribute to Africa's development:

- ***Responsible sourcing:*** *Ensure ethical supply chains, fair labour practices, and avoid conflict minerals. Africa is a continent blessed with a wealth of natural resources. The Democratic Republic of Congo (DRC) is a prime example. It holds an estimated 70% of the world's cobalt reserves, a critical component in the lithium-ion batteries that power our laptops, smartphones, and electric vehicles.[13] Yet millions of Congolese live in abject poverty, struggling to meet their basic needs;*

- ***Investing in local processing:*** *Create jobs, transfer technology, and add value to African resources by processing raw materials locally. For example, Veja (a French footwear company) sources organic cotton from family-owned farms in Brazil and manufactures its sneakers in factories across the country, ensuring fair labour practices and economic benefits for local communities. Veja's focus on local processing allows them to control quality and maintain a sustainable production cycle;*

- ***Supporting infrastructure development:*** *Partner with governments and NGOs to invest in roads, bridges, and energy projects, improving connectivity and fostering economic growth. For example: Siemens Stiftung (a German social foundation) partnered with the Kenyan government to provide off-grid solar power solutions to rural* *communities. This initiative improved access to electricity, empowering businesses, healthcare delivery, and creating educational opportunities;*

- *Fostering innovation and entrepreneurship: Provide mentorship, funding, and training to local African entrepreneurs. For example: GE's Africa Innovation Centre in Johannesburg provides a platform for African entrepreneurs to develop and scale their businesses. This real-world initiative empowers African innovators to address local challenges in areas like healthcare, energy, and water;*

- *Partnering for sustainable development: Collaborate with African stakeholders on initiatives like environmental protection, renewable energy, and climate change adaptation.*

By adopting these strategies, Western businesses can become partners in Africa's development. This creates a win-win situation, where businesses gain access to ethical resources and new markets, while African communities benefit from job creation, infrastructure development, and a more sustainable future.

THE EARTH IS FEMALE

Kowawa Kapukaja Apurinã

W*ords are spells, especially when they stem from our encounters with others. The cosmos are divergent and plural, but what distances humanity from itself is immediate consumption, supported by contemporary technologies and the culture of predation, which can be termed the Capitalocene: the era of Earth's predation and the accumulation of goods and status, devoid of spirituality.*

In the vastness of the Amazon, rivers follow their paths, and the waters are the lifelines for the inhabitants of the region. The forests and all the lives they shelter enchant themselves in harmony, far from technologies, diseases, and the scarcity of capitalist humanity. It is necessary to understand that we, human beings, are the only living beings who need accessories and countless theories to justify our presence on Earth, and to do this, we become predators of other species and ourselves. The waters flow, and one day they will reach the sea. The Earth is fertile, like a great womb of terrestrial life, and humanity's presence is the plague that destroys all horizons of this place with its machinery, contraptions, and empty rhetoric.

Will we end up in a great darkness of a starless sky, devastated cities, polluted seas, and widespread hunger and misery? Rationality becomes the justification for boundless predation, the development that distances, segregates, and excludes us. This is not the future we desire. Therefore, a change in thinking is fundamental, moving from the individual to the collective to connect with our ancient ancestries of well-being. We must understand that we are part of a whole, part of the body of Mother Earth.

We, the indigenous peoples of the global south, have learned to seek involvement within lightness and deep otherness, not just of the other but of all living and enchanted beings. For us, thought is collective; it is not the property of an individual or capital corporations. We practice the exercise of caring for each other (humans and non-humans). Everything is intertwined with the currents of affection and the flowing waters of caring for oneself and others. Western humanity has lost its way over time, forgetting its original shelters and channels of the Earth; valleys, forests, mountains, rivers, animals, and the consciousness of the subtle bonds that link them to places in nature. You need to reconnect with your noblest values, open up to connections with your origins, and be receptive to differences, for diversity is, has been, and will be the essence of life among us on the planet.

Caring for this planet means caring for everyone, with our fragilities and smallness. Recognising this is to recognise oneself collectively. The Earth is female, and we are all sons and daughters connected to all her fertility enchantments on this small blue planet. I am Kowawa Kapukaja Apurinã, daughter of Sakema, granddaughter of Kasatô, friend of the stars, lover of deep waters, and witch of ancient enchantments. May the Gods and Goddesses of all territories and universes, who are of the Good Words, teach us to walk on the only place we belong, our humanitarian cradle on Earth.

THE PROBLEM WITH STORIES FROM THE GLOBAL SOUTH

The problem with stories from the Global South is that many of us (in the Global North) just don't care that much about suffering that happens in the Global South. Stories from far away have less impact.

Here's a poem called *Flood Waters*:

Flood waters
Mothers and daughters
Pictures seen on the news
They don't care who dies
When they can't see their eyes
That's not a picture they choose

Just when she said
The riverbed's dead
Sipped on your favourite drink
Pass the pepper and salt
Who was at fault
Not me, don't ask me to think

Old people lying
And younger ones dying
you know there's salt in their tears
You don't care who dies
When you can't see their eyes
The rest of it, privileged fears

Sun higher overhead
Just another few dead
pinch of salt, on the lips of insanity
I must care who dies
Though I can't see their eyes
Assault for the voice of humanity

Note the couplet:

> **They don't care who dies**
> **When they can't see their eyes**

We all know this is true, to a greater or lesser extent. Naturally, we care more about those who are closer to us. We start with our friends and family, and then our local community. These are the targets of our love and affection. Most of us can bring fervour and passion to the 'love of our country', following the exploits of those who represent our countries in football (the soccer kind) and rugby, and athletics. We even get behind, and support, and cheer for our own respective continents in the Ryder Cup. We are outraged when our communities are threatened, disadvantaged, or discommoded.

But if they don't look like us, or they have different beliefs, or they come from the 'wrong side of town', or they are not our kind, or they come from afar, or we can't really see them, do we really care?

We know that in many places far or near, in our own countries, in each of our cities, maybe even on our streets or in our communities, there are people who are severely disadvantaged, economically, socially, ethnically, or as a consequence of climate change.

But if we can't see their eyes, do we care if they die?

Let's tell the story of Oliver, a young American boy who grew up in an upper middle-class family in New York.

Everyone loved Oliver, named by his mother after her favourite Dicken's novel. After three girls, she said, the arrival of Oliver was definitely a twist. Every time she said that, she chuckled. In Oliver's youth, he suffered from asthma, so his family moved out of Manhattan to Putnam County, New York. Living near Fahnestock State Park, the lush forest of oak, maple, and birch was just the healthy environment that Oliver needed. He grew to be a fit and healthy young boy, playing in goal for his local soccer team.

Oliver died in late 2023, just a few months after the Canadian fires. Beginning in March 2023 and increasing in intensity around June, the worst wildfire season in Canadian history affected Alberta, Ontario and Quebec. According to Oliver's mother, the smoke from it seemed to settle over Putnam County for months. We are not sure what killed Oliver, whether it was acute lower respiratory infection, aggravated asthma, or ensuing heart disease. Each of these are consequences of air pollution, which kills more Americans than guns or car accidents. In this case, climate change caused the fires and delivered the worst air pollution in New York's history. The smoke travelled down the east coast, stopped long enough in Putnam to cause the death of a young boy, before continuing on to the southeast and then across the Atlantic to Europe. Oliver's mother is now a mere shell, an empty vessel, looking for answers.

When you think about major injustices of history, you might recall racial segregation in the US, antisemitism and the Holocaust in Europe, or the worldwide brutality and exploitation of colonialism. But these, even taken together, are minor when you compare them to climate injustice, where those who are doing most damage to the planet suffer the least. Like segregation, antisemitism, and colonialism, climate injustice is about power, greed, and exploitation. Those who have – the wealthy nations, the rich companies or communities, the profligate consumers – are exploiting those who have nothing, or who are not equipped for the daily stress of living or surviving.

Today, those who have nothing – poorer countries, the colonised, the aged, those who are not allowed to vote, the indigenous, the poor and destitute, the homeless and hungry, the developing world, ethnic minorities, women, and those without access to education – are being severely disadvantaged by climate change, but also by actions that lead to climate change and social or economic disadvantage.

It is never too late to do the right thing. The place to start is with a justice mindset. As Professor Joyeeta Gupta,[14] states:

> *Justice is a necessity for humanity to live within planetary limits. This is a conclusion seen across the scientific community in multiple heavyweight environmental assessments. It is not a political choice. Overwhelming evidence shows that a just and equitable approach is essential to planetary stability. We cannot have a biophysically safe planet without justice. This includes setting just targets to prevent significant harm and guarantee access to resources to people and for just transformations to achieve those targets.*

If we want to slow our collective terminal illness, we need to transform our societies by focusing on social justice for the most affected communities first.

Remember, every action we take has a knock-on effect on someone somewhere. Someone is affected. Sometimes it is a positive effect; frequently it not. To guide our thoughts and actions we should consider the different affected communities.

THE RIGHTS OF AFFECTED COMMUNITIES

There are three lenses through which we should view how the activities of individuals, companies or nations might impact the rights of different communities:

- The economic, cultural and social rights of a community;
- The civil and political rights of a community;
- The rights of indigenous communities.

From the perspective of a business, the concept of rights overlaps significantly with the rights of workers in their own operations and in their value chain, as discussed in the previous chapter, **Chapter 7: Own Workforce & Workers in the Value Chain**, so I will not repeat that here. I will ask you instead to bring that context with you as you continue here. The topics covered in the next chapter, **Chapter 9: Consumers & End-users**, inevitably touch on many of the same issues visited here and similarly, **Chapter 10: Business Conduct** covers political engagement and lobbying, sometimes bedfellows of corruption and bribery, so I will only touch lightly on them here.

Climate change is fundamentally a human rights issue. Climate injustice is the greatest human rights injustice we have ever seen. Having an intersectional approach to affected communities is a big part of the equation that policymakers seem to miss. System change is the emergency we need to face, and we need to tackle it from the root cause: overconsumption, overexploitation and a privileged mindset.

The Economic, Cultural & Social Rights of a Community

Affected communities are

- **Local communities:** Those living adjacent to the organisation's operations, such as those near a mining site or a factory;

- **Indigenous peoples:** Tribal peoples in independent countries whose social, cultural, and economic conditions distinguish them from other sections of the national community, and whose status is regulated wholly or partially by their own customs or traditions or by special laws or regulations;

- **Communities in the value chain:** Those involved in the company's value chain, such as suppliers, contractors, or partners whose livelihoods may be impacted by the company's operations.

The economic, cultural and social rights of a community are the fundamental rights that enable individuals and groups to live a life of dignity and well-being. These rights include access to adequate housing, food, water, sanitation, healthcare, education, and employment. This involves ensuring that communities have equal access to economic opportunities, social services, and cultural participation.

It is probably worth pausing for a moment to think about how your company, and your stewardship of its capabilities and resources, might impact on your local community.

Is anyone in the local community stressed by a lack of food because climate change has restricted the ability of producers to produce food? Is the water in your neighbourhood clean and plentiful, or is it polluted by local industrial practices or agricultural effluent? Have local reservoirs dried up, or are they threatened? Does your company impact positively or negatively on any of these factors?

Now stretch your mind to think about communities that are not local to you. If you cannot see it, does that mean you don't care pay any attention to it? Of course not. What is it about geographical challenges, topological characteristics, or more specifically anthropogenic activities or governmental policies that impinge on the economic, cultural and social rights of a community? How do the operations of your business, or those of your value chain, augment or alleviate any impact?

Socio-economic disadvantages are compounded in many circumstances where stresses, such as extreme heat, disrupt one's normal environment. As an example, excessive heat is the biggest threat from climate change, and those less privileged will suffer more. Other areas threatened by extreme heat include:

- **Education and income:** Individuals with less education and income often face higher risks of heat-related mortality. This is partly due to limited access to air conditioning, health care, and other resources that can mitigate heat stress;[15]

- **Housing conditions:** Poor housing conditions, such as lack of proper insulation or ventilation, can exacerbate the effects of heatwaves, especially in urban areas where the heat island effect is more pronounced;[16]

- **Occupation:** People working in outdoor or physically demanding jobs are more exposed to heat stress, which leads to more heat-related illnesses and deaths;[17]

- **Age and gender:** Older adults, children, and women are often more vulnerable to heat-related mortality. Older adults may have chronic health conditions that are exacerbated by heat. Women are more likely to be caregivers and less likely to prioritise their own health during heatwaves.[18]

Affecting communities in real life

There are many recorded examples of cases where companies are being brought to trial for their operational activities that cause damages to the economic, social or cultural rights of community. While the outcome of the litigation is sometimes uncertain, and certainly protracted, the damage is usually real, and distressingly so. One story to tell is that of the Olympics in Rio De Janeiro, Brazil, in 2016.

The Olympic Game's legacy of displacement

You might expect that a construction company building a new sports stadium should assess its impacts on the local communities and their access to adequate housing. This could include evaluating whether the influx of workers has driven up housing prices and displaced residents, or whether the company's need for land or operations have damaged or destroyed existing housing. When it comes to major sports events like the Olympics or the World Cup, it is not always so benign.

Before and during the Olympic Games, the media coverage is mostly about the track and running stars, the pursuits of the pinnacle of performance by athletes, and the national pride of hearing one's own national anthem as someone from your tribe climbs the podium.

There is less coverage, however, about the people whose lives are thrown into chaos by the Olympics every four years: poor people who find themselves living in the wrong place, on land that the Games need for stadiums and parking lots. Poor people who are, per Olympic tradition, evicted and sent packing into a difficult new life.

An article in the *Washington Post*, 'The Price of Gold', is largely focused on the Olympic games in Rio, Brazil, but it also tells of the trauma around the sites of many other Olympic venues:

> In the lead-up to the 1988 Games, in Seoul, 720,000 people were forcibly moved. Before the 2008 Games, in Beijing, 1.5 million Chinese were reportedly shunted out of the way; resisters were handed one-year 're-education through labour' sentences. You could tell this story in either Seoul or Beijing, or in London, where a low-income housing development, Clays Lane, was erased to make way for the 2012 Games.

A research study[19] was conducted on Vila Autódromo, a small favela located next to the Rio 2016 Olympic Park, that was almost totally removed during the process of preparing the area to host the Games. The researcher interviewed 13 residents who passed through the process of eviction threats and displacement. Five still live in Vila Autódromo, whilst eight moved to social apartments provided by the city. The interviews revealed that the legacy of Rio 2016 for Vila Autódromo residents can be understood from three broad themes:

- Disempowerment of the community;
- Resistance and resilience during the process;
- Life after the Games.

The study concludes that the legacy of Rio 2016 for them is a very sad story.

Poor people have very little leverage against the International Olympic Committee, which oversees the Games and earned a total of $5.7 billion from the 2014 and 2016 Olympics. Even against the resistance of the residents, the city of Rio kept levelling Vila Autódromo that year.

Overall, during the seven-year preparation time (2009 to 2016), Rio city hall displaced more than 77,000 people from their houses in *favelas* or poor communities, arguing for the necessity of making space for infrastructural projects that were somehow related to Rio

2016, and 11 people were reported to have died during the construction.

Is Cargill the worst company in the world?
In an extensive article on Cargill, the American conglomerate, entitled 'Cargill: The Worst Company in the World' and written by Mighty Earth, a global environmental advocacy organisation, Mighty Earth's chairman, former Congressman Henry A. Waxman, says:

> *The people who have been sickened or died from eating contaminated Cargill meat, the child labourers who grow the cocoa Cargill sells for the world's chocolate, the Midwesterners who drink water polluted by Cargill, the Indigenous People displaced by vast deforestation to make way for Cargill's animal feed, and the ordinary consumers who've paid more to put food on the dinner table because of Cargill's financial malfeasance – all have felt the impact of this agribusiness giant. Their lives are worse for having come into contact with Cargill.*

The quote comes from the Foreword of an extensive report that backs up in detail a fairly audacious claim: that Cargill is the "Worst Company in the World".[20] You can judge that claim for yourself, but the quote neatly captures much of what we are trying to protect against when we are concerned with the economic, cultural and social rights of a community.

As a company, you should concern yourself with any activities that you undertake that will detrimentally impact on the community's access to adequate food and water, its security, safety and well-being, ensuring at all times that you engage with any affected stakeholders, and if found deficient in any of the above, you will need to report on the deficiencies and report on the measures taken to provide or enable remedy, such as compensation, rehabilitation, or other forms of redress.

The Civil & Political Rights of a Community

Civil and political rights refer to the fundamental freedoms and entitlements that allow individuals and communities to participate in the civic and political life of society. Some key civil and political rights we should consider are:

- Freedom of expression;
- Freedom of assembly and association;
- Protection of human rights defenders;
- Participation in decision-making processes;
- Access to information.

These rights are enshrined in international human rights frameworks such as the *International Covenant on Civil & Political Rights* (ICCPR) and the *UN Guiding Principles on Business & Human Rights* (UNGPs).

Unfortunately, there are many examples of how companies of all types across the world are impacting these rights in their local communities:

- **Mining:** Mining companies' operations in the Amazon rainforest are said to have violated the rights of indigenous communities by disrupting their traditional way of life and destroying their land. This includes impacts on their freedom of expression, freedom of assembly, and the rights of human rights defenders;

- **Oil:** Oil companies have severely impacted the rights of local communities by polluting their water sources and destroying their land. Human rights defenders' lives are at risk and freedom of expression or assembly is curtailed;

- **Agriculture:** An agricultural company with operations in India has been charged with infringing on the rights of local communities by displacing them from their land and destroying their livelihoods;

- **Construction:** Construction operations in South Africa have been accused of displacing local communities from their land and destroying their livelihoods;

- **Technology:** Some companies in the US are said to have exploited the rights of local communities by collecting and using their personal data without their consent.

The importance of respecting rights and engaging meaningfully with affected communities has been lost on these companies, but as the regulations and reporting obligations take hold, there will be nowhere to hide.

Governments as targets
At a more holistic level, governments are being taken to task for their roles in damaging the environment to such an extent that communities have felt it necessary to resort to the courts for action or compensation:

- **Netherlands:** The Urgenda Climate Case against the Dutch Government was the first in the world in which citizens, as an affected community, established that their government has a legal duty to prevent dangerous climate change. On 24 June 2015, the District Court of The Hague ruled the government must cut its GHG emissions by at least 25% by the end of 2020 (compared to 1990 levels). The ruling required the government to immediately take more effective action on climate change.

The Climate Case, which was brought on behalf of 886 Dutch citizens, made climate change a major political and social issue in the Netherlands and transformed domestic climate change policy. It inspired climate change cases in Belgium, Canada, Colombia, Ireland, Germany, France, New Zealand, Norway, the UK, Switzerland and the EU.

Following the ground-breaking judgment of the District Court, the Dutch Government decided to appeal the case. On 9 October 2018, The Hague Court of Appeal upheld the 2015 court decision. In other words, Urgenda won again. Then the Dutch government took its case to the Supreme Court and lost again. The government finally committed to taking steps to meet the target;

- **USA:** In March 2020, a lawsuit was filed by 16 young residents of Montana, aged between 2 and 18 years, represented by Our Children's Trust. They challenged a provision under the *Montana Environmental Policy Act* (MEPA) known as the MEPA Limitation, which prevented state agencies from considering the impacts of GHG emissions or climate change in their environmental planning.

  The plaintiffs based their challenge on a provision of the Montana *Constitution*, which protects "the right to a clean and healthful environment". This right has been recognised as a fundamental right by the Montana Supreme Court since 1999, allowing individuals and NGOs to directly challenge state laws that allegedly violate this right.

  On August 14, 2023, Lewis & Clark County District Court Judge Kathy Seeley ruled in favour of the plaintiffs, finding that the limitations on considering environmental factors when deciding oil and gas permits violated the constitutional right to a safe environment.

  This case is notable as the first climate-related constitutional lawsuit to go to trial in the US. The ruling was significant for the youth-led US climate litigation movement. It was expected that it might encourage similar actions in other states with environmental protections in their constitutions. That is exactly what happened in Hawaii in June 2024;[21]

- **Switzerland:** In April 2024, the European Court of Human Rights (EHCR) ruled in favour of a group of seniors who alleged that the Swiss government's failure to meet climate change mitigation targets was having an adverse impact on their health, well-being and quality of life. This landmark decision by the highest human rights court in Europe confirms not only that climate change is intimately linked to human rights, but effectively holds all European governments accountable to adopt more rigorous measures to combat climate change.

- However, in June 2024, the Swiss Parliament voted against the additional climate actions mandated by the court, saying the ECHR should not interfere with Swiss democracy. This action was shocking to many. No country has ever refused a judgment by the ECHR. Switzerland has a legal obligation to implement the ruling as it is a signatory to the ECHR.

  The Swiss now have two options: to leave the ECHR, which is unlikely, or to provide a plan by October 2024 on how they will enact the ruling. Hopefully by the time you read this, the correct action will have occurred.

The rise of SLAPPs

SLAPP stands for Strategic Lawsuit Against Public Participation. It refers to lawsuits that are intended to censor, intimidate, and silence critics, in this case representatives of an affected community, by burdening them with the cost of a legal defence until they abandon their criticism or opposition. These lawsuits are abusive because they can be used to stifle lawful scrutiny and publication on matters of public interest, such as corruption or wrongdoing.

In the case of a SLAPP, the plaintiff does not normally expect to win the lawsuit. The goal is to force the defendant into abandoning their criticism due to fear, intimidation, mounting legal costs, or exhaustion and to deter others from participating in public debate. SLAPPs threaten freedom of speech and democratic participation by suppressing information that should be public. They are particularly damaging to journalists, activists, and individuals who speak out on issues of public interest.

Examples of SLAPPs include:

- **Exxon's SLAPP against Arjuna Capital:**[22] The case of *Exxon vs Arjuna* involved a lawsuit filed by Exxon Mobil Corp against the activist shareholder group Arjuna Capital over a climate proposal. Exxon sued Arjuna Capital to prevent them from submitting a climate proposal at Exxon's annual shareholder meeting. The proposal called for Exxon to accelerate carbon dioxide (CO_2) emissions reductions. After Exxon filed the lawsuit, Arjuna Capital withdrew its proposal and made an "unconditional and irrevocable" pledge not to file a similar shareholder proposal in the future. Exxon then filed a status report stating that, although the shareholders had said they would not file the proposal in future years, the withdrawal did not provide Exxon complete relief. Exxon said it would continue with the suit because a ruling from the court was needed on whether the exclusions relating to ordinary business" or "resubmission" in the *Rules* of the Securities & Exchange Commission (SEC) would allow Exxon to exclude the proposal from its proxy statement.

In June 2024, a federal judge in Texas dismissed the lawsuit, ruling that the case was moot due to Arjuna's pledge. The judge stated that, without a live case or controversy, the court could not advise Exxon of its rights. While, at the end, this was the judgement that Arjuna needed to get out of the lawsuit, the net effect is that Exxon's tactics put an end to Arjuna's activism;

- **Energy Transfer's SLAPP against Greenpeace:**[23] The Dakota Access Pipeline (DAPL), proposed by Energy Transfer and its partners in 2014, would have carried crude oil from North Dakota's Bakken oil field to Illinois, and then down to the US Gulf Coast. DAPL was part of the fracking boom that began in the region in 2008 that also spurred the construction of oil export terminals and other infrastructure. From the very start, members of the Standing Rock Sioux Tribe, along with other Sioux Nations, opposed the pipeline.

  As time passed, anti-pipeline protests grew, gaining national and international attention as construction neared the river. The Obama administration denied land access for the pipeline, but the Trump administration reversed this decision upon taking office. Energy Transfer CEO Kelcy Warren had donated to the Trump's re-election campaign.

  In 2017, the pipeline was completed and became operational. Energy Transfer filed a suit against Greenpeace, and not the Standing Rock Sioux Tribe who had organised the protests. The case is still ongoing. According to Greenpeace: "We are being sued by Energy Transfer for nearly US $300 million related to the Indigenous-led 2016 protests at Standing Rock. Not only does this SLAPP attempt to rewrite the history of this movement led by the Standing Rock Sioux, but a loss at trial could prove destructive to Greenpeace in the US and have widespread impacts for the climate justice movement all around the world".

The Rights of Indigenous Communities

Indigenous communities were there first. They stewarded the land and the animals and the resources long before the colonisers arrived and took it all away. There is a large debt to be paid.

When you look up the word 'indigenous', the answer you get is clear.

indigenous

/ɪnˈdɪdʒɪnəs/ **adjective**

1. originating or occurring naturally in a particular place; native.
    'coriander is indigenous to southern Europe'

2. (of people) <u>inhabiting</u> or existing in a land from the earliest times or from before the arrival of <u>colonists</u>.
    'she wants the territorial government to speak with Indigenous people before implementing a programme'

Source: Oxford Languages

I like the simple definition:

> **Indigenous**: *(of people) inhabiting or existing in a land from the earliest times or from before the arrival of colonists.*

You might also take note of the example sentence that is used:

> *She wants the territorial government to speak with Indigenous people before implementing a programme.*

Those two sentences describe:

- The **cause** of many of the problems that most Indigenous communities have today: colonisation. There were no colonies and far fewer disadvantaged Indigenous communities before colonisation;

- The **solution** going forward: governments and businesses should listen to Indigenous communities prior to taking any actions. That does not go far enough though. Indigenous communities must have complete right of self-determination.

In the Western world, Indigenous communities are generally identified as tribal peoples in independent countries whose social, cultural, and economic conditions distinguish them from other sections of the national community, and whose status is regulated wholly or partially by their own customs or traditions or by special laws or regulations.

Alternatively, they may be considered to be 'indigenous' on account of their descent from the populations that inhabited the country, or a geographical region to which the country belongs, at the time of conquest or colonisation or the establishment of the present state boundaries. These peoples, regardless of their legal status, retain some or all of their own social, economic, cultural, and political institutions, and we are all the richer for it.

Despite the fact that indigenous peoples make up around 15% of the world's extreme poor and just 6% of the global population, they care for 22% of the Earth's surface, and are protecting 80% of the world's remaining biodiversity.[24] This highlights how indigenous communities have learned how to live alongside nature in a way that other communities have not, and if we needed a reason, it underlines why it is essential that we serve their needs fairly and respectfully.

Indigenous people (and marginalised communities too) are on the frontlines of the planetary emergency, and we must be very conscious that we respect their rights, which include:

- **Free, prior and informed consent:** This involves the right to be consulted, participate, and have control over their lands, territories, and resources. It is a manifestation of indigenous peoples' right to self-determination;

- **Self-determination:** This includes the right to free, prior and informed consent, as well as the right to manage their own affairs and make decisions about their future;

- **Cultural rights:** These include the right to participate in the cultural life of the community and to preserve their cultural identity;

- **Human rights:** Indigenous peoples are entitled to the same human rights as all other individuals, including the right to life, liberty, security of person, and an adequate standard of living;

- **Right to land and resources:** Indigenous peoples have the right to their lands, territories, and resources, which are essential for their survival and well-being.

These rights are recognised and emphasised in international instruments such as the ICCPR, the *International Covenant on Economic, Social & Cultural Rights* (ICESCR), and the *United Nations Declaration on the Rights of Indigenous Peoples*.

Are the Sami the last indigenous people in Europe?
Spreading across the Arctic regions of Sweden, Norway, Finland, and Russia, the Sami people have faced significant challenges in

protecting their reindeer herding practices, culture, and land against the encroachment of mining companies.

The Sami people have the right to pursue reindeer herding, which is essential to their culture and livelihood. However, their rights are often restricted by the Swedish government, which has granted mining concessions to companies like Beowulf Mining, threatening the Sami way of life. The mining activities force them to travel up North, where life is not possible for them and their herds. Reindeer herding is not only an economic activity but also a cultural practice that defines the Sami identity. The loss of reindeer herding would lead to the erosion of Sami culture and the loss of their traditional way of life. However, the Swedish government has failed to recognise their land rights, leading to conflicts over land use and ownership and the Sami people have had to stand up for themselves.

The UN has criticised Sweden for failing to protect the Sami people's rights, particularly in the context of mining activities, and has urged Sweden to halt mining projects that violate Sami rights and to engage in meaningful consultations with the Sami community.

If we are to have a liveable planet, Indigenous people need to be considered a key stakeholder and treated equitably. We have long way to go.

ESRS-S3 – AFFECTED COMMUNITIES REPORTING OBLIGATIONS

Ingrid De Doncker

Engaging communities is important because it builds trust and loyalty, enhances employee satisfaction, stimulates local economies, attracts talent, manages risks, fosters innovation, and ensures long-term sustainability. These benefits collectively contribute to the overall success and positive impact of businesses and organisations.

ESRS-S3 is the reporting standard that helps to ensure that companies are transparent about their social responsibilities and the effects of their operations on local communities. It enables users of the sustainability statement to understand material impacts on affected communities connected with the organisation's own operations and value chain, including through its products or services, as well as through its business relationships, and its related material risks and opportunities, including:

- How the organisation affects communities, in areas where impacts are most likely to be present and severe, in terms of material positive and negative actual or potential impacts;
- Any actions taken, and the result of such actions, to prevent, mitigate or remediate actual or potential negative impacts, and to address risks and opportunities;
- The nature, type and extent of the organisation's material risks and opportunities related to its impacts and dependencies on affected communities, and how the organisation manages them;
- The financial effects on the organisation over the short-, medium- and long-term of material risks and opportunities arising from the organisation's impacts and dependencies on affected communities.

The Affected Communities Sub-topics

ESRS-S3 covers three main sub-topics related to how a company's operations impact local communities:

- **Communities' economic, social and cultural rights:** This includes adequate housing, adequate food, water and sanitation, land-related and security-related impacts;
- **Communities' civil and political rights:** Examples here are freedom of expression, freedom of assembly, impacts on human rights defenders;
- **Rights of indigenous peoples:** Here we think about free, prior and informed consent, self-determination, cultural rights.

This standard applies when material impacts on and/or material risks and opportunities related to affected communities have been identified through the materiality assessment process laid out in ESRS 2 *General Disclosures*. This Standard shall be read in conjunction with ESRS 1 *General Requirements*, and ESRS 2, as well as the ESRS-S1: *Own Workforce*, ESRS-S2: *Workers in the Value Chain* and ESRS-S4: *Consumers & End-users*. The requirements of this section should be read in conjunction with the disclosures required by ESRS 2 on Strategy (SBM). The resulting disclosures shall be presented alongside the disclosures required by ESRS 2, except for SBM-3

Material impacts, risks and opportunities and their interaction with SBM, for which the organisation has an option to present the disclosures alongside the topical disclosure.

It is important to understand the *Minimum Disclosure Requirements* (MDRs) in ESRS 2, Chapter 4.2. When an organisation identifies a sustainability matter as material, 34 MDR data points (DPs) for Policies, Actions, Targets, and Metrics (PAT-M) are applicable if the organisation discloses on policies, actions and targets. If it does not provide disclosure on policies, targets or actions, then it needs to disclose the reasons for not doing so, as per the corresponding 10 DPs of ESRS 2 MDR PAT paragraphs 62 and 81.

ESRS-S3 outlines clearly, in five *Disclosure Requirements* (DRs), the narrative and numeric DPs an organisation should comply with. There are 45 *Shall* DPs, and they are all narrative. There are 18 additional *May* DPs. The MDR PAT DPs are to be disclosed under S3-1, S3-4, S3-5 when the sustainability matters are material.

Figure 8.1 : ESRS-S3 Reporting Requirements

ESRS-E4	Resource Use & Circular Economy		
	Communities' economic, social and cultural rights	Communities' civil and political rights	Rights of indigenous peoples
	All below are subject to materiality for each of the sub-topics.		
	STRATEGY		
ESRS2-S3-SBM-2	Interest and views of stakeholders.		
ESRS2-S3-SBM-2	Material impacts, risks and opportunities and their interaction with strategy and business model.		
	IMPACT, RISK & OPPORTUNITY MANAGEMENT		
ESRS-S3-1	**Policies** related to affected communities.		
ESRS-S3-2	**Processes** for engaging with affected communities about impacts.		
ESRS-S3-3	**Processes** to remediate negative impacts and channels for affected communities to raise concerns.		
ESRS-S3-4	**Taking action** on material impacts on affected communities, and approaches to managing material risks and pursuing material opportunities related to affected communities, and effectiveness of those actions.		
	METRICS & TARGETS		
ESRS-S3-5	**Targets** related to managing material negative impacts, advancing positive impacts, and managing material risks and opportunities.		

Figure 8.1 shows the structure of the ESRS-S3 DRs and DPs that must be reported, if deemed material by the double materiality assessment.

ESRS-S3 aligns with internationally recognised standards and guidelines, such as the UNGPs, ILO conventions, OECD *Guidelines for Multinational Enterprises*, the Global Reporting Initiative (GRI), the Task Force on Climate-related Financial Disclosures (TCFD), the United Nations SDGs, particularly those on SDG8: *Decent Work & Economic Growth* and SDG11: *Sustainable Cities & Communities*.

ESRS-S3 and the CSDDD also are closely linked. Both aim to enhance corporate accountability and transparency regarding the impacts of business operations on communities and the environment. Both emphasise the importance of engaging with stakeholders, particularly affected communities, to understand their concerns and address potential adverse impacts.

Finally, ESRS-S3 and the CSDDD are designed to be compatible with other EU sustainability initiatives, such as the EU *Taxonomy* and the *Sustainable Finance Disclosure Regulation* (SFDR). This integration ensures a cohesive approach to sustainability reporting and due diligence across different regulatory frameworks.

---

[1] *Essay on Tragedy of the Commons* – Free Essay Example – Edubirdie, accessed June 15, 2024, https://edubirdie.com/examples/essay-on-tragedy-of-the-commons/.

[2] According to Disaster Philanthropy, Pakistan's 2022 monsoon season produced significant rainfall, devastating floods and landslides, affecting millions of people. The floods affected all four of the country's provinces and approximately 15% of its population. https://disasterphilanthropy.org/disasters/2022-pakistan-floods/.

[3] *Kenya's bad urban planning and human pressure led to floods*, https://www.fastcompany.com/91117592/kenya-floods-urban-planning-human-pressure.

[4] *Addressing the Short- and Long-Term Impacts of Kenya's Floods*, https://cfkafrica.org/addressing-the-short-and-long-term-impacts-of-kenyas-floods-cfk-africas-response/.

[5] *Kenya: Floods cause widespread devastation in* Nairobi, MPR News. https://www.mprnews.org/story/2024/04/25/kenya-floods-cause-widespread-devastation-in-nairobi.

[6] *Kenya: Floods cause widespread devastation in Nairobi*, MPR News, https://www.mprnews.org/story/2024/04/25/kenya-floods-cause-widespread-devastation-in-nairobi.

[7] *Kenya's bad urban planning and human pressure led to floods*, https://www.fastcompany.com/91117592/kenya-floods-urban-planning-human-pressure.

8   *UN Human Rights team issues report on post-election violence,*
     https://www.ohchr.org/en/press-releases/2009/10/un-human-rights-team-
     issues-report-post-election-violence-kenya.

9   *Waki Report*: https://www.knchr.org/Portals/0/Reports/Waki_Report.pdf.

10   *Our Stories*: Kenya – US Agency for International Development,
     https://www.usaid.gov/kenya/our-stories?block_config_key=aZ-
     omnGBìYm_wSLA1a gQXyhkz-
     ttqZBWh8REobM8CyY&field_content_category_target_id_1%5B1158%5D=1158
     &field_tags_target_id%5B37191%5D=37191&page=1&sort_by=created&sort_orde
     r=DESC.

11   *UN Human Rights team issues report on post-election* violence,
     https://www.ohchr.org/en/press-releases/2009/10/un-human-rights-team-
     issues-report-post-election-violence-kenya.

12   https://en.wikipedia.org/wiki/Resource_curse.

13   *USGS Cobalt Mineral Commodity Summary 2023,*
     https://pubs.usgs.gov/periodicals/mcs2023/mcs2023-cobalt.pdf.

14   Professor Joyetta Gupta is Co-Chair of the Earth Commission, Professor of Law
     & Policy in Water Resources & Environment at IHE Delft and Professor of
     Environment & Development in the Global South at the University of
     Amsterdam.

15   *Social inequalities in heat-attributable mortality in the city of Turin,
     northwest of Italy: a time series analysis from 1982 to 2018,*
     https://ehjournal.biomedcentral.com/articles/10.1186/s12940-020-00667-x.

16   *Heat Exposure and Socio-Economic Vulnerability as Synergistic Factors in
     Heat-Wave-Related Mortality*, https://www.jstor.org/stable/40284160.

17   *Climate Change, Occupational Heat Stress, Human Health & Socio-
     Economic Factors*, https://link.springer.com/referenceworkentry/ 10.1007/978-
     3-030-05031-3_37-1.

18   *Social inequalities in heat-attributable mortality in the city of Turin,
     northwest of Italy: a time series analysis from 1982 to 2018,*
     https://ehjournal.biomedcentral.com/articles/10.1186/s12940-020-00667-x.

19   *Rio 2016 Olympic Legacy for Residents of Favelas: Revisiting the Case of Vila
     Autódromo Five Years Later*, https://www.mdpi.com/2076-0760/12/3/166.

20   *Cargill: The Worst Company in the World*, https://stories.mightyearth.org/
     cargill-worst-company-in-the-world/.

21   *Navahine v Hawaii Department of Transport*,
     https://navahinevhawaiidot.ourchildrenstrust.org/.

22   *Exxon Mobil Corp. v Arjuna Capital, LLC*, https://climatecasechart.com/
     case/exxon-mobil-corp-v-arjuna-capital-llc/.

23   *Energy Transfer v Greenpeace*, https://climatecasechart.com/case/energy-
     transfer-equity-lp-v-greenpeace-international/.

24   *Australia's State of the Environment Report*, https://soe.dcceew.gov.au/
     climate/management/national-and-international-frameworks#-cli-21-figure-
     21-indigenous-peoples-and-the-environment.

9

CONSUMERS & END-USERS

Orla Carolan

One Christmas a few years back, I read a newspaper article, 'No new clothes for a year', about a person who had only purchased or swapped second-hand clothes over the previous 12 months in order to reduce waste and stop buying things that she clearly did not need. I read the article more than once, and thought it was something I should try. However, a few days later, I found myself at the January sales making the usual impulse purchases of winter coats and last season boots at knock-down prices. It would save me next winter and they were an investment at a fraction of full cost. I clearly was not ready to embrace a 'conscious consumer' mindset or turn this idea into action. It was few years too early for me.

I don't think I am the only one who has an intention to do good, to lessen my impact, to reduce waste, or to spend less on things I do not need. Nor am I the only one who has such intentions that don't translate into actual actions.

There has been plenty of research conducted in recent years in this area to understand buyer motivation and how 'sustainability' or 'sustainable outcomes' influence our buying decisions and behaviours. When it comes to an environmentally or socially responsible lifestyle, the space between those intentions and action can be a grey area, rather than a green one. In a cost-of-living crisis or recessionary times, not surprisingly consumers prioritise cost-saving over green or social values. In a 2023 worldwide survey,[1] 70% of consumers who took part cited sustainable living as important to them but a whopping 61% said they lacked the awareness or motivation to actually do it.[2] A bit like what happened to me.

I see this play out even further in my own home. I have two teenage daughters who like to shop. And when they shop, they want their purchases to arrive in real time at little or no cost. They are not unaware of where the garment or accessory has come from and that someone their own age who is lowly paid may have been the person who made it, but it doesn't change their buying behaviour and they will eagerly await the Amazon van or courier delivery, and check the post box daily until it is safely in their possession. They will probably wear what has arrived a handful of times, or maybe even just once, before ordering its replacement, usually from the same website, after seeing their favourite influencer online twirling around in the latest trend.

Thousands of such influencers work for these global online fashion brands, targeting young buyers like my daughters. They post daily on social media sites showing off their 'hauls', which usually include piles of boxes containing bigger piles of clothes, gadgets or cosmetics they have supposedly purchased for next to nothing but were probably 'gifted' free to market to their young *audiences. And their followers will follow, ordering the same items from the same websites in large quantities.*

According to a 2022 report[3] on popular global fashion companies, the most searched brand worldwide (across 113 different countries) was the Chinese fast-fashion retailer Shein. Shein and other such brands can add thousands of lines to their apps on a daily basis. This is definitely not a model that we can think is in any way sustainable from an environmental perspective. And it also has suffered from negative media coverage, due to poor working conditions and labour law violations.

Orla Carolan

FROM ACCOUNTING TO SUSTAINABILITY – FINDING MY OWN VALUES

It might be useful for context to explain how I have arrived (more recently) to sustainability, and a career in this area, one which I hope will sustain me until I retire, which thankfully is not in the near-term horizon.

I have a banking and financial services background and have worked in finance and corporate reporting for most of my career, the majority of which was in the investment banking space in administration and accounting for hedge funds whose investors were high net worth individuals. The balance sheet numbers never seemed real to me, like it was actually someone's money, that they could be *that* wealthy and still drive and thrive on more return as markets moved in their favour. I never felt totally at ease in this work, which was a bit too 'capitalist' and maybe wasn't where I should be. I was also searching for something else, not knowing what that was, but it had to be where I could make an impact in a positive way on other people, wider society or just giving back and seeing someone else achieve because I was able to help them to do so.

After leaving this 'first' career, I worked as an executive and career coach which was closer to my purpose of helping others, a time I thoroughly enjoyed but funnily enough I missed the 'large company' vibe. So I moved into professional services and, as part of my new role, I got to spend the guts of a year working with an amazing team in the Central Bank of Ireland on a project to understand the impact on consumers of investment funds – that is, retail and wholesale investors when things went wrong. Things could go wrong for many reasons – for example, the fund manager or investment company could commit a fraud or other misconduct, leading to loss or failure of the investment product and ultimately causing harm to its investors. A wider economic shock (for example, a property market crash) could lead to failure of investment funds with large exposures to residential property, also causing an impact and loss to investors. I loved this work, and there was a purpose in it that was more than just earning fees, which is what I was used to from working in the bank or an advisory practice.

Overall, the Central Bank of Ireland and other European and global supervisory authorities have a sharp focus on consumer protection, some of which is born out of previous catastrophic failures of the banking system and the personnel within those financial institutions.

As part of its work, the Central Bank of Ireland has defined its 'key drivers of consumer risk' in its latest *Consumer Protection Outlook Report* (2023).[4] These are areas of focus for the regulator and the entities it supervises but probably are also appropriate to think about for any business with respect to their customers and at what points there may be more risk of those consumers being harmed.

These key drivers of consumer risk are:

- Poor business practices and weak business processes;
- Ineffective disclosures to customers;
- The changing operational landscape;
- Technology-driven risks to consumer protection;
- The impact of shifting business models.

These drivers focus on governance but also link into strategy and business model and other social topics reflected within the new *European Sustainability Reporting Standards* (ESRS). These drivers were defined by the Central Bank in its role as the supervisory authority to regulated financial institutions with the intention that "sustained concrete action by regulated firms would make a material positive difference for consumers of financial services". The ESRS and other wider social sustainability standards and guidelines also aim to achieve broadly similar objectives for all consumers and end-users.

I am not sure at this stage what number career I am at; I would probably say it is a 'third' twist. It happened a little by accident but has brought me to a place where impact is the highest priority. As part of my professional services role, I also took up a secondment in 2022 with the European Financial Reporting Advisory Group (EFRAG), around the time when EFRAG took on the responsibility of advising the European Commission on what should be included within the ESRS to reflect the requirements set out within the *Corporate Sustainability Reporting Directive* (CSRD) for organisations to report against certain environmental, social and governance topics. EFRAG is a standard-setter, responsible for the enormous task of drafting sustainability standards for Europe and working closely with other jurisdictions and standard-setters, including the International Sustainability Standards Board (ISSB) and Global Reporting Initiative (GRI).

I spent around 18 months in total at the EFRAG Secretariat, in differing capacities, working with an amazing team, initiating the sector-specific standard development programme whilst the wider team literally moved mountains to finalise and release the first set of sector-agnostic ESRS, which organisations in scope will apply beginning this year FY 2024.

It was an incredible learning experience, observing and being part of the research and disclosure development work and has given me an opportunity to now work in this area. After initiating the CSRD service line within the professional services firm I worked for, I had an opportunity to join the company I work for now: Future Planet. The organisation, and my role in it, are wholly about impact, with core values aligned to my own. The values that we, as an organisation, live every day and aim to embed in our interactions with our customers, stakeholders and among ourselves are respect, authenticity, impact, nurturing and of course optimism. So it has been a good move, and I have found my place and a role with the right purpose. No more bad 'capitalist' feelings for me.

CONSUMERS & CONSUMERISM

Why Do We Care about Consumers?

A customer is the most important visitor to our premises. He is not dependent on us. We are dependent on him. He is not an interruption to our work. He is the purpose of it. He is not an outsider in our business. He is part of it. We are not doing him a favour serving him. He is doing us a favour by giving us the opportunity to do so.

Mahatma Gandhi

We care about consumers, as without them businesses would not exist.

The Traditional Theory of Consumerism

Traditional economics views consumerism as a predominant driver of the economy, fuelling economic growth. Consumerism itself is the theory that individuals who consume goods and services in copious quantities will be better off. Capitalist economies rely on customer spending and encourage their populations to spend above their fundamental requirements to maintain the economy's continued growth.

A great early example of consumerism in action is the automobile industry and later the mobile phone industry. Both, through their business strategies, develop new products with superior technology and novel features, enticing people to update their models even when what they currently have still functions proficiently.[5]

The traditional view and definitions of consumerism are certainly outdated and narrower in focus than what is true in the 21st century but some things still hold true. Nonetheless, consumerism clearly does not account for sustainable outcomes, encouraging overconsumption to drive profit and performance for organisations and economies in general.

However, we still need to hold on to some of these concepts, even in a more sustainable world. Without customers or demand for a company's products or services, organisations would not exist or be able to survive. And economies and employment would not be maintained, grow, or prosper.

Overproduction & Overconsumption

> *What consumerism is at its worst is getting people to buy things that don't actually improve their lives.*
>
> **Jeff Bezos**

Overproduction is the production of goods that exceeds the needs of the consumers who are consuming them. It was the leading cause of the Great Depression – factories and farms produced more goods than the people could afford to buy, so prices fell, factories closed their doors and workers were laid off, which led to an endless cycle of poverty and want.

Overconsumption is what happens when an ecosystem can no longer sustain the use of its resources. It strips the earth of natural resources, such as forests, fish, soil, minerals, and water, which collapses ecosystems, ruins habitats and endangers the survival of countless species that contribute to an intricate, vibrant circle of life.[6]

When we overproduce and overconsume, we harm the planet and the people who inhabit that planet, including ourselves.

I keep returning to the fashion industry, but it is one of the best and most tangible examples (in addition to food) of absolute overconsumption, which has far reaching environmental and wider social impacts.

According to the founders of Community Clothing, a Lancashire-based fashion brand, the fashion industry made roughly 100 billion garments last year, and 30 billion didn't even make it into shops but went straight to the incinerator or landfill.[7] What a shocking statistic but, honestly, it is not surprising.

What about Sustainable Consumption?

Every time you spend money, you are casting a vote for the kind of world you want.

Anna Lappe

In my introduction, I referred to the 'space between intention and action' when it comes to consumer behaviour: people want to do the right thing but do not always act, for many different reasons. Most research appears to imply that younger generations, including Gen Z and millennials, make up the demographic most vocal about sustainable consumerism. Interestingly, though, a study released by global consultancy Bain & Company in November 2023 seems to dispel those perceptions, citing that concerns about climate change did not significantly vary by age, with 68% of Boomers and 69% of Gen X reporting being very or extremely concerned about the environment compared to 74% of Millennials and 72% of Gen Z. Not surprisingly, the report also found that, despite the willingness and intention to pay for more sustainable products, a significant gap still exists in consumers' ability to do so, with companies on charging on average 28% premiums for more sustainable products.

The response of older generations to this survey does not surprise me in any way. Many older consumers grew up in harder times, living through deep recessions, high unemployment and staggering interest rates on mortgages and other types of credit. Every penny spent was planned and nothing wasted. I know growing up that this was absolutely the case in my family home and, even without the same financial restrictions now, these habits still persist. We all could achieve so much more if we lived in this way, being thoughtful about everything we purchase and consume and trying to avoid waste at all costs.

Most research in this area points to the difficulties consumers have in deciphering how to shop more sustainably, including being able to interpret and understand product labelling. As a consumer myself, I sometimes feel it is extra work to try and seek out sustainable products and then when I find them am not sure how sustainable they really are. The EU Commission is making progress here, aiming to begin to remediate this lack of information for consumers with the *Ecodesign for Sustainable Products Regulation* (ESPR).

This regulation should enable the setting of performance and information conditions known as 'ecodesign requirements' – for almost all categories of physical goods (with some exceptions, such as food and feed, as defined in *Regulation 178/2002*). One of ESPR's aims is to improve the availability of information on product sustainability, which hopefully will aid consumer choices allowing them to take action.

In addition, the ESPR aims to:

- Improve product durability, reusability, upgradability and reparability;
- Make products more energy and resource-efficient;
- Address the presence of substances that inhibit circularity;
- Increase recycled content;
- Make products easier to remanufacture and recycle;
- Set rules on carbon and environmental footprints;
- Improve the availability of information on product sustainability.

The ESPR also includes other additional measures, including:

- Digital identity cards ('Digital Product Passports' – DPPs) for products, components, and materials, which will store relevant information to support products' sustainability, promote their circularity and strengthen legal compliance;
- Rules to prevent the destruction of unsold products;
- Measures around Green Public Procurement, enabling mandatory criteria to be set for EU authorities that purchase the products it will regulate.[8]

The ESPR has been published in the *EU Official Journal* and a tentative timeline has been set for implementation, with the setting up of an Ecodesign Forum planned for the second half of 2024. The first workplan for this Forum is expected to be issued in early 2025.[9]

Sustainable consumption has to be our future, something we will revisit later in this chapter.

THE EU REGULATORY CONTEXT

The EU promotes the protection of consumers in conjunction with national governments. Over the past 50 years, the EU has put in place a robust set of policies and rules to provide a high level of protection for EU consumers and to enable them to benefit from the social and economic progress Europe and its internal market have achieved. This includes an overarching product safety policy and legislation, which prevents unsafe products reaching consumers and promotes the high quality of European exports. Strong consumer law sets an EU-wide framework to combat unfair commercial practice, unfair contract terms and misleading advertising, both in domestic and cross-border situations, whilst securing consumers' rights to withdraw from contracts and seek adequate redress. The recently adopted *Consumer Rights Directive* has substantially strengthened consumer rights, in particular by harmonising a number of rules applicable to online contracts. The EU is also involved in promoting consumers' rights to information and education and it supports consumer organisations in the Member States.[10]

Consumer law is therefore nothing new and most predate the CSRD. National governments and regulators also supplement these EU laws with requirements relevant to local markets in areas where they identify requirement for additional protection measures – for example, national level *Consumer Protection Codes*.

Other more recent regulation such as the CSDDD, the ESPR, the *European Accessibility Act* and no doubt additional regulatory requirements as they emerge will continue to strengthen the focus on consumer and investor protection.

The Corporate Sustainability Reporting Directive

The CSRD amends the EU *Accounting Directive*, introducing new provisions for organisations with respect to sustainability reporting – more specifically on what sustainability information organisations need to include going forward within their annual management report. One of these new provisions relates to disclosure topics across Environmental, Social and Governance (ESG). EFRAG'S role is to articulate and embed CSRD's new requirements into disclosures within the ESRS.

In doing this, EFRAG must consider other globally recognised principles and frameworks:

- Principles include those on responsible business conduct, corporate social responsibility, and sustainable development;

- Frameworks referenced include the SDGs, the UN *Guiding Principles on Business & Human Rights* (UNGPs), the OECD *Guidelines for Multinational Enterprises*, the OECD *Due Diligence Guidance for Responsible Business Conduct* and related sectoral guidelines, the *Global Compact*, the International Labour Organization's (ILO) *Tripartite Declaration of Principles concerning Multinational Enterprises & Social Policy*, the ISO 26000 standard on social responsibility, and the UN *Principles for Responsible Investment*.

However, consumers and end-users or specific topics relating to the impact of business on consumers and end-users and dependencies of business on its customers are not specifically called out in the CSRD in the same way, for example, as climate change mitigation, working conditions or gender equality.

The Inclusion of Consumers & End-users as a Topic

As a business cannot survive without demand for its goods or services, it also cannot survive without its customers. How that business operates inherently impacts those customers either in a positive or negative way and creates both risks and opportunities for the business based on how it operates.

Aside from the direct impact on consumers and end-users or the risks or opportunities to organisations based on that impact, consumers are also a key and central stakeholder and user of financial and non-financial information.

More sophisticated consumers and/or investors will or may use financial information produced by organisations to make buying decisions. In contrast, regular citizens or customers are unlikely to directly consult organisations' annual management reports without specific purpose but may leverage this information through third parties providing advice, such as financial advisors or non-governmental organisations.[11]

Wider Governance Topics & Consumers

Disclosures around business conduct matters is outside of topics outlined in ESRS under the social standard ESRS-E4 – *Consumers & End-users* but is part of ESRS-G1 – *Governance* (see **Chapter 10**). This and other governance topics also have relevance for consumers.

Poor business conduct is a good example of this, whereby unethical or poor internal controls or practices can have an outward or extended impact into how customers are treated. Thus governance topics should also be considered in the context of consumers and end-users when understanding materiality and relevant impacts, risks and opportunities to the organisation.

Poor business conduct & the consumer impact

During the 'Celtic Tiger' era in Ireland, poor controls, ineffective oversight and loose risk management practices at certain financial institutions resulted in lending practices that contributed to a banking collapse when a difficult recession hit.

The Irish experience is an example of a traditional credit-driven crisis, where structural real estate imbalances combined with cheap but short-term international sources of funding led to weakened lending practices as banks competed for limited business opportunities in the real estate sector, while authorities did not intervene soon enough to mitigate the resultant build-up of excessive risks.[12]

These weakened lending practices had a significant impact on normal retail banking customers who borrowed money during this time when property prices were extremely high and interest rates were low. When initial mortgage terms ended, and prices were falling, many of these customers were either charged the wrong rate of interest on mortgage repayments or were not offered or denied lower rates of interest which they should have been allowed to avail of. These practices later resulted in a number of financial institutions and banks receiving significant fines from the regulator with respect to overcharging tens of thousands of customers. Unfortunately, many of these customers found themselves paying higher interest charges at a time when a recession had started and property prices were falling significantly. This was also against the backdrop of growing unemployment, in particular in the construction sector. More than 15 lenders were found to have charged some customers more expensive rates than should have been offered or made available to them. For some customers, the financial impact was so grave that they entered mortgage arrears and ended up losing their homes.

ESRS-S4 – CONSUMERS & END-USERS

ESRS-S4 defines consumers as:

> *... individuals who acquire, consume, or use goods and services for personal use, either for themselves or for others, and not for resale or commercial purposes. Consumers include actual and potentially affected end-users.*[13]

ESRS-S4 does not separately define 'end-users' aside from the reference above within the consumer definition, but 'end-user' is generally defined as:

> *... the person or organisation that uses a product or service.*[14]

ESRS-S4 – *Consumers & End-users* is one of four social standards that form part of the first 'set' of standards to be applied by organisations in scope for reporting under the CSRD. These initial standards are sector-agnostic in nature and so do not specifically call out relevant topics that are more material to any type of product or service or consumer but simply outline potential topics that are likely to be relevant across sectoral and industry groupings.[15] Future ESRS at sector level will likely include additional and more specific topics relevant to business activities and should help organisations in completing their materiality assessments. For now, since what we have are sector-agnostic standards, when conducting a double materiality assessment an organisation needs to determine whether the topics outlined in ESRS for consumers and end-users are material from an impact, risk or opportunity perspective to people and the environment and/or their organisation. They also need to independently review and determine any entity- or sector-specific material topics in addition to what is outlined in ESRS and disclose accordingly. Sector-specific regulation and/or global sector standards or other relevant frameworks can be used to guide these entity-specific disclosures – for example, the Sustainability Accounting Standards Board (SASB) in the US.

Consumers and end-users are important to an organisation, both from an impact and financial perspective.

Organisations have ethical and legal duties towards consumers who purchase or use their products and services. When they care about consumers, they are fulfilling those duties which has a positive impact on their business and reputation and ultimately can drive better performance and financial results. On the flip side, negative impacts through unethical or bad behaviours may lead to negative effects on consumers and end-users, leading to serious financial effects for an organisation through reputational damage, brand erosion and, in certain cases, business failure.

As a basic approach and as outlined within ESRS,[16] organisations need to:

- Understand how they affect consumers and/or end-users in a positive or negative way;
- Understand how the organisation can itself be impacted based on its dependencies on consumers and/or end-users;
- Determine the financial and non-financial effects of both of these types of impact.

Disclosures specific to consumers and end-users are included within the ESRS-S4 topical standard. In addition, organisations will need to make certain disclosures as they relate to consumers and end-users when including mandatory information required by ESRS 2 *General Disclosures*. Such disclosures are not subject to a materiality assessment but need to be made by all organisations reporting under the CSRD.

ESRS 2 disclosures as they relate to consumers and end-users include those under;

- **Basis of Preparation (BP):** Including whether consumers and end-users as a topic and the sub-topics within have been assessed to determine if they are material, how the organisation's business model and/or strategy accounts for impacts relating to consumers and end-users and a list of relevant policies in relation to this topic;
- **Governance (GOV):** Including at a more generic (all topic) level how the administrative and management bodies are constructed in terms of skills, expertise and oversight responsibilities and are responsible for performance monitoring, incorporating known risks, impacts and opportunities into strategic decision-making and how their own incentive schemes are linked to sustainability matters, including targets set;
- **Strategy & Business Model (SBM):** Including at an organisational level some additional disclosures relevant to consumers and end-users – for example, specific information around product and services offerings, customer categories and significant markets and customer groups. Interdependencies and resilience of organisational strategies and business models with respect to its consumers and end-users (in addition to other material topics) and the impact of both on consumers and end-users;

- **A detailed overview** of the process, oversight and key decision-making approach in finalising Impacts, Risks and Opportunities under the IRO disclosures is required. Specifically, the outcome of the materiality assessment process is specified for each topic under ESRS, including consumers and end-users.

The structure of ESRS includes additional and more specific disclosures with respect to each topic under the ESRS 2 *General Disclosure* areas within the individual standards.

Material Topics under ESRS-S4 – Consumers & End-users

ESRS-S4 – *Consumers & End-users* has three 'sub-topics', each with an additional three sub-sub-topics against which disclosures need to be made if they are deemed material to the organisation reporting under ESRS.

Across the topics described in this chapter, organisations should distinguish between whether impacts, risks and/or opportunities are systemic and widespread or if they are isolated and relate to specific business relationships, in addition to whether they apply to certain or all customer groups.

Additional EU Directives and regulation already are in place for some of these topics and reporting areas as set out in ESRS. For example, privacy is governed by the *General Data Protection Regulation* (GDPR), which sets strict guidelines on data protection and privacy. Freedom of expression and freedom of speech is regulated by various national laws, while consumer protection laws are well-embedded and in all countries. Health and safety is governed by product safety regulations such as the EU *General Product Safety Directive*. Making products and services accessible to all consumers, including those with disabilities or other special needs is a hot topic and the requirements of the *European Accessibility Act* are edging closer with a June 2025 implementation date.

Topics & Sub-Topic Overview

Topic 1: Information related impacts for consumers and/or end-users
This topic relates to:

- Privacy and the protection of personal information of consumers;
- Freedom of expression and safeguarding of consumer rights to express themselves freely;

- Access to quality information – for example, the provision of accurate and accessible information about products and services.

We have all seen, heard and read in the media about major data breaches and 'ransom' attacks on global organisations and public sector bodies, whereby large volumes of personal and sensitive information of customers have been leaked online for all to see. These data breaches can have far-reaching consequences for the organisation itself from a financial perspective, including fines and litigation but also reputational and brand damage. External impacts on customers and other connected parties also can be significant, with their personal health, financial or other data being shared publicly causing stress and anxiety and potentially more far-reaching financial impacts.

I am sure, like me, you can think of many examples you have heard or read about in the media of compromised personal data and how many consumers have been impacted, from government agencies to national police forces, to social media and retail giants. These all are organisations we engage with every day and trust with our data.

Topic 2: Personal safety of consumers & end-users
This topic relates to:

- The health and safety of consumers with respect to products or services that may be or have been harmful to consumers' health;
- Security and protection from physical harm;
- The protection of children from harmful products or services.

I find it difficult to understand how any organisation can value the safety or life of a child differently in one country, region, or continent *versus* another. It's as if they feel they can 'get away' with more (or less) in a less developed or less wealthy part of the world. The value of a child's life is the same, wherever you are. And maybe this is also to do with regulation and the quality standards applied to food production, labelling and selling that certain poor practices can go undetected in one country *versus* another. But whether these standards are in place or differ from region to region, selling a sub-standard product that would not be acceptable in its country of origin constitutes unethical business.

Nestlé adds sugar to infant milk sold in poorer countries

> *Nestlé, the world's largest consumer goods company adds sugar and honey to infant milk and cereal products sold in many poorer countries, contrary to international guidelines aimed at preventing obesity and chronic diseases, a report*

has alleged. Campaigners from Public Eye, a Swiss
investigative organisation, sent samples of the Swiss
multinational's baby-food products sold in Asia, Africa and
Latin America to a Belgian laboratory for testing. The results,
and examination of product packaging, revealed added
sugar in the form of sucrose or honey in samples of Nido, a
follow-up milk formula brand intended for use for infants
aged one and above, and Cerelac, a cereal aimed at children
aged between six months and two years. In Nestlé's main
European markets, including the UK, there is no added sugar
in formulas for young children. While some cereals aimed at
older toddlers contain added sugar, there is none in products
targeted at babies between six months and one year.[17]

Interpreting nutritional information on any food packaging can be difficult – in particular, where the product composition is complex and is, by its nature, enhanced to boost nutritional value. The World Health Organization (WHO) guidelines for the European region say no added sugars or sweetening agents should be permitted in any food for children under 3. Where lack of guidelines may exist in other regions, these European standards surely should apply and, from an ethical standpoint, an organisation selling a product globally that is subject to such guidelines surely should know they have a moral obligation to treat the children across these markets in the same way.

The Nestlé case is still under investigation but highlights where double standards may or do potentially exist that could harm children and their health in one country but not another.

Social media needs to come with a mental health warning
I recently watched a documentary and read articles in the media about the social media platform TikTok and, more specifically, how it uses algorithms to assess user behaviour. Recommended content on the channel can be based on what users have previously watched or engaged with. This was specifically in relation to young and, in some cases, more vulnerable users and in the context of mental health challenges they may be facing whilst using this platform.

I use TikTok myself and, honestly, I like its algorithm. I watch cooking videos – usually the ones that promise I can make a wholesome family meal in less than 10 minutes with little or no washing up. And it delivers: our evening meals are usually based on one of my favourite food influencers' recipe of the day. But I have never thought twice when I sign in on any given day and a whole host of dinner preparers I have never seen before are on my feed.

But I am not 13, or 16, and thankfully right now not suffering with mental health, anxiety or other related disorder. But I have two teenagers who can while away a day looking at TikTok and the content suggested to them using the algorithm and I am sure that, within their wider friend and social groups who also use the platform to a similar extent, there are vulnerable users.

In filming this documentary,[18] three new TikTok accounts were created, and profiles set, with only a date of birth to enter by the user to confirm they were over the minimum use age of 13 years. The users did not search for topics or interact with videos but viewed videos presented to them on the 'For You' feed, which suggests content based on the profile set up, previous content viewed, etc. When video content relating to loneliness, feelings of isolation or parental relationships were shown, the users simply watched them twice. Within minutes, similar content was being presented to each user, with the severity of content escalating further as more videos were watched. I genuinely found this shocking, that children could access this content with ease – in this case, without actively seeking it out. Users can very quickly find themselves in a rabbit hole of negative content that may feed anxieties they are already experiencing.

Aside from this example which leads into the sub-topic of the protection of children from harmful products and services, there are many more we can reference when it comes to health and safety of consumers in general and information available to customers through information on the products or services they buy. Another good example is that of Johnson & Johnson where allegations have been made that they failed to warn customers of the harmful effects of one of its products.

Information for consumers about health & safety risks
In 2022, Johnson & Johnson announced it would stop selling its talc-based baby powder amid ongoing battles and pending lawsuits over the product. Pending lawsuits dating back over 25 years alleged that its branded baby powder containing talc had caused ovarian cancer.[19] The allegations against Johnson & Johnson are that it failed to properly warn consumers about potential health risks associated with the talc-based baby powder. In total, it is expected that Johnson & Johnson will pay out an estimated $700m to resolve the investigation across 40 US states.[20] Customers would not have willingly purchased this product, I am sure, had they known or been informed about these risks.

Even though Johnson & Johnson have agreed this settlement in the case in certain states in the US, it still maintains its talc products are safe and do not cause cancer. Additional law suits and class actions are still pending.[21]

Topic 3: Social Inclusion of Consumers & End-users

This topic brings non-discrimination into play, ensuring:

- Equal treatment of consumers;
- Accessibility to products and services, regardless of background, ability, disability, or other factors;
- Responsible marketing practices that are not designed to mistreat or mislead consumers when making purchasing decisions.

How was your airport experience?

Sinead Burke is an Irish writer, academic and disability activist popular for her TED talk, *Why Design Should Include Everyone*. She opens her talk with the words: "I want to give you a new perspective" and that is exactly what she does. She talks, in detail, of her experience in using an airport and highlights just how much the design of the 'airport experience' inhibits her autonomy, does not in any way meet her basic needs or allow her a dignified airport experience. She, as a customer of public airport services, is not treated equally – whether that is in using the bathroom where she is unable to lock the door or in ordering a cup of coffee which is delivered to her on a counter that is out of reach. She also refers to having to crawl on her hands and knees onto a chair in order to sit down, risking her personal safety in doing so. Her story highlights that she has in no way been considered in the design of these airport services, which she should be able to avail of with ease whenever she goes on holiday. Something most of us take completely for granted. It is truly a powerful message and one that definitely left me with a "new perspective".

Selling, mis-selling and labelling of financial products

Financial literacy means the knowledge and skills needed to make important financial decisions. Every day, thousands of people decide where to open a bank account, which mortgage to choose or where to invest their money and how to save for retirement.[22]

When I was a child, my parents had a financial advisor. Every so often, he would call to our house with a briefcase full of paperwork and brochures on financial products he thought relevant to our family. He would be smartly dressed in a suit and tie and smoked a cigar during the consultation. My mother, who was a stay-at-home parent for the most part, wanted to take out a savings policy, for self-protection – so that, in case anything happened to my father, she would have funds to access in her own name at a later date. When that later date came, she had been paying into the plan for probably 20+ years. She approached the product provider to ask what it was worth, and was told it was worth nothing. To her surprise and probably more-so disappointment, she had been sold an insurance product and, because she had lived beyond a certain age, it had expired, and there was now no benefit payable. This had quite an impact: she felt responsible for putting her trust in someone and not asking any questions.

Of course, this was a long time ago (probably around 1980), and we have moved on since then with increased regulation on selling practices in particular with respect to financial products, with more education available to help consumers understand what they are purchasing and, more importantly, their consumer rights. We are also more aware of the type of institutions and individuals we are dealing with and have developed accountability frameworks such as the Senior Executive Accountability Regime (SEAR) in Ireland, which assigns decision-making responsibilities at an individual level to those in control functions, including decisions with respect to conduct matters.[23] And, of course, the *Corporate Sustainability Due Diligence Directive* (CSDDD) established a "corporate due diligence duty".

The core elements of this duty are identifying and addressing potential and actual adverse human rights and environmental impacts in the company's own operations, their subsidiaries and, where related to their value chain(s), those of their business partners. These directives hopefully will further develop responsibilities and mandate disclosure for responsible parties. When individual responsibilities are assigned, there may be less chance of misconduct happening as people have personal, not collective, responsibilities for outcomes – that is, they cannot hide.

Greenwashing in the financial services sector
As this book is focused on sustainability, it would be amiss not to discuss the issue of greenwashing when it comes to financial products and the impact of greenwashing when it comes to investors in those financial products or even retail banking insurance or investment product customers.

The European Banking Authority (EBA) published a report in May 2023 on its progress on greenwashing monitoring and supervision within the EU. Chapter 2 of the report includes greenwashing trends and provides examples of greenwashing in the financial sector. There are too many examples in this report to include here but those that stand out when I think about normal banking customers, looking to invest money or build their pensions whilst trying to be part of the sustainability transition, include:

- Misleading statements on sustainability characteristics – for example, green retail loans and mortgages (advertised as such) that are not used to finance goods, products, activities or properties that qualify as (fully) green *or* saving products labelled as green although the institution does not clearly commit on the extent to which the savings collected will be used to finance sustainable projects;

- Misleading statements on future sustainability commitments – for example, institutions making public commitments to reduce scope 3 emissions and/or reach net zero emissions for a given retail portfolio (for example, mortgages or car loans) where the transition plan is not credible;

- Investment products being false or inaccurate statements on the extent to which the service (for example, portfolio advice or investment) considers clients' sustainability preferences *or* investment funds being marketed as green, although the green-related considerations are not significant in the manager's investment decisions.[24]

Here's an example of greenwashing in the investment funds sector:

> *Investment giant Vanguard is on the hook for potentially millions of dollars in damages after the Federal Court found it misled investors about its $1 billion ethical bond fund, in the corporate watchdog's first greenwashing court victory.* [25]

There are many examples of greenwashing. Recently, in Australia, the Federal Court found the global investment giant Vanguard contravened the law by making misleading claims about certain ESG exclusionary screens applied to investments in a Vanguard Index Fund. Investments held by the Fund were based on an index called the Bloomberg Barclays MSCI Global Aggregate SRI Exclusions Float Adjusted Index (Index). Vanguard had claimed the Index excluded only companies with significant business activities in a range of industries, including those involving fossil fuels, but has admitted that a significant proportion of securities in the Index and the Fund were from issuers that were not researched or screened against applicable ESG criteria.

In plain English, Vanguard misled its investors and potential investors, by including companies within the portfolio in sectors it had vowed to exclude and not adequately conducting its screening process to ensure this was the case. This was the first such case brought by the Australian Securities & Investments Commission (ASIC) on misleading marketing and greenwashing claims in the financial services industry.

I know I said that time and regulation has moved on since my mother trusted her financial advisor in the 1980s but ordinary people believe their banks and their investment advisors; they trust they know what they are doing, are qualified and act ethically. Greenwashing was not a thing back then; we just hoped we were sold the right product to meet our needs. This adds an additional layer of complication and complexity for us as investors and consumers. I hope we can rely on our regulators to continue their work in this field. The planet definitely depends on this one.

Greenwashing outside the financial services sector
Greenwashing and general mis-selling of financial products garners lots of media attention and profile, maybe more so than some other sectors due to the high level of regulation in the sector in general.

In 2019, McDonalds famously introduced its first paper straws, which were found not to be recyclable. In 2021, a report issued by the Changing Markets Foundation looked at clothing from major high-street fashion brands to check the truthfulness of their sustainability claims and found 60% of claims overall were misleading. Retail giant H&M was alleged to be one of the worst offenders, with a shocking 96% of their claims not holding up. In early 2020, Ryanair audaciously announced itself to the British public as Europe's "lowest emissions airline". The claim was more or less made up and the UK's Advertising Standards Authority (ASA) promptly banned the ads. And there are so many more examples.[26]

In reading these examples and considering what we have talked about around financial products, an old saying springs to my mind: *Buyer beware!*.

CAN WE BE OPTIMISTIC ABOUT THE FUTURE?

Earlier in this chapter, we talked about why businesses care about consumers, the traditional theory of consumerism and the effects of both overproduction and over consumption on people and the environment. We have seen many stark examples about the mistreatment of and misinformation to consumers causing sometimes serious and grave impact. Risks and opportunities with respect to consumers and end-users and across other environmental, social and governance topics stem from past actions, either positive or negative, and future events, driven by the organisation itself or wider economic or social factors.

To sustain their business, organisations need to learn how to manage all of these factors, with limited resources. But to survive, they will need to find more sustainable ways of working and sustainability needs to become core to business strategy if we are to meet our goals in reducing our environmental and wider impacts to an acceptable level.

According to McKinsey, companies with high ESG ratings consistently outperform the market in both the medium and long term. While sustainability strategies might be an investment in the short term, they can lead to long-term benefits.[27] This is not surprising.

The benefits of having such a strategy and being sustainable are also not surprising, including brand protection by avoiding negative impacts and risks, being a purpose-driven organisation to create or improve competitive advantage, accessing new markets where there is growing demand for sustainable goods, among others.

Organisations need to help consumers on this journey, whether they are direct customers for products or services or indirect customers through other sales or distribution channels, and whether this is through better information and product labelling, avoiding greenwashing or supporting circular economy initiatives.

New regulation and reporting requirements will also help in this regard. Where organisations don't have a sustainability strategy, they will need to develop one where reporting requirements require it. This will have implications for smaller organisations in their value chain that will need also to have a strategy and to collect data on their initiatives for reporting purposes. A butterfly effect should ensue.

But consumers also have the power to influence how their favourite brands produce the goods they love, both individually and collectively. And many consumers can make choices about what they buy from whom.

I think there is a reason to be optimistic in this regard. Consumer sentiment has changed and is continuing to take pace. I am definitely personally optimistic for 2024 that I will achieve my goal to buy "no new clothes for a year".

ESRS-S4 – CONSUMERS & END-USERS REPORTING OBLIGATIONS

Ingrid De Doncker

The ESRS-S4 standard details a set of disclosures that companies must report with regards to their effects on consumers and end-users. This includes both positive and negative impacts, as well as any risks and opportunities that arise from these interactions.

The standard enables users of the sustainability statement to understand material impacts on consumers and end-users connected with their own operations and value chain, through its products or services, as well as through its business relationships, and its related material risks and opportunities, including:

- How the organisation affects the consumers and/or end-users of its products and/or services in terms of material positive and negative actual or potential impacts;
- Any actions taken, and the result of such actions, to prevent, mitigate or remediate actual or potential negative impacts, and to address risks and opportunities;
- The nature, type and extent of the organisation's material risks and opportunities related to its impacts and dependencies on consumers and end-users, and how the organisation manages such risks and opportunities;
- The financial effects on the organisation over the short-, medium- and long-term of material risks and opportunities arising from its impacts and dependencies on consumers and/or end-users.

Consumers & End-users Sub-Topics

the ESRS-S4 standard, *Consumers & End-users*, covers three main sub-topics related to how organisations (actually and potentially) impact or are impacted by (actual or potential risks and opportunities) the consumers and end-users of its products and services:

- **Information-related impacts on consumers and end-users:** Here we think of privacy, freedom of expression and access to (quality) information;
- **Personal safety of consumers and end-users:** This includes health and safety, security of a person and protection of children;

- **Social inclusion of consumers and end-users:** This relates to non-discrimination, access to products and services and responsible marketing practices).

Figure 9.1: ESRS-S4 – Consumers & End-users Reporting Requirements

ESRS-S4	Consumers & End-users		
	Information-related Impacts on Consumers and End-users	Personal Safety of Consumers and End-users	Social Inclusion of Consumers and End-users
	All below are subject to materiality for each of the sub-topics.		
	STRATEGY		
S4-ESRS2-SBM-2	Interest and views of the stakeholders.		
S4-ESRS2-SBM-3	Material impacts, risks and opportunities and their interaction with strategy and business model.		
	IMPACT, RISK & OPPORTUNITY MANAGEMENT		
ESRS-S4-1	Policies related to consumers and end-users.		
ESRS-S4-2	Processes for engaging with consumers and end-users about impacts.		
ESRS-S4-3	Processes to remediate negative impacts and channels for consumers and end-users to raise concerns.		
ESRS-S4-4	Taking action on material impacts on consumers and end-users, and approaches to mitigating material risks and pursuing material opportunities related to consumers and end-users, and effectiveness of those actions.		
	METRICS & TARGETS		
ESRS-S4-5	Targets related to managing material negative impacts, advancing positive impacts, and managing material risks and opportunities.		

This Standard shall be read in conjunction with ESRS 1 *General Requirements*, and ESRS 2, as well as ESRS-S1: *Own Workforce*, ESRS-S2: *Workers in the Value Chain* and ESRS-S3: *Affected Communities*. The requirements of this section should be read in conjunction with the disclosures required by ESRS 2 on Strategy (SBM). The resulting disclosures shall be presented alongside the disclosures required by ESRS 2, except for SBM-3 Material impacts, risks and opportunities and their interaction with SBM, for which the organisation has an option to present the disclosures alongside the topical disclosure.

It is important to understand the *Minimum Disclosure Requirements* (MDRs) in ESRS 2, *Chapter 4.2.* When an organisation identifies a sustainability matter as material, 34 MDR data points (DPs) for Policies, Actions, Targets, and Metrics (PAT-M) are applicable if the organisation discloses on policies, actions and targets. If it does not provide disclosure on policies, targets or actions, then it needs to disclose the reasons for not doing so, as per the corresponding 10 DPs of ESRS 2 MDR PAT, paragraphs 62 and 81.

ESRS-S4 outlines clearly, in five *Disclosure Requirements* (DRs), the narrative and numeric DPs an organisation should comply with. There are 44 *Shall* DPs, of which 39 are narrative and 5 are semi-narrative, as well as 19 additional *May* DPs. The MDR PAT DPs are to be disclosed under S4-1, S4-4, S4-5 when the sustainability matters are material.

---

[1] Nielseniq (NIQ) (September 2023). How to turn green consumer intentions into sustainable actions, https://nielseniq.com/global/en/insights/report/2023/how-to-turn-green-consumer-intentions-into-sustainable-actions/.

[2] Economist Impact (March 2024). *How Can Companies Create More Conscious Consumers?*, https://impact.economist.com/sustainability/circular-economies/how-can-companies-create-more-conscious-consumers.

[3] Shein's Fast Fashion Domination Comes at a High Cost, *TIME*, referencing a report complied by Money.co.uk, 30 November 2022, https://www.money.co.uk/credit-cards/most-popular-fashion-brands-2022.

[4] Central Bank of Ireland, Consumer Protection Outlook Report 2023, https://www.centralbank.ie/regulation/consumer-protection/consumer-protection-outlook-report.

[5] *The Momentum*, Why Consumerism Is Ingrained Into Western Society, https://www.themomentum.com/articles/why-consumerism-is-ingrained-into-western-society.

[6] *Net Impact* (November 2020). Consequences of Overproduction and Overconsumption, https://netimpact.org/blog/overproduction-overconsumption-consequences.

[7] Patrick Grant, *How Customers Create More Conscious Consumers*, 13 March 2024. https://impact.economist.com/sustainability/circular-economies/how-can-companies-create-more-conscious-consumers.

[8] European Commission. *Ecodesign for Sustainable Products Regulation*, https://commission.europa.eu/energy-climate-change-environment/standards-tools-and-labels/products-labelling-rules-and-requirements/sustainable-products/ecodesign-sustainable-products-regulation_en.

9   European Commission. *Ecodesign for Sustainable Products Regulation*,
    https://commission.europa.eu/energy-climate-change-environment/ standards
    -tools-and-labels/products-labelling-rules-and-requirements/sustainable-
    products/ecodesign-sustainable-products-regulation_en.

10 European Commission. *The Consumer Rights Directive*,
    https://commission.europa.eu/law/law-topic/consumer-protection-
    law/consumer-contract-law/consumer-rights-directive_en.

11 European Commission. *The CSRD Directive, EU 2022/2464,* https://eur-
    lex.europa.eu/legal-content/EN/TXT/?uri=CELEX%3A32022L2464.

12 BIS (Ocober 2020). *The Banking Crisis in Ireland*, FSI Crisis Management
    Series, https://www.bis.org/fsi/fsicms2.pdf.

13 EFRAG. *Appendix VI (ESRS)* – Acronyms and glossary of terms, efrag.org.

14 As defined In Oxford Languages, https://languages.oup.com.

15 EFRAG. *ESRS 1 Application Requirements Appendix B: Sustainability matters
    covered in topical ESRS*, https://www.efrag.org/en/sustainability-
    reporting/esrs-workstreams/sector-agnostic-standards-set-1-esrs.

16 EFRAG. Reference to ESRS – 4 / 1, efrag.org

17 *The Guardian* (April 2024). https://webstories.theguardian.com/stories/
    uk/2024/apr/17/nestl-adds-sugar-to-infant-milk-sold-in-poorer-countries-
    report-finds/; and https://www.theguardian.com/global-development/2024/
    apr/17/nestle-adds-sugar-to-infant-milk-sold-in-poorer-countries-report-finds.

18 RTE Investigates (April 2024). *RTÉ Prime Time experiment reveals disturbing
    content recommended to 13 year old TikTok users in Ireland,*
    https://about.rte.ie/2024/04/18/rte-prime-time-experiment-reveals-disturbing-
    content-recommended-to-13-year-old-tiktok-users-in-ireland/

19 *The Hill* (January 5, 2024). J&J proposing to pay $6.5B to resolve almost all talc
    ovarian cancer suits, https://thehill.com/policy/healthcare/4636549-johnson-
    and-johnson-baby-powder-lawsuits-settlement/

20 *Forbes* (January 8, 2024). Johnson & Johnson Will Pay $700 Million To Resolve
    Baby Powder Marketing Probe, Report Says,
    https://www.forbes.com/sites/tylerroush/2024/01/08/johnson--johnson-will-
    pay-700-million-to-resolve-baby-powder-marketing-probe-report-says/.

21 AOL News (June 11, 2024). Johnson & Johnson reaches $700 million talc
    settlement with US states (aol.com), https://www.aol.com/news/johnson-
    johnson-reaches-700-million-171205413.html.

22 European Commission. Financial Literacy, https://finance.ec.europa.eu/
    consumer-finance-and-payments/financial-literacy_en.

23 Central Bank of Ireland. Individual Accountability Framework,
    https://www.centralbank.ie/regulation/how-we-regulate/individual-
    accountability-framework.

24 European Banking Authority. Progress Report on Greenwashing,
    https://eba.europa.eu/sites/default/files/document_library/Publications/Report
    s/2023/1055934/EBA%20progress%20report%20on%20greenwashing.pdf.

25 Australian Securities & Investment Commission. https://asic.gov.au/about-
    asic/news-centre/find-a-media-release/2024-releases/24-061mr-asic-wins-
    first-greenwashing-civil-penalty-action-against-vanguard/.

26 Akepa. Greenwashing examples for 2023 & 2024: Worst products & brands,
    https://thesustainableagency.com/blog/greenwashing-examples/#ryanair.

27 HBS Online (November 2019). *The Importance of Sustainability in Business*,
    https://online.hbs.edu/blog/post/business-sustainability-strategies.

10

BUSINESS CONDUCT

Ingrid de Doncker

When I was five years old, my father died. It seems maybe a little unbelievable now looking back, but I wonder if what I learned in those early years is what formed my outlook on life. Even though I was very young, I feel he left me with values and principles that I have carried with me. He loved to travel, discovering the great unknown. He was an engineer and invented lots of small things. He loved music, jazz, and he was a great dancer. He was very socially involved, an organiser of events, involved in the community and giving back where he could.

It is reasonable to assume that, at the age of 5, he was my hero. I believe I gained a textured perspective from my now long-absent father. I also love all the things he loved. I love to dance in the rain, and discover new things. I always try to understand the 'why's' and the 'why not's'. I am pulled towards equity, respect and fairness. I have an active aversion to bullies, selfish behaviour and injustice. I am very aware of my privileged life and have a need to understand all sides of our shared ESG story.

This is what has driven me in my professional life – as a procurement and supply chain professional for over 25 years – to uncover instances of corporate and individual overconsumption, largely a disease of the Western world, that are a manifestation of selfishness, injustice, inequity or disrespect. In most cases, it is unintended and subconscious. Nevertheless, people suffer and resources are wasted. My passion is to do what I can to help companies change that. We can reduce suffering and resource wastage and drive sustainable change in businesses, while being cognisant of their mandates and constraints that challenge us.

Ingrid De Doncker

INTRODUCTION

In 2019, when my Future Planet co-founder Donal Daly and I started out, sustainability as now understood did not exist, or rather it existed but was not understood, particularly by business leaders. Although this was long before the *European Sustainability Reporting Standards* (ESRS) were defined, nonetheless there still were many standards, documents, principles, regulations and directives. Those in the know talked about the EU *Green Deal*,[1] the Organisation for Economic Co-operation and Development[2] (OECD) guides, United Nations[3] (UN) publications, the *Intergovernmental Panel on Climate Change*[4] (IPCC) reports, the Global Reporting Initiative[5] (GRI) and the UN Sustainable Development Goals (SDGs).[6] The Sustainable Accounting Standards Board (SASB) was in the mix too, but mainly applied in the US.

It was very clear to us why it was so difficult for businesses to know where to start. There was too much information, largely written by, or structured for, academics, researchers or scientists. For businesses, it was a hugely bewildering domain.

We thought it might be easier for companies if they could think about sustainability in a way that mapped to their business, so we created our 'Live-Buy-Design' model designed to help companies to:

- **Live** better in their organisations;
- **Buy** better from their suppliers; and
- **Design** better products for their customers.

The funny thing is that, after we transitioned Live-Buy-Design to ESRS, as ESRS became the *lingua franca* for sustainability, the Live-Buy-Design structure re-emerged as a description of Value Chain activities – Upstream, Own Operations, and Downstream or Buy-Live-Design. In the chart below, you would just swap the positions of the 'LIVE' and 'BUY' columns.

Live-Buy-Design outlined a path to good business conduct that served as a catalyst for sustainable change by fostering a culture of responsibility, innovation, and long-term thinking, in the business (Own Operations), from the supply chain (Upstream) and for their products and customers (Downstream). We sometimes still reference this approach when customers want more clarity on how sustainability should map to the way their business works.

Figure 10.1: The Live-Buy-Design model

	1. LIVE Better	2. BUY Better	3. DESIGN Better
PEOPLE	1.1 Labour Practices, Employee Development	2.1 Social & Shared Value	3.1 Customer Waste
	1.2 Employee Health & Safety	2.2 Human Rights & Community Relations	3.2 Community Health
	1.3 Diversity, Equality, Inclusion	2.3 Stakeholder Engagement & Collaboration	3.3 Market Communications
PLANET	1.4 GHG Scope 1, 2 Management	2.4 GHG Scope 3 Management	3.4 Product Environmental Footprint
	1.5 Energy Management	2.5 Waste Management	3.5 Sustainable Forestry & Land Use
	1.6 Water Stewardship	2.6 Climate Adaptation	3.6 Biodiversity
	1.7 Air Quality & Pollution	2.7 Sustainable Logistics	3.7 Sustainable Packaging & Single Use Plastics
PROSPERITY	1.8 Risk Management & Sustainable Strategy	2.8 Sustainable Procurement	3.8 Circular Economy
	1.9 Privacy and Data Security	2.9 Materials Sourcing & Optimisation	3.9 Business Resilience & Innovation
	1.10 Corporate Governance	2.10 Business Ethics, Transparency, Compliance	3.10 Responsible Sales & Product Labelling

Sustainable Development Goals (SDGs), Global Reporting Initiative (GRI), International Organisation for Standardisation (ISO), Sustainability Accounting Standards Board (SASB), Greenhouse Gases Protocol (GHG), Carbon Disclosure Project (CDP), Science Based Targets (SBTi), Task Force on Climate-Related Financial Disclosures (TCFD), International Sustainable Standards Board (ISSB), Corporate Sustainability Reporting Directive (CSRD), International Financial Reporting Standard (IFRS), Climate Disclosure Standards Board (CDSB), et al

Figure 10.2: The European Sustainability Reporting Standards

Environmental	Social	Governance
E1: Climate Change	**S1: Own Workforce**	**G1: Business Conduct**
Climate change adaptation	Working conditions	Corporate culture
Climate emissions (mitigation)	Equal treatment and opportunities for all	Protection of whistle-blowers
Energy	Other workers related rights	Supplier relation management incl. payment terms
E2: Pollution	**S2: Workers In The Value Chain**	Political engagement, lobbying
Pollution of air	Working conditions	Corruption and bribery
Pollution of water	Equal treatment and opportunities for all	Animal welfare
Pollution of soil	Other workers related rights	
Pollution of living organisms	**S3: Affected Communities**	
Substances of concern	Civil and Political Rights	
Substances of very high concern	Economies, social, and cultural rights	
Micro-plastics	Rights of indigenous commodities	
E3: Water and Marine Resources	**S4: Consumers and End-users**	
Water consumption	Information related impacts	
Marine resources	Personal safety	
E4: Biodiversity and Ecosystems	Social inclusion	
Direct impact drivers of biodiversity loss		
Impacts on the state of species		
Impact on extent and condition of ecosystems		
Impacts and dependencies on ecosystem services		
E5: Resources and Circular Economy		
Resource inflows, resource use		
Resource outflows of products and services		
Waste		

In the intervening years, there have been many developments in sustainability and environmental, social and governance (ESG) regulations. As you will know from **Chapter 1: The Customer is the Planet**, the ESRS have evolved and are now the main reference point for sustainable business practices. As a GRI professional and having assessed the Task Force on Climate-related Financial Disclosures[7] (TCFD) in businesses, I was delighted to see this common language emerging and particularly pleased that the content of ESRS – including how it relates to the Value Chain – is substantially the same as Live-Buy-Design, albeit structured differently under the pillars of ESG, as shown in **Figure 10.2**.

WHAT IS GOOD BUSINESS CONDUCT?

Why do businesses exist? They exist to create value. This value creation serves multiple purposes, both for the business itself and for society as a whole. Businesses are in business to create value by satisfying needs and wants, generating profit, creating employment, driving innovation, contributing to economic development, fulfilling social responsibilities, and creating value for shareholders and stakeholders alike. If we agree on the reasons why business exists, then business conduct relates to how businesses behave and interact with different stakeholder groups and the environment. It's about doing business in a way that is ethical and socially responsible, while protecting the environment.

'People buy from people – people sell to people'. However, doing business is not just about making money; it is about prospering, while being conscious of the impact on society and the environment. This thinking is applied in the double materiality assessment principle of the *Corporate Sustainable Reporting Directive* (CSRD). That is, we must consider both perspectives: how climate and societal change affect the financial performance of a business and, equally, how business decisions impact on climate and society.

At its core, ethical business conduct is about upholding integrity, transparency, and accountability within a business' operations and value chains. By caring about customers, employees, suppliers, and communities, businesses can build trust and have long-term success.

As explained in **Chapter 1**, businesses should consider the long-term impact of their actions, in line with the Iroquois tribe's Seventh Generation principle,[8] evaluating their potential effects deep into the future. This principle sets the stage for discussions on sustainability, corporate responsibility, and intergenerational justice, by serving as a reminder of the importance of considering the long-term consequences of present actions and the imperative of leaving a positive legacy for future generations.

Investors and shareholders have an important role in business. They can be the guardians of long-term value, and stewards of the governance compass. They can encourage companies to adopt responsible business conduct. If they are so inclined, they can use their power to promote good behaviour by voting for ethical practices. However, if we commit to double materiality, we also need to include all stakeholders, not just shareholders. By considering the needs of customers, employees, suppliers, and communities, companies can build trust and enhance their reputation, driving sustainable growth and value creation in the long term.

All good businesses need to be accountable, take responsibility for their actions and follow the laws and regulations within which they operate. Today these regulations, sustainability standards, and guidelines encourage companies to do more to help society and protect the planet. Guidelines and principles from organisations like the OECD, the UN, and the World Business Council for Sustainable Development (WBCSD) give businesses a framework for good behaviour.

In essence, we can say that ethical business conduct is business development that espouses sustainability. Businesses must strive to maintain ethical standards, uphold social responsibility, and promote sustainable practices. Doing so promotes innovation, value creation, and sustainable and inclusive growth. This sustainable growth will adhere to legal frameworks, and consider the impact on planetary boundaries and the broader responsibilities to society. Through transparency, accountability, and integrity, companies can nurture their operations while reflecting on the impact on investors, customers, employees, communities, and governments and, of course, the environment.

According to the ESRS, the primary topic in Governance is Business Conduct. Within this topic, there are six sub-topics:

- Corporate culture;
- Protection of whistle blowers;
- Animal welfare;
- Political engagement, lobbying;
- Supplier relation management, including payment terms;
- Corruption and bribery.

CORPORATE CULTURE

Let me start with a famous quote from the Austrian-American management consultant, educator, and author Peter Drucker, who said:

Culture eats strategy for breakfast.

Actually, according to the Drucker Institute (and they should know), Peter Drucker never said that. What he *did* say, in the *Wall Street Journal*, Thursday, March 28, 1991,[9] was:

Culture – no matter how defined – is singularly persistent.

Much more nuanced and certainly less catchy.

Drucker understood, however, that no matter how well-designed your strategy, it will fall flat without a good culture. At the end of the day, employees are the most important factor that impacts the success of a business, and employees are the embodiment of your culture. In other words, you need to get your corporate culture right.

We have all seen examples of bad company culture, from movies like *The Wolf of Wall Street*,[10] based on the real-life story of Jordan Belfort, a former Wall Street trader, who later was found guilty of crimes related to stock market manipulation and fraud, to other stories of harassment, intense pressure, and absolute prioritisation of profit over purpose and people. These are not nice environments to be in, and in the long-term, as employees' morale declines, and company reputation suffers, the business inevitably fails.

Culture does not happen by accident. Principles matter, but policies and procedures do too.

Principles are at the core. In our company, Future Planet,[11] we have established what we call the RAINO principle. It stands for the five core values that we espouse and guide our employees to embed in their interaction with all stakeholders, internal and external.

Figure 10.3: The Future Planet RAINO Principle

R	Respectful
A	Authentic
I	Impactful
N	Nurturing
O	Optimistic

Culture, of course, starts at the top. In many ways, creating a corporate culture is one most impactful roles of leadership. It is leadership's real job to establish clear ethical standards and values that guide the behaviour and decision-making of the management team and employees, and act as a guide for stakeholders in the value chain, both suppliers and customers alike. When you, as a leader, can clearly define your expectations for honesty, integrity, fairness, and respect in all business dealings, you are well underway to building alignment to your mission, vision, and values. Your sustainability strategy is a great opportunity to set goals, agree actions and define metrics in a set of policies that govern your interaction with the planet.

'The tragedy of the commons'[12] is a concept developed by Garrett Hardin in 1968. It is the idea that shared resources inevitably will be misused and overused by a few, leading to ecological disaster for all. Companies with a strong corporate culture combat the tragedy of the commons by regarding environmental stewardship as being of similar value as financial benefits. This not only relates to reducing carbon footprint, minimising waste, and implementing eco-friendly initiatives that contribute to a healthier planet, but can also include employee engagement, as well as customer or community initiatives that have a positive impact on local ecosystems and communities.

In large organisations, embedding culture – because it doesn't just happen – requires clear policies and procedures, rules of engagement, boundaries, and responsibilities. In today's dynamic landscape of shifting regulations and evolving business tactics, companies must deal with a myriad of policies, practices, and procedures. Often these policies have grown incrementally, are spread through the organisation, are often incohesive, and sometimes are contradictory. This brings inconsistencies in style, lack of ownership, and inadequate compliance that, in turn, can compromise ethical standards.

In large companies also, well-managed policies are the lifeblood of compliance and growth. They establish, clarify, and convey expectations, define risk boundaries, elucidate governance and responsibility, and steer preferred behaviours. These elements are crucial for fostering a compliant culture, safeguarding the organisation, and attaining business goals. It takes a strong leadership team to put them in place and it takes a mature leadership to incentivise cultural behaviour.

Putting the right policies and governance framework in place can create a culture of compliance and prevents nefarious practices from emerging. For many, It is the boring side of doing business; the so-called administration or paperwork, the revision-controlled corporate policies, internal procedures, mandatory training programmes and compliance requirements. However, it is a sure sign of leadership when they take a stand and are held accountable for their company, its culture, their objectives, and its position in the market.

Shaping Culture through the Right Policies

One of the challenges in creating policies, of course, is that you need to cater for multiple audiences: employees, the business and the planet. To reach that high bar, you must prioritise the development and implementation of robust business conduct policies, which should clearly outline the company's values, expectations, and procedures for addressing ethical lapses, misconduct, conflicts of interest, and discrimination. Regular training and communication are key to ensuring that all employees, from the C-suite to the frontlines, understand and adhere to these policies. Additionally, businesses should foster a culture of accountability, where employees feel empowered to speak up about concerns without fear of retaliation.

'Feeling valued' is a very powerful, though invisible, currency that pays dividends when given freely. A culture of ethics and integrity not only enhances brand reputation and competitive advantage, it also fosters innovation and collaboration. Moreover, a positive corporate culture can serve as a powerful tool for attracting and retaining top talent in a highly competitive job market. And some companies do value all their employees; you may have read recently that LEGO[13] has linked its compensation and incentives to sustainability efforts to include all salaried employees globally. In the end, the benefits of a strong corporate culture far outweigh the costs of implementing and maintaining it.

Bad Corporate Culture at Uber

We all know Uber and know also that Uber is no stranger to controversy. There have been multiple accusations of sexual harassment at the firm[14] and questions over its 'stop-at-nothing' approach to expansion. The latter allegedly saw it using illegal technology to evade law enforcement, poach drivers from competitors and spy on users.

There were also accusations regarding Uber's 'bro' culture – a social dynamic often associated with groups of young men who exhibit stereotypically masculine behaviours. This subculture is often associated with toxicity and exclusion also. The allegations included complaints that senior members of staff had made sexist jokes and visited a brothel in Seoul. Even though some were not proven, the claims affected the price of the company's shares, which were traded privately at the time.

In February 2017, former Uber engineer Susan Fowler[15] published a blog post detailing her experiences of sexual harassment, discrimination, and retaliation during her time at the company. Fowler's allegations sparked a broader conversation about workplace culture and gender discrimination in the tech industry. The revelations prompted Uber to launch an internal investigation led by former US Attorney General Eric Holder to examine the company's workplace practices and culture.

The Holder Report,[16] released in June 2017, documented systemic issues within Uber's workplace culture, including instances of sexual harassment, bullying, and discrimination. The report outlined recommendations for addressing these issues, such as improving diversity and inclusion initiatives, strengthening HR policies, and enhancing leadership accountability.

In the wake of the scandal, Uber's CEO and co-founder, Travis Kalanick,[17] faced mounting pressure to resign due to his perceived role in fostering a toxic workplace culture and his handling of the crisis. He ultimately stepped down as CEO, following a tumultuous period marked by controversies and management upheaval.

In response to the scandals and controversies, Uber implemented a series of reforms aimed at improving its corporate culture, enhancing regulatory compliance, and rebuilding trust with stakeholders. The company has hired new leadership, revamped its HR policies, and launched initiatives to promote diversity, equality, and inclusion in the workplace. Uber also has sought to improve transparency and accountability through enhanced reporting mechanisms and engagement with regulators and advocacy groups.

The Uber scandal underscores the challenges that companies face in managing corporate culture, addressing workplace misconduct, and navigating complex regulatory environments. It serves as a cautionary tale for tech companies and other organisations about the importance of fostering a positive workplace culture, promoting diversity and inclusion, and upholding ethical standards in all aspects of business operations.

THE PROTECTION OF WHISTLEBLOWERS

Would you want to be a whistleblower? You might be seen as a hero who exposes wrongdoing, a protector of people's rights, or an agent of change who might instigate new regulations for safety measures. On the other hand, some people view whistleblowers as traitors or 'snitches', who are disloyal to their employers or organisations, or troublemakers who disrupt workplaces and damage morale and create unnecessary conflict. We all have heard of Edward Snowden[18] or Julian Assange.[19] Villains or heroes, being a whistleblower can have detrimental impacts on people's lives.

But, from an organisation's point of view, there are many reasons why it is important to have strong whistleblower protection in place. Whistleblowers often are the first to identify and report illegal or unethical activities within your organisation. Knowing that employees can safely report misconduct can discourage others from engaging in such behaviour, particularly if the wrong-doers are brought to account. By identifying problems early on, whistleblowing can help you to improve internal controls and compliance procedures.

It is certainly not a simple decision to become a whistleblower, but thankfully there are emerging protections in place. In the EU, the pertinent guidelines come from the *Whistleblower Directive*. While the directive has been hailed as a significant step forward in protecting whistleblowers within the EU, its real-world impact depends on several factors, including how it is implemented by individual Member States and how organisations adopt internal reporting policies. It is too early to say whether the Directive will be a 'game-changer' for whistleblower protection and achieve the expected high standards of protection.

Whistleblowing at Boeing

The situation at Boeing underscores the challenges whistleblowers face in exposing corporate wrongdoing and the importance of robust protection mechanisms to ensure safety and accountability.

In 2019, whistleblowers, including a former quality manager, raised concerns about Boeing's manufacturing processes, alleging that the company prioritised speed over safety. A Boeing engineer testified at a US Senate hearing about being ignored and physically threatened after raising safety concerns. He described witnessing workers jumping on plane parts to fit them, which he referred to as the 'Tarzan effect'.[20]

As you may know, Boeing's planes have been in the media spotlight due to technical problems, including a door blowing off soon after take-off, emergency landings, and incidents where passengers sustained injuries and deaths. Lion Air Flight 610 crashed in October 2018, and Ethiopian Airlines Flight 302 crashed in March 2019, both Boeing 737 Max aircraft, killing a total of 346 people. The focus of the crash investigations was the flight control software, the Manoeuvring Characteristics Augmentation System (MCAS).

After the 737 Max tragedies, the US House Transportation Committee released an investigative report, documenting "a disturbing pattern of technical miscalculations and troubling management misjudgements" by Boeing, combined with "numerous oversight lapses and accountability gaps by the Federal Aviation Administration (FAA)".

Recent audits and investigations have confirmed quality control issues at Boeing, despite the company's denial of unsafe work practices, and whistleblower disclosures have brought significant attention to safety and quality control issues within Boeing, leading to public and regulatory scrutiny; not least of which was the FAA investigations into Boeing over falsified inspection records. While not directly stated, such high-profile cases often lead to internal policy changes and a re-evaluation of corporate practices to prevent future incidents.

In the wake of the Boeing 737 Max scandals, the company announced in mid-2024 that Boeing CEO Dave Calhoun was due to step down at the end of the year as part of a broad management shakeup. Chairman of the board, Larry Kellner, won't stand for re-election this year, and Stan Deal, CEO of the commercial airplane unit, is already gone.

However, it's important to note that whistleblowing also can have negative consequences for the individuals involved, as seen in the tragic deaths of two Boeing whistleblowers under mysterious circumstances.[21] These events highlight the risks faced by individuals who come forward and the need for robust protections. Despite these risks, their courage can drive positive change and reforms in corporate behaviour, so it is important that your organisation has robust whistleblower protections in place.

ANIMAL WELFARE

We all agree that the welfare of animals is important. The EU has established a comprehensive set of rules and regulations aimed at protecting the welfare of animals, covering various aspects of animal care and treatment. This includes measures to prevent cruelty, minimise suffering, and provide appropriate living conditions, healthcare, and humane handling for animals used in agriculture, research, or other contexts relevant to an organisation's activities.

On January 1, 2012, the EU implemented significant changes to its regulations regarding the housing of laying hens, when *Council Directive 1999/74/EC* (the '*Chicken Cages Directive*') came into full force, prohibiting the use of conventional battery cages for laying hens across the EU. I remember it well, as I was working for the largest food and drink retailer in Ireland at the time.

Additionally, the directive mandated that all egg production units be registered with competent authorities and have a distinguishing number to enable traceability back to the farm of origin. While the transition to enriched cages represented an improvement in animal welfare standards, there was uneven transition across Europe. The immediate trade effect was that certain countries that had not implemented the Directive, overnight could not export, resulting in supply disruption and increases of approximately 40% in egg prices across the EU.[22] This sharp rise in prices was attributed to the reduced supply of eggs as producers struggled to comply with the new regulations and the higher costs associated with enriched cages or alternative systems.

Since 2005,[23] there has been growing concern within the EU regarding the long-distance transport of live animals for slaughter or other purposes. In response, the European Commission has proposed a ban on the export of live animals from the EU to non-EU countries. This proposed Directive aims to address the significant animal welfare issues associated with prolonged transport times, which can expose animals to exhaustion, dehydration, injury, and disease. It seeks to eliminate the export of live animals from the EU, instead promoting the trade of meat, carcasses, and genetic material through the development of cold chain infrastructure. This approach would not only improve animal welfare by reducing the stress and suffering associated with long-distance transport but also would create new job opportunities in the meat production and preservation sectors within the EU. However, the proposed ban comes with complex economic, regulatory, and trade implications. Balancing these factors will be essential to achieving the desired outcomes, while minimising the negative impacts on farmers and related industries.

POLITICAL INFLUENCE & LOBBYING

Engaging in political influence and navigating lobbying activities is a complex interplay between government, business, and special interests in the political landscape. People, and people in business, must carefully navigate the 'dos' and 'don'ts' to ensure ethical and transparent practices. Failing to do so can lead to legal scrutiny, fines for non-compliance with lobbying disclosure laws, and reputational damage due to perceived undue influence on policy-making.

Did we not see a blatant example of this in early 2024 when former US president Donald Trump rubbed shoulders with oil executives at Mar-a-Lago in Florida and told the attendees at dinner to raise $1 billion to help him take back the White House,[24] and in return promised to reverse the pause on liquefied natural gas (LNG) export terminal permits on "the first day" back in office, increase auctions for oil drilling in the Gulf of Mexico and green-light Alaskan oil drilling, and ditch emissions targets for car manufacturers that are projected to spur on the EV transition?

Another example you may have read about is Shell's secret lobbying against policies that would hold it accountable for its environmental impact, while issuing public statements about embracing climate action – a clear demonstration of hypocrisy and lack of integrity. According to the Friends of the Earth[25] in 2018:

> *Shell claims publicly that it embraces the* Paris Climate Accord, *but what occurs behind the scenes is quite different. According to research, Shell spent some $22 million in 2015 on lobbying activities against climate policies. Of the 25 largest corporations, Shell, Exxon, IBM, Total and Pfizer have – via their industry associations – the largest negative impact on climate policy.*

Shell has been aware of the dangers of climate change for more than 30 years, as revealed by confidential internal documents and its own film *Climate of Concern*.[26] However, the company continues to focus on fossil fuels. Its attempts to shirk responsibility and shift blame to factors beyond its control undermine its credibility as a responsible corporate citizen.

Providing direct financial or in-kind support to political parties or candidates without proper disclosure, engaging in indirect political contributions through intermediary organisations without transparency, or asking for donations for political favours, and failing to consider the alignment between public statements on material impacts, risks, and opportunities and lobbying activities are all practices that should be avoided.

On the other hand, if you do engage transparently and ethically with policy-makers and regulators, and you comply with lobbying disclosure requirements and industry standards, that will lead to positive outcomes. It is important here to collaborate with stakeholders and advocate policies to align business interests with societal values. A company that openly discloses its lobbying activities, adheres to strict ethical guidelines, works with diverse stakeholders to promote policies that balance business needs with social responsibility is an attractive provider of products or services, even if not all of its policy goals are achieved.

Your first step is to share all the 'dos' and 'don'ts' of good business conduct in your business with your employees and your other stakeholders. Think about it in relation to your own family, your own household; what would you put in place to ensure all rules of the house are clear and understood and followed by everyone? Once everyone understands and adheres to the 'dos' and 'don'ts', your business can navigate this complex regulatory and compliance landscape while upholding your values, maintaining stakeholder trust, and contributing to the sustainable business practices and societal well-being that will also benefit your business financially.

Political Influence & Lobbying Gone Bad

One of the more recent scandals involving political influence and lobbying activities involves Cambridge Analytica,[27] a British political consulting firm that specialised in data mining, analysis, and strategic communication for political campaigns and other clients. The company gained notoriety for its work on behalf of political candidates and organisations, including its role in the 2016 US presidential election, and the Brexit referendum in the same year in the UK.

The scandal erupted in March 2018 when news reports revealed that Cambridge Analytica had obtained personal data from millions of Facebook users without their consent. The data was harvested through a third-party app, which collected information not only from users who installed the app, but also from their friends' profiles, resulting in the unauthorised collection of vast amounts of personal data.

Cambridge Analytica allegedly used the harvested data to create psychological profiles of individual voters, which were then used to target them with personalised political advertisements and messages. The company claimed to have developed sophisticated algorithms and techniques to micro-target voters and influence their behaviour, including their voting preferences and political opinions.

The revelations about Cambridge Analytica's data practices raised concerns about the potential impact on democratic processes and electoral integrity. They prompted regulatory investigations and inquiries by government authorities in the US, UK, and other countries. Facebook faced scrutiny over its data privacy practices and its handling of user data, leading to calls for greater regulation of tech companies and online platforms.

In the aftermath of the scandal, Cambridge Analytica filed for bankruptcy and ceased operations. Facebook faced backlash and public outrage over its role in the data privacy breach and its failure to protect user data. The scandal prompted Facebook to implement changes to its platform and policies to strengthen data privacy protections and enhance transparency and accountability in its data practices.

The scandal underscored the vulnerabilities of digital platforms and the risks of data exploitation for political purposes. It raised important questions about the ethical use of data, the regulation of tech companies, and the influence of money and special interests in democratic processes. The fallout from the scandal continues to shape discussions about data privacy, online disinformation, and electoral integrity in the digital age.

THE MANAGEMENT OF RELATIONSHIPS WITH SUPPLIERS

This is the reason why I was happy to write this chapter; this is my comfort zone! For years, throughout various sectors and roles, I had the privilege of engaging with thousands of suppliers, throughout the sourcing processes of different organisations in different sectors.

It goes without saying that I had to apply different criteria for various sectors during the procurement process to achieve a value-for-money contract. The knowledge and expertise required for purchasing and negotiating food products were distinct from those needed for evaluating leasing contract proposals for rigid transport. When I concluded the negotiation rounds to determine the cents per millimetre rubber revenue from recycling tires for hundreds of trucks annually, I could not apply that experience to my next project: a specification review for capabilities and skills requirements in the tender for pension administration services. Similarly, negotiating a facilities management contract for a group of airports was different from leading negotiations to establish the minimum health and safety criteria for transporting and storing chemicals on-site, especially when transitioning the contract from Chinese to local chemical suppliers.

Often procurement and supply chain professionals are considered a 'Jack of all trades and master of none' – competent in many skills but not excelling in any particular one. Every day, we try to address different impacts, mitigate various risks or try to take advantage of opportunities. Sometimes, our time is fully absorbed in dealing with supply chain disruptions that can happen at any link in the supply chain, planning delays, product quality issues, increased costs, changed specifications, excess and obsolescence budgets, and so on. Other days, we are knee-deep in managing risks such as supplier failures, non-compliance with contractual obligations, unethical practices in the supply chain, payment delays or disputes. On good days, we get stuck into focusing on realising long-term beneficial opportunities, such as strengthening supplier relationships through collaboration, implementing ethical sourcing practices, conducting due diligence on suppliers, or optimising payment processes to ensure timely and fair payments.

For me, the most rewarding time was the time I spent collaborating with suppliers; understanding, evaluating, learning, agreeing, and disagreeing. It needs the same focus and energy as a personal relationship. There needs to be communication, clarity, commitment, respect, and trust. It takes time and it takes two to tango, so let's dig deeper into each of these key factors:

- **Communication:** Open and frequent communication is the foundation of any successful supplier relationship. Businesses that encourage open communication with their suppliers can better understand each other's needs, challenges, and goals. Companies that communicate clearly and transparently are more likely to build trust and foster collaboration with their suppliers. A mutual understanding allows for more effective problem-solving and decision-making, ultimately leading to a more efficient and productive supply chain;

- **Commitment:** A shared commitment to success is essential for building long-lasting supplier relationships. Companies that demonstrate a genuine commitment to their suppliers' well-being and growth are more likely to attract and retain high-quality partners. This needs to happen at every level of the company. Everyone benefits when top-down goals are shared, and bottom-up collaboration drives valuable partnerships. It enables joint innovation, risk mitigation, and shared value creation;

- **Clarity:** This is a skill that is highly underestimated. Often people talk a lot, but say very little. Their lack of clarity can stem from ineffective communication skills, overcomplicating information, or assuming the other person understands without providing clear context or explanations. Take the guess-work out of the communication by setting clear expectations and goals which are crucial for aligning suppliers with your business goals. Companies that establish clear guidelines through code of conducts, or can translate their ESG targets and metrics in a simple and effective way, are more likely to achieve successful outcomes. A study by McKinsey[28] found that companies in the top quartile for ESG performance were 5% more profitable than those in the bottom quartile. Additionally, companies with a strong ESG focus had higher market valuation multiples, indicating that investors are willing to pay a premium for sustainable and responsible companies;

- **Respect**: Treating suppliers with respect and fairness is essential for building strong, long-lasting relationships. Most companies are focused on treating their customers well. Many have departments specifically to deliver customer service and customer success, so should this not be the same for suppliers? Respect throughout the value chain is a crucial aspect of conducting business responsibly and ethically. It involves treating all stakeholders – including suppliers, employees, customers, and the environment – with dignity and respect. Let's not forget that business success depends on having great relationships with suppliers and customers alike;

- **Trust:** Trust is the glue that holds supplier relationships together. Companies that build trust with their suppliers are more likely to enjoy the benefits of a strong, resilient supply chain. Let's not forget that most of the risks for many companies lie in their supply chain; not only sustainability-related risks, but also economic and social risks. At every link in the supply chain, there is a company that requires the same level of trust that customers give to you when they buy your products or services. Never assume trust is a given. Trust is developed over time through consistent and reliable interactions between equal partners;

- **Continuous improvement:** Finally, suppliers and buyers should continuously seek ways to improve the relationship, processes, and products, ensuring the partnership remains dynamic and effective. By fostering strong relationships with suppliers, you can tap into a diverse pool of expertise, ideas, and resources, effectively leveraging the collective brainpower of multiple stakeholders to drive continuous improvement for a sustainable and competitive advantage.

Volkswagen's Supplier Relationship Management Scandal

Supplier relationship scandals exists across all sectors. Have you seen the Netflix television series *Rotten,*[29] which travels deep into the heart of the food supply chain to reveal unsavoury truths and exposes hidden forces that shape what we eat? As a lecturer at several universities for sustainable procurement and supply chain, it is a 'must see' series for my students to understand the scale, scope, irremediability, and likelihood of abuses that happen in food supply chains.

On 23 May 2024, the *Critical Raw Materials Act*[30] came into force, aimed at ensuring a diverse, secure, and sustainable supply of critical raw materials for the EU's industry, especially strategic sectors, such as clean technologies, digital, defence and aerospace industries. The Act is a strategic, comprehensive response to the escalating global demand for critical raw materials and the complex geopolitical factors impacting their supply. Cobalt is one of those critical raw materials and a key component used in lithium-ion batteries for electric vehicles (EVs). The demand for cobalt has surged with the growth of the EV market; however, cobalt mining operations,[31] particularly in the Democratic Republic of Congo (DRC), have long been associated with human rights violations, child labour, and unsafe working conditions.

In 2020, a lawsuit[32] was filed against Volkswagen in the US on behalf of Congolese families who alleged that their children were killed or injured while mining cobalt used in Volkswagen's electric vehicles. The lawsuit accused Volkswagen of knowingly benefiting from forced labour and child exploitation in its cobalt supply chain and failing to conduct adequate due diligence to prevent human rights abuses.

This case could be examined under multiple areas of the ESRS. However, I include it here as the root cause of all these grave issues was VW's lack of responsible sourcing policies and its basic disregard for supplier relationship management. The incidence of bad supplier management and violations included:

- **Human rights violations:** Reports have documented widespread human rights abuses in cobalt mining operations, including child labour, unsafe working conditions, and environmental pollution. The lawsuit against Volkswagen highlighted the company's alleged complicity in these abuses through its procurement of cobalt from suppliers in the DRC;

- **Supply chain transparency:** The scandal underscores the challenges of ensuring transparency and accountability in complex global supply chains, particularly in industries like automotive manufacturing where companies rely on a vast network of suppliers and subcontractors;

- **Corporate responsibility:** Volkswagen faced criticism for its role in perpetuating human rights abuses and exploitation in its cobalt supply chain, raising questions about the company's commitment to ethical sourcing, responsible procurement practices, and adherence to international labour standards.

In response to the lawsuit and public scrutiny, Volkswagen[33] pledged to investigate the allegations and address any violations of its responsible sourcing policies. The company reiterated its commitment to human rights, sustainability, and corporate social responsibility but acknowledged the need for greater transparency and oversight in its cobalt supply chain. This was too little too late for families whose children were abused, forced into labour, or even worse, killed.

More recently, in June 2023, a complaint[34] was filed by the European Centre for Constitutional & Human Rights, a non-governmental organisation, with a German regulator arguing that German companies Volkswagen, BMW, and Mercedes-Benz were violating their obligations under Germany's due diligence law by failing to tackle supply chain links to forced labour in the Xinjiang Uyghur Autonomous Region of China.

These cases highlight the importance of ethical sourcing, supplier management, and due diligence in preventing human rights abuses, and ensuring social and environmental responsibility throughout the supply chain. They underscore the need for companies to take proactive measures to identify and address risks of exploitation and misconduct in their procurement practices.

CORRUPTION & BRIBERY

One of the biggest business scandals that I can remember was the Enron scandal[35] in 2001. Corruption and bribery, however, is not a thing of the past. We hear about it all the time in the news, be it allegations or convictions. It is very much a threat to good business conduct, to democracy, and to sustainable business.

Prevention and detection of corruption and bribery are critical aspects of corporate governance and risk management. These practices are essential to mitigate legal and regulatory fines, protect reputation, safeguard against financial losses, and prevent fraudulent activities that can harm your business, your stakeholders and the environment. By addressing risks such as bribery, corruption, embezzlement, fraudulent financial reporting, money laundering, and conflicts of interest, companies proactively manage threats to their integrity and competitive advantage.

We all know that anti-bribery and fraud policies and procedures do not happen by themselves; they need to be created. Strong leadership again matters here. A clear governance framework needs to be implemented across the full value chain and regular risk assessments and audits need to identify vulnerabilities and areas of concern to enable organisations to take proactive measures to address potential issues.

Policies on corruption and bribery should be communicated effectively to relevant stakeholders, including employees, contractors, suppliers, and other parties with a vested interest in compliance. Using a range of communication tools and channels, such as flyers, newsletters, dedicated websites, social media, and face-to-face interactions, helps to ensure that policies are understood and implemented across the value chain.

In this context, it is essential to identify functions or regions within the organisation that are at risk due to their tasks and responsibilities. By understanding these 'functions at risk' or 'regions at risk', companies can tailor their prevention strategies to effectively address specific vulnerabilities. Internal and external control procedures provide transparency and demonstrate the right commitment to detecting and preventing corrupt practices. Training activities on ethical conduct and compliance should be presented in a manner that highlights regional differences or workforce categories. Companies need to think beyond their own employees and enable their value chain by offering training programs as part of a supplier development program. Quizrr[36] offers a Supplier Code of Conduct training programme designed to educate supply chain stakeholders, including management and workers, on upholding ethical standards. Ultimately, it is the commitment to ongoing training and compliance reporting that provides valuable insights for stakeholders, and demonstrates the business commitment to prevent fraud and bribery.

Institutionalised Bribery Practices at Glencore

The biggest bribery scandal I have come across in recent years was the Glencore scandal.[37] Glencore, a commodities trader, pleaded guilty to a decade-long scheme of bribing foreign officials. The widespread bribery and corruption spanned multiple countries, primarily in Africa and Latin America. The scandal highlighted systemic corruption within Glencore, with senior executives authorising bribes to secure business advantages and manipulate markets across these regions.

The Glencore scandal had far-reaching consequences for the company, including significant financial penalties, legal repercussions, and reputational damage. Glencore agreed to pay more than $1.5 billion in total to resolve bribery and market manipulation investigations by authorities in the US, UK, and Brazil. In the UK, Glencore Energy UK Ltd was ordered to pay a record £281 million penalty for bribery offences in Africa. In the US, Glencore was sentenced to pay $700 million, consisting of a $428 million fine and $272 million in forfeiture, after pleading guilty to foreign bribery charges. Glencore also reached a $180 million settlement with the DRC to resolve corruption allegations from 2007 to 2018. And as part of the US plea deal, Glencore will be subject to an independent compliance monitor for three years to oversee its anti-corruption efforts.

The scandal exposed Glencore's "endemic" culture of bribery and corruption, severely tarnishing its reputation. There were calls for Glencore to be removed from the Extractive Industries Transparency Initiative (EITI)[38] due to its unethical conduct being inconsistent with EITI principles. Glencore also faced criticism for failing to provide adequate redress to the affected countries and communities impacted by its corrupt practices.

On 24 May 2022, Glencore announced agreement with authorities in the US, UK and Brazil to resolve investigations into past practices at certain Group businesses. Since then, Glencore has updated its ethics and compliance[39] programme and policies.

ESRS-G1 – BUSINESS CONDUCT REPORTING OBLIGATIONS

ESRS-G1 – *Business Conduct*[40] is about telling people how a company behaves in its business. This standard enable users of the organisation's sustainability statements to understand its strategy and approach, processes and procedures as well as its performance in respect of business conduct.

Business Conduct Sub-topics

The standard focuses on the following matters, collectively referred to in this Standard as 'business conduct'. Article 16 of ESRS 1, in relation to G1 impacts, risks and opportunities and mandatory reporting, outlines clearly the six sub-topics we should consider under this standard:

- **Corporate culture:** The values, convictions, and ethical principles and codes of conduct that define the goals and operational conduct of a business. It encompasses the policies, strategies, and practices that shape how a company operates and interacts with its stakeholders;

- **Protection of whistleblowers:** The legal safeguards and mechanisms in place to protect individuals who report or disclose information about wrongdoing, illegal activities, or unethical practices within an organisation or institution;

- **Animal welfare:** G1 requires companies to transparently disclose their governance, policies, processes, and performance related to animal welfare, if it is a material topic for their business operations and stakeholders. This aims to promote better corporate practices and accountability in managing animal welfare impacts;

- **Political engagement and lobbying activities:** Companies are required to provide transparency on the activities and commitments related to exerting its political influence with political contributions, including the types and purpose of lobbying activities;

- **Management of relationships with suppliers, including payment practices:** Companies need to disclose information on how they manage relationships with suppliers, including payment practices and transparency in the upstream value chain;

- **Corruption and bribery:** Reporting should detail how the company ensures compliance with anti-corruption and anti-bribery measures and should focus on prevention and detection, including training and Incidents.

The requirements of this section should be read in conjunction with and reported alongside the disclosures required by ESRS 2 on Governance (GOV), Strategy (SBM) and Management of impacts, risks and opportunities (IRO).

It is important to understand the *Minimum Disclosure Requirements* (MDRs) in ESRS 2, *Chapter 4.2*. When an organisation identifies a sustainability matter as material, 34 MDR data points (DPs) for Policies, Actions, Targets, and Metrics (PAT-M) are applicable if the organisation discloses on policies, actions and targets. If it does not provide disclosure on policies, targets or actions, then it needs to disclose the reasons for not doing so, as per the corresponding 10 DPs of ESRS 2 MDR PAT, paragraphs 62 and 81.

ESRS-G1 outlines clearly, in six *Disclosure Requirements* (DRs), the narrative and numeric DPs an organisation should comply with. There are 39 *Shall* DPs, of which 25 are narrative, 8 are numeric and 6 are semi-narrative, as well as 10 additional *May* DPs. The MDR PAT DPs are to be disclosed under G1-1, G1-4 when the sustainability matters are material.

Figure 10.4: ESRS-G1 Reporting Requirements

ESRS-G1	**Business Conduct**
	All below are subject to materiality for each of the sub-topics.
	Corporate Culture, Protection of whistle blowers **Animal welfare, Political engagement** **Supplier relationship management with payment practices** **Corruption and bribery**
	GOVERNANCE
G1-ESRS2-GOV-1	The role of the administrative, supervisory and management bodies
	IMPACT, RISK & OPPORTUNITY MANAGEMENT
ESRS-G1-1	Business conduct policies and corporate culture.
ESRS-G1-2	Management of relationships with suppliers.
ESRS-G1-3	Prevention and detection of corruption and bribery.
	METRICS & TARGETS
ESRS-G1-4	Confirmed incidents of corruption or bribery.
ESRS-G1-5	Political influence and lobbying activities.
ESRS-G1-6	Payment practices.

On a final note. ESRS-G1 aligns closely to another international standard, the OECD's *Due Diligence Guidance for Responsible Business Conduct*,[41] which provides practical support to enterprises on the implementation of the OECD's *Guidelines for Multinational Enterprises*[42] by providing plain language explanations of its due diligence recommendations. Implementing these recommendations can help enterprises avoid and address adverse impacts related to workers, human rights, the environment, bribery, consumers and corporate governance that may be associated with their operations, supply chains and other business relationships. The guidance includes additional explanations, tips and illustrative examples of due diligence.

1　https://commission.europa.eu/strategy-and-policy/priorities-2019-2024/european-green-deal_en.

2　https://www.oecd.org/about/.

3　https://www.un.org/en/.

4　https://www.ipcc.ch/.

5　https://www.globalreporting.org/.

6　https://sdgs.un.org/goals.

7　https://www.fsb-tcfd.org/.

8　https://7genfoundation.org/7th-generation/.

9　https://shorturl.at/O0iTm.

10　Belfort, J. (2007). *The Wolf of Wall Street*.

11　https://futureplanet.com/.

12　'The Tragedy of the Commons'. *Science* 162 (1968): 1243–1248. Hardin, Garrett, & John Baden, eds. *Managing the Commons*. San Francisco

13　https://www.knowesg.com/companies/lego-incentivises-entire-workforce-for-climate-action-22052024.

14　https://www.theguardian.com/technology/2017/jun/06/uber-fires-employees-sexual-harassment-investigation.

15　https://www.susanjfowler.com/blog/2017/2/19/reflecting-on-one-very-strange-year-at-uber.

16　https://shorturl.at/bKktv.

17　https://shorturl.at/KGYhU.

18　https://www.politico.eu/article/vladimir-putin-russia-citizenship-us-whistleblower-edward-snowden/.

19　https://shorturl.at/H45Qt.

20　https://www.bbc.com/news/live/world-us-canada-68838169.

21　*What We Know After Death of Joshua Dean, Second Boeing Whistleblower to Die in Two Months*, https://www.snopes.com/news/2024/05/07/boeing-whistleblower-deaths/.

22　https://www.rte.ie/news/business/2012/0320/314901-egg-business/.

23　https://eur-lex.europa.eu/EN/legal-content/summary/eu-rules-on-the-protection-of-animals-during-transport.html.

24　https://www.politico.com/news/2024/05/09/trump-asks-oil-executives-campaign-finance-00157131.

25　https://www.foei.org/eight-shell-scandals/.

26　https://www.youtube.com/watch?v=A24fWmNA6lM.

27　https://www.nytimes.com/2018/04/04/us/politics/cambridge-analytica-scandal-fallout.html.

28　https://shorturl.at/JzH6G.

29　https://www.netflix.com/ie/title/80146284.

30　https://single-market-economy.ec.europa.eu/sectors/raw-materials/areas-specific-interest/critical-raw-materials/critical-raw-materials-act_en.

31　https://www.theguardian.com/global-development/2021/nov/08/cobalt-drc-miners-toil-for-30p-an-hour-to-fuel-electric-cars.

32   https://bit.ly/3yCL1pN.
33   https://www.volkswagen-group.com/en/publications/corporate/supply-chain-and-human-rights-2145/download?disposition=attachment.
34   https://bit.ly/4bof4Qx.
35   https://www.britannica.com/event/Enron-scandal.
36   https://www.quizrr.se/supplier-code-of-conduct.
37   https://www.glencore.com/investigations.
38   https://eiti.org/.
39   https://shorturl.at/vh2od.
40   https://shorturl.at/lpmwq.
41   https://www.oecd.org/investment/due-diligence-guidance-for-responsible-business-conduct.htm.
42   https://www.oecd.org/investment/mne/.

11

WHAT IF...?

Minou Schillings

Just like most kids, my favourite question growing up was 'Why?' But, unlike the other kids around me, I never grew out of this phase. I couldn't stop asking 'Why?', simply because the currently dominant way of living doesn't make any sense to me. Why do we spend so much time behind screens? Why are we so competitive? Why are there cars everywhere? Why do people still go hungry whilst we produce plenty of food to feed the world? Why do we force pigs into slaughterhouses? Why do we go into war? Why do we exploit other human beings?

I have never gotten a satisfying answer to any of these questions. Because you can only answer these questions in a semi-sensible way, by grounding your logic in the consumer-oriented hyper-capitalist and mechanistic worldview. Accepting a worldview as an unmovable baseline for your logic is something that even 4 year old Minou didn't accept.

In The Netherlands, where I was born and raised, the hyper-capitalistic mechanistic worldview is dominant. It is a society strengthened in the belief that humans are 'above' wider nature by literally 'defeating' the sea and living below sea level. Growing up struggling with this narrative helped me to recognise that we can only question our current worldview if we simultaneously explore alternatives. From Why?, to What If...?, to How Might We...?

Minou Schillings

WHAT IF...?

In a world grappling with the consequences of relentless development and anthropocentric practices, the need for alternative and especially a wider range of visions for the future has never been more pressing. This chapter explores the possibility of transition to regenerative futures, inviting readers to imagine a world where the pursuit of wholeness takes precedence over the narrow quest for answers. Drawing on diverse perspectives from indigenous wisdom to Western ecological thinkers, it explores the possibility of a future of many ways of living in harmony with earth, based on reciprocity and interconnectedness.

What if you woke up in the year 2050 and found the world in peace and balance? When we dream about regenerative futures, we imagine a society in which the well-being of life sits at the core. A world where people, communities, businesses and governments choose collaboration over competition, compassion over envy, curiosity over judgement, multigenerational caring over short-term thinking.

A society in which people are more familiar with the names of plants than the names of brands; where we compare ourselves, not to each other, but only to who we were the day before; and where we sense and prioritise life.

We wake up in the morning, feeling rested after a night of breathing crisp fresh air. The food we are eating is nourishing, heals the soil, enhances biodiversity and brings our families and communities together. Our lives flow from doing fulfilling work – activities that nourish our happiness. We recognise the need to heal our relationships and our traumas in collective ways, knowing that peace is a continuous and shared process that needs to be nurtured constantly. In short, imagine a world in which we as humans, found our way back, to ourselves, to each other and to all other forms of life.

When I wake up in the world of my wildest imagination, I open my eyes in the morning to the sound of birds chirping, the canopy of the forest right above me. I marvel at the tree tops through a sky window of highly isolating glass, covered in mini solar tiles. The rest of the roof and all outside walls are flourishing with native species, cooling the house, cleaning the air and boosting my happiness and the lives of birds, hedgehogs, butterflies and other insects.

I step out of bed into the shower, quickly rinsing off with captured rainwater. I am once again grateful for the foresight of the community in valuing the vital importance of water, resulting in a water retention system supporting the lives of the humans and more-than-human species in the area. The system consists of lakes and wadis, rain barrels, vertical gardens, rooftop terraces, reforested areas, highly diverse food forests and the end of the 'traditional' flush toilet, now just an echo of the past. Composting poo is back in fashion, fulfilling an important role in the growth cycle of vegetables, fruits, grains and nuts. Out of the shower, I get dressed in timeless fashion, designed for longevity in both style and material. My favourite? To this day still, the jacket my mom wore on her wedding day – 30+ years in use and still going strong.

Most of my days are a nourishing balance between laptop, canvas and land-based work. Online, I collaborate with people across the world, working on experiences designed to enhance the regenerative capacities of individuals, communities and businesses. Behind my canvas, I simply paint, unrestrained by commercial expectations. On the land, I care for the soil, the garden, the chickens and the sheep.

After detoxing from a digital overdose and frisbeeing my laptop out of the window, I retreated to a farm for a couple of years. Soon realising that simply farming sounds beautiful, but wasn't what fulfilled me, I realised that I both love wider nature and technology, gardening and facilitation, writing and community weaving. It turns out that mono kills life, diversity enhances life. This also applies to the range of activities we are involved in during our days.

The nomadic, highly-dynamic lifestyle has always drawn me. Luckily, the birth of multiple eco-village networks around the world makes it now possible to travel slowly and to live with others in a way that regenerates both my own well-being and the eco-systems I am a part of.

The eco-village I woke up in this morning is an experimental collection of treehouses, built organically at different layers, starting a couple metres above the soil. The houses are both built in the trees and covered by trees and other native species. Imagine the creators of Avatar, Pipi Longstocking and Dune coming together to build a village for tree-huggers! All the houses are connected by bridges. Everything you need is within a 15 minute walk/shared zipbubble (zipline meets car)/bicycle journey. The ground below the treehouses is 90% rewilded, with an abundance of edible and non-edible species; the other 10% is cared for by regenerative farmers in collaboration with other species like cows, chickens, worms, pigs, butterflies and bees.

Living in villages, where capacities, efforts and goods are shared, results in a lot less pressure. Stepping out of the rat-race opened up a wide range of possibilities for play, rest, creation and experimentation. Once I started unlearning and re-imagining life, artificial desires and vanity goals ceased to exist. Every time I let go of a marketing or career-driven desire, something beautiful happened. I had more time, more headspace and more energy to enjoy the truly fulfilling and meaningful. For me, this means lots more time to cook, paint, play hide and seek, hike, talk to strangers, build treehouses, write, experiment, forage, share meals with loved ones and hike again.

The widespread notion that humans are a plague on the earth, incapable of living in harmony with wider nature, both diminishes the regenerative ways of our ancestors and the potential of future generations. We live in a world in which almost every institution is designed to squander our imagination. Traditional education, standardised testing, 9 to 5 careers, political polls; none of these systems leave much room for our imagination. But that doesn't mean we don't have it. We do – and even better, we can nourish our imagination capacities just like a muscle.

WHAT IS REGENERATION?

The seriousness and complexity of the meta crisis dawned on me while I was studying in Malta at the Institute for the Development of Thinking. Having grown up surrounded by forested areas, I feel most at home around trees. It hit me hard when I arrived in Malta and it felt there were more cars than trees. The island called 'the rock' is mostly buildings and, unsurprisingly, rocks. For the first time, I deeply felt the longing for rewilding. I always wanted to use my career as a force for good. This deepened by what I can only describe as an existential crisis: fear for the future; fear for the livelihood of the children I might have one day; fear for the health and lives of all living beings, now and generations to come.

Out of this fear, I started my business called The Green Sprint – a highly speed-oriented, controlling and pushy name. Everything needs to be greener faster. I started to facilitate accelerated innovation processes to develop sustainable products faster. I did exactly what so many well-intentioned people are doing, trying to solve the problem with the same kind of thinking that created it. Instead of shifting horizons, I helped businesses to sprint in the same direction faster, a bit greener, but still perpetuating overconsumption and extraction. The transformative process of every innovation process was blocked by our unchecked business-as-usual biases, assumptions and worldviews.

Accelerated innovation processes are a great way to make the current reality better, but what we need is other realities – realities that open up once we shift horizons. We can hold the space for these realities to emerge by changing the questions, unlearning our extractive beliefs, recognising the past, deepening our imagination for other futures, re-imagining the way we live, work, unite and inhabit this earth. In this chapter, we are sharing stories and ways that can help you to shift horizons.

Imagine ...

Imagine sentient aliens, travelling across the universe, coming to visit Earth now. For the first time ever, they set foot on earth, stepping into 2024. How do you imagine they will respond?

Will they look at each other, utterly confused, wondering, why this species is hoarding life and jeopardising their own existence? Will they flee back to their spacecraft, bewildered and worried lest they catch the infection that has struck this odd species?

We don't even need to imagine visiting aliens to make the point. We can simply ask people and communities living in organic and circular ways how they see 'modernity'.

Our odd species is still maturing and, throughout the 19th, 20th and first half of the 21st century, has suffered a long, extractive and stubborn puberty. Just as teenagers sometimes behave in ways that make absolutely no sense, we as humans behave in ways that must seem ridiculous and dangerous to other species.

The way we currently live on, and relate to, the other beings on this planet makes no sense. We are actively countering our own ability to thrive – and even to survive. We are creating conditions in which life suffers and decays. Eco-systems are on the verge of collapse (planetary boundaries) and the sixth mass extinction is unfolding before our eyes.

Our current societal systems are pushing these degenerative patterns. As long as humans keep interfering with wider nature in destructive ways, we are degenerating life on earth. The regenerative lens is an invitation to humans to create the conditions conducive for life to thrive. This isn't something new: it is just new to us, who have been born and raised into a hyper-individualistic and commercial society that started to drift away from the wisdom of nature long ago.

How would you explain regeneration to a 5 year old?
Imagine you are in a city. There is concrete, asphalt and pavement everywhere. These dense materials block all forms of life from thriving – though the occasional fearless flower manages to make its way up in the space between the paving stones. But most life is squandered. The soil is pressed down and suffocated. Water can't get into the earth; it flows off and creates floods with every downpour.

Regeneration is like flipping all these pavements out, caring for the soil beneath it and making sure that plants, butterflies, hedgehogs and worms come back out to play.

Besides bricks, pavements and concrete, what else do you think is stopping life in today's world? Windows that birds crash into. Roads snails can't cross. Natural parks where wolves aren't welcome. Oceans unsafe for whales. River dams blocking salmon in their yearly migration. Besides these visible things, there are many invisible systems blocking life from thriving.

Sustainability is a state of equilibrium – a state of balance. It is a state in which an eco-system can exist – although always temporarily – since nature is never at rest. Degeneration is the process of moving away from sustainability, while regeneration is the process of moving towards a sustainable state. Where the sustainable state can be understood as a destination, regeneration is a constant movement – a lifelong journey of becoming and arriving.

> *A regenerative human culture is healthy, resilient and adaptable; it cares for the planet and it cares for life in the awareness that this is the most effective way to create a thriving future for all humanity.*

Daniel Christian Wahl

Regenerative human cultures are shaped by communities and, in our current world, these communities often take the shape of businesses. Businesses have a tremendous amount of influence on our shared narratives, systems and societies. To change our future, we need to re-imagine how we come together - changing from teaming up in profit-driven businesses, to uniting in communities grounded in the regeneration of life.

A regenerative business acknowledges the interdependence of systems. It constantly seeks to understand its place within the system and the well-being of other life forms it depends on and interacts with. It uses this knowledge as a guide for decision-making. It creates value for all stakeholders involved, with restorative, inclusive and resilient principles at its roots.

> *Regenerative leaders bring vitality and well-being to all our living systems. In so doing, we wake up to what it really means to be fully human.*

Laura Storm & Giles Hutchins, *Regenerative Leadership: The DNA of Life-affirming 21st Century Organisations*

Regeneration is a what, how, why, where and who. It is an all-encompassing lens on life, a decision-making compass and guide supporting you in our collective journey to create the conditions for life to thrive.

Difference & Overlaps between Sustainability, Circularity & Regeneration

When roaming the halls of a sustainability conference, you most likely will encounter a debate around the distinctions between sustainability, circularity and regeneration. While it may seem like a matter of terminology, words hold significant weight and shape the way we think. It would be a great loss if individuals driven by impact and the vision of a thriving future for all beings are unable to collaborate because of unnecessary misalignment in terminology. If sustainability professionals struggle to find common ground, how can we expect the rest of the world to join the movement?

Sustainability is predominantly discussed in line with the definition put forth by the Brundtland Commission in 1987:

> *Sustainability means meeting the needs of the present without compromising the ability of future generations to meet their own needs.*

Achieving a sustainable state, where both present and future generations can thrive, requires a life-sustaining balance. This means avoiding any external interventions or actions that disrupt the eco-system, as each instance of such interference leads to degeneration. A degenerating system experiences a loss of vitality and deteriorates further. When an eco- or social system becomes degenerated, regeneration is the necessary movement towards rebalancing the sustainable state. Regeneration, simply put, involves healing a system or being and creating the conditions for life to flourish.

The shift from focusing on sustainability to regeneration means a shift from goal-oriented action to condition-oriented processes. This is a significant difference as it reclaims caring for the planet as an integrated part of being a living system (human/organisation/government). We temporarily turned sustainability into a tick-box exercise and now it's time to shift horizons and embrace the regenerative lens in every way possible. I understand regeneration as a capacity-building process with deep love, understanding and respect for life on earth and a strong connection to place, context and beings. The focus of regeneration is to dismantle the barriers to thrivablity and to create the conditions for life to flourish. For the next couple of decades, this means co-existing and collaborating with the goal-oriented sustainability and flow-focused circular approaches. Different approaches to the meta-crisis are rarely mutually exclusive. We love silver bullet solutions but, in facing the meta crisis, it's vital we acknowledge that we simply don't know which mix of approaches is going to help us emerge from the mess we created.

For further exploration of living systems awareness and regenerative futures, consider reading the following books:

- *Thrivability*, Michelle Holiday;
- *Designing Regenerative Cultures*, Daniel Christian Wahl;
- *Braiding Sweetgrass*, Robin Wall Kimmerer;
- *Restoring the Kinship Worldview*, Wahinkpe Topa (Four Arrows) & Darcia Narvaez, Ph.D.

MUSINGS ON REGENERATIVE FUTURES – 1

Brunni Corsato[1]

What if you woke up tomorrow morning in a regenerative and thriving society? What would that world look like?
A regenerative world to me means a more integrated world, one where all our steps and practices are taken considering our environmental surroundings but also the people around us and those who will come after we are gone.

To regenerate is to combine ancestral wisdom with society's current knowledge to ensure our planet and all its inhabitants – humans, animals, plants and more – can thrive. Beyond just environmental measures, that also means slowing down to allow time for deep thinking, curiosity, playfulness and pleasure. Humanity's best solutions come from that. Slowing down also reflects on how we consume, ultimately leading to a smaller, more localised way of engaging with what we buy, what we eat, and how we travel. Regeneration needs to be immanent to be transformative.

Can you describe a day of your life in this future? How does this life feel?
Life feels lighter and more fulfilling. Knowing that the regeneration of the planet is top priority for us as a society, I'm even more motivated to contribute to the greater good, and so is everyone else. Jobs across the board are informed by this lens, and the effects of collective action can be felt daily, contributing to global momentum.

Don't let the enormity of the work ahead make you overwhelmed. Tap into hope and patience, and focus on doing 1% better than the day before. Understand what you can contribute that would generate the most impact in the long run to regenerate the environment and do just that – day in, day out. This work is bigger than any individual, but don't let that discourage you. Begin. Good luck.

WHOEVER OWNS THE PAST HAS TWO FEET ON THE CHEST OF THE FUTURE

Tiago Paes Vilas Boas

I was born in the ancestral lands of the Guarani people, once a thriving forest, now known as São Paulo State, Brazil. The country takes its name from a tree (Paubrasilia echinata) that was nearly driven to extinction within the first decades of colonisation. These lands were originally called Yby Marã E'ymam, or Land Without Sorrows. For 500 years, sorrow has entrenched itself in these lands, and peace has been elusive. In my youth, I realised I could not escape from conflicts with the police, in my work, and with the state.

My right to being and my community, along with indigenous and quilombo communities, were – and still are – perceived as a threat to the relentless progress of development projects rooted in colonialism, extraction, and violence. Though the narrative has changed over time, the violence against our bodies persists. Poverty, racism, and injustice were constants in my community – sometimes normalised, but increasingly confronted. The realisation that the job market would not heal the wounds or address the structural racism I faced led me to refuse to renounce my community, culture, and identity, even as the state and justice systems sought to normalise the colonial project.

The violence of colonial systems in my youth, juxtaposed with the compassion of the many communities I belong to, led me to facilitate reciprocal and organic relationships between individuals, communities, and nature. For more than a decade, I have sought to weave wisdom and an intercultural worldview, learning from indigenous elders from around the world to facilitate processes of change, design circular solutions, and foster reciprocal and learning relationships.

> **The most effective way to destroy people is to deny and obliterate their own understanding of their history.**
>
> **George Orwell**

When a few aim to own history, a brutal act of politics of memory is imposed – who should be remembered and who is forgotten – followed by erasing the diversity of ways of being and then the transition to an imposed single story. In the recent past, Nazism sought to reconstruct a new narrative for Germany, envisioning a mono and supremacist society. Today, Western countries employ singular narratives of progress, democracy, freedom, science, and ways of being as tools for colonisation. These narratives are wielded to justify interventions, invasions, assassinations, coups, and sanctions against what they label as 'underdeveloped' countries and the alternatives to their plan: the indigenous and traditional communities and their ways of being.

Behind these actions often lie motives of resource exploitation, ideological and cultural expansion, and geopolitical power plays. Manipulations, lies and erasure — most of us still live inside of colonial projects based on such an agenda. Humans against humans, humans against everything, humans own everything.

Who has the right of memory and who does not? Who can and can't dream about a regenerative future?

I invite those who can dream to not just reimagine a future, but to use your position and privilege to build mutual relationships and work for the liberation of those that cannot dream yet. A simple example is to search for partners in your sector that work with communities in conditions of poverty, and stability, not in transactional relationships, often exploitative, but liberated ones.

This quest for a regenerative future is a journey of reflection and reckoning that requires courage, humility, and willingness. It invites us to interrogate our assumptions and confront our biases. Let our acts of everyday life be the base stones of a more just future.

For further exploration of alternative narratives and indigenous perspectives, consider reading the following books that offer valuable insights into decolonising history and challenging dominant narratives:

- Orientalism, Edward W. Said;
- How Europe Underdeveloped Africa, Walter Rodney.
- Life Is Not Useful, Ailton Krenak.

The timeline of your life is not a straight line, after all; it is a series of ebbs and flows, backs and forths, heres and theres. You are nowhere and everywhere all at once, and that means that most of the time, the best you can do is be present to the moment, be open to the unlearning and the learning, and trust that you're doing the work of Love.

Kaitlin B. Curtice, *Living Resistance: An Indigenous Vision for Seeking Wholeness Every Day*

MANY PATHS, MANY WAYS: INDIGENOUS & TRADITIONAL KNOWLEDGE SYSTEMS & PRACTICES

Tiago Paes Vilas Boas

More than acknowledging the indigenous and traditional knowledge and science, this section is also about yarn, entangling and connecting diverse ways of living in reciprocal ways that work not just for humans but for all our extended relatives: mountains, rivers, birds, plants, etc.

First, I want to honour the earth, who always provides and cares as a beloved mother. The earth is a living being, not a separate entity but the very base of my existence. Then my second acknowledgement is for the violence and the resilience and resistance of many indigenous and traditional people who keep balanced ways of living in deep reverence, respect, responsibility and reciprocity to earth. I want to emphasise the diverse people of the territories, whose indigenous names I don't know, such as Curaçao, Suriname, Bonero, St. Martin, Aruba, Indonesia and many others, where the nation-state, Netherlands, where I am writing, has enforced more than 300 years of atrocities such as slavery and colonisation. My last acknowledgement is for those who sit in many circles through time and have shared and kept the knowledge and science – to name a few from whom I am still learning and trying to honour this gift: Láné Sáan Moonwalker, Joshua Konkankoh, Paula Underwood, Kowawa Apunirã, Nego Bispo and Abdias do Nascimento.

This practice of honouring the territory and its relationships could take hours in traditional and indigenous communities. It is an understanding of a deep and continuing relationship that makes us beings.

Now is your turn. I would like to invite you to take a moment to reflect and acknowledge the land beneath your feet – the very earth that sustains you and the trees, birds, water and so on. Take a moment to express gratitude for it, while also acknowledging the harm you have done to it. Leave this book and find a place that feels comfortable to sit or perhaps walk and reflect on that for 10 minutes, then come back. How was it?

I hope that this exercise sparks a meaningful reflection in the way you walk on the land that you are. There is no separation between the land we are and what we are. It's important to value the relationships you are a part of, including those with plants, rivers, air, technology, furniture, and animals, etc.

'Interbeing' is a term that is not yet in the dictionary. However, if we combine the prefix 'inter' with the verb 'to be', we get a word that conveys the idea that all things exist in a state of interconnected being, where everything is interwoven and mutually dependent.

Who are the indigenous and traditional communities who have cared for the land you are on? I encourage you to seek out this knowledge; it can unleash a small thread of reconciliation with your history that you might not be aware that you seek.

Imagining the future demands an ability to grapple with unprecedented challenges, a task at which many businesses have fallen short due to their narrow understanding of living systems – not just within their own operations, but within the broader context of life itself.

Paula Underwood, a wisdom-keeper from the 10,000-year-old tradition of the Haudenosaunee people of North America, was tasked with sharing her knowledge with all who would listen – "to all listening ears", as Paula would say. This is a system of practices that had enabled generations to weather floods, famines, and other trials by employing a multitude of unique perspectives, to address challenges collectively.

Paula believes that organisations could thrive if they transformed into learning communities – circles where old and new perspectives are shared, seeing with old and new eyes, fostering mutual gratitude and understanding that, while we cannot know everything, our collective diversity equips us to navigate the complexities of life more effectively.

According to Paula's sharings, the Haudenosaunee community were organised into clans: the Wolf, Bear, and Turtle. The Wolf could today represent the planners, managers, and implementers; the Bear clan embodied innovation and creativity; and the Turtle clan comprised critical thinkers, activists, and individuals who anchored the group in its foundational values and vision.

Together, they sought the wisdom of the Eagle, embodying qualities of vision and insight, to help them navigate the challenges of the future. Paula used to say that "wisdom is knowledge put into practice".

Also, the Bears would experiment with ideas over extended periods, fully immersing themselves in the consequences before presenting their findings to the community. This deliberate approach ensured that decisions were made with a thorough understanding of their implications – a practice that prompts us to consider how we might have approached the development of artificial intelligence differently had we truly lived and experienced its potential impacts before implementation.

MUSINGS ON REGENERATIVE FUTURES – 2

Joy Njeri[2]

What if you woke up tomorrow morning in a regenerative and thriving society. What does that world look like?
We see each other as one, stewards co-creating a thriving Earth. We are part of nature, deeply interconnected with everything around us. Imagine a world where drilling a hole in the boat (exploiting resources) wouldn't just sink one person, but all of us – that is the illusion of separation we are living.

Can you describe a day of your life in this future? How does this life feel?
Sunlight streams through bioluminescent curtains, illuminating the vibrant green wall inside my home. The gentle chirping of birds mingles with the hum of bees flitting amongst the rooftop garden. A sense of shared purpose vibrates through the air. Children play in community gardens, while neighbours gather to barter organic produce grown on their balconies. My day begins with a mindful meditation amidst the lush rooftop garden, feeling a deep connection to the earth. My commute is a joyful ride on a solar-powered bicycle through the corridor full of flowers, colour and life.

Businesses are the beating heart of our communities. They are the bustling marketplaces where ideas are exchanged, solutions are born, and needs are met. Like a mirror reflecting societal values, businesses have the power to shape the future they envision. Imagine business leaders as conscious value creators. By responding to and creating for the good of society, they can become powerful agents of positive change. This doesn't negate the importance of financial sustainability but rather emphasises a more holistic approach to value creation.

> The corporation is an invention of man and must be controlled by man.
>
> **Chester I. Barnard**

For a good dose of inspiration and imagination consider reading:

- *From What is to What if*, Rob Hopkins;
- *Ministry of Imagination Manifesto*, Rob Hopkins;
- *Active Hope*, Joanna Macy;
- *Moral Imaginations* newsletter, Phoebe Tickell.

SHIFTING HORIZONS FROM EXTRACTIVE TO REGENERATIVE: UNLEARING MODERN-DAY 'TRUTHS'

Arriving in regenerative futures isn't a linear journey with a set destination. We can't mechanically shift from degenerative to sustainable, restorative and finally to regenerative – although the comfort of business frameworks suggests otherwise. Shifting horizons requires an open-mind, tremendous courage, deep compassion and a willingness to (un)learn from birth to death. As we all know, but often refuse to live by, change is the only constant.

In this chapter, we will explore the departure from extractive business-as-usual, rooted in coloniality, racism, patriarchy, hyper-individualism and limitless capitalism, a world defined by an overdose of mechanistic masculine energy and a prevailing individualistic productive consumer story.

The illiterates of the 21st century will not be those who cannot read and write, but those who cannot learn, unlearn and relearn.

Alvin Toffler

To realise a radically different, regenerative, and just future, we need to provide a space for our wildest imaginations to flourish. As long as we cling to old narratives of a dying world, we'll remain trapped in a cycle, unable to achieve the profound change needed to truly heal our planet. Thus, we must embark on a journey of (un)learning, shedding the stories, mindsets, and beliefs that no longer serve us.

Unlearning doesn't mean forgetting. It means consciously deciding which beliefs, assumptions, habits and stories no longer serve life on earth. It's crucial that we deal with our current challenges, accumulated over centuries of injustice, racism, colonialism and many other forms of oppression, so that we heal these relations, repair and take care of these open wounds. Otherwise, 10% of humans, those who are in enormous position of power and privileges, will continue escaping from their responsibility and continue to sell dreams of exclusivity to the earth.

By listening and sharing understanding with Grandmother Láné Sáan Moonwalker, an indigenous elder, from the lineages of Apache, Yoeme, and Ashkenazi, a healer, environmental guardian and spiritual teacher, I shared the views that we suffer from not relating to nature, and sustaining transactions instead of relations, avoiding our responsibility with all beings, forgetting to practice reciprocity instead of sustainability, and escaping from having a difficult conversation about the violence committed to Mother Earth. We need to foster intergenerational and non-human relationships as a way to create peace for the next generations dreaming about the future. Many of the current degenerative narratives are shaped by extractive histories that carry lessons, not to forget but to learn from.

Exercise / Question

Where, when, why and how have you unlearned? What 'truths', assumptions, beliefs or stories did you question, learn from, deconstruct and eventually leave behind?

Examine what ways of being and doing you are questioning today.

Don't worry about unlearning and moving on quickly. Unravelling the beliefs and worldviews that shape your life is a journey deserving of time and slowness. Remember this isn't a journey to move forward fast. Shifting horizons is a cyclical journey, slowly deepening below the surface of the visible.

(Exercise inspired by Kaitlin B. Curtice's book, *Living Resistance, An Indigenous Vision for Seeking Wholeness Every Day* .)

For further exploration of (un)learning and the transformation of worldviews and cultures consider reading:

- *Restoring Our Kinship Worldview: Indigenous Voices Introduce 28 Precepts for Rebalancing Life on Planet Earth,* Darcia Narváez & Wahinkpe Topa;
- *Courage to Transform: The 2023 Sustainability Report,* Forum for the Future, which explores various worldviews and transformation approaches;
- *A Systems View of Life,* Fritjof Capra & Pier Luigi Luisi;
- *Hospicing Modernity: Parting with Harmful Ways of Living,* Vanessa Machado de Oliveira (not for the faint hearted).

The Narrative Dictates the Answers

We used to think that the Earth was flat. Throughout history, humanity has collectively clung to beliefs that shaped our understanding and influenced decisions, behaviours, and systems. We thought that women couldn't travel on trains without their uterus falling out, we prosecuted 'witches', thought cigarettes cured asthma, and drilled holes into people's heads to release evil spirits. These stories permeated society, shaping our reality. However, just as these beliefs were debunked over time, we must challenge and transform the narratives that currently govern our world.

In today's society, women still have to stand up, every day, to the fact that masculine energy is running the global (shit)show – but the patriarchy hasn't always been dominant. One example of a matriarchal society is the Iroquois, who were organised matrilineally, with familial descent traced through the mother's line. Women held significant roles in decision-making and property ownership. Clan mothers played a crucial part in selecting chiefs and had authority in council meetings.

Today, the Mosuo people in China's Yunnan province are often cited as an example of a contemporary matriarchal society. In Mosuo culture, family lineage is traced through the maternal line, and property is passed down through daughters. Women have considerable influence in household affairs, economic decisions, and social structures. They hold key roles in community governance, and their opinions are highly valued in decision-making processes within the society. A world dominated by masculine mechanistic energy isn't a given, it's a temporary finite state.

When I feel the world is going increasingly dark, more technocratic, consumeristic and controlling, I remind myself change is a pendulum, swinging from one extreme end to the other. For a while, it will semi-stabilise, slowly swinging in the broad middle – until an event or change in the world brings the energy back into the swing, rocking it up higher and higher to the extreme ends.

The narratives of the dying world of business-as-usual won't simply fade out. They will fade, come back stronger, fade away, make a come-back and slowly, over time, changes start to last. The transition we are envisioning here isn't one of years or decades. I can imagine the journey to a humanity guided by a living systems view of life taking generations, perhaps even centuries. Therefore, regeneration is more than a goal; it's a movement. And it's our choice to help this movement and the potential regenerative futures come to life, even if we can't live to see them fully flourish.

Exercise

I'd like to extend an invitation for you to join me on a journey to the end of this century. We're going on a remarkable adventure into a completely transformed world.

Just 50 years ago, the unimaginable occurred: People united, businesses wholeheartedly adopted regenerative practices, and governments prioritised eco-consciousness over self-interest.

Now, I want to ask you to close your eyes for two minutes and step into this new reality.

- What did you see? Smell? Hear?
- What was there? What wasn't?
- Who was there? Who wasn't?
- How did being there feel?

IMAGINATION AS A RADICAL ACT

We are blinded by a disingenuous narrative blocking our ability to imagine and relate. In this story, capitalism, war, poverty, destruction of wider nature, inequality, oppression and unequal opportunities are a 'given'. To be human means to compete, to fight, to go to war, to be envious and always put yourself first. This narrative has been stifling compassionate relating and our collective ability to imagine and unite behind better stories.

This sharp story of hatred and competition doesn't reflect what it means to be human. It does, however, painfully reflects our current zeitgeist. This prevailing growth-oriented capitalistic worldview, in which humans became Consumers and governments turned Corporate has only been dominant since the early 20th century – a period so short, it is as insignificant as a blink on the cosmos' timeline. A very confused cosmic blink! During this confused and destructive blink of modernity and consumerism, humans have lost a sense of themselves and what it means to be a living being.

In each era, dynamics are in place that uphold the *status quo*. Despite this, there is one absolute given, things will change. It's our choice how we show up to this reality. Do you allow yourself to truly dream, to imagine a radically different world? Do you dare to re-imagine your business, our economic system or even our whole society?

Sharing dreams and potential futures far removed from today's reality are an easy target. Radical ideas are often torn down by statistics, beliefs and convictions grounded in old paradigm narratives. That these ideas can't flourish in today's reality doesn't prove they are an impossibility.

By shifting our focus from 'What Is' to 'What If?' (Rob Hopkins, *From What Is to What If*, 2021), we explore bold possibilities and reimagine the future:

- What if business leaders encouraged moral rebellion?
- What if we embrace Mother Earth as our guiding compass for decision-making?
- What if all board meetings were held in a forest?
- What if our daily needs were realised by local citizen-led cooperatives?
- What if diverse and marginalised communities became the leaders in shaping the future of our societies?
- What if the media prioritised stories of love and hope?
- What if we redesigned our cities and infrastructure to mimic the vibrant and regenerative patterns of the natural world?

The only way to make sense out of change is to plunge into it, move with it, and join the dance.

Alan Watts

Which stories and beliefs are holding our imagination back?

TRANSFORM FOR REGENERATIVE FUTURES

Transforming for regenerative futures is a life-long journey. On this journey, we will constantly identify new business-as-usual narratives to unravel and unlearn. Woven with this unlearning journey is the constant reconnecting to the regenerative capacities that form the essence of all living beings – such as living with the rhythm of nature, nature literacy, entanglement with more than-human-species and reciprocal relationship-building. Humans, and other species of whom the scientific community is barely starting to understand their consciousness, additionally hold unique capacities that have regenerative potential when applied in the right relationship. Capacities like creativity, storytelling, compassion, imagination and deep listening will play a truly vital role in the transition to regenerative futures.

How Might We Help People of All Generations to Develop Capacities for Regeneration?

There is no list of 10 capacities one needs to develop to become a catalyser for regeneration. Regenerative capacities are highly context- and place-based. They are fluid and constantly evolving. Having said this, there are principles and capacities that we share globally, among humans and some more-than-human beings. The overview in this chapter is a selection that can be a starting point for your journey, though it is not an extensive or complete list.

Over the last couple of years, I have realised that definitions are a terrible starting point for deep transformations. They are often too hard to grasp from the business-as-usual perspective. Too often, they are dismissed because, from that perspective, they don't make sense.

Changing the answer is evolution. Changing the question is revolution.

Jorge Wagensberg

Incremental changes that hold us firmly in the *status quo* are partly the result of not changing the questions we are asking ourselves, both in business and on a societal level. We are focusing so strongly on making progress in a forward movement that we forget to shift horizons and change directions. Going beyond the visible and exploring the invisible pattern, structures, systems and worldviews (spheres of change) requires us to slow down, stop, observe and sit with the questions. When changing questions, we are literally diverting out of a loop, and opening up potential futures. We are designing futures through the lens of the questions of the now. These futures aren't where we think the results of our questions and thinking will land. By unconsciously basing the questions on lenses, assumptions and unravelled history, we are shaping the future.

Be patient toward all that is unsolved in your heart and try to love the questions themselves, like locked rooms and like books that are now written in a very foreign tongue. Do not now seek the answers, which cannot be given you because you would not be able to live them. And the point is, to live everything. Live the questions now. Perhaps you will then gradually, without noticing it, live along some distant day into the answer.

Rainer Maria Rilke

Before you move on. I want to invite you to think and share the questions that are alive in you right now:

- What are the questions you have been living?
- What questions are you afraid or hesitant to explore?
- What questions spark joy and excitement in you?

Stewards for life

"Jane is in the forest, where it is raining. Jane isn't wearing a coat, she doesn't have an umbrella, and she isn't standing under a tree or canopy to cover her head, but the rain does not touch Jane. Why?"

Take a couple of minutes to think about this question. Why is the rain not touching Jane? Once you have pondered on a couple of answers to this questions, continue reading this chapter.

We hold the capacities for thrivability, but they are covered under a thick layer of career goals, vanity metrics and rat-race dreams constantly reinforced by 10,000 marketing messages a day, our current education system and social media. This is the reason you might have not guessed why the rain didn't touch Jane. We are so used to looking at the world through an anthropogenic lens that we lost the ability to see and care for the perspectives of the more-than-human. Jane is a fish.

(This is a lateral thinking riddle inspired by the work of the Maltese scholar, Edward de Bono.)

> *If you design a system to do something specific, don't be surprised if it does it. If you run an education system based on standardisation and conformity that suppresses individuality, imagination and creativity, don't be surprised if that's what it does.*
>
> **Sir Ken Robinson**, *Creative Schools: Revolutionising Education from the Ground Up*

The dominant education, work and political systems are designed to shape people into productive parts of the economy. Is this what life on earth needs? I love to see not only education, but work, as well as our role as citizens and voters, as a life-long (un)learning journey in which we are constantly developing the capacities that help life on earth, including ourselves, to flourish. Unfortunately, developing our ability to steward life is not one of the main pillars of the education system, nor does it often have a high priority during our professional careers. In a world facing collapse, this is a tremendous loss. We humans are living beings with the ability to regenerate. We can be a keystone species that enables life to thrive.

What would the world look like in which we considered, cared and designed for all living beings?

What would a world look like in which humans intentionally developed their capacities to regenerate from birth to death?

There is no set list or roadmap to this inner development journey. Just as regeneration is rooted in context and place, so are the capacities and skills that enhance life. This chapter is an invitation to you to start exploring your own potential as a steward for regeneration. Here, we are exploring a few capacities gathered from regenerative practitioners that I have encountered on my journey. This list is by no means complete, nor does it do justice to the complexity of all the perspectives now, future and past of people and communities living in right relationship with wider nature. Instead of giving you tips and methods on how to start developing the capacities to become stewards of life, I want to invite you to explore and truly sit with the questions. Not directly looking for solutions, instead go beyond the visible and allow yourself to move from one question into the next. At one point, without having to force it you will naturally start to come to answers. Have the courage to give it time.

Living Systems awareness

As much as we like to believe the world is a place we can categorise, box and divide, a reality that we can shape and control in a linear cause-and-effect manner, there are actually no hard lines, no real separations between anything. Everything exists in relationship. Once you are aware of the interconnectedness of life, deep compassion and countless ways to care and connect unfold. Living Systems awareness means the ability to recognise life as a universe of systems, formed by parts in relationship.

> *A system is an interconnected set of elements that is coherently organised in a way that achieves something. If you look at that definition closely for a minute, you can see that a system must consist of three kinds of things: elements, interconnections, and a function or purpose.*
>
> **Donella H. Meadows**, *Thinking in Systems: A Primer*

Systems awareness is one of the most important capacities in our 'toolkit' for regenerative futures. Understanding patterns, systems, structures, worldviews and relations between them helps you navigate transformative impact. So:

- How can we deepen our understanding of the ecosystems we are a part of?
- How do we deepen our ability to recognise the interconnectedness of life?

- How do we enhance symbiosis between human and more-than-human systems?

Reading suggestions:
- *Thinking in Systems: A Primer*, Donella Meadows
- *The Systems View of Life*, Fritjof Capra & Pier Luigi Luisi

More-than-human perspectives
Do you bring the perspectives of other beings into your sustainability conversations? In the design of spaces and products for humans, other living beings are often not considered. We design on a human timescale, for human usefulness and human preference. This narrow lens is at the expense of other living beings now and in futures to come. Transition to regenerative futures requires us to step out of the human lens and consider more-than-human perspectives. Similar to when we are communicating in two different languages, we have to come up with different ways to bridge the communication gap and create a deep understanding of the more-than-human beings we are interconnected with. So:

- How do we honour wider nature's calling and protect life from being overshadowed by the short-term needs and desires of human stakeholders?
- How do we learn to listen to the calls of the earth?
- How do we better understand which more-than-human voices need to be amplified and integrated in designing businesses, strategies and commons?
- How do we design for humans and more-than-human beings?
- How do we transcend the limitations of the anthropogenic timeframe?

Exploration Suggestions:
- Onboarding Nature Toolkit - onboardingnature.com

Playfulness
Life doesn't spring from spreadsheets. It springs from play, especially play in relation to others. When you feel stuck, remind yourself that you are never stuck; there are always possibilities. When you are feeling stuck, it just means you can't see these possibilities yet and you need to play. Stuckness simply is an invitation to dance and play with the questions. So:

- What if all business leaders and politicians played hide-and-seek for two hours every week?

- How can play help adults unlearn our desire for predictability and certainty?

Life thrives by diversity

Life, society, creativity, food and arts all thrive by diversity. The best way to kill the magic of life and make way for nothingness is by choosing the mono path of sameness. Through the regenerative lens, we are constantly seeking to enhance diversity. Business-as-usual has made the Earth an increasingly monotonous human-centred place, a planet where the consumer human worldview is the only truth, the one perspective we design for. Now we are slowly seeing and accepting what many indigenous communities have always known: that we are living on a multi-world Earth, where the natural, spiritual, human, and perhaps some worlds that we don't even know of (yet), coexist simultaneously and interconnected. It's therefore vital that we hold space for a variety of worldviews and perspectives. So:

- Whose worldviews are currently dominant?
- Whose world views are currently oppressed?
- How do we amplify the softer voices?
- How can amplifying diversity become our decision-making compass towards inclusive pathways?

Deep compassion

> Compassion is all-inclusive. Compassion knows no boundaries. Compassion comes with awareness and awareness breaks all narrow territories.

Amit Ray

Ask yourself:

- How can we deepen compassion for more-than-human beings?
- Are we willing to face our own pain and discomfort for the thrivability of life?
- How can we better integrate the voices of beings affected by our decision making?

Interbeing

> We are faced with a choice: continue down the conventional path of alienation from life, despite that pathway's inevitable devastation; or forge a new path of greater alignment with life, with all its promise and potential.

Michelle Holliday

Ask yourself:

- How do we learn globally and connect locally?
- How do we meet in transformations without the limitations of language and temporary worldviews?

Intuition

Consultancies, risk analysis, data reports and KPIs make it hard for people to listen to and trust their intuition. Everything is done to take uncertainty out of the equation. Predictability and replicability is key. Even recruitment – a deeply human process – is now increasingly data-driven. This obsession with clarity and predictability is stifling our ability to trust our intuition. In times as complex as the time we live in, it is exactly our intuition that we need to trust. Compassion and living systems awareness doesn't spring from Excel sheets; it arises from being connected to our intuition. So:

- How do we rediscover and commit to our intuition?
- What stories, beliefs and assumptions are disconnecting us from our intuition?
- How do we tap into our intuition to navigate an increasingly complex and uncertain landscape?

Rooting indigenous wisdom

The path to weave modern ways to ancestral ways is to weave, learning from each other and build new knowledge that works now, where you are.

Tiago Paes Vilas Boas

Ask yourself:

- How do we create space for indigenous knowledge?
- How do we work with indigenous communities in reciprocal ways to co-create the path to a future?
- How do organisations reconnect to the multi-perspective history of the land they are existing on?

Multigenerational caring

Imagine you are hiking in the Alps. You are walking on a beautiful path on top of a mountain ridge. By accident, you drop a glass bottle on the path. It breaks into pieces. You know that tomorrow people will walk barefoot on this path. Without hesitation, you clean up the glass; you don't want to harm anyone.

But, what if these people will not be walking there barefoot tomorrow, but 100 years from now? Would you still clean up the glass?

This story is a variation of a thought experiment often used in discussions about ethics, environmental responsibility, and future impact. Multigenerational caring means considering and caring for generations to come. In the Haudenosaunee philosophy of the Iroquois, this is called the Seventh Generation principle: the decisions we make today should lead to a healthy future for the next seven generations. So:

- How do we deepen our compassion for the living beings that aren't born yet?
- How do we listen to the memories of the generations before us and the dreams of the generations to come?

Exercise

You have been telling the people that this is the Eleventh Hour, now you must go back and tell the people that this is the Hour. And there are things to be considered . . . Where are you living? What are you doing? What are your relationships? Are you in right relation? Where is your water? Know your garden. It is time to speak your Truth. Create your community. Be good to each other. And do not look outside yourself for the leader.

Hopi Elder Wisdom

WHAT IF...?

Everything needed to live regeneratively on this earth already exists. It has existed as long as living beings roamed the earth. We are living beings, entangled with all the other life forms. When we observe other animals, we see they embody the intelligence that enables them to live with the rhythm of life. We humans are no different; this intelligence lives within us. It's just so bizarrely and artificially noisy in this world that we are struggling to connect to it. If we could only find the quietness in ourselves, each other and wider nature, we could recognise what truly matters: Life.

On my courageous days, I seek questions. On the days I feel low and fragile, I seek the answers. So:

- What if we lived the questions instead of seeking for the answers?
- What if we embodied our journey to find alternative ways of living and being?

---

1   Brunni Corsato is a creative writer, visual artist, researcher and strategist, passionate about creativity, the new Internet and meaning-making systems.
2   Joy Njeri is a champion for collective action for a regenerative revolution with purpose.

ABBREVIATIONS

ASA	Advertising Standards Authority
ASIC	Australian Securities & Investments Commission
BII	Biodiversity Intactness Index
BP	Basis for Preparation
$CaCO_3$	calcium carbonate
CBD	*Convention on Biological Diversity*
CCUS	carbon capture, use, and storage
CDP	Carbon Disclosure Project
CEO	chief executive officer
CFC	chlorofluorocarbon
CFO	chief financial officer
CH_4	methane
CO	carbon monoxide
CO_2	carbon dioxide
CO_2e	CO_2 equivalent
COP	Conference of the Parties
CPG	consumer packaged goods
CPU	central processing unit
CRPD	*Convention on the Rights of Persons with Disabilities*
CSDDD	*Corporate Sustainability Due Diligence Directive*
CSRD	*Corporate Sustainability Reporting Directive*
DACS	direct air capture and storage
DAPL	Dakota Access Pipeline
DfD	design for disassembly
DIY	do-it-yourself
DP	Data point
DPP	Digital Product Passport
DR	Disclosure Requirement
DRC	Democratic Republic of Congo
EBA	European Banking Authority
EEZ	Exclusive Economic Zone
EFRAG	European Financial Reporting Advisory Group
EHCR	European Court of Human Rights
EITI	Extractive Industries Transparency Initiative
EPA	Environmental Protection Agency
EPR	extended producer responsibility
ESG	environmental, social and governance
ESPR	*Ecodesign for Sustainable Products Regulation*

ESRS	European Sustainability Reporting Standards
EU	European Union
EV	electric vehicle
EWG	Environmental Working Group
FAA	Federal Aviation Administration
FSB	Financial Stability Board
GBVH	gender-based violence and harassment
GDP	gross domestic product
GDPR	*General Data Protection Regulation*
GHG	greenhouse gas
GMV	gross merchandise value
GOV	Governance
GRESB	Global Real Estate Sustainability Benchmark
GRI	Global Reporting Initiative
HFC	hydrofluorocarbon
HIV	human immunodeficiency virus
HR	human resources
HRDD	human rights due diligence
ICCPR	*International Covenant on Civil & Political Rights*
ICESCR	*International Covenant on Economic, Social & Cultural Rights*
IEA	International Energy Agency
IFRS	International Financial Reporting Standards
IFRS-S	International Financial Reporting Standards – Sustainability
IIRC	International Integrated Reporting Council
ILO	International Labour Organization
IMO	International Maritime Organization
IoT	Internet of Things
IPCC	Intergovernmental Panel on Climate Change
IRO	Impact, Risk and opportunity
ISSB	International Sustainability Standards Board
IT	information technology
ITUC	International Trade Union Confederation
kg	kilogram
km	kilometre
km²	square kilometre
LCA	life-cycle assessment
LEAP	Learn-Evaluate-Act-Publicly report
LED	Light-emitting diode
LNG	liquefied natural gas
MARPOL	*Marine Pollution Prevention Convention*
MCAS	Manoeuvring Characteristics Augmentation System
MDG	Millennium Development Goal

MDR	Minimum Disclosure Requirements
MEPA	*Montana Environmental Policy Act*
MPA	marine protected area
MT	Metrics and Targets
N_2O	Nitrous oxide
NCP	Nature's Contribution to People
NFRD	*Non-Financial Reporting Directive*
NGO	non-governmental organisation
NOAA	National Oceanic & Atmospheric Administration
NOx	nitrogen oxides
NZE	Net Zero Emissions by 2050 Scenario
OECD	Organisation for Economic Co-operation & Development
OGM	operational-level grievance mechanism
OHCHR	Office of the United Nations High Commissioner for Human Rights
PAT-M	Policies, Actions, Targets & Metrics
PFAS	Per- and polyfluoroalkyl substances
PFC	perfluorocarbon
PLA	polylactic acid
PM	particulate matter
POPs	persistent organic pollutants
ppm	parts per million
PPP	public-private partnership
RA	Rockwell Automation
RAFI	Human Rights Reporting & Assurance Frameworks Initiative
RAINO	Respectful / Authentic / Impactful / Nurturing / Optimistic
RAM	random access memory
ROI	return on investment
SASB	Sustainability Accounting Standards Board
SBM	Strategy and Business Model
SBT	science-based target
SBTi	Science-Based Targets Initiative
SBTN	Science-Based Targets Network
SDG	Sustainable Development Goal
SDS	Sustainable Development Scenario
SE	Schneider Electric
SEAR	Senior Executive Accountability Regime
SEC	Securities & Exchange Commission
SEK	Swedish krona
SF_6	sulphur hexafluoride
SFDR	*Sustainable Finance Disclosure Regulation*
SIN	Substitute It Now

SLAPP   Strategic Lawsuit Against Public Participation
SME   small and medium enterprise
SOx   sulphur oxides
STEM   science, technology, engineering, and mathematics
STEPS   Stated Policies Scenario
TCFD   Task Force on Climate-related Financial Disclosures
TNFD   Taskforce on Nature-related Financial Disclosures
UDHR   *Universal Declaration of Human Rights*
UK   United Kingdom
UN   United Nations
UNEP   United Nations Environment Programme
UNFCCC   *United Nations Framework Convention on Climate*
         Change
UNGPs   *UN Guiding Principles on Business & Human Rights*
UNICEF   United Nations International Children's Emergency Fund
US   United States
VMS   vessel monitoring system
VOC   volatile organic compound
VRF   Value Reporting Framework
WBCSD   World Business Council for Sustainable Development
WEF   World Economic Forum
WHO   World Health Organization
WMO   World Meteorological Organization

ABOUT THE AUTHORS

Sustainability is such a broad topic, and the planet is such a big place, that writing this book would not have been possible if we had not managed to combine the knowledge of many experts.

Over the next few pages, you can read about the authors, and learn about their background and particular areas of expertise.

The authors are listed in the order they appear in the book.

Donal Daly

Ingrid De Doncker

David Carlin

Carlos Terol

Harald Friedl

Elena Doms

Dr William Beer

T.A.O. Garraty

Oliver Dauert

Marije De Roos

Elin Bergman

Anna Triponel

Minou Schillings

Joy Njeri

Kowawa Kapukaja Apurinã

Tiago Paes Vilas Boas

Orla Carolan

Donal Daly

Donal is co-founder and CEO of
Future Planet, an AI-based
sustainability software company.
Prior to Future Planet, he founded
five global software companies
that together served more than
two million users in corporations
around the world.

A graduate of University College
Cork (Engineering) and KU Leuven,
Belgium (SDGs), he has been a
strategic advisor to the Irish
Government in technology and
sustainability and is author of multiple Amazon #1 Bestsellers.

Donal founded the Altify Foundation, a charitable and volunteer
programme and is a long-term supporter of human-rights and social
enterprises. As Entrepreneur-in-Residence in UCC, he mentors
emerging businesses, particularly in the area of sustainability and
green-tech.

Ingrid De Doncker

With more than two decades of
pioneering work in sustainable
procurement and supply chain
management, Ingrid De Doncker
has significantly advanced global
sustainability initiatives.

As the cofounder and Head of
Research and Innovation at Future
Planet, she plays a crucial role in an
ESG team that developed a
platform that empowers
organisations to create and
implement robust sustainability
strategies by structuring and managing their ESG data to effectively
track and measure metrics, auto-generating transformation plans,
and ensuring compliance with CSRD requirements.

A sought-after speaker both nationally and internationally, Ingrid
is a lecturer at three of Ireland's universities. Her inclusive leadership
and innovative approach to sustainability has earned widespread
recognition, including the prestigious Irish Times Innovation Award

in 2022. Ingrid's extensive advisory work on environmental, social, and governance (ESG) issues across numerous organisations, along with her expertise in public and private procurement in Ireland and Europe, underscores her significant contribution to promoting responsible business practices and sustainable procurement.

David Carlin

David Carlin is an acknowledged authority on climate change and its implications for the financial system. He is the founder of Cambium Global Solutions, an advisor to governments, corporates, and financial institutions on climate and ESG topics.

He has authored numerous reports that provide practical tools for financial actors looking to address climate change and has run capacity-building programmes for financial institutions and supervisors around the world.

David led the creation of UN Environment Programme's Finance Initiative (UNEP FI)'s Risk Centre as the head of Risk. Over the past years, he has worked with over 100 global banks, investors, and insurers on climate scenarios, climate risk assessments, and climate governance.

He is an advisor to UNEP FI's TNFD pilot program on nature and biodiversity related risks as well as the Net-Zero Banking Alliance (NZBA). He has also been a technical advisor to the Glasgow Financial Alliances for Net Zero (GFANZ). David is also a contributor to Forbes and a senior associate at Cambridge's Institute for Sustainability Leadership (CISL) as well as a visiting fellow at King's College London.

David has worked as a Principal in Finance, Risk, and Public Policy for Oliver Wyman and in Model Risk Management for PNC Bank. His background is in quantitative modelling and decision science.

Carlos Terol

Carlos has been on a changemaker journey for over 10 years, passionate about inspiring people to create a positive impact in the world.

Carlos is the Founder of Good Ripple, a global platform to connect changemakers that has grown from zero to 3,200+ members from 104 countries in 18 months. He is also a Climate Fresk Facilitator, a Speaker and a Top Corporate Sustainability Voice on LinkedIn with over 30,000 followers.

Harald Friedl

Harald is an internationally renowned circular economist. He is advising the United Nations in several countries and is working with top companies on their road towards circularity.

Harald has co-initiated the global yearly "Circularity Gap Report", one of the most referenced publications in the field of circular economy. Harald has extensive consulting experience as CEO of the do-tank Circle Economy in Amsterdam.

He spearheaded the circular transition in his home country, Austria, when he served as Circular Economy Accelerator for the Austrian Government in 2022.

Elena Doms

Elena Doms was born and raised in the Arctic. Throughout her career she led a social impact youth NGO and worked as a Director at Mastercard, merging digital and sustainable transformations. Seeing her childhood home melt away and becoming a mother inspired Elena to quit her corporate job in search for impact.

In partnership with C-biotech, she launched +EARTH+ with a crazy bold mission: To create the largest Soil & CO2 cleanup with nature. +EARTH+ is an award-winning start-up that works with scientists, technology companies, industry, farmers and cities on restoring soils with plants. These plants are then turned into circular construction materials that help decarbonize our cities.

Elena is also a LinkedIn Top Green Voice, helping educate and inspire others for climate action. A sustainability keynote speaker and storyteller, who gathered audiences up to 4,500 people. An Arctic Artist, who paints icebergs and Northern Lights, sharing the beauty and the tales of the polar regions. And an Ambassador of Habitats Foundation, helping restore biodiversity.

Dr William Beer

Dr William Beer is the Owner and Founder of Tunley Environmental and is responsible for the overall strategy and growth of the business. Will is obsessed with continuous improvement and takes pride in managing and adapting to change across all departments of Tunley Environmental.

Being the "smartest person in the room" gives you nothing so Will surrounds himself by people who, in his words, are "better than him" to ensure the Tunley Environmental continues to

improve its service competencies. Learning from others has, and continues to be a critical success factor in Tunley Environmental's growth.

With a professional background in multi-departmental transformation and an academic background in advanced full factorials, large datasets and combustion modelling, Will continues to apply innovation, change management and exploration skills to his role as the CEO of Tunley Environmental.

T.A.O. Garraty

Tara Garraty, BSc, MSc Conservation Biology, PhD Conservation Biology (Pending), is a seasoned sustainability and conservation scientist with a specialised background in ecology and conservation biology.

Tara holds a BSc and MSc degree in Conservation Biology, focusing on ecosystem services and ecosystem health, and is in the process of submitting her PhD in Conservation Biology, titled "An Ecological Model: Quantifying Links Between Biodiversity, Hydrological Events, and Climate Change within the Peruvian Amazon," which focus on the impacts on biodiversity in a changing climate.

Tara's career has concentrated on research and education in tropical and marine conservation, climate change, sustainability science, ecosystem function, biodiversity, and general ecology. Her in-depth research, which includes extensive statistical ecological and climatic modelling, offers a comprehensive understanding of the impacts of climate change on crucial tropical ecosystems.

Driven by her passion for preserving the planet, her main career goals are to contribute towards global conservation and sustainability objectives, educate public platforms on essential environmental issues, and promote sustainable practices through fieldwork, education, and research.

Oliver Dauert

Oliver Dauert is the founder & CEO of Wildya. In his role, he leads the strategy and business execution of the start-up.

He is a LinkedIn Top Green Voice & passionate biodiversity builder.

Additionally, Oliver manages a business consulting agency for biodiversity businesses and NGOs (Wild Business Mates).

Prior to Wildya, Oliver worked in travel tech for Evaneos (B-Corp), managing transformative projects during the COVID crisis. As well as working in mobility tech (Moovel by Daimler), e-commerce (Saltwater Shop) & non-profit industry (Red Rhino Society/ESN).

Marije De Roos

Marije de Roos, AKA The Circular Fashion Detective, is a Dutch economist turned circular fashion pioneer. Her mission is to make landfills obsolete and hence she has developed a passion for materials and supply chains.

Marije's startup Positive Fibers® combines science, design, and technology to put the ECO into eCommerce one positive product at a time. She is also the author of the forthcoming book *Farm-to-Fashion*, which helps fashion professionals to make truly circular fashion and lifestyle products that do more good than harm to the environment and people in the supply chains.

Elin Bergman

Elin Bergman is known for being Sweden's "circular economy queen", is named LinkedIn Top Green Voice and is a recognized international keynote speaker.

She works as a Circular Impact Officer and spokesperson of the Swedish circular economy network Cradlenet, and is also one of the co-founders of the Nordic Circular Hotspot, a collaboration platform for accelerating circular economy in the region.

Elin has also recently become a Founding Member of the Circular Economy Coalition - an international coalition of value-aligned individuals and organisations collectively advancing the circular economy through shared tools and resources, bridging the Global North and Global South. For many years she worked as WWF Sweden's circular economy expert, where she developed the international circular economy network Baltic Stewardship Initiative, to enable the recirculation of nutrients in the Baltic Sea region in the agri-food sector.

Anna Triponel

Anna Triponel is an internationally renowned business, human rights and climate expert and founder and CEO of Human Level. Over the past decade, she has travelled the globe to advise hundreds of companies – as well as their investors and lawyers – on what it means to take a people-centred approach to business. Anna advises companies on human rights strategies, weaving human rights into climate strategies and just transition, and ways to adapt business models to be future fit.

She is an Advisor to Board members, VPs and General Counsels, and is a regular keynote speaker and featured commentator in the

media. Anna is a Mediator for OECD National Contact Point instances, an International Human Rights Expert for a range of operational-level grievance mechanisms and sits on a number of advisory committees. She has lived and/or worked in the majority of countries on the African continent, running human rights impact assessment and stakeholder empowerment processes.

As a consultant at the Harvard Kennedy School of Government, she worked with John Ruggie on the development of the 2011 UN Guiding Principles on Business and Human Rights. As Senior Advisor at the leading centre of expertise on the UNGPs Shift, she played an instrumental role in the development of the 2015 UN Guiding Principles Reporting Framework.

She has been a corporate lawyer in New York at Jones Day, an international human rights lawyer working across Africa and Asia at *pro bono* Nobel Peace Prize nominee firm PILPG, and a development lawyer in Washington DC at the World Bank. She holds three bars as a lawyer (New York, England & Wales, France – currently non-practising lawyer). Degrees include an LL.M. in International Law (American University Washington College of Law); Masters degree in international business / human rights law (University of Paris X); Business Sustainability Management (Cambridge Institute for Sustainability Leadership) and MBA (Essentials from London School of Economics).

Minou Schillings

"If you never change your mind, why have one". This quote by E. De Bono best describes Minou's approach in a nutshell. As a Regenerative Transition Facilitator, Imagination Activist and Community Weaver, Minou invites and enables business leaders, founders and intrapreneurs to (un)learn business as usual, imagine radically different futures and transform to become stewards for regeneration.

Minou, born and raised in a forested area of the Netherlands, has embraced a slow nomadic life grounded in travelling and community living for the last 8 years. She chooses collaboration over competition and the train over a corner office. Minou's Dutch roots ensure you're in for a direct, no-nonsense, and Down-To-Gaia experience. She's a disarming speaker on a mission to make the complex accessible, the unimaginable possible and the future radically different and better for all life on earth.

With a Master's in Creativity and Innovation from the Edward De Bono Institute and a Bachelor's in Food Innovation (Malta) from HAS Green Academy (Hertogenbosch), Minou is armed with a unique skill set to lead you on a transformative journey. As a Systems thinker, guest lecturer, Keynote speaker and (un)learning experience designer, Minou holds provoking, safe, confronting and surprising spaces for businesses and individuals to transition towards regenerative thinking, leaving business-as-usual in the dust.

As the founder of The Green Sprint, author of the newsletter *Shifting Horizons for Regenerative Futures*, co-lead of Taste The Shift and Co-initiator of the Regenerative Marketing Movement, she commits herself with full compassion and curiosity to an experimental, collaborative, (un)learning approach to exploring pathways to regenerative futures.

Minou has been described as the definition of positivity. Not the façade annoying positivity, but the zero-bullshit, inspiring one that not only captures your attention but also instantly puts a smile on your face. There is one simple reason she remains this positive, an unrelenting belief in the compassion, kindness and care of humans. It's not knowledge we need to unlearn, but greed, hyper-individualism and short-term thinking, deep down we do remember how to take care of life on earth.

Joy Njeri

Joy Njeri Njihia is more than just a name; it represents a commitment to spreading joy and positive change wherever she goes. Joy come from Kenya, which has breathtaking landscapes. Her journey has taken her through civil society, corporate corridors, and entrepreneurial ventures, with each chapter deepening her understanding of my mission.

With over two decades of experience, Joy worked with data at L'Oreal East Africa to boost profits and build small businesses. As the founder of Fruity Pap, she was instrumental in converting food waste into value for local businesses. Aside from spreadsheets, her true calling is to advocate for justice, human rights, and equality. The International Criminal Court (ICC) and Kituo Cha Sheria were her allies in this endeavour.

"Togetherness is life" is based on Kikuyu wisdom. Community fuels Joy's belief that collective action ignites transformative change. Having a social science degree has helped Joy bring her philosophy into her work. Joy is currently a partner with What Matters, actively working to create transformative change. She also helps to create environments in which creativity and empathy thrive, and everyone, regardless of background, feels seen and valued.

Joy's business acumen, social consciousness, and collaborative spirit fuel her collaborations with organisations and individuals, helping shape the world we want to live in.

Kowawa Kapukaja Apurinã

Kowawa Kapukaja Apurinã was born indigenous of the Apurinã ethnicity from Middle Purus in the state of Amazonas, Brazil.

Her work primarily focuses on indigenous education, environmental education, racial issues, affirmative actions, and indigenous women. She is a founding member of the Pupykary Institute of the Apurinã People, co-founder of the Brazilian Articulation of Indigenous Anthropologists (Abia), and co-founder of the Indigenous Artivism collective.

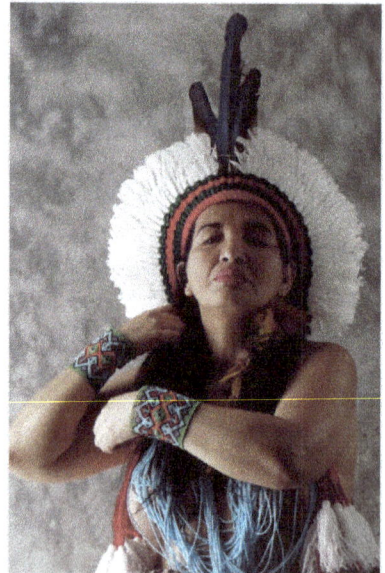

Kowawa serves as CEO of FemeNI/Fair of Black and Indigenous Women Entrepreneurs and curator/member of Ruidosa Alma/Trans Performance. She is a Ph.D. student in Anthropology at the Federal Fluminense University

(UFF)/Sorbonne Paris 3, with a Bachelor's degree in Law, a teaching degree in Visual Arts, and a Master's degree in Anthropology, all obtained at the Federal University of Pelotas.

Kowawa also holds a Master's degree in Education & Technology from the Sul-Rio-Grandense Federal Institute, with experience in Arts, Anthropology, Education & Law. Her research interests include indigenous peoples, violence, and indigenous ancestries.

Besides her academic pursuits, Kowawa is an artist, educator, and cultural producer.

Tiago Paes Vilas Boas

Tiago was born in the ancestral lands of the Guarani people, once a thriving forest, now known as São Paulo State, Brazil. The country takes its name from a tree (*Paubrasilia echinata*) that was nearly driven to extinction within the first decades of colonization. These lands were originally called *Yby Marã E'ymam*, or Land Without Sorrows.
For 500 years, sorrow has entrenched itself in these lands, and peace has been elusive. In his youth, Tiago realized he could not escape conflicts with the police, in his work, and with the state. The violence of colonial systems, juxtaposed with the compassion of the many communities he belonged to, led him to facilitate reciprocal and organic relationships between individuals, communities, and nature for more than a decade. He has sought to weave wisdom and an intercultural worldview, learning from indigenous elders around the world to facilitate processes of change, design organic solutions, and foster reciprocal and learning relationships.

Orla Carolan

Orla Carolan is Executive Director - ESG Strategy & Compliance at Future Planet, working with clients on double materiality assessments and planning for implementing the Corporate Sustainability Reporting Directive (CSRD).

Orla has over 20 years' experience in finance and corporate reporting roles for multinational organisations mainly in financial services. In this time Orla has managed implementation of accounting standards and more recently worked with clients on the implementation of CSRD and the European Sustainability Reporting Standards (ESRS).

Orla also has experience in standard setting having worked with the European Financial Reporting Advisory Group (EFRAG) on the ESRS development programme, experiencing first-hand how the requirements of the CSRD are being transposed into reporting requirements for organisations.

Orla is a chartered certified accountant and regularly delivers training and Continuing Professional Development (CPD) to the accounting profession. She is also a part time lecturer for Chartered Accountants Ireland on their new CDP Diploma in Sustainability Reporting.

www.ingramcontent.com/pod-product-compliance
Lightning Source LLC
Chambersburg PA
CBHW061112220326
41599CB00024B/4004